OLIVER GOLDSMITH

His Life and Works

1. Portrait of Goldsmith by Sir Joshua Reynolds. (National Gallery)

OLIVER GOLDSMITH

His Life and Works

A. Lytton Sells

London   George Allen & Unwin Ltd
Ruskin House   Museum Street

First published in 1974

© George Allen & Unwin Ltd 1974

ISBN 0 04 928030 9

PR3493
.84
1974b

Printed in Great Britain
in 12 point Fournier type
by T. & A. Constable Limited

TO IRIS

Preface

When I was asked by Malcolm Barnes to write for Allen and Unwin a book on Goldsmith's life and works, I did not at first realise that little exists which one can regard as critical or satisfactory. The many biographies which have appeared seem defective in several respects. They either omit information which is readily available, or ignore essential features of his life and character, or fail to see the real problems which should be considered; they are too prone to pass over or make light of his faults. After much study, it became clear that one would have to go back to the sources, and – what is equally important – think out his character afresh, and without regard to accepted opinions.

The primary source is the memorandum which Thomas Percy, on 28 April 1773, took down from Goldsmith's dictation. This manuscript has been printed by Professor K. C. Balderston in *The History and Sources of Percy's Memoir of Goldsmith*,[1] and it is notable for its extreme brevity and reticence. After Goldsmith's death Percy began to supplement it with information supplied by Maurice Goldsmith and by Mrs Hodson. Early in 1777 Johnson took over the duties of biographer and, through the good offices of Malone – the most careful scholar of his day – obtained further details relative to his late friend's life at Trinity College, Dublin. After Johnson's death in 1784 Percy resumed the task, collected material from additional sources and after delays, for which he was not responsible, published his *Memoir* as an introduction to the 1801 edition of Goldsmith's works.

The value of Percy's *Memoir* is that it contains the testimony of contemporaries; its peculiarity, that the material is so

[1] Cambridge University Press, 1926.

sparse. Sir James Prior in the first long *Life of Goldsmith* (1837, 2 volumes) added a vast amount of information which he found in Boswell's *Life of Johnson*, in Northcote's *Life of Reynolds*, in Cradock's *Memoirs*, and in other books, or obtained from Mrs Gwynne (née Mary Horneck) and other persons who remembered the poet. John Forster added further details; and still more have become available with the publication of Boswell's private Papers, of Mrs Thrale's records and of Sir Joshua Reynolds's 'Portrait' of his friend.

But despite this wealth of material, there are still strange blanks in Goldsmith's life, and questions which remain unanswered. They can be properly discussed only when we come to the relevant moments in Goldsmith's career, though they may be summarised as follows:

1   How far can we rely on Goldsmith's own account of his adventures; for example, on what happened after leaving Trinity College and before going to Edinburgh?

2   Where and how did he learn French, written and spoken – a language and a literature on which he relied in most of his writings from beginning to end?

3   What did he do, and even where exactly did he go, between leaving Leyden about the beginning of February 1755[1] and reaching Dover a year later? On 2 March 1785 Malone told Percy: 'Dr Johnson used to say that he never could get an accurate account of Goldsmith's history while he was abroad.' Yet the Grand Tour was usually a highlight in a man's life. Why was Goldsmith so averse from talking about it?

4   Goldsmith owed more to his mother than to any other person. It was she alone who insisted on his schooling, so as to enable him later to go to College. Without her, he would never have received the serious education and acquired the culture which enabled him to become a writer. Why, in later years, when she was living in poverty and beginning to lose her sight

1 According to Prior.

did he do nothing to assist her? It was fully in his power to
do so.

5 When did James Scott ask Goldsmith to write in support
of the ministry – stated to be Lord North's – which was being
attacked by Wilkes and 'Junius'? A recent biographer suggests
the end of 1767. But Wilkes was then in France and North was
not Prime Minister. And why did Goldsmith refuse?

6 What were Goldsmith's relations with women, and particularly with Mary Horneck? This was not an ordinary
relationship.

All these questions are more or less wrapped in mystery. The
fact is, that for Goldsmith's inner life, his thoughts and feelings
in solitude, there is only guesswork. He kept no journal, he left
no memoir other than the impersonal notes which he confided
to Percy; and few of his letters have survived. We are handicapped by the knowledge that we cannot often give credence to
what he tells us about himself, unless it is corroborated by
others. Several instances will be given. He was an inveterate
liar, and would no doubt have agreed with that other Irishman
who 'had too much respect for Truth to drag her out on every
paltry occasion'. Yet many people found him 'lovable' and his
friends included men and women of high character and intelligence. Finally his works, and more particularly *The Vicar of
Wakefield*, have enjoyed an international celebrity and, what is
even more rare, won a kind of personal affection for their
author.

In preparing this study I have had recourse to Professor
Arthur Friedman's edition of *The Collected Works* (Oxford,
1966, 5 volumes) which has the advantage over J. W. M. Gibbs's
otherwise excellent edition (London, 1885, 5 volumes) in that
it offers a better arrangement of the material and more abundant
and up-to-date annotations: to these, all writers on Goldsmith
must be indebted. There remain doubts as to some of the
anonymous articles and essays which Gibbs, following Percy

and others, believed to be by Goldsmith, and the eighteen new pieces which, after careful study, Professor R. S. Crane identified as his.[1] Friedman accepts and includes the articles published by Crane, but excludes some of those, notably the 'Poetical Scale' and the seven papers 'On the Study of the Belles-Lettres' which were printed by Gibbs. There is no proof as regards the above ascriptions. It seems regrettable that Friedman accepts as by Goldsmith the long, carping review of Kedington's Homer – which reflects no credit on the reviewer – but not the learned papers 'On the Study of the Belles-Lettres' which are superior to most of Goldsmith's journalistic writings. The matter is not, however, of great importance. The 'Essays' which Goldsmith acknowledged as his own would scarcely have been remembered if they had not been by the author of *The Deserted Village*. On the other hand, the translation of Vida's *Scacchiae Ludus*, which Gibbs had good reason for printing as by Goldsmith, but which Professor Friedman excludes, is an excellent piece of work, and the evidence for Goldsmith's authorship is such as to justify our ascribing it to him.

[1] *New Essays by Oliver Goldsmith*, University of Chicago Press, 1927.

Acknowledgements

I have been greatly assisted by the staff of the libraries of Durham University and Cambridge University for the many facilities which they have afforded; by Dr Hans Lieb, Staatsarchivar of Schaffhausen, for information about the Falls of the Rhine, which proves – unfortunately – that Goldsmith did not see them 'frozen right across'; and by Professor F. C. Spooner, of the Department of Economic History in the University of Durham, who has very kindly calculated for me the relative value of money between Goldsmith's times and our own; as a result of which it is now clear that he was well paid for his work and, after about 1767, a comparatively well-to-do man. It is a pleasure also to recall the kindness of the Very Reverend R. L. P. Milburn, Master of the Temple, who received me in his house, showed me the grave believed to be that of Goldsmith, outside the Temple Church, and assisted me in the search for illustrations. For these I gratefully acknowledge the services of the British Museum, the National Portrait Gallery, the Courtauld Institute of Art, and the Cambridge University Library. I would also like to extend my thanks to the Rt. Hon. Lord Tollemache for permission to reproduce a painting from his collection; *The Masquerade at Ranelagh*. I am also grateful to the editor of the journal *Review of English Studies*, for allowing me to reprint a substantial part of an article first published by them in 1935 as Appendix I: 'The History of Francis Wills'; and to the editor of the *Durham University Journal* for permission to reprint Appendix II, 'A Note on Goldsmith's Influence on the French Stage', first published by them in 1941. Valuable information has also been obtained by an old friend, Father Denys Gonthier, who, being in Paris, has made extensive enquiries on my behalf. (See page 27.) Finally, I owe a suggestion connected with Goldsmith's attitude to Sterne, and its possible influence on *The Vicar of Wakefield*, to I. Lytton Sells. To my wife, indeed, I owe a very great debt. She has read the whole work in manuscript and corrected many

sions and shortcomings. In addition she has assisted me in my interpretation of Goldsmith, and she also pointed out the impossibility of his having seen the Falls of the Rhine frozen right across, and the bearing of this on the chronology of his Grand Tour. Careful re-reading of *The Vicar of Wakefield*, relating it to Goldsmith's circumstances at the time of composition, has enabled me to see the novel in a light other than the accepted one, and as the work of a disillusioned rather than of a good-natured man.

On the other hand it has been a pleasure to record his relations with Mary Horneck, accepted in Goldsmith's circle as a woman of some culture, who was to prove a softening and refining influence in his later life, if not a possible missed romance.

Contents

Illustrations

Part One

❧THE LIFE❧

Chapter 1

An Irish Boyhood

❧ 1728-45 ❧

I

When Oliver Goldsmith was born, in the very heart of Ireland, the country was still in the state of quiescence, or rather paralysis, that followed the upheavals of the past century and a half. To the subjects of Elizabeth I, Ireland was a country near at hand and so easier to colonise than North America. Catholic estates had been confiscated on a gigantic scale; but no acts of violence had left so deep a scar on Irish memories as the seizure of the six counties of Ulster, the destruction of the clan-system and the planting of colonies of Scots[1] and English. Although Charles I, one of the most tolerant of men, had felt some sympathy for the Irish, the London Parliament showed none. 'Popery' was not to be tolerated. In the struggle which began in 1641 and lasted until 1652, murders provoked reprisals, numbers of Protestants were killed and Catholics massacred in great numbers. By 1652, out of a population of about a million and a half, 600,000 had died in war or perished from starvation, some 35,000 had emigrated, whilst scores of boys and girls had been sold as slaves.

Charles II would have liked to make some amends, but public opinion in England was against him, and in Ireland the administration and the House of Commons were solidly Protestant and opposed to any change. By the Act of Settlement most of the best land was now in the hands of Englishmen; and a further Bill of 1663 deprived 3,000 small landowners

[1] Who, however, may have felt they were returning to the fatherland.

of their property. So that whereas, prior to 1641, most of the land fit for agriculture had belonged to the Irish, now most of it had been acquired by Protestant settlers. The Catholic religion was tolerated, but no Catholic schools were permitted. When James II landed with a French army in 1689, he was naturally greeted with enthusiasm. A new Parliament, mainly Catholic, met in Dublin and passed measures less vindictive than might have been expected. But the reaction was short-lived. The defeat of James's army and the capture of Limerick were the prelude to an era of extreme oppression. The Irish army migrated to France, as well as most of the Irish nobles; the remainder were nearly all reduced to poverty, and the common people were thus deprived of those who could have led or protected them. Further measures subjected Irish Catholics to the severest restrictions; impoverished, ignorant and deprived of educational facilities, they were now incapable of resistance. Since Parliament, and the administrative and the learned professions, were open only to Protestants, it was not surprising if some of the Catholic gentry who had survived and been educated abroad, conformed at least temporarily to the Anglican Church. Robert Nugent seems to have been one of these. The country was still so impoverished that many families, like that of Arthur Murphy – another friend of Goldsmith and one who had been educated in France – moved to London, as did scores of their penurious countrymen.[1]

Conditions were, however, improving, at least in parts of the country. The Duke of Devonshire was an enlightened viceroy (1738-45) who in time of famine alleviated distress out of his own pocket; while the Earl of Chesterfield who succeeded him proved an excellent administrator. Even so, many districts remained scenes of dire poverty and squalor. The Protestant squires or 'gentry', a dissipated and self-indulgent class, like their English counterparts, often oppressed

[1] W. E. H. Lecky, *A History of Ireland in the Eighteenth Century*, London, 1902, vol 1, *passim*.

their Irish tenants.[1] On the other hand, a spirit of toleration on the part of many Protestants was steadily growing. They assisted Catholics in the purchase of land, and protected them from the savagery of the penal laws. Edmund Burke's mother was a Catholic and he in due course married a Catholic girl. George Berkeley, the most eminent metaphysician of his age, recommended in Dr Madden's *Querist* (1735) that Catholics should be allowed 'to purchase forfeited land' and also be admitted to the full privileges of education at Trinity College.[2] It seems likely that the class of Anglican clergy to which Goldsmith's parents belonged, were on good terms with the Catholic peasantry.

Such was the state of Ireland when Goldsmith came into the world. Although scarcely touched on by his biographers, this background is relevant to the conditions in which he grew up. By the time he was a schoolboy and was learning French from the priests, he must have become acutely aware of it. This awareness helps to explain his often excessive benevolence to the poor, and his freedom from anti-Catholic bias.

II

In the early seventeenth century a certain Juan Romeiro, who happened to be in Ireland with a Spanish nobleman, decided to stay. He married a Miss Goldsmith, turned Anglican, and was given a living in County Mayo. The Goldsmiths had been established in Ireland since at least 1540. In the seventeenth century they tended to be hereditary clergymen, and were soon as Irish in temperament as the natives. The Reverend John (Juan) Goldsmith's grandson was a fairly well-to-do man who led an easy life and imprudently begat thirteen children. Charles, one of his sons, although educated at Trinity College, Dublin, seems to have had no money, no forethought, and

---

[1] Ibid., pp 284, 291–94.
[2] Ibid., pp 300–18.

little practical ability. As easy-going as his father, he lived, like Micawber, in the expectation that something would turn up.

What turned up, in 1718, when Charles was about twenty-eight, was Ann Jones, daughter of the Reverend Oliver Jones. It looked as though she had expectations, and Charles married her; whereupon her uncle, who was rector of Kilkenny West, gave the couple the use of a house at Pallas in County Longford. It was here that they lived for about twelve years and here that their son Oliver was born, apparently on 10 November 1728. He had an elder sister, Catherine, and an elder brother, Henry. Charles and Maurice were younger brothers.

Hitherto, the Reverend Charles had made a living by acting as curate in near-by parishes and from the produce of a farm of fifty acres which his mother-in-law had given him. But in 1730 – again through his wife's relations – he was appointed curate of Kilkenny West, and moved to a better house outside Lissoy (since renamed Auburn) with a farm of seventy acres. It stood on the plain near Lough Ree, in a region commemorated in *The Deserted Village* and recalled in *An History of the Earth and Animated Nature*.

Young Oliver, handicapped by a thickset body and irregular features, not to speak of the example of a happy-go-lucky father, impressed his first schoolmistress as 'impenetrably stupid'. A little later, however, at the village school at Lissoy, the master seems to have been helpful. Thomas Byrne, an old soldier – he had been quarter-master in Lord Galway's regiment in the War of the Spanish Succession – was a great raconteur, diverting his pupils with tales of the O'Donnells and other heroes of old Ireland. A fairly good Latinist, he could translate Virgil into English verse; and it was perhaps he who first gave Oliver a taste for versifying, which he began to exercise while still a small boy. What is even more likely is that Byrne's stories and the tales which Oliver heard from wandering entertainers – professional story-tellers in both senses of the word – blurred in his mind the borderline between fact and fiction and encouraged a propensity for romancing.

On holidays or summer evenings he liked to wander in the countryside, seeking a glimpse of an otter in the river, listening to the cries of water-birds and thrilling with terror as did 'the whole village', he tells us, at the 'dismally hollow' booming of the bittern. Unhappily, when he was nine, an attack of small-pox left his face badly marked for life. After he recovered, his parents sent him to a diocesan school at Elphin, where he was regarded as having talent. Why he was moved to Campbell's school at Athlone is a mystery; it was Campbell's illness two years later, in 1741, that led to his attending Patrick Hughes' school at Edgeworthstown for the rest of his schooldays, that is from the age of thirteen to seventeen.

This was the longest and most serious schooling that he received. He here acquired a real knowledge of Latin and is said to have enjoyed Horace and Ovid, Livy and Tacitus. Without these studies he could scarcely have become so clear and elegant a prose writer. Mr Hughes drew him out and gave him con-fidence, and Goldsmith afterwards told Thomas Percy that Hughes had been the most helpful of his teachers. His holidays were spent at Ballymahon and here one or two Catholic priests who had been educated in a French seminary, taught him French, a language in which he was to grow proficient: such is the tradition reported by Washington Irving,[1] and no other explanation seems to fit the facts.

Writers on Goldsmith appear not to have understood how dependent he was to be, throughout his career, on a knowledge of French literature. It was as a reviewer of French as well as English works, and as a translator, that Griffiths first employed him. He used French authors in most of his popular compila-tions, including even the histories of England; and these well-paid publishers' enterprises were the principal and most

[1] *Oliver Goldsmith: a Biography*, New York, 1844, vol 1, ch 5. The statement is repeated by Forster.

lucrative sources of his income. Furthermore, he relied exten-
sively from the outset on French writers for his original work:
for his journalistic ventures and essays, and for *The Citizen of
the World*. The principal plots of both his comedies are taken
from Marivaux, with minor details from Brueys and Le Grand.
His library, at the time of his death, contained at least 103 items
in French, many in two or three volumes, some in fifteen,
nineteen and twenty-one.

Thus, without a good knowledge of the language and an
extensive acquaintance with eighteenth-century French literature and scientific writings, not only would his work have been
materially different, but one does not see how he could have
made a living at all. For *The Vicar of Wakefield*, for the two
long poems and for the two plays, the payments though
individually substantial, could not possibly have kept him in
London for the eighteen years which he spent there.

It is not that a reading knowledge of French was at all
unusual in the eighteenth century. It was the international
language of polite society and was tending to replace Latin in
scientific publications. Men like Gray, Horace Walpole and
Gibbon knew it as well as Goldsmith, if not better. Many
people were of course better acquainted with the country itself.
But no one depended on the literature, imaginative, historical
and scientific, to anything like the same extent. In this respect
Goldsmith was quite exceptional.

One does not pick up a foreign language from the air or
learn to speak and understand it without personal tuition. Here
one must go back to the beginnings, that is, for Goldsmith, to
his school holidays between 1741 and 1745. On the oral founda-
tion laid at this time he was able to build up a knowledge of the
written language, as will be seen later, at Trinity College and in
Holland.

Where had the priests learned French? Since no Catholic
seminaries were permitted at this time, young men who wished
to take orders went to the Continent, most of them to France.

Here they had the choice of eight or nine colleges, including the two in Paris which were the most important: the old Collège des Lombards in the rue des Carmes, and the Communauté des Clercs in the rue du Cheval-Vert. The building still exists.[1] As the course of study in preparation for the priesthood often lasted nine or ten years, most of these men, on their return home, must have known and spoken French as well as their native tongue. It is unlikely that a boy of fourteen or fifteen, as indolent as Oliver, could have learned French on his own initiative; yet in the winter of 1753-54, when he was preparing to leave Edinburgh, he wrote to Thomas Contarine: 'I . . . intend to visit Paris, where the great Mr Farhein, Petit and Du Hammel de Monceau instruct their pupils in all the branches of medicine. They speak French, and consequently I shall have much the advantage of most of my countrymen, as I am perfectly acquainted with that language. . . .'[2]

It was probably during the years spent at Patrick Hughes' school, that he heard of Turlogh O'Carolan, a kind of Irish Homer, blind like Homer, who travelled from place to place on horseback. He carried with him his harp and a repertory of heroic tales which he recited in gentlemen's halls, in return for board and lodging. Other songs – 'for he could improvise' – were designed to compliment the family which was entertaining him. 'He was,' writes Goldsmith, 'at once a poet, a musician, a composer, and sung his own verses to his harp.' His astonishing memory and facetious turn of mind were once illustrated when he visited an Irish nobleman on the same day as a distinguished musician. He at once challenged the latter

---

[1] My information about it, and about the number of Irish priests who were trained in France – some 180 in the period preceding the Revolution— I owed in 1921 to the late Father Patrick Boyle who very kindly helped me as a research student. It is not now, however, an *Irish* College. The Reverend Father Denys Gonthier, of Assumption College in Worcester, Mass., has made detailed researches for me, and he finds that it is now occupied by Sisters of the Sacred Heart, by Polish priests and refugee clergy from Poland.

[2] *The Collected Letters of Oliver Goldsmith,* ed Katherine C. H. Balderston, Cambridge, 1928, p 15.

'to a trial of skill'. The musician played on his violin [airs from] Vivaldi's fifth concerto.[1] Carolan then played them on his harp, without a mistake, though he had never heard the concerto before; and he followed up this achievement by playing an improvisation of his own à la Vivaldi. An inveterate whisky drinker, he in the end drank a cup too many. He had died, 'the last of the bards', in 1738, and Goldsmith was sufficiently impressed by what he had heard to devote a short paper to him in *The British Magazine* for July 1760.

On his way home for his last vacation from Edgeworthstown, Oliver allegedly had an adventure so comical, but so true to type, that his biographers have nearly all accepted it. The distance was about twenty miles and he had the use of a horse; but the roads were very bad and, as a friend had given him a guinea, he decided to travel in style. On reaching Ardagh he enquired of the first person he met for 'the best house' in the place, and this person, a humourist named Cornelius Kelly, directed him to the home of Mr Featherstone, the local squire. Suspecting no trick, Oliver dismounted at the front door, called to the stableman to look after his horse, walked into the house and asked the gentleman he saw there to 'get something comfortably good in a hurry, for that he was very hungry'. Whereupon Mr Featherstone, amused by his visitor's swagger, decided to play up to him. Oliver then ordered a bottle of wine and invited his host and the latter's wife and daughters to share supper with him. He even ordered two more bottles; and before going up to bed, requested that a hot cake be prepared for his breakfast. It was only next morning that, on asking for his bill, he discovered the mistake and was overcome with confusion.

Such, in brief, is the story contained in his sister Catherine's narrative, written over forty years after the event.[2] Goldsmith's biographers regard it as the source of Marlow's blunder in *She*

---

[1] Goldsmith wrote that Carolan played over on his fiddle the fifth concerto of Vivaldi (*British Magazine*, July 1760).

[2] Reprinted by Miss Balderston in an Appendix to the *Collected Letters*, pp 166–8.

Stoops to Conquer, and it may be, at least in part. But what seems possible in the glamour of the footlights is less acceptable in real life. Inns usually carry a sign over the front door. It is just conceivable that he took the Featherstone's house for an inn; but that, after entering, he could remain under such an illusion for more than half-an-hour seems incredible. It is more likely that, if he ever made the initial mistake,[1] he soon discovered his blunder, but that the Featherstones overcame his embarrassment by entertaining him for the night; and that on his return home he invented the rest of the story. Oliver was a born *mystificateur*[2] and an inveterate plagiarist. If he had read a story or a play of the kind (such as Dancourt's *Maison de Campagne*) he was capable of ascribing it to himself; this also is a possible explanation.

It was a few months after this that Catherine eloped with Daniel Hodson, whose father was a man of property. The Reverend Charles, though deeply annoyed, felt he should settle some money on his daughter by way of reparation. He undertook to provide her with £52 a year, a kindness very prejudicial to Oliver who, in the natural course of things, would have proceeded to Trinity College as a paying student. The family now hesitated about this. But Ann Goldsmith, aware of her son's unusual talents, urged the need of a university education, and in the event it was resolved that he should apply for entry by examination as a sizar. The prospect did not appeal to him.

To an ambitious boy, however, the plan presented great advantages. The sizars were required to sweep the floors and wait on the Fellows' table. In return for these, not onerous, duties, they received board, lodging and tuition free. It is true that they did not wear splendid gowns like the young noblemen; but, as Constantia Maxwell observes, 'many famous men

---

[1] Once, when staying at Bath with Lord Clare, he mistook the Earl of Northumberland's house for Lord Clare's. They were side by side and looked the same. But the Northumberlands put him at his ease.

[2] His detailed and circumstantial account of how he had heard Voltaire arguing with Fontenelle in Paris is a complete fabrication.

have been sizars – notably Sir Isaac Newton at Trinity College, Cambridge. . .' The term had come from Cambridge as had many of the official duties and customs of the Irish College.[1] It was the dress even more than the inferior status from which Oliver recoiled. He knew he was stocky and ill-favoured – people reminded him of it – and he was very conscious of the role dress plays and its importance to one's appearance. In later life this became an obsession with him.

In the present juncture his uncle, the Rev Thomas Contarine, intervened. He was the grandson of an Italian monk, a member of the Contarini family, patricians of Venice. This Contarini had fallen in love with a nun who was also noble; they had married and taken refuge in France. Here the wife died. The widower crossed to London; but, cold-shouldered there, he decided to seek his fortune in Ireland. At Chester, where travellers took ship for Dublin, he fell into conversation with a Miss Chaloner who spoke fluent Italian and had the further advantage of being related to the Provost of Trinity College. It may be assumed that Contarini, like many Venetian nobles, possessed both mental and physical distinction. Miss Chaloner married him; he himself having turned Anglican, was given a living near Elphin. His grandson, a good scholar and a friend of Bishop Berkeley, had married Charles Goldsmith's sister, Jane. He was at this time prebend of Oran, near Elphin, and was fairly well-to-do. He had taken a liking for young Oliver. Under his persuasion, the boy agreed to be educated at what was then the most eminent University in the British Isles. At the beginning of June 1745, he set out for Dublin.

[1] Constantia Maxwell, *A History of Trinity College, Dublin: 1591–1892*, Dublin, 1946, pp 44–5. The Rev Patrick Brontë was a sizar at Cambridge, as was Sterne.

Chapter 2

Dublin and its Aftermath

1745-52

The country round Lissoy was pleasant enough, as one can judge from Goldsmith's picture of it in *The Deserted Village*; but the road to Dublin traversed forlorn and desolate regions. In former days the greater part of Ireland had been covered with magnificent forests. The Irish loved their woodland haunts; but most of the trees had now been ruthlessly felled. Here and there, by the roadside, one passed a miserable hovel where the whole family, with its dogs and pigs, lived in the one room, and the smoke from the peat-fire escaped through a hole in the roof. But Dublin was a fine city. With a hundred thousand inhabitants, it was easily the second largest in the United Kingdom. It is true that the old town which, with its narrow streets, must have resembled London before the Great Fire, was dirty and malodorous like all big places. But Dublin was beautified by the new Parliament House, completed in 1739, by the new quarter which housed the gentry with their carriages and sedan chairs, and by the vast area of St Stephen's Green.[1] London, as we shall see, enjoyed no such amenities: it was also a great deal filthier, overhung by a dense pall of murk, a breeder of disease and 'devourer of men'.

Goldsmith could live here in far better surroundings than he was to find in London. He also, as a student, enjoyed advantages greater than in any English or Scottish university. Trinity College, with its spacious courts, covered a wide area of

[1] Lecky, op. cit., pp 319–20.

ground. The Library, enriched by recent generous donations from private libraries, was subsidised by the Parliament, while a new and handsome Reading Room had been opened in 1732. The syllabus had also been improved, with the addition of chemistry, botany and anatomy, and the establishment of a laboratory and an anatomical theatre.[1] It is recorded in a work on *The Ancient and Modern State of Ireland* (1759) that 'the students are carefully instructed in the more refined parts of Classical Learning; Oriental, Ancient and Modern Languages; Criticism; Sacred and Profane History; Oratory; Logick; Ethics and Metaphysics...' as well as the sciences, mathematics, law and theology.[2] By contrast with their counterparts in Oxford and Cambridge, the professors and lecturers were active in teaching – one of them a little too active for Oliver's taste. The entrance examination was a much more searching test than in the English universities, and the whole standard was higher. Lord Chesterfield when Viceroy observed that 'the Irish schools and universities are indisputably better than ours'. That Ireland then produced some of the most brilliant thinkers and writers of the age, like Swift, Berkeley, Burke, Sheridan and Goldsmith himself, was due in no small part to the excellence of the instruction and to the facilities afforded by the Library for reading outside the required texts – facilities of which young men like Burke and Goldsmith, with their passion for books, were able to avail themselves.

On 11 June 1745, Oliver passed the entrance examination which consisted of translations from Greek and Latin texts. He was now admitted as a sizar and would be free, in due course, to compete for a scholarship or exhibition. He was given a room at the top of No. 35 staircase, which he probably shared with an old schoolfellow named Beatty. For an undergraduate on the classical side, the first year syllabus included a study of the *Aeneid*, the *Odes* of Horace, and in Greek of

---

[1] Lecky, op. cit., p 321.
[2] Maxwell, op. cit., p 148.

Epictetus; some logic from Burgesdicius, the bugbear of students, who despised it; and some mathematics. Oliver was a good student if at times 'thoughtless' and heedless. But he was unfortunate in his Tutor, the Reverend Theaker Wilder, a violent and bad-tempered man, unlike his colleagues. Wilder ridiculed young Goldsmith in class, and Wilder's tastes were the opposite of his pupil's; he preferring logic and mathematics to the Latin poetry which Oliver loved. This perhaps explains why, in his essay on *The Present State of Polite Learning in Europe*, Goldsmith was to write that 'Mathematics seems a science to which the meanest intellects are equal'.

But he was not always suffering under Wilder. Oliver seems to have known one or two of the other tutors; he made kind and useful friends, especially Edward Mills, a distant cousin; while his good voice and gift for rendering Irish songs brought him a certain popularity. Apart from all this, we have no exact knowledge of how he spent his leisure hours, which were many. Already a great reader, he browsed in the library; and since, during the ten years or so that followed his graduation, no library seems to have been at his disposal – except, for two or three months, Thomas Contarine's – we must ascribe to this period more than the beginnings of that wide knowledge of English poetry which made of him a competent book reviewer and essayist. And where, if not here, did he acquire that exceptional knowledge of French which he possessed by the time he reached Edinburgh? The spoken language he had learned from the priests, to some extent; the written language he could acquire only from books; and it is unlikely that the priests would have lent him many: Bossuet's *Sermons* and *Oraisons funèbres*, perhaps; Boileau's *Art poétique* and *Satires* possibly. The Library of Trinity College opened a wider field, as did the City Library; for French classical literature had reached Dublin in the early years of the century, if not before. Berkeley, who entered Trinity College in 1704, was influenced, in the formation of his philosophy, by Descartes and especially by

B

Malebranche, as well as by Locke and the metaphysical articles in Bayle's *Dictionnaire*; it is significant that when visiting Paris he made a point of calling on the author of the *Recherche de la Vérité*.[1] To return to Goldsmith – Prior tells us that when in Holland (1754) he widened his knowledge of French literature. In default of any other explanation, it follows that the foundations of this knowledge were laid in leisure hours at Trinity College. It is difficult to see where else he could possibly have picked up so out-of-the-way a book as Marana's *Espion Turc*.

Dublin offered much in the way of popular entertainment, from cock-fighting and bull-baiting to musical recitals, and drama at the Smock Alley Theatre, which was then under the management of Thomas Sheridan, father of the dramatist. Here, in the winter of 1745, Garrick appeared in some Shakespearean tragedies, and Mrs Bellamy in Congreve's *The Way of the World*.[2] If Oliver heard them, he has left no record of it; nor did he know Burke, who had entered Trinity College in 1744.

There were indeed too many distractions in Dublin. Oliver needed a tutor who would interest him more in his work, and a father who would warn him against indolence. Charles Goldsmith no doubt gave good advice, but a good example would have been better. Early in 1747 he died, leaving his wife and younger children in much reduced circumstances. Far from being steadied by this misfortune, Oliver now became more irresponsible. It was impossible for his mother to continue sending him an occasional remittance, and moreover he never knew how to husband what resources he had. He sometimes pawned his books, sometimes composed ballads which he sold for five shillings each. Then, in May, he took part in a student riot. Dublin undergraduates were mischievous and violent, and the authorities had no such means of controlling them as existed at Cambridge and Oxford. The present riot was no

---

[1] A. A. Luce, *Berkeley and Malebranche*, Oxford, 1967.
[2] J. E. Walsh, *Sketches of Ireland Fifty Years Ago*, Dublin, 1847, pp 7–8.

mere fight with the butchers – a more usual source of trouble[1] – but with the police. The leaders caught one or two constables and ducked them in a cistern; they then tried to break into the town gaol, known as 'the Black Dog'. Some of them were actually killed. Oliver was lucky to get off with a reprimand,[2] and to be able, in June, to compete for a scholarship.

He was awarded an exhibition, but the records show that during the rest of the year his attendance at lectures was irregular. Prior records a story to the effect that he became entangled with some woman and that his friends had to disengage him from a marriage that would have been disastrous. One night in the winter he gave a party, contrary to College regulations, for men and girls from the city. The noise of dancing and merriment roused Mr Wilder, who drove the revellers downstairs and dealt their host a resounding buffet. Always sensitive to indignity – he was now after all about nineteen – he decided to emigrate, *or so it is said*. But this was more easily thought of than executed. The sale of a few clothes realised little cash and in the end he set off for home with only a shilling in his pocket. The journey seems to have taken about a week, and Oliver reached his brother Henry's house with little on his back and nothing in his stomach.

Henry fed and clothed him, then took him back to Dublin and induced Wilder to overlook the misdemeanour. Peace thus re-established was of short duration. One day in the spring of 1748 when Wilder was lecturing on physics, he asked Oliver to define the centre of gravity. Oliver could not. Theaker gave the explanation, and then: 'Now, blockhead,' he asked, 'where is *your* centre of gravity?' The reply, too improper to have been recorded, brought the house down, and also the tutor's wrath. The months that followed brought no further *éclat*, but young Goldsmith had not changed. He worked when so

[1] Lecky, op. cit., p 322.
[2] BM Additional MSS 42517. Cited by R. M. Wardle, *Oliver Goldsmith,* Lawrence (Kansas) and London, 1957, pp 35 and 302, note 33. See Maxwell, pp 133–9, for a detailed account of student rowdiness.

minded, is supposed to have translated Macrobius and to have been able to 'turn an ode of Horace into English better than any of' the others. This one can believe. But he was always short of money. Mills sometimes supplied him and more often gave him breakfast. One morning, when Oliver did not appear as invited, Mills discovered him not exactly in bed, but inside the mattress which he had ripped open. And here was the explanation: on the previous evening he had met a woman with five very small children. She said she had arrived from the country, that her husband was in hospital and that she had no shelter and no money. Oliver had none, either. But he took her to the College, gave her all his blankets and what clothes he could spare. This was only the first of many occasions when he acted as a private welfare agent, sometimes at his own expense, sometimes at other people's. He had learned this vice from his father. His heedless alms-giving in later life to spongers and beggars partly accounts for his being, at the time of his death, at least £2,000 in debt.

Yet his literary attainments were considerable and he did well in the examinations held in December 1748. Prior states that he took his Finals soon afterwards and his B.A. in February; but this is doubtful. It appears that early in 1749 he went to stay with Contarine whose library provided ample means of study for the final examinations. It would be a searching test; and since Oliver had pawned his Greek Lexicon and probably other books, a resource of this kind was essential. It therefore seems likely that he passed his Finals not on 27 February 1749, but on the same day in 1750, and that he then received his B.A. and returned home.

The father of the 'Man in Black' in *The Citizen of the World*, whose story is supposed to contain personal reminiscences, had been disappointed 'in the middling figure I made at the University.' Goldsmith had figured quite well, academically. He had procured from his books and lectures the literary equipment that was to make him the most versatile writer of his age. But there were other sides to the picture. If he had been left to himself, he would not have troubled to go to the university; once there, he had to be helped, encouraged and pushed, to take a degree. Freed from direct home influence, he had not been subject to the personal discipline which, at Oxford and Cambridge, the colleges and university Proctors imposed on undergraduates. He had mixed with low-class Dubliners and upperclass College rowdies, and from them acquired faults which clung to him throughout life: an addiction to gambling and a sort of heedless irresponsibility.

His brother may have welcomed him; his mother, who had pinched and saved for him, can hardly have felt much enthusiasm. The problem now was how to provide for his future. As he was the most feckless of a family notorious for its lack of practical sense, and as he apparently had no notion of a career and no desire to do anything, the prospects looked decidedly dim. For a time he lived with the Hodsons at Lissoy. Country life, with no regular employment, was entirely to his taste; and when the family urged him to take Holy Orders, he objected, possibly because, like the Man in Black, 'to wear a long wig when I liked a short one, or a black coat when I generally dressed in brown, I thought a restraint upon my liberty'; but more probably because he felt no vocation for a life that would involve, in addition to clerical duties, school teaching and perhaps farming. Once again, however, Thomas Contarine used his influence, and Oliver presented himself for ordination to Dr Synge, the Bishop of Elphin. The Bishop decided that he was too young, but he may have had other reasons. Oliver is said to have been wearing a pair of scarlet breeches. He seems to have been capable of anything.

It was a great relief to have been rejected by the Bishop. He could now wander by the Inny or the Shannon, play the flute, and try to catch otters. Some of his evenings he spent reading what books he could find, accounts of travel, novels and eastern tales – the latter being much in vogue. At other times be amused himself with Robert Bryanton, an old friend and now the squire of Ballymahon; Oliver at this time was living there with his mother whose previous home at Lissoy had been taken over by the Hodsons. Goldsmith and Bryanton are said to have organised a circle at George Conway's inn at Lissoy, and one can well believe that Oliver, with his repertory of songs, became the life and soul of these parties. They furnished hints, Washington Irving surmised, for the scene of the 'Three Jolly Pigeons' in *She Stoops to Conquer*. The guess is likely, and it proved so tempting that in after years the Irish tavern was renamed the 'Three Jolly Pigeons', much as Lissoy was renamed Auburn.

Of these junketings in low company Mrs Goldsmith and Henry disapproved, and it was again Contarine who found a remedy. He arranged for Oliver to be engaged as tutor in the house of Mr Flinn, a man of property in Roscommon. This suited Oliver. The salary was good, he ate with the family and in the evenings played cards with them. One night, however, after he had been living with the Flinns for about a year and had just been paid, he lost at cards all his money, and his temper. He accused his opponent of 'unfair play' – whatever that may have meant. There was a row and he threw up his job. But the fact that he was given a good horse and £30 in cash suggests that the complaint was not ill-founded.

Thirty pounds was a large sum in those days, and some of it would have been helpful to Ann Goldsmith who was living near the poverty line. But Oliver vanished from the region. Six weeks later he turned up at his mother's house without the horse he had been given and without the money. She was, Mrs Hodson wrote some forty years later, 'much concern^d at his folly & c^d not be readily reconcild to him, but his Brother and Sisters so contrived to meet at his Mothers to bring on a reconciliation. . . .' Mrs Goldsmith insisted on an explanation, and 'he then told his mother if she c^d cooly sit down & listen he wd resolve the many questions asked'. Here was his story:

He had gone to Cork, sold the horse and paid the Captain of an American ship for his passage. The winds being contrary, the ship was delayed for three weeks, when Oliver, returning from a jaunt into the country, found that it had sailed in his absence. He lingered in Cork until he had only two guineas left; then bought for £2 a miserable nag which he named Fiddleback, and with a crown in his pocket set off for the house of a college friend who lived only eight miles away. Not far out of Cork he met a poor woman with 'eight little clean children', who told a pitiful story of her husband being in gaol for debt and herself dependent on him. Oliver gave her half a crown. Now as his friend had often invited him to come and stay for the summer, he felt sure of a welcome and a loan. On reaching the friend's house, he was set upon by a 'large mastiff', rescued by a grim old serving-woman and embraced by the friend. The latter, who was allegedly recovering from a severe illness, enquired for his news, but on being asked for a loan, walked about in silence. Dinner appeared at last, or rather a small bowl of sago, some sour milk and a hunk of stale bread. At eight o'clock his host suggested that they should go to bed, since his rule was 'to lye with the lamb & rise with the lark'. Next morning Oliver said that he was proposing to leave, a proposal which the other warmly commended, while declining to lend the guinea which Oliver requested. He would however lend a horse; whereupon, going to his room, he took from under the bed an oak walking stick. Oliver was of a mind to lay this across his friend's shoulders; but at that moment there came a knock at the street door and a gentlemanly neighbour, a 'counsellor-at-law' was shown in. The friend introduced Oliver, and the neighbour invited them both to dine with him at his seat, 'a most beautiful place'. After a first-rate meal which restored Oliver's strength and spirits, the counsellor's two 'lovely daughters' played on the harpsichord so sweetly that they brought tears to their father's eyes, since they reminded him of his dead wife. The friend took his leave, but Oliver, being urged to stay, remained for three days with this hospitable family. When he was about to depart the Counsellor offered him his purse and insisted that he should take what he needed; also a horse and servant to accompany him. But he nobly demurred to accepting more than 'three half guineas'.

This narrative contains no dates and no names. Much of it flows on in a continuous sentence unbroken by punctuation, and the spelling is bad; but it is the only genuine record we possess.[1] Thomas Percy printed a *letter*, addressed to Mrs Ann Goldsmith and containing much the same narrative, correctly written and with initials to designate the friend and the Counsellor; but this has now been proved a forgery. Percy showed it to Malone, an outstanding scholar, who declared that he did not believe a word of it.[2]

To continue Mrs Hodson's statement: 'And now Dr Mother says he since I have struggld so hard to come home to you why are you not better pleas^d to see me, and pray says the Mother have you ever wrote a letter of thanks to that dear good man. . ., no says the D^r I have not then says the Mother you are an ungratefull Savage a Monster. . .'

The family and the friends who were present upbraided Oliver 'for which he for a full half houre sat listning to with grate composure and after they had vented their Passion he beg^d they wod sit down and compos themselv^s for what he told them was only to amuse them and that there was not one word in it; how ever he afterward assur^d me of its veracity'.

There is nothing to assure us of it. That Oliver should have decided to emigrate without taking leave of his mother is strange; that he should have paid for his passage to America and then missed the boat is however in keeping with his

---

[1] Reprinted by Miss Balderston in an Appendix to the *Collected Letters,* pp 170–6.
[2] Prior (vol I, pp 119–25) reproduced Malone's letter to Percy and the alleged letter to Mrs Goldsmith, to which he is supposed to have added the signature 'Oliver Goldsmith'. This 'letter' seems to have been composed, on the basis of Mrs Hodson's narrative, by an Irishman, Thomas Campbell, who evidently thought it would look more circumstantial than Mrs Hodson's.

character. But the fantastic experiences at the 'friend's' house, the providential arrival of the 'Counsellor', the 'lovely daughters' who played the harpsichord, the generous offer of money by a stranger, with the loan of a horse – all this sounds like romantic fiction. Small wonder if Malone disbelieved it.

For some time after his escapade, whatever it may have been, Oliver lived with the Hodsons. Then the Lawders persuaded Contarine, who had been outraged by Oliver's behaviour, to forgive him; and it was decided that he should be sent to London to study law. He was 'acquipt . . . handsomely' and provided with £50 by Contarine; but in Dublin where he was to embark, 'he unfortunately met a Mr S. at a Coffie house they both fell into play and los every shill^g of fivty pound, so once more return^d to his Mother a hart broken dejected being. . . .' Mrs Hodson adds that he 'undertook to behave with more circumspection'; but his conduct had outdone that of the Prodigal Son. For his mother, it was the last straw, and she refused to have anything more to do with him.

The misadventure in Dublin must have occurred in the winter of 1751–52, when Oliver was about twenty-three. He lived for 'some months' with Henry at Pallas; then quarrelled with him and moved, either to the Hodsons' at Lissoy, or more probably to Thomas Contarine's house at Kilmore. Contarine's daughter Jane, married some eighteen years before to Mr Lawder, was fond of Oliver, and in later years he remained in touch with her and her husband. Now, in 1752, the word went out again that something had to be done with Oliver. Isaac Goldsmith, Dean of Cloyne and a man of distinction, a cousin of the family, suggested a medical career. And so it was decided that Oliver should go to Edinburgh. It might take him three years to qualify as a physician and surgeon. Contarine undertook to provide £10 a year, other members of the family £15, and in the autumn of 1752 Oliver was packed off to Scotland, with a little money in hand and a great deal of good advice.

A fact which emerges from all this is that family relations were very close-knit in Ireland and that the family had a great sense of responsibility for all its members; but also that Oliver himself had very little.

Chapter 3

Edinburgh and Leyden

❧ 1752-54 ❧

When Oliver Goldsmith reached Edinburgh, entering probably by the West Port in the early morning, a 'cawdy' or
porter took his luggage from the coach and led him to a
lodging-house. Having engaged a room he sallied out to
explore the city. From St Giles's the view along the High
Street and the Canongate down to Holyrood Palace was much
as it is today; but from the esplanade of the Castle one saw,
immediately below the precipice, no neat public gardens but
the dark Nor' Loch, which stretched as far as the dam at
Halkerston's Wynd. Beyond the loch rose the low ridge on
which the 'New Town' was to be built. Sooner or later, from
that northern side, he would survey Edinburgh in all its
grandeur: the old city on its ridge and, away to the east,
Arthur's Seat and Salisbury Crags. It was the most splendidly
situated city in the British Isles, full of 'noble prospects', as
a Scotsman later pointed out to Samuel Johnson. But Goldsmith had no feeling for mountains or wild landscapes.

When it was time to return to his lodgings, he realised that
he had forgotten the name of the street and even that of his
landlady; however, a providential encounter with the 'cawdy'
whom he had employed enabled him to get back. The place
had no amenities. Two other students lodged there, but the
landlady, who provided dinner, produced a 'gigot' of mutton
at the week-end and made it serve in one form or another for
the whole week. Oliver moved to better quarters.

In an undated letter to Daniel Hodson he wrote that during the day he was 'obliged to attend the public lectures', but at night was alone in his lodging, with no society other than a folio, a skeleton, his cat and his 'meagre landlady'. But life was not expensive, since board, lodging and laundry cost only £22 a year, which seems to have been as much as, if not more than, the usual figure. On 8 May 1753 he wrote a fuller account of himself to Thomas Contarine. He was living 'as recluse as the Turkish Spy in Paris' – a reference to G.-P. Marana's book –; almost unknown save to the few who attended the lectures. But it is evident from what follows that a great number attended the classes of Alexander Monro. This distinguished man was professor of anatomy, but he often discoursed on other branches of the curriculum. He was, says Oliver, a skilful physician who attracted students from the Continent and 'even from Russia'. This was due not only to great knowledge but to a gift for clear exposition. Oliver had no great opinion of Andrew Plummer, the lecturer on chemistry, nor of Charles Alston, the professor of botany and materia medica. He proposed therefore to continue attending Monro's lectures for a second winter and then to proceed to Leyden to study under Albinus, the professor of anatomy. Meanwhile he finds the study of medicine 'the most pleasing in nature so that my labours are but a relaxation and I may truly say the only thing here that gives me pleasure.' One wonders. To this letter he added a postscript to explain that since his arrival he has had to buy everything, including shirts, and is therefore drawing £6 on his uncle. Continuing this letter, apparently after an interval, he relates that he has 'been a month in the Highlands', travelling mostly on 'a horse of about the size of a ram'.

Very different in tone is a letter of 26 September 1753 to the gay Robert Bryanton. He is obviously speaking from his heart when he confesses to 'an hereditary indolence (I have it from the mother's side)'. This last remark was so clearly untrue that it may have been meant as a joke. He will not weary Robert by describing 'this unfruitful country', with its heath-covered hills and 'valleys scarce able to feed a rabbit'. But he thinks well of the people, both poor and rich. The gentlemen are much better bred than the same class in Ireland. Dancing is popular, and balls are frequently held in 'the Edinburgh Assembly'. The ladies sit at one end of the room, the men at the other. After a time the Directress selects 'a gentleman and lady to walk a minuet, which they perform with a formality that approaches despondence.' Then others join in, and finally all take part in a country dance. Oliver maintains, presumably as a joke, that Scottish ladies 'are ten thousand times handsomer than the Irish'; but mentions having seen the Duchess of Hamilton – a celebrated Irish beauty – with 'her battered husband'. He enquires about George Conway, of the Lissoy inn, and in a PS. asks Bryanton to 'give my service to my Mother if you see her for as you express it in Ireland I have a sneaking kindness for her still' – a remark to take one's breath away.

If his first winter in Edinburgh had been, according to him, studious and austere, he was certainly amusing himself with other students in 1753 and, according to Percy's *Memoir*, 'too often mixing in scenes of dissipation'. Towards the end of November he paid his tailor's bill, had his old hat relined and silver-laced, bought thirteen yards of cloth, some of it claret-coloured, some white, also a new hat and, a fortnight later, a pair of fine worsted hose. While some of these purchases may have been necessary, it is more likely that he wished to appear to advantage at the Duke of Hamilton's. It seems that he had been introduced as a fellow countryman of the Duchess, one of the beautiful Miss Gunnings, of County Roscommon, and that she and her husband entertained him as an amusing story-teller and singer of Irish ditties. In a letter to Contarine, written probably in the New Year, he says that for 'more than a fortnight' past he has been at the Duke's house every other day, treated there 'more as a *jester* than as a companion'; but 'I disdained so servile an employment; 't was unworthy my calling as a physician.' He had not, however, disdained having dinner or supper there on each occasion.

He had begun the letter to Contarine as follows:

'My dear Uncle,

'After having spent two winters in Edinburgh, I now prepare to go to France the 10th of next February. I have seen all that this country can exhibit in the medical way, and therefore intend to visit Paris, where the great Mr Farhein, Petit, and Du Hammel de Monceau instruct their pupils in all the branches of medicine. They speak French,[1] and consequently I shall have much the advantage of most of my countrymen, as I am perfectly acquainted with that language, and few who leave Ireland are so. . . .'

From a subsequent letter to his uncle it appears that he embarked on a Scottish vessel, the 'Saint-Andrew,' which was sailing for Bordeaux. After two days at sea a storm drove them into Newcastle-on-Tyne, where he went ashore with 'six agreeable companions'. On the following evening they were making merry in a tavern when a sergeant, followed by a dozen grenadiers, burst in and arrested them. Goldsmith's companions were Scotsmen in the French service who had come home to enlist soldiers for France. He himself was held in prison for a fortnight before he could prove his innocence. Meanwhile the 'Saint-Andrew' had sailed (like the American ship at Cork) and, or so it has been alleged, foundered with all hands at the mouth of the Gironde: not the only occasion when the credulity of Goldsmith's biographers has been subjected to a certain strain. Fortunately another vessel was due to leave for Holland, so he took a passage on this, reached Rotterdam after nine days, and travelled by land to Leyden, whence he wrote

[1] According to Prior, he intended to suggest that French was used instead of Latin, as in most other faculties.

the above account. His letter, which contains a detailed description of Holland and the Dutch, was postmarked 6 May 1754 and addressed from 'Madame De Allion's' at Leyden.

A simple calculation shows that he had reached Leyden about 18 March and from this it follows that he had not seen everything he describes in the letter of 6 May. He writes, for example: 'In winter, when their canals are frozen, . . . all people are on the ice; sleds drawn by horses, and skating, are at that time, the reigning amusements. They have boats here that slide on the ice, and are driven by the winds. When they spread all their sails they go more than a mile and a half a minute, and their motion is so rapid that the eye can scarcely accompany them.' One suspects that Oliver's eye had no opportunity of doing so, since the ice had probably thawed, or begun to thaw, when he arrived. On the other hand, he travelled a little in one of the horse-drawn canal-coaches, observing the countryside. 'Nothing can equal its beauty. Wherever I turn my eye fine houses, elegant gardens statues grottoes vistas present themselves, but enter their towns you are charmed beyond description.'

He must have known that he would have no language difficulty: all educated Dutch people knew French and some preferred to write in it, like Justus van Effen whose works he was to plagiarise, and Isabella van Tuyl van Zuylen – 'Belle de Zuylen' for short – the future Madame de Charrières, whom Boswell was to court in 1764 and who later published a number of novels in French. Whether the professors lectured in Latin, Goldsmith does not say. He considered them lazy, except for Gaubius who taught chemistry. He does not mention Albinus, although the latter enjoyed a European reputation. The teaching he thought inferior to that of Edinburgh. There were only four British students.

Instead of attending a regular course of lectures and taking a degree, he devoted much time to reading and especially, according to Prior,[1] to improving his knowledge of French literature. He could also have taken lessons there. French occupied an important place in Dutch education, and we know the names of three masters, one of them English, one Dutch, who were teaching it in Leyden about this time.[2] Holland moreover was an important outlet for the French book trade and a centre for the publication of periodicals in French. It may be that Goldsmith encountered Jean Marteilhe, an old refugee, whose *Mémoires* he subsequently translated. A certain Abraham Marteilhe, perhaps a son of Jean, had been inscribed in the Law School in 1749; but the *Album Studiosorum* of Leyden does not mention Goldsmith's name; nor indeed shall we find him registered or even mentioned in the records of any Continental University.

His opinions of the Dutch were mixed. The better class imitated the French but were less easy and more ceremonious. The lower class were extremely odd. You see a creature wearing on a head of lank hair 'a half-cocked . . . hat laced with black ribbon, no coat but seven waistcoats and nine pairs of breeches'. The object of 'this well-cloathed vegetable's appetite' wears a large cap trimmed with lace, and twice as many petticoats as her lover wears breeches. She carries about with her a small stove, at which her lover lights his pipe. A Dutchwoman's appearance is the exact opposite to a Scottish woman's; the former being 'pale and fat', the latter 'lean and ruddy'. And this is not the only contrast. In Scotland 'you might see a well-dressed Duchess issuing from a dirty close and here a dirty Dutch man inhabiting a palace.' Goldsmith concludes by saying he is not sure how long he will stay in Leyden; 'however I expect to have the happiness of seeing you at Kilmore if I can next March.'[3]

If in May he intended to return home after a year's study in

---

1 Vol I, p 168.
2 K.-J. Riemens, *Esquisse historique de l'enseignement du français en Hollande depuis le XVIe jusquau XVIIIe siècle*, Leyden, 1919, ch V.
3 Letter to Thomas Contarine, 6 May 1754 (*Collected Letters*, pp 19–25).

Holland, he changed his mind before long, whether because he still wished to see Paris or because the example of Baron Holberg led him to imagine that he could tour a large part of Europe on foot without money and with only a flute and a good voice to recommend him. Ludvig Holberg had begun life as a poor boy in Bergen. He had learned French, acquired some knowledge of music and had then set off on a tour of the Continent, visiting many parts of France, Germany and Holland. In later life he settled in Copenhagen, where he made his name as a dramatist, composing a number of comedies much in the manner of Molière. The king ennobled and pensioned him.

Now it so happened that Holberg was in Leyden in 1754 and died there; and since Goldsmith afterwards wrote an account of him, it seems evident that while in Leyden he was told of Holberg's adventures.

How he managed to support himself in Holland is, like so much else in his early life and even later, a matter of conjecture. He is said to have brought £33 from Edinburgh, and this would last some time. He may then have given lessons in English and made money at cards. Dr Ellis, one of his fellow students, sometimes lent him small amounts. Once, when he made a considerable sum by gambling, and Ellis advised him to save it, he promised to do so and then gambled it away. Even so, Ellis retained a favourable impression. Despite his peculiarities, he said, Goldsmith was remarked for 'an elevation of mind . . . a philosophical tone and manner; the feelings of a gentleman'. Without the assistance of this generous Irishman, one does not well see how Oliver could have got away from Leyden. Ellis seems to have given him a few pounds to start him on the journey; but almost immediately, on passing a shop where tulip bulbs were for sale, he ordered a packet to be sent to Contarine as some return for the latter's kindness. This stripped him of all but a pound. At the beginning of 1755,[1] however, the weather may have been good, and he set out with

1 Prior says 'about February', but without proof. Early January seems more likely.

a small pack containing a flute and one clean shirt, in a more cheerful frame of mind than he was to return from the Continent twelve months later.

However piecemeal our knowledge of Goldsmith's doings between his leaving Trinity College and his leaving Leyden,[1] the year 1755 may well be called 'the Unknown Year'. He kept no journal of his travels, and the letters he wrote home – and he apparently wrote several – have all been lost. Thus an account of his tour depends mainly on hearsay, on occasional reminiscences, which sound authentic, in his subsequent writings, and on inferences from George Primrose's narrative of his tour, which are to be treated with caution.

[1] The accepted view, by Prior, Gibbs and others, is that Goldsmith remained in Holland until early 1755. But he may have left Leyden before this date, when he sent the bulbs to his uncle Contarine on the eve of his departure; these would hardly have been on sale after October or November.

Chapter 4

The Grand Tour

❧ 1755 ❧

To reach Paris, he had to cross the Austrian Netherlands, where he probably passed through Louvain, Brussels and Antwerp, then back into Holland to see the candle-lit caverns at Maestricht. But there is no record of his doings other than an article in No. II of *The Bee* on 'Happiness in a great measure dependent on Constitution', in which he writes:

I remember to have seen a slave in a fortification in Flanders, who appeared no way touched with his situation. He was maimed, deformed and chained; obliged to work from the appearance of day till nightfall, and condemned to this for life; yet with all these circumstances of apparent wretchedness, he sung, would have danced but that he wanted a leg, and appeared the merriest, happiest man of all the garrison. What a practical philosopher was here! a happy constitution supplied philosophy, and though seemingly destitute of wisdom, he was really wise.

In most of Goldsmith's biographies the account of his doings in France, Switzerland and Italy is inadequate, or ambiguous, or inaccurate. Reaching Paris about the end of February, he no doubt found the streets dirty and evil-smelling like those of Dublin and, as he later discovered, those of London. But this would not have concerned him overmuch. Life in Paris was gay and brilliant. His natural impulse would be to seek out his countrymen at the Communauté des Clercs, in the rue du Cheval-Vert. A mention of the priests of Bally-mahon, not to speak of his own brogue, would secure him an entry, and his Irish songs and amusing stories, a welcome. One may assume that these priests found him a cheap lodging in the Latin Quarter and occasionally entertained him to meals. Many Irish priests haunted the streets and the small hotels around the Sorbonne. One remembers, in this connexion, Jean-Jacques Rousseau's experience on his return from Venice in 1744. He had taken a room in his old hotel, where Thérèse Levasseur was employed as laundress. The Irish and Gascon abbés had teased her and Rousseau had defended her; then they had turned their raillery on him. But Goldsmith was naturally more at ease among his compatriots than Rousseau had been. He understood the raillery which had ruffled Jean-Jacques. With the French in general he probably got on better than did the average Englishman.

From deference to his uncle and perhaps with a view to serious study he must have listened to a few lectures and watched a few demonstrations at the Ecole de Médecine; but he cannot have been a regular pupil of either Antoine Ferrein or Antoine Petit; or of H.-L. Duhamel du Monceau. He appears, however, to have attended some of the popular lectures de-livered by Guillaume-François Rouelle, who was demon-strator in chemistry at the Jardin du Roi, now the Jardin des Plantes. 'I have seen as bright a circle of beauty at the chemical lectures of Rouelle as gracing the court of Versailles', he writes in his *Enquiry into the present state of Polite Learning*. What is of special interest here is that Diderot attended this course and made full notes of it, notes which were printed and published in 1870. Now as Goldsmith says in his memoir on Voltaire that he heard Diderot arguing with Fontenelle in Paris, it is possible that someone pointed out Diderot to him. This is a charitable conjecture to account for what otherwise appears to be a mere fiction. If he did not actually hear Diderot, a long and circumstantial passage in the *Memoirs of M. de Voltaire* is almost entirely an invention.

Nearer the truth is his account of hearing Mademoiselle Clairon at the Théâtre Français, which was then housed in the rue des Fossés-Saint-Germain, near the Latin Quarter. In his essay 'On our Theatres' in No. II of *The Bee*, he gives a detailed and enthusiastic description of her manner in tragedy, and considers her very superior to any English actress of the time. It looks as though he also attended performances of Molière's *L'Avare* and *Le Médecin malgré lui*; in his 'Remarks on our Theatres' in No. I of *The Bee* he compares the *jeu* of the French actor in these pieces with that of an English actor in *The Miser* and *The Mock Doctor*, which were Henry Fielding's adaptations of them, and this with a minuteness which suggests that he had actually seen them. It is tempting to suppose that he went to see Marivaux' *Le Legs* which was on the repertory of the same theatre, because the main or 'romantic' plot of *The Good-Natured Man* is taken from it; whilst at the Comédie Italienne in the rue Mauconseil (for which Marivaux was the principal purveyor) he also probably saw *Le Jeu de l'Amour et du Hasard*, a play which was to provide the 'romantic' element in *She Stoops to Conquer*. The theatre was evidently more attractive than the Ecole de Médecine.

It is unlikely, at the same time, that he gave up reading during his continental tour. He was a great book-lover and books in Paris were unbound and cheap. Copies of Marivaux' three periodicals, perhaps of the plays above mentioned, or even of Gresset's *Ver-Vert* and Piron's *La Métromanie*, of which he displayed a personal knowledge not long after his arrival in London, were among his likely purchases. Being small and light, they could be easily carried about in his knapsack.

While strolling through the woodlands that surround Paris, he was amazed, he says, by 'the immense quantity of game', birds and deer, no doubt, remarkably tame because protected by law, as one of the privileges of the nobility. And he was certainly aware of the intellectual movement in Paris and of its subversive character.

How he made ends meet during these days, like so much else about his doings, can only be guessed at: probably by gambling, certainly by borrowing. It is unlikely that he was admitted into any home of the upper bourgeoisie or into one of the great literary salons, to which Horace Walpole had the entrée. The following passage in the *Memoirs of M. de Voltaire* (1759, published in 1761) should therefore put us on our guard at the outset:

'The person who writes this Memoir, who had the honour and the pleasure of being his acquaintance, remembers to have seen him in a select company of wits of both sexes at Paris, when the subject happened to turn upon English taste and learning. Fontenelle who was of the party and who [was] unacquainted with the language or authors of the country he undertook to condemn, with a spirit truly vulgar began to revile both. Diderot, who liked the English and knew something of their literary pretensions, attempted to vindicate their poetry and learning, but with unequal abilities. The company . . . were surprised at the silence which Voltaire had preserved all the former part of the night, particularly as the conversation happened to turn upon one of his favourite topics. Fontenelle continued his triumph till about twelve o'clock, when Voltaire appeared at last roused from his reverie. His whole frame seemed animated. He began his defence with the utmost elegance mixed with spirit, and now and then let fall the finest strokes of raillery upon his antagonist; and his harangue lasted till three in the morning. I must confess that, whether from national partiality, or from the elegant sensibility of his manner, I never was so much charmed, nor do I ever remember so absolute a victory as he gained in this dispute.'

How disappointing to realise that this scene, so vivid that one can almost see and hear the famous protagonists, was not witnessed by Goldsmith in Paris or anywhere else! Voltaire had left Paris in 1750 and after spending three years at the court of Potsdam, had quarrelled with Frederick and made for Switzerland, reaching Geneva on 12 December 1754. He had begun by taking a house at Monrion, below Lausanne; and in March 1755 (when Goldsmith was in Paris) had settled at 'Les Délices' near Geneva. From 1750 until 1778 he never set foot in Paris. Even so, one is loth to conclude that when Goldsmith wrote he had had the honour of knowing Voltaire, he was lying.[1] He may have been introduced to him later when near Geneva.

In 1785 Malone wrote to Percy, who was then collecting material for his *Memoir* of Goldsmith: 'Dr Johnson used to say that he never could get an accurate account of Goldsmith's history while he was abroad.' Apparently no one could. It is possible that before leaving Paris he fell in with some Englishman who presumably had money, and accompanied him to Switzerland – or so one story has it. But this is as uncertain as all the others are suspect. However that may be, Goldsmith probably left Paris towards the end of April and made his way up the valley of the Marne with the intention of crossing the Vosges to Strasbourg. The weather must have been springlike and life perhaps enjoyable.

Gay sprightly land of mirth and social ease,
How often have I led thy sportive choir
With tuneless pipe, beside the murmuring Loire.

[1] Prior (vol I, p 181) wrote: 'It would appear he had the honour of an introduction to Voltaire in Paris . . .' and cites in support of this view (or rather illusion) the letter to the *Public Ledger* of 17 January, 1760 in which the writer speaks of hearing Voltaire at Monrion – supposing apparently that Monrion was in or near Paris. If on some occasion unrecorded, Goldsmith heard Diderot and Fontenelle arguing about the English, it has been suggested by Dr Loyalty Cru, the American critic, that it is not only unlikely that Diderot was so easily worsted, but that he probably scored the success which Goldsmith ascribes to Voltaire (*Diderot as a Disciple of English Thought*, New York, 1913, pp 80–4).

The Loire had famous literary and poetical associations, – and was needed for a poor sort of rhyme – but Goldsmith's itinerary cannot have taken him along its course. The Marne sounds just possible. From Strasbourg he crossed the Rhine and spent some days in Baden, listening to the professors at Freiburg or Tübingen and forming a low opinion of their intelligence.

'But let the Germans have their due; if they are dull, no nation alive assumes a more laudable solemnity, or better assumes all the decorums of stupidity. Let the discourse of a professor run on never so heavily, it cannot be irksome to his dozing pupils. . . . I have sometimes attended their disputes at gradation. . . . [These] are managed between the followers of Cartesius whose exploded system they continue to call the new philosophy, and those of Aristotle. Though both parties are in the wrong, they argue with an obstinacy worthy the cause of truth. . . .'

On this page of *Polite Learning* he assumes, with Voltaire and other luminaries of the Enlightenment, that Descartes's philosophy as a whole had been discredited.

Prior states that Goldsmith passed into Switzerland at Schaffhausen, apparently because in the *History of the Earth and Animated Nature* he writes of the cataracts of the Rhine, 'one of which I have seen exhibit a very strange appearance; it was that at Schaffhausen, which was frozen quite across, and the water stood in columns where the cataract had formerly fallen'. This is fiction. The Rhine itself never freezes, and the famous Falls which are just south of the city, are never frozen quite across. In a hard winter – and the early months of 1755 were unusually cold – the volume of water may be a tenth of the volume in summer. The water then escapes through nicks in the rocky lip of the Falls.

'The Rhine then no longer plunges over the whole breadth of the Falls, but only through little passages and ravines, while the smaller falls on either side dry up and become iced over; and also the rocks on to which spray falls and freezes; so that, if you are looking from the Schaffhausen side, it appears not unlike a completely frozen waterfall. . . .'[1]

One may guess that he visited Bâle and then crossed the Jura on his way to Geneva. He recalled, again in *Animated Nature*, flushing woodcocks 'on Mount Jura in June and July'; and if this is true, it affords further proof that he was not at Schaffhausen before the middle of May. He probably reached Geneva by way of Berne and Lausanne, which would be a fairly direct route. According to Prior, 'he remained for some time' in Switzerland, 'visiting Basle, Berne and other places of note, but fixing (sic) more permanently at Geneva' – which implies five or six weeks in all. How could he have lived there for so long? One can believe that the easy-going peasantry of France had fed and sheltered him, the more so as a Frenchman's heart always opens to one who speaks his language. But the Swiss are a business-like people, not accustomed to providing food and shelter for nothing; and moreover all northern and most of central Switzerland is German-speaking, and Goldsmith did not know German. Neither Prior nor Professor Wardle, Goldsmith's most recent biographer, appear to have seen this difficulty, namely that Goldsmith could not possibly have borrowed and begged his way across Switzerland, or for that matter in Geneva. Hence one inclines to accept the story that he was with some English traveller, and to infer that this gentleman may have carried him in a coach or post-chaise and paid his expenses. It is just conceivable, on the other hand, that he had borrowed in Paris a sum large enough to meet his

---

[1] This information has been sent me by Dr Hans Lieb, Staatsarchivar of Schaffhausen, in a letter of 1 September 1972. 'Oliver Goldsmith's description of the *Rheinfall* cannot be taken literally,' he observes. Apart from this, Goldsmith cannot have reached Schaffhausen before May, and the ice would by then have melted. It seems possible that someone told him what the falls had looked like in February and March. Or he may have seen them on his return journey in January.

needs; but unlikely that he had received a remittance from
Ireland, because he had exhausted that source of supply, and if
money *had* been sent, Mrs Hodson would have remembered it
when writing to Percy. Here and at nearly every turn in the
Grand Tour we are faced with insoluble difficulties.

From *The Traveller* it is clear that he admired the Swiss, but
not their country. After summing up the Italians, he writes:

> My soul, turn from them! turn we to survey
> Where rougher climes a nobler race display,
> Where the bleak Swiss their stormy mansions (sic) tread,
> And force a churlish soil for scanty bread:
> No product here the barren hills afford,
> But man and steel, the soldier and his sword;
> No vernal blooms their torpid rocks array,
> But winter ling'ring chills the lap of May;
> No zephyr fondly sues the mountain's breast
> But meteors glare, and stormy glooms invest.

This is not the Switzerland he traversed between Bâle and
Geneva. Much of the Swiss plateau affords rich pasturage and
arable land, with orchards and patches of forest; there are vineyards near Neuchâtel (which he may have seen) while the
'Côte' from Lausanne and Vevey eastward is covered with
vineyards. Even the mountains as early as April are bright with
flowers. The verses are intended as a contrast with the 'lush-
ness' of Italy. 'Sensual bliss' degrades the Italians; but 'churlish
soil' and 'barren hills' ennoble those who force a living from
them. All this is 'very bookish,' and yet *The Traveller* was
apparently begun in Switzerland. In dedicating it to his brother
Henry in 1764 he was to write: '. . . as a part of this poem was
formerly written to you from Switzerland, the whole can
now . . . be only inscribed to you.' It is not a description of his
travels, but a philosophical study of national characters. There
is nowhere in it a sensation of things seen. Suggestions of

landscapes here and there are vague and conventional. At a time when Thomas Gray had been enchanted with the 'romantic' gorge that leads up to the Grande Chartreuse (1739); at a time when Windham and Pococke had made it fashionable for visitors to Geneva to see the glaciers of Chamonix,[1] Goldsmith had no feeling for mountain scenery. Take the following lines:

> E'en now, where Alpine solitudes ascend,
> I sit me down a pensive hour to spend;
> And, plac'd on high above the storm's career,
> Look downward where a hundred realms appear:
> Lakes, forests, cities, plains extending wide,
> The pomp of kings, the shepherd's humbler pride.

If this is not an imaginary 'prospect', it may have been founded on the memory of a view from the ridge of the Jura above Geneva. From near the Col de la Faucille one could look down on France on both sides, on Geneva and Lac Leman to the south-east, and to the mountains of Savoy ('the pomp of kings'?) beyond.

When Goldsmith reached Geneva, towards the end of June (?), the great topics of local interest were the glaciers of Chamonix and Monsieur de Voltaire. If he was unaware that Voltaire had recently settled in the region, people would soon have told him. In a letter to the *Public Ledger* of 17 January 1760 we read: 'I remember to have heard Mr Voltaire observe, in a large company at his house at Monrion, that at the battle of Dettingen, the English exhibited prodigies of valour; but they soon lessened their well-bought conquest by lessening the merit of those they had conquered. Their despising the French then, he continued to observe, was probably the cause of their defeat at Fontenoy. . . .'

---

[1] William Windham and Peter Martel, *An Account of the Glaciers or Ice Alps in Savoy*, London, 1744.

This letter has been ascribed to Goldsmith and the views expressed in it are in line with his known opinions. Voltaire, however, was not living at Monrion, now a part of Lausanne, that summer.[1] He had settled at 'Les Délices', a house a short way below Geneva, where the Arve joins the Rhône; it is possible that Goldsmith called on him there; that Voltaire received him kindly; and that there perhaps he heard his host defending the English against some detractor other than Fontenelle. One hesitates to regard his statements of having heard Voltaire as complete fabrications.

The documentary evidence of his doings in France, Switzerland and Italy is of the slightest. He was always reticent about his travels. In the memorandum of his life which he dictated to Thomas Percy on 28 April 1773 we read, after a few lines regarding his studies in Edinburgh and Leyden:

He then went (about 1755) to *Padua in Italy*, where [in Italy?] he staid 6 months & saw *Venice, Florence, Virona* [*sic*] *& all the North Part of Italy*. His Uncle dying while he was at Padua, he was obliged to return back thro France &c on Foot, lodging at Convents chiefly of the Irish Nation. After spending in this peregrination [the whole tour?] near a year he came to settle in London this was about the breaking out of the War in 1756. . . .[2]

One notices two curious things here: first, that he told Percy nothing about his sojourn in Paris or his travels through

[1] He, however, returned to stay there from 16 December to the end of February 1756. But at least one critic doubts whether the above letter is in fact by Goldsmith. Assuming his authorship, it is still singular that he should make specific mention of Monrion, as Voltaire was at this time established at 'Les Délices'. It may be that Voltaire made intermittent journeys to Monrion for business reasons, and that on one of these occasions Goldsmith saw him. He might have been taken there by the young man with whom he is said to have been travelling from Paris – perhaps by coach as Lausanne is some distance from Geneva. Or, of course, Goldsmith might have got the story by hearsay.

[2] See Katherine C. H. Balderston, *The History and Sources of Percy's Memoir of Goldsmith*, Cambridge, 1926, p 15.

Germany and Switzerland; second, he implies that he stayed six months in Padua, or in Italy, it is not clear. A scrutiny of the dates and of the time at his disposal will show that he may have spent as much as five months in Italy, and of these, at most two in Padua. It is true that his statement can be supplemented from other sources, such as reminiscences in the *Animated Nature*, some of which can be accepted; inferences drawn from George Primrose's account of his adventures which, however, must be treated with caution; a few indications from *The Traveller*, equally suspect; and details collected by Percy, including the anecdotes and rumours which he found in Samuel Glover's short *Life of Dr Goldsmith*, published in 1774. But Percy regarded Glover's book with suspicion and he rejected the story that while in Geneva Goldsmith was put in charge of a 'parsimonious young Englishman' and went with him to Marseille. Percy was right: such a journey would have taken him far out of his way.

We may reasonably suppose that Goldsmith lingered about three weeks in Geneva and then set out for Italy, about the beginning of August. The Mont Cenis was the favourite route at that time. Gray and Horace Walpole had gone that way in 1739, and Dr Burney was to cross that pass in 1770. We might infer that Goldsmith did the same. This means that on leaving Geneva he entered Sardinian territory and after passing Chambéry, followed the valley of the Arc to Lanslebourg and from there climbed the mule-track up the pass. It was not very high or very difficult, though travellers thought it terrible. It led down to Susa, with its Roman Arch, and the great city of Turin. Here the Dora Riparia joins the Po; and in *Animated Nature* we find hints that he came this way. He describes the 'floating bee-houses' which he says he saw in Piedmont – barges carrying from sixty to an hundred hives which the bee-keepers steer down slow-flowing streams, so as to pass meadows rich in honey-bearing flowers.

To reach Padua the obvious road lay almost due east to

Milan and thence by way of Brescia, Verona and Vicenza. If, however, we are to believe that he visited Florence, he would have taken the more southerly route through Piacenza and down the old Via Aemilia to Bologna, then across the Apennines to Florence. He would have had to return to Bologna and thence by Modena and Mantua would have rejoined the other road at Verona and from there made his way to Padua. It is impossible to know how he found food and shelter. Goldsmith's biographers have assumed that he was given 'a gratuity in money, a dinner and a bed for the night' for his 'skill in disputation' in convents and universities. But the evidence goes to show that during his eighteen years in London he was generally ineffective in conversation and at times made himself absurd by trying to shine in argument.[1] Garrick cannot have been entirely mistaken when he wrote that Goldsmith 'talked like poor Poll'. This being so, one cannot suppose that in a public debate, in Latin, in a foreign country, he can have displayed a fluency and eloquence of which he was devoid among Londoners. When Dr Johnson in later years declared: 'Sir, he *disputed* his way across Europe,' he must have believed that George Primrose's account in *The Vicar of Wakefield* of how he contrived to live during his tour of Italy,[2] was autobiographical. Of this, we have no proof whatever. The facts point to the conclusion that Goldsmith can only have lived either by begging, or by rendering some services, probably menial, to the convents or other institutions from which he

---

[1] Cf. Boswell, *A Tour to the Hebrides with Samuel Johnson* (1785), where they sometimes spoke of Goldsmith; and also the *Life of Johnson*, Oxford, 1934–50, vol II, p 196.

[2] 'My skill in music could avail me nothing in a country where every peasant was a better musician than I; but by this time I had acquired another talent . . . which was a skill in disputation. In all the foreign universities and convents there are, upon certain days, philosophical theses maintained against every adventitious disputant; for which, if the champion opposes with any dexterity, he can claim a gratuity in money, a dinner and a bed for the night. In this manner therefore I fought my way towards England; [and] walked along from city to city' (Chapter XX). Goldsmith would perhaps have liked to proceed in this way, and may have tried – but without success.

sought assistance; or in both ways. One even wonders whether such institutions were numerous enough to provide food and shelter all the way. It would be pleasant to think that, like Saint Anthony on his way from Portugal to Padua, Goldsmith often lived on the fruits of the earth.

Whether he visited Florence or not, he cannot have avoided seeing Verona, with its superb Piazza della Signoria, its house of Juliet and the stupendous Roman Amphitheatre; in Vicenza, the masterpieces of Palladio, his Teatro antico and the Rotonda on the hill above; and in Padua the Byzantine domes of Sant' Antonio and Santa Giustina. Yet he never in later life is reported to have spoken of these marvels, nor are they even mentioned in *The Traveller*.

One may suppose that he visited Venice, both because of the fame of the Serenissima and for the sake of his uncle's ancestry. In any event, he seems to have pushed north into the mountains,

. . . where the rude Carinthian boor
Against the houseless stranger shuts the door –

a repulse which he later told Hickey that he had actually experienced.

It was probably in late September that he returned southward and settled in Padua to attend lectures at the Medical School.[1] He did not matriculate, nor did he sign his name in the Bidello's Register. Even so, it is certain that he *was* there; that now or, more probably, earlier, he actually wrote to Daniel Hodson for a remittance to pay for his return home; that Hodson collected all the money he could and sent it (in the form, no doubt, of a letter of credit); that it never reached him, and that he suffered great privations.

---

[1] During one of my visits there I examined all the archives, those in the Palazzo centrale of the University, those in the Cathedral (which relate to the University) and those in the Biblioteca municipale, without finding a trace of him.

It is difficult to imagine that anyone living in Padua at this time did not hear frequently of the spectacular success which Carlo Goldoni had been experiencing in Venice. After his return there in 1748 he had produced some of his most famous comedies, including *La Bottega del caffè*, *Il Bugiardo* and *La Locandiera*; and in 1755 he was the principal purveyor for the Teatro San Luca. Yet Goldsmith mentions him only once, in the 1774 edition of *An Enquiry into the Present State of Polite Learning*, as one of five Italian writers who 'deserve the highest applause' – and with no further comment. A paper entitled 'The History of Cyrillo Padovano, the noted Sleep-Walker', which appeared in *The Westminster Magazine* for February 1774, has been ascribed to Goldsmith, and one is tempted to suppose that it is Goldsmith's and that he first heard of this Carthusian monk while staying in his native city.[1]

Goldsmith may have remained in Padua for two months or a little longer, but by mid December he had to return by the most direct route, that is, by Verona and Milan; and it seems likely that he crossed the Alps by way of Domodossola and the Simplon;[2] and that he may again have seen the Falls of the Rhine. But all this is conjectural. He somehow contrived to traverse north-eastern France, availing himself perhaps of the hospitality of convents, and so reached Rouen – from which city he wrote to Ireland – and then made his way to Calais. He landed at Dover about 1 February 1756, travel-stained, emaciated and much the worse for wear. He might not have stayed in England if the remittance from Hodson had reached him; he may well have feared that his family's silence boded no good for a returning prodigal. In a letter to his brother-in-law, dated 27 December 1757, he wrote: '. . . let me only add that

[1] On the other hand, it appears that the description is really based on two separate cases, one apparently German, the other that of an Italian named Arlotto.

[2] A contemporary quoted by Prior speaks of Goldsmith's crossing 'the mountains of Rhaetia'. This would mean that he entered or left Italy by the Splügen. He could not have gone that way from Geneva; while in winter the Via Mala would be difficult and perhaps impassable.

my not receiving that supply was the cause of my present establishment in London'.[1]

What had he gained from his travels? Had he enjoyed them? He does not appear to have been thrilled by the varied and beautiful scenery or by the noble cities he had visited; or to have been interested in architecture and painting. Unprovided with letters of introduction, he apparently met no professional people, no writers except possibly Voltaire, no members of the nobility; and this is why his judgement of the French, the Swiss and the Italians is sketchy and superficial. Yet he was a fairly shrewd observer of men, even if often gullible; and, had he taken the trouble to keep a journal, it would have furnished a wealth of material for his later writings. One feels that for an educated and well-read man of twenty-six, he had wasted a unique opportunity. Above all, he had not studied medicine either at Leyden, or Paris, or Padua long enough to take a degree, and he had apparently not even troubled to obtain a certificate of attendance from any of the professors. His singular aversion from describing to anyone his doings on the Grand Tour – a topic on which even the laconic were wont to turn loquacious – strongly suggests that for some reason he had not greatly enjoyed it.

[1] *Collected Letters,* p 27.

C

Chapter 5

England in 1756

During the eighteen years which Goldsmith was to spend in England, he never fully adapted himself to English life; yet the conditions of the time, political, social and economic, often affected him closely and he in turn reacted to them in his writings. A glance at these conditions will explain what few modern readers, other than historians, may be aware of.

Since the resignation of Sir Robert Walpole the Whig oligarchy of great nobles and landowners who dominated Parliament had split into factions, and the Duke of Newcastle, now head of the Government, was not the man to deal with a renewal of hostilities with France. War broke out later in 1756 and this brought William Pitt, a man of daemonic energy, into power. In July 1757 he formed a coalition with Newcastle.

Political parties as one knows them today can scarcely have been said to exist. The Whig factions were sometimes bitterly at odds with one another. The Tories had been discredited by the two abortive attempts at a Stuart restoration, but they had been strengthened by the accession to their ranks of the lower gentry. In the previous century these country squires had enjoyed considerable political influence, and had generally been attached to the Whig party in 1689; only to find that power was passing into the hands of the magnates. It was natural that they should turn Tory.[1] But they secured no share in government prior to about 1766.

The franchise was based on a property qualification, electors were not always free to vote as they liked, and the distribution

[1] J. H. Plumb, *England in the Eighteenth Century*, London, 1950, p 19.

of seats was archaic. The territorial magnates, some of whom owned four or five pocket-boroughs, could nominate promising young men and have them elected. William Burke and his younger brother Edmund, who later became friends of Goldsmith, both entered Parliament in 1763 through the patronage of Lord Verney. This did not mean that they became delegates or 'creatures' of Verney. Edmund Burke spoke and voted as he liked; his sympathy with the Americans and support of Catholic emancipation were not such as to commend him to majority feeling. Yet he was more representative than exceptional. The membership of the Commons was distinguished for its ability, sense of public duty and independence of judgement. Samuel Johnson approved of the system; he said that 'if he were a gentleman of landed property, he would turn out all his tenants who did not vote for the candidate whom he supported'. Was he altogether wrong? The system did not work badly, and Parliament exercised an authority which it no longer possesses.

What Goldsmith, who was a Tory, thought of all this one does not know, but there is nothing to suggest that he disliked it. He did, however, object to political *parties*, and, while chronically short of money, he refused a generous offer of money, provided he would write in support of a government of which he apparently shared the views. A little later he reproved Burke, not for being a Whig, but because he 'to party gave up what he owed to mankind'.

One could stand aloof from the political system but not from the economic conditions of the age. Agriculture was still the principal industry, and here an agrarian revolution was taking place. The industrial revolution was also in its early stages.[1] New urban industries were springing up and polluting the environment, especially in London, as Goldsmith learned to

---

[1] But the really revolutionary changes, notably in the production of iron and the invention of textile machinery, took place in and after 1769. (J. H. Plumb, op. cit., pp 78–80).

his cost. Commerce was flourishing. The growth of large and prosperous middle classes was altering the complexion of society. Many a great merchant bought an estate and adopted the manners and habits of a nobleman. A wealthy banker like Coutts was *persona grata* in the highest circles. There was no clear border-line between the bourgeoisie and the gentry. But, as already observed, the possession of land remained the key to political power.

Historians used to represent the Enclosure Acts as having destroyed a happy and prosperous peasantry and forced thousands to emigrate or to seek some wretched employment in the towns. Goldsmith in *The Deserted Village* draws a picture of this kind, a picture which provoked incredulity in London. It was certainly exaggerated. At the beginning of the century the medieval system of strip-farming in great open fields had still prevailed. The yield was meagre and inadequate to the needs of a population which began to increase rapidly after 1740. In the first decade of the century, only one Enclosure Act was passed; between 1750 and 1760, one hundred and fifty-six; between 1760 and 1770, four hundred and twenty-four.[1] The effect was certainly to dispossess a number of small tenants and even freeholders; but also to increase the size of individual farms and to render agriculture more productive and more prosperous than in former times. One doubts if there was any serious decrease in the rural population prior to the nineteenth century. A visible effect of the enclosures was that they transformed the landscape, the vast open fields being replaced by smaller fields, usually planned in rectangles and surrounded by hedges or walls, much as one sees them today.

Large and prosperous farms were not a novelty in Goldsmith's day. Flamborough and Williams in *The Vicar of Wakefield* were clearly no peasants or small-holders. It sounds as if Selby, who farmed at Hyde near the Edgware Road and with whom Goldsmith lodged for months at a time after 1770,

[1] J. H. Plumb, op. cit., p 82.

was a successful man. That he sold dairy produce and perhaps meat and poultry at good prices in London is a likely conjecture. All such farmers had benefited from the enclosures.

Country villages were dominated by the squire and the parson; especially by the former, who would also be the local JP (and a Tory). He was often a boorish creature like Fielding's Western and Goldsmith's Lumpkin; but as the century advanced, this class was acquiring culture and good manners. Hardcastle, in *She Stoops to Conquer*, serves as an example of what was happening.[1]

A similar improvement could be observed, after a time, among the clergy. In the early part of the century the National Church was distinguished neither for piety nor learning. The bishops were political nominees. The Government took care to appoint Whigs, and expected them to vote for it – which they usually did. As such sees as Oxford and Bristol were worth only £400 a year, and one or two even less, one had no chance of promotion to, say, Winchester (£30,000) or Durham (£50,000), if one took a line of one's own. The country clergy, often the younger sons of noblemen, differed little in habits and morals from the hard-drinking, loose-living squires who were their companions. They were required to administer communion only three times a year, and not to preach very often. Some supplemented their stipend by tilling a small farm, like Goldsmith's Dr Primrose. Parson Adams and Parson Trulliber, depicted so realistically in *Joseph Andrews* (1742), were probably true to life; as was the whole rural community of squires, clergy and peasants in *Tom Jones* (1749). There were certainly here and there conscientious incumbents who devoted their leisure, not to fox-hunting, but to the study and translation of the classics: like Dr John Burton, the editor of Sophocles (1758) and John Langhorne who translated Bion and Plutarch. Goldsmith was to review the work of both these Hellenists.

---

[1] In 1805, R. L. Edgeworth was to write: 'Instead of country squires we now have country gentlemen.'

They were probably exceptional. But the preaching of Wesley and the rise of Methodism had a salutary effect on the Anglican Church. Thomas Percy (1729–1811), Goldsmith's friend and biographer, was distinguished for his research into old English ballads and Icelandic literature, and Gilbert White (1720–93) for his writings on natural history. Though these were isolated figures, the quality of the clergy as a whole was changing for the better.

How far was Goldsmith right in preferring country-life to city-life? Existence in a country village must have been stiflingly circumscribed, but less so in the better country towns. The deplorable condition of the roads isolated all the provincial towns in bad weather, sometimes for long periods, and this led them to develop a cultural life of their own, as witness Erasmus Darwin's circle at Lichfield. Many gentlemen preferred to live in small towns, because these were quiet and healthy; and such places with their Assembly Rooms and Literary Societies became social centres more agreeable than they are today. Hence the appearance of a more refined domestic architecture in Nottingham and especially in Stamford; in Bath still more. Bath was the most fashionable resort for Londoners, and we shall find Goldsmith frequently staying in a place famous in connexion with Beau Nash.

Primary and secondary education were well catered for by the old public schools and grammar schools, and by over one hundred and fifty new ones. These, with the many private boarding-schools, prepared boys for entry into the learned professions. There were also boarding-schools for girls, which taught languages, dancing and music. Kate Hardcastle, who knew French, had presumably been at one of these. But since the middle class of merchants and shopkeepers was growing, the need for a more modern and utilitarian education was being supplied by schools run by nonconformists, like Dr Milner's academy at Peckham, where Goldsmith was employed for a time. In most schools the syllabus included a little mathematics, some English and French, but especially the Latin and Greek classics, which remain the best means of forming character and taste, and of teaching boys how to think and how to write. Generally speaking, the grammar schools and public schools supplied an education adequate for most purposes, so that while, on leaving school, many boys entered the Inns of Court – 'the third University' – comparatively few proceeded to Oxford or Cambridge.

Here the colleges provided, in their fellowships, agreeable and somnolent sinecures. Most of the undergraduates were sons of the nobility and gentry, but scholarships or influence admitted a number of poor or middle-class boys, and these included men of distinction like Thomas Warton at Oxford, and at Cambridge, Christopher Smart and Thomas Gray, the most learned of our poets. Cambridge was also the home of mathematical studies, and the Mathematical Tripos (1747) which took precedence of all others, demanded serious study. In other respects, however, students did much as they liked, and no one was obliged to take a degree. A nobleman might not spend more than four or five terms at the university. In Parliament, he could quote aptly from Cicero, Horace or Juvenal, but this aptitude he owed more to his school than to his university. The latter did, nevertheless, add a certain polish. Among Goldsmith's friends or contemporaries, Collins, Johnson, Percy and Gibbon studied at Oxford; Sterne and the poets here mentioned at Cambridge.

If literary merit were publicly rewarded, this was often due to patronage, as it is today due to personal influence. Thomas Gray owed his professorship to the Duke of Grafton; Gibbon entered parliament as member for Liskeard through the influence of the Eliot family. Goldsmith was one of the few who made his way by merit alone. It is true that Johnson assisted him powerfully in 1762; but Johnson very fairly admitted that Goldsmith would have got on in any event, only more slowly.

As regards literature in general, high-class journalism had

appeared under Queen Anne. The middle years of the century saw the expansion of a periodical literature of reviews and magazines, and somewhat later of political journals, like the *Briton* and the so-called *North Briton* which became a power to be reckoned with. The increase in the reading public led to the opening of public libraries, sometimes very fashionable and luxurious. Not only was the book-trade expanding, but publishers – usually known as 'booksellers' – were offering very large sums to capable authors, especially for popular compilations. Goldsmith arrived at a time when he could, and did, profit from this situation. The principal writers of the age were mostly of humble or middle-class origin, but success opened a way for them into society, sometimes into the best; and the same held good for such artists as Joshua Reynolds and George Stubbs. Thus we find Stubbs in constant demand in country houses, and Goldsmith and Reynolds mixing with gentlemen and nobles.

The tone of literature had greatly improved since the late seventeenth century. In drama the gross cynicism of Wycherley and his successors had disappeared. Fielding's clear-sighted realism was as moral in its bearing as Richardson's puritanical manner, though one could hardly say as much of Smollett's novels. While satirical poetry remained as ferocious as ever, the authors of narrative and elegiac verse vied with one another in delicacy and refinement. The popularity of 'sentimental comedy', a genre ridiculed by Goldsmith, testified to a desire on the part of the theatre-going public for a moral ideal in advance of the practice of the age. The state of private morals was certainly low; cynical in the upper strata of society, squalid in the lower. Middle-class conduct seems to have been better; but, if one makes allowance for his moralising intention, there was probably much truth in Hogarth's pictures. It has been customary to disparage eighteenth-century morals: they were no worse than today's.

To sum up: the English were then a robust and enterprising

people; they were growing wealthy and powerful; the nation was on the upgrade.

With this bare outline of conditions in Goldsmith's time, nothing has as yet been said about the metropolis. Between England's 'green and pleasant land' and the 'great wen' of London the contrasts were extreme. London was the largest city in Europe and by far the biggest in England. Out of a total population, in England and Wales, of about six and a half millions, London contained some 677,000. The poorer classes were concentrated in and round the City proper, but also off Holborn, in streets running into the Strand, and in parts of Westminster. The outskirts of the City, east and west, were, however, the worst. All European cities were insanitary, but London was filthy beyond anything now imaginable. Workshops turned their waste into the ditches and the backwaters of the Thames; ordinary citizens dumped rubbish in Lincoln's Inn Fields, in Tothill Fields, or simply threw it into the kennels. For the poorer classes, personal hygiene was impossible, clothes and bodies were inevitably verminous. Infant mortality was extremely high, adults were short-lived, and prior to 1750 the death-rate exceeded the birth-rate.[1] London was well described as a 'devourer of men'. To other evils was added the smog. Coal-smoke from the tenements and factories created a dense murk which hung over the central districts and was aggravated by fogs in winter. Visitors from the Continent were more amazed by this, apparently, even than by the vice, crime and violence that prevailed, especially after nightfall. P. J. Grosley, who visited London in the early 1760s, described the great cloud of smoke that enveloped the city like a mantle, 'a cloud which, recoiling upon itself, suffers the sun to break out only now and then, which casual appearance procures the Londoners a few of what they call "glorious days"'.[2]

[1] M. Dorothy George, *London Life in the XVIIIth Century*, London, 1925, pp 81–98, and *passim*.
[2] P. J. Grosley, *A Tour to London* (1765), translated 1772.

These conditions revolted even the natives; Pope and others described them with disgust. Worst of all perhaps was the stench from the Fleet Ditch, 'a naucieous and abominable sink of nastiness', full of offal and dead dogs. Food, exposed on open stalls, was often fly-blown, and these conditions produced outbreaks of low fever and occasionally of typhus.[1] Pure water being unobtainable, one was obliged to drink beer, or tea or coffee made with boiled water. The poor flew to gin which was cheap, and the production of which had become a major industry. It promoted crime and violence,[2] and can be compared in its effects with the modern vogue of hard drugs. Tea-drinking probably did more than any other part of the diet to improve the nation's health.

Such in bare outline, and omitting the more horrific features of the London scene, were the conditions of life in 1756. Biographers of Goldsmith have said little or nothing about them, but Goldsmith himself experienced the reality. Born a countryman, he had spent most of his twenty-seven years in country parts. For the next seven years, until Newbery found him a room at Islington (1762), he lived in some of the most sordid districts and among the poorest people. Small wonder if he was once ill for several weeks and if, as soon as he had enough money, he made frequent excursions into the provinces and in later life spent most of his summers in the near-by countryside.

It is true that conditions in London, including the paving of the streets, were greatly improved after 1762; and that he himself occupied comfortable chambers in the Temple from 1765 onwards; true also that he enjoyed the social life of literary London. But he would scarcely have subscribed to Johnson's saying, that 'a man who is tired of London is tired of life'.

[1] Dorothy Marshall, *English People in the XVIIIth Century*, London, 1956, pp 167–8. In the preceding pages I have been much indebted to this excellent work.
[2] M. D. George, op. cit., pp 27–34.

Chapter 6

Hard Times

❧ 1756-61 ❧

England, when Goldsmith stepped ashore in February 1756, was for him virtually a foreign country, and the outlook was bleak. He would have preferred to make for home, trusting to Henry or the Hodsons to receive him, and then setting up as a physician, one of those death-dealing practitioners whom Molière had loved to ridicule. But while he had contrived to wangle and 'dispute' his way across western Europe, no English purse would open for a shabby Irishman with a dreadful accent. In some boys' school in Kent he was engaged as an usher, having named as a referee Dr Radcliff of Trinity College, Dublin. But realising a little later that he had not given his real name to the school, he wrote to Radcliff asking him to ignore any enquiry. His duties meanwhile proved thankless. We can probably believe what he says in No. VI of the *Bee*, that the boys ridiculed and played tricks on him, and even that the master laughed at him. He resigned or was dismissed, and gravitated to London, the most populous of European cities, renowned for its wealth and notable for its wickedness.

Of the wealth there was at first not a sign. He probably entered by the East End. After the cities of Italy, with their noble churches and lordly palaces, London looked mean and sordid. It is likely that his first and most lively impressions were those which he afterwards ascribed to his Chinese philosopher:

'Judge then how great is my disappointment on entering London, to see no signs of that opulence so much talked of abroad; wherever I turn, I am presented with a gloomy solemnity in the houses, the streets and the inhabitants; none of that beautiful gilding which makes a principal ornament in Chinese architecture . . . in the midst of their pavements a great lazy puddle moves muddily along; heavy-laden machines . . . crowd up every passage; so that a stranger . . . is often happy if he has time to escape from being crushed to pieces.' *Citizen of the World*, Letter II.

This was no exaggeration. The kennel ran down the middle of the street, and any refuse was thrown into it. There were no 'side-walks', only an occasional post to serve as protection for pedestrians. Such a scene on a raw, wet morning in late winter would be enough to daunt anyone 'without friends, recommendations, money or impudence,' to quote a letter which Oliver wrote to Hodson at the end of December 1757. He thought of suicide, and small wonder. His skill with the flute was of no use to him since there were no regular orchestras and those which were improvised did not contain a flautist. Besides, it is believed that he played only by ear and could not read musical notation. Eventually a chemist on Fish Street Hill employed him as an assistant; and then, hearing luckily that Dr J. F. Sleigh, who had helped him in Edinburgh, was in London, he called on him. When Sleigh at last recognised this woebegone figure for the gay young student he had known, he gave him money (and probably a meal). Thus encouraged, Oliver set up as a doctor in Southwark. It appears that Beatty, his former room-mate in Dublin, met him soon afterwards and was told that 'he was practising physic, and doing very well'; an exaggeration, since few of his patients could pay much, if anything; and his clothes were obviously shabby.

It has been surmised that he applied to Trinity College about this time for the degree of M.B., but there is no evidence of its being awarded. He, however, considered himself a doctor because he soon afterwards sought an appointment as physician with the East India Company, and was actually accepted, but had to resign, being unable to pay his passage. By calling himself 'Doctor' he made up for his physical and social unimportance. An ingenious Italian has observed that man's principal care is *costruirsi* – to build himself up. This was Goldsmith's idea. Meanwhile, to supplement his meagre takings, he acted as proof-reader at Samuel Richardson's Press, and here he met the aged author of the *Night Thoughts*. Dr Farr, another Edinburgh acquaintance, recalled Goldsmith's calling on him 'early in January', probably 1757, and having breakfast. Goldsmith showed him the manuscript of a tragedy which he had submitted to Richardson, and spoke of his plan 'of going to decipher the inscriptions on the written mountains' in Arabia. A handsome allowance was available for the purpose. It is true that Goldsmith knew no Arabic, but this difficulty must have seemed as trifling as his lack of any solid qualifications as a physician.

More useful was his meeting another Edinburgh student whose father, Dr Milner, ran a school for nonconformists in Peckham. Dr Milner being ill at the time, his son engaged Oliver to undertake the teaching, while Mrs Milner managed the business side. To teach Latin, English, and even French, he was well qualified. But he often diverted the pupils with stories and flute-playing, and so wasted his money on beggars that Mrs Milner proposed that he should let her take care of it. Fortunately, while taking his meals with the Milners, he was noticed by Griffiths, a bookseller and owner of the *Monthly Review*. Observing from his conversation that he was unusually cultured and had a wide acquaintance with literature and an exceptional knowledge of French, Griffiths offered him employment as a writer of articles and book-reviewer, with a room over the shop in Paternoster Row and a salary of £100 a year. Oliver began work there in April and contributed a large number of articles and reviews of works both English and French. But Griffiths occasionally altered or corrected his copy, and this irked him, as did the monotony of the work, and he left the shop in the autumn.

His translation of the *Mémoires* of Jean Marteilhe, probably at Griffiths' request, is an important landmark in his career: first because it reveals him as a born translator, able to digest – in this instance – a long and badly written work and present its essentials in good English; second, because it was a long book and he produced his copy in a remarkably short time. This capacity for hard work, both literary and mechanical, was to increase with the years. The mere quantity of work accomplished in composing his *History of the Earth and Animated Nature* between 1771 and 1773, in addition to other undertakings, was a staggering achievement.

After leaving Paternoster Row he had found lodging in a garret in Salisbury Square, near Fleet Street, and had undertaken to write for the brothers Dodsley a work on the then state of literature in Europe, based mainly on his continental experiences. Now perhaps for the first time it occurred to him to take up writing as a profession, although he must have earlier divined that here lay his real talent.

Writing home earlier in the year he had given the impression of being prosperous; and now his younger brother Charles was sent over for Oliver to launch him on a career. He can hardly have been welcome. The Hodsons had told Oliver that his sister Jane, who had thought she was marrying a fortune, had been mistaken and needed help, while his mother had lost the farm at Pallas from which she had derived a small living. Decidedly, the Reverend Charles had left his widow a legacy of misfortunes.

On Christmas Day (1757), from the Temple Exchange Coffee House, Oliver wrote to Daniel Hodson, having learned how much his good brother-in-law had done to raise money and send it to him in Italy. It is in this letter that he explains why he had settled in London, touches on the privations he had suffered and relates how he was making 'a shift to live'. He is feeling homesick; this 'maladie du pays' is unaccountable, since Ireland is not a fine country, there is no good company, conversation is bawdy, wit and learning amount to nothing. Yet he would rather be on 'the little mount' at Lissoy than on Flamstead Hill; and his desire to return – as he hopes to do next summer – is simply because the Hodsons and a few others live there. He feels 'real uneasiness' about Jenny and his mother, and would wish to redress their situation; but 'at present there is hardly a Kingdom in Europe in which I am not a debtor'.[1]

The letter was embarrassed, which was natural. It was injudicious to mention that he had heard Signora Colomba Mattei at the Italian Opera.

In the New Year (1758) he went back to teach at the Milners' school, a helpful stop-gap. His hopes he was pinning on the success of 'The Present Taste and Literature in Europe' as he now called it; much, if not most, of the material was in hand, based on what he had read and heard while travelling. Back at Salisbury Court in the late summer and frequenting the Temple Exchange Coffee House, he wrote in succession to his cousin Edward Mills, to Robert Bryanton, to Jane Lawder, to Hodson and, later on, to his brother Henry; having previously communicated with a bookseller named Bradley in Dublin. The motive for this orgy of letter-writing was to obviate the peril of his book's being pirated in Ireland and to promote its sales there so as to bring him a reasonable return.

To Mills (7 August) he begins by speaking of his correspondent's affairs, a topic of primary interest to the recipient of a letter; only after two or three pages does he broach the real business. A prospectus, or simple announcement, of his forthcoming work has been prepared and of this an hundred copies will be sent to Mills, who is asked to circulate them among likely people. A similar request has been sent to Dr Radcliff,

[1] *Collected Letters*, pp 26–32.

to Lawder, Bryanton, Hodson and Henry Goldsmith.[1] From a subsequent letter to Henry (13 January 1759) it transpires that he will be dispatching 250 copies to Bradley and that his friends are asked to send the money they collect to this book-seller. This he calculates should amount to £60 and he may soon need it. Had he allowed for the expenses of postage and for Bradley's charges? And was the book to be priced at say four shillings and six pence? It would be interesting to know.

The letters are amusingly varied. To Robert Bryanton (14 August) he writes with affection. His friend has not written. Does he know whom he has offended? Does he realise that 'the Scaligers and Daciers [of the future] will vindicate my charac-ter, give learned editions of my labours, and bless the times with copious comments on the text?' He goes on to sketch the beginning of a lecture on himself:

'Oliver Goldsmith flourished in the eighteenth and nineteenth centuries. He lived to be an hundred and three years old, and in that age may justly be styled the sun of literature and the Confucius of Europe. Many of his earlier writings, to the regret of the learned world, were anonymous. . . . The first avowed piece the world has of his is entitled an "Essay on the Present State of Taste and Literature in Europe" – a work well worth its weight in diamonds. . . . In this he proves that block-heads are not men of wit, and yet that men of wit are actually blockheads.'[2]

This letter is also of interest because it looks to the future. He is already talking about 'my Chinese Philosopher'.

The next missive (15 August) which is to Jane Lawder at Kilmore, divulges the difficulties of living on a pittance. 'I have already given my landlady orders for an entire reform in the state of my finances. I declaim against hot suppers, drink less

---

[1] *Collected Letters*, pp 32–5.
[2] Ibid., pp 36–41.

sugar in my tea, and cheek my grate with brickbats.' His walls are hung, not with pictures but with 'maxims of frugality'.[1]

In the letter to Hodson he speaks of his appointment as physician and surgeon to a factory of the East India Company 'on the coast of Coromandel', mentions the heavy initial expenses but also the dazzling prospects 'which induce me to leave a place where I am every day gaining friends and esteem and where I might enjoy all the conveniences of life'. After asking Hodson to circulate 'an hundred proposals' for his book, he enquires urgently for news of the family. If Maurice will only learn to write and spell correctly, he will try to procure him employment in London. Finally, and not too soon: 'Pray let me hear from my Mother since she will not gratify me herself and tell me if in anything I can be immediately serviceable to her.'[2] Not a very practical suggestion from a man on his beam-ends.

The response to all this correspondence was discouraging. Mills and the Lawders seem not to have replied at all, and for the moment he had no money for the passage to India. In this impasse he applied to the College of Surgeons for a position as 'hospital mate' and was invited to appear before the examiners. As a decent coat was needed for the interview, he asked Griffiths to be his surety with a tailor. Why Griffiths agreed remains a mystery, since he was not on good terms with Goldsmith, who probably owed him money. According to Prior, Goldsmith had given the publisher to understand that he had received, or expected to receive, an army appointment and had to be properly dressed. It was understood, in any event, that after the interview he would return the coat to the tailor. But now the worst happened. On 21 December 1758 the examiners found him 'not qualified' as 'mate to an hospital'.

The sane course was to return the coat and set to work on four books which Griffiths had asked him to review. Instead of

[1] Ibid., pp 41–8.
[2] Ibid., pp 49–55.

this, he put the coat in pawn. One may suppose that he was in a perfectly desperate situation. Yet if he was actually starving he could have applied to one of the new friends of whom he had spoken in writing to Hodson: Dr Grainger, for example, or possibly Smollett, who would certainly have given him a meal. However that may be, he was accosted soon after drawing money for the coat by a Mrs Martin, who related a pitiful story about her husband being in prison for debt and herself in a terrible quandary; and he gave her what was in his pocket. Women whose husbands were in prison seem to have had a fatal attraction for him. This was the second time it had happened and the second time that he had given away articles of clothing. It was probably now that he raised a loan from some friend, leaving as security the four books he was to review.

Before long the tailor grew anxious and sent his account to Griffiths. Goldsmith's early biographers have reproved Griffiths for his subsequent behaviour or treated him as 'a grinding bookseller'; but his indignation is understandable. He wrote angrily to Goldsmith, reproaching him with his conduct and asking for the books to be returned. Goldsmith promised to send them back before long; whereupon Griffiths threatened to prosecute him. (One may assume that the publisher had now taken the coat out of pawn, returned it to the tailor, and footed the bill.)

Goldsmith replied in an abject and pitiful letter:

'Sir,
'I know of no misery but a gaol to which my own imprudence and your letter seem to point. I have seen it inevitable this three or four weeks, and by heavens request it as a favour. . . . I tell you again and again I am now neither able nor willing to pay you a farthing, but I will be punctual to any appointment you or the taylor shall make; thus far at least I do not act the sharper. . . . No, Sir, had I been a sharper, had I been possessed

of less good nature and native generosity, I might surely now have been in better circumstances. I am guilty I own of meannesses which poverty unavoidably brings with it, my reflections are filled with repentance for my imprudence but not with any remorse for being a villain. . . .'

He adds that when his book with Mr Dodsley is published, 'perhaps you may see the bright side of a mind when my professions shall not seem the dictates of necessity'; and in a postscript: 'I shall expect impatiently the result of your resolutions.'

The letter was hardly of a kind to mollify Griffiths, but seeing there would be no gain from putting the delinquent in prison, he negotiated. The outcome was a notice in the *Public Advertiser* for 7 February 1759:

'Speedily will be published, Memoirs of the Life of M. de Voltaire; with critical observations on the writings of that celebrated Poet, and a new Translation of the *Henriade*. Printed for R. Griffiths, in Paternoster Row.'

By the terms of the contract Griffiths must have recovered the expenses in which he had been involved and reserved a reasonable profit, while paying Goldsmith as much as £20; but he did not forgive the misdemeanour, and in after years the *Monthly Review* traduced Goldsmith's character and sometimes disparaged his works. The fact that the Irishman had begun to write for Alexander Hamilton's *Critical Review*, a Tory monthly and a rival of Griffiths' *Monthly*, must have displeased him. Goldsmith, however, being freed from the threat of imprisonment, had recovered himself enough to write to Henry (13 January 1759) a long, rambling letter in which he speaks of his 'settled melancholy' and 'gloomy habits of thinking', but makes no mention of his treatment of Griffiths. As the book on *Taste and Literature in Europe* is expected in February, he proposes to have 250 copies dispatched to Dublin, the outlook being now less promising than he had hoped; but he is still resolved to go to India. 'It gives [me] some pain,' he continues, 'to think I am almost beginning the world at the age of thirty-one' – an indication that he had been born in 1728 or possibly 1727.[1] He pictures himself as having 'a pale melancholy visage with two great wrinkles between the eyebrows, with an eye disgustingly severe'; and speaks of passing his days 'among a number of cool designing beings' – Griffiths and the tailor, one supposes. Turning rather abruptly to the question of Henry's little boy, he considers that he should do well at Trinity College, 'if he be assiduous and divested of strong passions'; but if he have 'ambitions, strong passions and an exquisite sensibility of contempt', that is, if he be sensitive to ridicule, then he should not go to that college. Much can be done 'by a proper education at home. A boy . . . who understands perfectly well Latin, French, Arithmetic and the principles of the civil law, and can write a fine hand, has an education that may qualify him for any undertaking.' But he should never be allowed to touch a novel, since novels describe a happiness that never exists. Children should not be told that human nature is excellent, but taught thrift and economy. 'Let his poor wandering uncles example be placed before his eyes.' Oliver is willing to help Maurice if he comes over; but: 'My Mother I am informed is almost blind, even tho' I had the utmost inclination to return home I could not, to behold her in distress without a capacity of relieving her from it, would be too much to add to my present splenetic habit.' After a reference to 'poor Jenny', he announces that 'there is a book of mine will be publish'd in a few days. The life of a very extraordinary man. No less than the great Mr Voltaire. You know

---

[1] And not in 1730, the date preferred by American critics. There is no documentary proof of when he was born; but it could not have been to his interest to pretend to be thirty-one, if he were only twenty-eight.

already by the title that it is no more than a catchpenny. However I spent but four weeks on the whole performance for which I receiv'd twenty pounds.' It appears that in an earlier letter to Henry he had spoken of an 'heroicomical poem' which he was planning. He now gives a specimen of it – verses which, slightly amended, were to appear in Letter XXX of *The Citizen of the World* where they are recited by 'the poet' at a meeting of the Club of Authors. Oliver concludes his letter by observing that 'Poetry is much an easier and more agreeable species of composition than prose . . .'[1] – which for most of our great writers seems to be true.

There are odd points in this letter. He says he has 'taken chambers in the temple and [Maurice] shall lodge with me until something is provided.' How in the low state of his finances he could have paid for such rooms is impossible to understand. We know that by the latter part of February he was lodging in Green Arbour Court and that his landlady was the Mrs Martin whom he had assisted with such dire consequences to his relations with Griffiths.

He had begun, meanwhile, to write notices on new books for the *Critical Review*, one, on Stephen Barrett's translation of Ovid's *Heroides*, appearing in the January number. Ovid, he observes, has been singularly unfortunate in his translators, and his bad luck continues with the present one, who is headmaster of a school in Kent. Several passages which he quotes establish the point. And he takes this review as an occasion for animadverting on the low state of public taste which applauds industry rather than merit, and makes it possible for mediocrity to be published while genius is left to starve. But he had very warm praise for the Reverend J. Langhorne's translation of Bion's elegy on the Death of Adonis. This notice appeared in the *Critical Review* for March, and as Langhorne's book had been published by Griffiths and as Langhorne was a regular

[1] *Collected Letters*, pp 156–64.

contributor to the *Monthly*, one might have expected Griffiths to be pleased. But the *Critical Review* and the *Monthly Review* were at daggers drawn.

Goldsmith was now becoming better known. Already in August 1758, when writing to Daniel Hodson,[1] he had mentioned that he was gaining new friends and sometimes enjoying 'refined conversation'. He had apparently met Dr Grainger as early as this, and also Dr Smollett. But nothing much is known of his acquaintances prior to February 1759 when, on the twenty-first, he was invited to dinner by Grainger who introduced him to the Reverend Thomas Percy, then rector of Whitby in Northamptonshire: a day to be marked with a red letter. Percy was to become one of his truest and kindest friends, as well as his first reliable biographer. Following the meeting at Grainger's, Percy called on him, in his sordid lodging at Green Arbour Court, at a moment when Goldsmith was correcting the proofs of the venture now entitled an *Enquiry into the Present State of Polite Learning in Europe*, which was to appear on 2 April. There could be fewer contrasts more incongruous than that between an ambitious survey of contemporary letters in Europe and the squalid room which housed its author. Goldsmith offered him the chair and himself sat in the window while they talked. Percy afterwards recalled the entry of Mrs Martin's little girl with a request for a loan of coal in a chamber-pot.

During the following spring and summer Goldsmith continued to write notices of new books for the *Critical Review*, notable among them being a friendly, if discriminating notice on Arthur Murphy's play *The Orphan of China*. He may have met Murphy soon after this. In the autumn he started a new weekly magazine, written entirely by himself and published by John Wilkie. The plan was to produce something on the lines of Marivaux' *Spectateur français* – his main source of materials

---

[1] *Collected Letters*, pp 49–50.

and ideas – which had appeared in 1722 when Marivaux too had been making his debut in journalism. The contents also were sometimes similar, though Goldsmith imparted more of variety to each week's number, which contained from three to eight articles, with five as an average: moral tales, book-reviews, reflexions on the theatre, translations and articles translated without acknowledgement. He called it *The Bee*, suggesting that he would take his honey wherever he found it: which is exactly what he did: lifting passages from volume V of the *Encyclopédie* (twice), from Justus van Effen (three times), and from others, including Marivaux who was to be his great standby. Today the book makes agreeable reading; but Goldsmith was not yet known to the public, sales were poor and the number for 24 November was the last. After this, the eight numbers were collected and published by Dodsley in December.

Meanwhile the *Memoirs of the Life of M. de Voltaire* which was to accompany Purdon's translation of the *Henriade*, was in hand. The latter appeared in September, but the *Memoirs* saw the light only in 1761 when it was serialised in the *Lady's Magazine*.

Such periodicals were in great demand at this time, five or six being in circulation when the *Lady's Magazine* began to appear on 1 October, with Goldsmith as a principal contributor and perhaps as editor. As he also wrote for the *Busy Body* and was known to Smollett and Newbery – an enterprising publisher – as an essayist with a gift for producing work of a high standard at short notice, these men offered him something like regular employment. On 1 January 1760 Smollett's *British Magazine* made its début, while on the sixth, Newbery launched the *Public Ledger*. He may also be said to have launched Goldsmith, because the latter now began to publish in his magazine those 'Chinese Letters' which appeared regularly throughout the year and less frequently until the autumn of 1761. The whole series, following the model of Montesquieu's

Lettres persanes, but adapted to the current vogue for anything Chinese, offered more of variety and less of artistic unity than Montesquieu's masterpiece. Yet it is one of his best works. It revealed him as a master of humour, and it attracted the attention of Samuel Johnson.

Chapter 7

Music, Drama and Politics:

✼ 1757-60 ✼

During his first four or five years in London, Goldsmith sought what diversion he could, when he had money to spare. He had visited Ranelagh and Vauxhall Gardens, open to anyone who could pay; and he had frequented the Italian Opera House which, in 1751, had afforded Giuseppe Baretti, a future acquaintance, the means of coming to London. 'Of the Opera in England' he had written so knowledgeably in *The Bee* as to give the impression that he was a serious critic. 'Some years ago,' he writes, 'Italian opera was fashionable, and dreaded by the play-houses. At present the house seems deserted.' In other countries the best poets compose the words and the stage-settings are magnificent. With us they are cheap, and the singers mostly 'indifferent'. He expresses surprise that since 'Metastasio is so well known' and so admired in England, the managers put on any operas but his. The singers should be confined to their parts, and not allowed to choose their own songs, nor to indulge in those 'unnatural startings' and lengthened out 'shakes', so painful to the ear. 'Neither Corelli nor Pergolesi ever permitted them.'

The art of *bel canto* had indeed been abused since Alessandro Scarlatti brought it to its apogée; with which view Oliver evidently agreed.

Composers, he continues, should cultivate greater simplicity than they do. They should follow the example of Rameau, who achieves surprising effects with harmonies which 'are often

only octave and unison'. Even so, a good manager, or con-
ductor, could make a success of opera in England if he went
the right way about it. Most of the performers have some merit.
'Signora Matei[1] is at once both a perfect actress and a very fine
singer'; but Cornacini, with a melodious voice and a vast range,
is a poor actor. Goldsmith doubted whether opera would ever
become popular with us.

It does not appear, however, that he himself was really
interested in opera or in oratorio – then much in favour – or
in instrumental music. At the same time he gave the appearance
of knowing a good deal about music, or was able to get the
subject up. This is clear from his paper 'On the different
Schools of Music' which appeared in the *British Magazine* for
February 1760. He distinguishes three 'Schools': that of
Pergolesi in Italy which he places in the first rank; of Lully in
France which he regards as elegant but monotonous (?); and
of Purcell, the precursor of Handel, in England. An anonymous writer strongly objected to 'a foreigner [Handel] who
has not yet formed any school' being placed at the head of the
English; and he also criticised other observations of Goldsmith's. The latter's detailed replies seem to display an appreciation of his subject. Purcell's excellence, he thought, lay in
melody, Handel's in harmony. And as Handel had lived so long
in England – from 1710 until his death in 1759 – he should be
considered as naturalised. 'Consequently Handel may be placed
at the head of the English school.'

The theatre attracted Goldsmith more than other forms of
entertainment. It is clear from the strictures contained in his
Enquiry into the Present State of Polite Learning that he had
frequented Drury Lane, and probably Covent Garden, and
that he had heard Garrick and disapproved of his despotic
attitude towards playwrights. A new play, he said, 'must
undergo a process truly chemical before it is presented to the
public. It must be tried in the manager's fire; strained through a

---

[1] Mattei is the usual spelling.

licenser, suffer from repeated corrections. . . . Getting a play on in three or four years is a privilege reserved only for the happy few who have the arts of courting the manager as well as the muse. . . .' And he added further on: 'Our actors assume all that state off the stage which they do on it; . . . every one is *up* in his part. I am sorry to say it, they seem to forget their real characters.'

All this was clearly aimed at Garrick who was both actor and manager. Others agreed with Goldsmith. Horace Walpole had gone further. 'Garrick,' he said, 'is treating the town as it deserves and likes to be treated, with scenes, fireworks, and his own writings. A good new play I never expect to see more; nor have seen since the "Provoked Husband" which came out when I was at school.' But Walpole could offend Garrick with impunity, whereas Goldsmith, although he had not named the great man, could not. When he asked for his support in applying for the post of Secretary to the Society of Arts, Garrick refused to assist him. Much later, at the time of the *Good-Natured Man* and *She Stoops to Conquer*, he was again unhelpful.

On the other hand he had assisted dramatists like Samuel Foote who had dared to criticise him. In 1747 Foote had mimicked and ridiculed Garrick at the Haymarket. In 1757 he had produced one of his own plays at Drury Lane, and in October 1758 Garrick had engaged him, again at Drury Lane, and even lent him £100 to enable him to give a show in Edinburgh. The likelihood is that Garrick was afraid of Foote's powers of caricature. He knew that his virtuosity would enable him to appear on occasion at Covent Garden, as he did in 1762 when he produced his adaptation of Corneille's *Le Menteur*; and on other occasions at the Haymarket, though only in the summer months.

In these circumstances it is likely that Goldsmith saw and heard Foote, possibly in a version of *Le Cocu imaginaire* (Drury Lane, 1761) or in Fielding's versions of *Le Médecin malgré lui* and *L'Avare*; or, at the Haymarket in the summer of 1761, in Foote's own three-act comedy, *The Minor*. It is true that he nowhere speaks of Foote; but neither does he speak of other famous people whom he certainly saw during his years of obscurity.

Though he tells us little of his own doings at this time, we learn a good deal of his views on foreign policy. He had followed the course of the war which broke out soon after he reached London and was to last until 1762. The war distressed him because he liked the French, admired the brilliance of their literature, and hoped for an ultimate reconciliation. This explains the tone of an article in the *Busy Body* for 20 October 1759. News of the Battle of Minden and the capture of Quebec had inspired public rejoicings, and Goldsmith relates how he had visited a Punch-House and two Coffee-Houses and listened to conversations in the street, in order to hear what Demos was thinking. An old waiter said it would be easy to send forty men-of-war to Paris, where they could take the city and depose Louis XV. A shoemaker on the other hand had feared an invasion of England: '. . . tell me, if the French papishes had come over d--n my blood, what would have become of our religion?'

Goldsmith foreseeing a final victory, advocated generous terms of peace. These 'are never made with so good a grace as from a victorious army. It is very possible for a country to be very victorious and very wretched.'

This article was followed by a letter which appeared on 17 February 1760 in No. V of the *Public Ledger*. He praises the courage and humanity of his countrymen but regrets that many of them 'talk of the French with detestation', condemn them 'as guilty of every vice, and scarce [allow] them any national virtue'. Such assertions displease him because they are false and because in some companies he is obliged to sit silent. 'To beat the French, and to scold them too, is out-heroding Herod.' In lighter vein he draws the portrait of Jack Reptile the gallophobe. In a bout of fisticuffs he has knocked down three Frenchmen – or so he says. How can such people live on salad and frogs? He hates everything French except the wine, and on this he gets drunk three times a week.

In an essay 'On National Prejudices' printed by the *British Magazine* for August 1760 he relates a discussion with a pseudo-patriot who grossly disparaged the Dutch, the Germans, the French and the Spaniards, declaring that the English 'excelled all the rest of the world' in every virtue. Goldsmith replied with an estimate which it would be difficult to dispute. Most impressive, however, is a passage printed by Prior as part of an *Introduction to the History of the Seven Years' War*, but which seems to have been written, like the above articles, about 1760 before anyone knew how long the war would last. It would be a mistake, he thinks, to annex the French possessions in North America because the threat they represent to the American colonists, who are far from submissive, obliges them to remain loyal to the mother-country. Once their fear of France is removed, they will no longer have any need of England. Goldsmith advocates a policy of moderation. The French establishments in America should be restored, but the greatest efforts should be made to curb and contain France's dangerous military preponderance in Europe.

One doubts if Goldsmith had thought out this for himself. Such views must have been held by many farsighted people. If not consciously a Tory at this time, he shared the Tories' preference for a peace policy.

Chapter 8

Great Expectations

❧ 1761-62 ❧

Being now in receipt of a more regular income, Goldsmith exchanged the squalor of Mrs Martin's lodgings for rooms in Wine Office Court, where he lodged with a kinswoman of Newbery. A further advantage of his new status was that he met such writers and scholars as his countryman Murphy, and especially Christopher Smart, who had married Newbery's step-daughter. How well he knew Smart and on what terms they stood, seems to be unknown. After a brilliant début at Cambridge where he was Praelector in Rhetoric and a Fellow of Pembroke, Smart had ruined his career by addiction to drink and involvement in debt; although Thomas Gray and his other friends at the college did all they could to extricate him. He was now drifting into religious mania and heading for insanity. In London where he sometimes frequented Johnson's circle, he would go down on his knees, even in the street, to praise God, and entreat his friends to do the same. Johnson was amused: 'I would as lief pray with Kit Smart as with anyone,' was his comment. But neither he nor Goldsmith could foresee that Smart would produce such amazingly original poems as *A Song to David* and the *Jubilate Agno*.

While Goldsmith now enjoyed a wider circle of literary acquaintances, he had become singularly vulnerable to spongers, especially if they were Irish. A Dubliner named Pilkington presumed on his having met him to ask for the loan of two guineas. He said he had promised a great lady to procure two white mice, she being a connoisseur of strange animals. Now the mice had come from India and were awaiting delivery on a ship in the Thames. All that Pilkington needed was money to buy a cage, and decent clothes in which to present himself to 'a Duchess'. In this story of white mice anyone but Goldsmith would have smelled a rat. Instead, he merely protested that he had only a half-guinea in his pocket, but he agreed to pawn his watch for a few hours, and Pilkington, thus provided, vanished without returning.

More informative than some of these instances of his heedlessness in money matters is the record of an evening spent with other acquaintances, some of them probably Irish, at Blackwall, when, after a 'white-bait dinner' and several bottles of wine, he began to animadvert against *Tristram Shandy* as an obscene novel, 'derogatory to public taste'. Others disagreed, argument degenerated into a brawl and Goldsmith was roughly handled. This episode throws light on his ideas of the novel. He had not liked *Tom Jones*, he thought Smollett coarse, and Sterne he did not think even funny. Whatever the alleged shortcomings of Goldsmith's own private life, the novelist, he felt, should offer his readers a picture, not indeed of 'a happiness which never existed', but one from which the grosser features were expunged.

On 31 May 1761 he invited to supper at Wine Office Court several guests including Percy and Johnson, whom he now met possibly for the first time. They took to each other at once. Amusingly enough, Johnson had appeared in a new suit and a new wig, explaining to the astounded Percy that 'Goldsmith, who is a very great sloven, justifies his disregard of cleanliness . . . by quoting my example,' and adding that he wished to set him a better one.

Goldsmith had written admiringly of Johnson and a few others in *The Bee*; but Johnson had also been greatly impressed by the Chinese Letters. Whether or not he had already met Goldsmith, he now became his friend, protector and – if one may use the word – his promoter; while Goldsmith, though less subservient than Boswell, seems to have been usually over-awed by him. Johnson, as everyone knows, dominated the limited circle of London *literati* – limited, because apart from Goldsmith, the principal writers of the age – Gray, Walpole, Sterne, Hume, Robertson and Gibbon – either did not live in London or rarely put in an appearance, and in any case did not trouble themselves about Johnson.

With the general public however, his prestige stood high. The *Dictionary* had made his name, his talent for conversation sealed his reputation. Like most of his contemporaries he stood for reason and common sense and he had the art of saying things, often important, in memorable language. In this lies his title to fame. It was remarked recently in the *Times Literary Supplement*, that he was the luckiest of authors: that he had the finest biographer ever, who had at his elbow the finest scholar of the day (Malone), and now has had the prince of editors. But for these circumstances, and perhaps for his *Lives of the Poets*, he would now be virtually unknown, except to research scholars. Today most people see him through the eyes of Boswell's book, which is a panegyric. While apparently concealing none of his hero's faults, he still conveys the impression of a very great and good-hearted man.

Reference to independent witnesses shows this to be delusive. Thus in 1762 Norton Nicholls, then an undergraduate at Trinity Hall who had just met Thomas Gray, wrote to W. J. Temple, his friend in London: 'I did not find him as you found Johnson, surly, morose, Dogmatical or imperious. But affable, entertaining and polite.'[1] No one thought of describing Johnson as affable. 'His manners,' wrote Horace Walpole, 'were sordid, supercilious and brutal.' Mrs Harris, wife of a Salisbury scholar, was shocked by his 'dreadful voice . . . [he was] more beastly in his dress and person than anything I ever

---

[1] Quoted by W. Ketton-Cremer in *Thomas Gray: a Biography*, Cambridge, 1955, p 191.

beheld. He feeds nastily and ferociously.' And it is significant that Erasmus Darwin's circle at Lichfield felt no liking for 'the arrogant Dr Johnson.' What most people suffered from, however, was his manner in arguing a point. With great learning and a retentive memory, he talked less for the pleasure of exchanging ideas than for the expectation of delivering a knock-out, which he usually did. But if, as occasionally happened, anyone was getting the better of an argument, he would shout him down. On one occasion he complained: 'Sir, I am not used to be contradicted,' which provoked the retort: 'Better for yourself and friends, Sir, if you were. . . .' Yet no one suffered from him as did Mrs Thrale who for over twenty-five years mothered him, fed him, and made gallons of tea for him; and whom after the death of her husband he treated so outrageously when he heard that she planned to marry Piozzi, an excellent man, that one questions his sanity. It can be said, in palliation of much of his behaviour, that he had fits of 'vile melancholy', which were one sympton of a permanent neurosis.

Such was the 'Great Cham' who now became Goldsmith's friend and literary champion. While he was to lend him decisive support on two or three critical occasions, his example in personal manners can hardly have been helpful. Goldsmith was awkward and heedless by nature, handicapped also by his early environment, and he probably learned most in the way of the social graces from the examples of Reynolds and of the Horneck family. He wished, naturally enough, to improve his standing and appearance, and this explains his passion for fine clothes; which he carried to excess. Between 1761 and 1774 his tailor's bills tell a story of astounding extravagance.

Meanwhile he was fighting his way upwards and neglecting no possible opening. In 1760 he had applied for the post of Secretary to the Society of Fine Arts and had sought Garrick's influence on his behalf; but Garrick, annoyed by a previous criticism of his management of the theatre, refused. Goldsmith

D

next appealed to Lord Bute for a subsidy to enable him to visit the Near East, where he thought that one might discover useful arts, unknown in Europe. Lord Bute was not interested. If, a few years later, he had asked the Earl of Northumberland, the new Lord Lieutenant of Ireland, he would certainly have received a grant. But Goldsmith was not apt to do the right thing at the right time.

The year 1762 was to be for Goldsmith a year of chequered fortunes, personal and literary, and of episodes ludicrous or alarming. While engaged in abbreviating Plutarch's *Lives* for a *Compendium of Biography* which Newbery had planned, he was taken ill, and a man named Collier completed the work. For the rest of the year he seems to have worked by fits and starts, and to have failed lamentably to make ends meet. Some Red Indian chiefs, known as the Cherokee Kings, were in London that summer, dressing and wearing their war-paint to the delight of the public; one of them was so gratified by Goldsmith's admiration that he embraced him warmly, leaving on his cheek a smear of oil and colour. It was soon after this that he paid a visit to Bath, one of the two or three most fashionable resorts of the time, and here it occurred to him to learn what he could about Richard Nash, the former master of the ceremonies, with a view to a biography. This he wrote and published so quickly that the October number of the *Critical Review* noticed the book by regretting that 'a writer of genius' should have been 'tortured to give substance to inanity'. But the twenty-eight guineas which he was paid – though only later – consoled him for the torture. Meanwhile, in this same month of October he was so badly out of pocket that he could not pay Mrs Carnan the rent of his room and was threatened with arrest and imprisonment.

There appears to have been a 'bailiffs' scene,' less amusing and probably 'lower' than the one in *The Good-Natured Man*, and the delinquent sent an SOS to Johnson. The latter, according to Boswell, sent a guinea in advance and came as soon as he was able. Goldsmith he found comforting himself with a bottle of madeira; and when Johnson asked if he had any likely manuscript in hand, he produced from a drawer the manuscript of a novel. Boswell says that, after glancing through it, Johnson took it to Newbery and came back with £60 in cash; but a record, more reliable in this instance, proves that Goldsmith cannot have received more than twenty guineas and that the remaining £40 or forty guineas were paid only at intervals over the next three years.[1] It is, moreover, unlikely that the 'novel' – presumably *The Vicar of Wakefield* – was complete at this time; and finally no one has explained why Goldsmith, who disapproved of the novel as a genre in general, and of Fielding, Smollett and Sterne in particular, should himself have undertaken to write a novel.

The appearance of *Tristram Shandy* seems to the present writer to afford a convincing explanation. Volumes I and II had been published at York on 1 January 1760 and their author, a hitherto unknown Yorkshire parson, had immediately leapt into fame. His real sin was not in having written an 'obscene' novel,[2] but in having been magnificently fêted by all the fashionable people in London who should have been fêting Goldsmith. Volumes III and IV had come out early in 1761 and been greeted with the same enthusiasm. Goldsmith would therefore show that he could produce a much better novel than Sterne's. As in *Tristram Shandy*, the scene would be in Yorkshire and the narrator would be a Yorkshire vicar. To those readers who were bemused by the smooth blarney of Goldsmith's style, it would be a real novel, 'pure' as *Tristram Shandy* was not. To those who saw into Goldsmith's real intentions, which today are clear enough from the absurd situations and the sly observations and innuendoes of the

[1] See pp 251–2 for a full discussion of this point.
[2] It contained two scandalous and slightly indecent, but hardly obscene, allusions to Yorkshire notables, but for the most part it was whimsical and Rabelaisian. Sterne possessed a wonderful command of the language, which threatened to rival Goldsmith's.

vicar, it would be a parody of a romantic novel, in which all the characters would serve as butts for ridicule. Goldsmith seems already to have been convinced – as he was known to be in later years – that whatever other people could do, he could do better. Apart from this, there is no evidence that he aspired to be a novelist.

Some of his biographers have been scandalised that a 'novel' destined to appear in almost every language and to be constantly read and re-read should have been sold for so little as £60 (actually sixty guineas).[1] But '*Habent sua fata libelli.*' Johnson probably appreciated the humour and thought that the adventures of the Primrose family might appeal to conventional taste, but even he afterwards declared that he saw 'nothing natural' in it, and he was right. Newbery must have doubted whether it would hit the public taste, and for many years it was coolly received. The price he paid for the book was generous. Goldsmith himself regarded Newbery as a benefactor. Yet, more even than a benefactor, he needed a business-manager, and this was exactly what Newbery undertook to be. Probably in early December he arranged for Goldsmith to lodge with a Mrs Fleming in an apartment in Canonbury House. This was a range of old buildings, dominated by a tall brick tower, at Islington, then a country village. It would be difficult for him to spend as much money out here as in the City, while at the same time he would be more disposed to work. He agreed in fact to work for Newbery and to allow the latter to manage his income, paying his rent (£50 a year) and other bills, and making him an allowance for pocket money.

Newbery had done him a good turn earlier in the year, on 5 March, by publishing the Chinese Letters in two volumes as *The Citizen of the World*. The book was anonymous but its authorship was probably an open secret. It was the only English work of its kind comparable with the *Lettres persanes*, and

---

[1] Sixty guineas at that time was equivalent in purchasing power to about £659 in 1970, and rather more today (see Appendix III). It was a good price for a first novel.

it revealed its author at the height of his powers. He never in later years wrote better or with more humour and vivacity. The *British Magazine* considered it 'light . . . reading, partly original, partly borrowed', which was more or less true, since many French writers had been put to contribution. Yet there is in it more of originality than of plagiarism. The response of the English public was rather lukewarm, but a French translation was reprinted four times within the first five years.

Seen therefore in perspective, the year 1762 had not been such a bad one. As a man of letters, Goldsmith was made. He had been hailed as 'a writer of genius', he was calling himself 'Doctor Goldsmith' and others were so addressing him. His star was at last in the ascendant. And now that Newbery was acting as his banker and would not perhaps object to an occasional overdraft, he ceased to worry about money. He came into London for Christmas and on Christmas Day dined with Thomas Davies who ran a bookshop in Bloomsbury. It was a popular resort of the *literati*, the more so as Mrs Davies, a major attraction of the place, presided at the tea-table. It was on this occasion that Goldsmith met Boswell, to whom we owe a great deal of information about him.

Chapter 9

Meeting the Right People

⁂ 1763-65 ⁂

James Boswell, son and heir of Lord Auchinleck, had first come to England in 1760 and during a stay of three months had secured introductions to Laurence Sterne and to the Duke of York. He had returned to London in November 1762 in the hope of obtaining a commission in the Guards, of wearing a splendid uniform and dazzling the charmers. But his father put a stop to such notions, and James then fell back on lion-hunting. He wished especially to add 'the great Dr Johnson' to his bag, for he greatly preferred authors to books.

He had already begun to write down everything he heard, *at the time*, and everything he did, including his lowest amours; and he had a rare talent for dramatising himself and for show-ing off his whims and superstitions, all 'with some slight touch of insanity', as Sir Walter Scott shrewdly suspected. But his passion for interviewing famous people, and for reporting their sayings, was perhaps unique. Without his *Life of Johnson*, many of Goldsmith's sayings and doings would have been lost.

On the occasion of this first meeting he reports Goldsmith as in a carping and contentious mood. The conversation having turned on poetry, Goldsmith criticised Shakespeare on the ground of his 'pantomime' and allowed him no 'great merit'. Gray's *Odes* were 'terribly obscure'; poetry had fallen on evil days. Pope seems to have represented Goldsmith's ideal, while his views on Shakespeare may have been influenced by Voltaire or have been a reaction against Garrick. Boswell thought

Goldsmith had 'some genius' but that in his remarks on Shakespeare he was 'a most impudent puppy'.[1] In the following May (1763) he insinuated himself into Johnson's acquaintance.

Boswell – Mr Johnson, I do indeed come from Scotland, but I cannot help it.
Johnson – That, Sir, I find is what a great many of your countrymen cannot help.

Boswell lay down under this, continued to court the man, and at last, on 25 May, after spending most of the night drinking port with him at the Mitre, was accepted on the intimate basis he desired. It was on this occasion that, Goldsmith being mentioned, Johnson said that he 'is one of the first men we have as an author at present, and a very worthy man too. He has been loose in his principles, but he is coming right.' Whether he referred to moral or literary principles, is obscure. In any case, the remark indicated that Boswell should cultivate Goldsmith; which he proceeded to do by a visit to Canonbury House. Goldsmith gave him tea and they talked about Hume and other writers. A few days after this, Johnson, Boswell and Goldsmith met for dinner at the Mitre. Johnson then took Goldsmith to Miss Williams' rooms to take tea with this dependant of his, and Boswell felt humiliated at being left out: 'Dr Goldsmith, being a privileged man, went with him this night, strutting away and calling to me with an air of superiority... "I go to Miss Williams...," but it was not long before I obtained the same mark of distinction.'

This episode took place on 1 July; on the sixth Boswell invited Johnson, Goldsmith, Davies and Ogilvie to dine at his rooms in Downing Street. But Boswell and other friends had made so much noise the night before that the landlord had threatened them with arrest; so the party now thought it

---

[1] *Boswell's London Journal*, 1762–63, ed F. A. Pottle, New York, 1950, pp 105–6.

prudent to adjourn to the Mitre. Here, after an argument about politics, Ogilvie began to praise his native land. There was very rich country round Edinburgh, he observed: an opinion which Goldsmith, who had no feeling for scenery, denied. Ogilvie was not to be subdued. Scotland, he maintained, presented a great many noble, wild prospects – a truth which, however, provoked Johnson's famous rejoinder, that the noblest prospect for a Scotsman was the high road to England.[1] Such anecdotes throw a great deal of light on character.

Goldsmith, emboldened by Newbery's protection, was going to enjoy himself in the months to come. Heedless as ever, he ordered wine, sassafras for tea, entertained his acquaintances, drew money to pay his tailor's bills, and generally overspent. By the end of the year Newbery found that while he had paid his protégé £111 1s 6d, the latter's earnings had amounted to no more than £63. (Now in the 1760s £111 was equivalent to about £1,150 of our currency, in terms of purchasing power; £63 was equivalent to about £665[2]). The debit was carried forward. Goldsmith devoted the summer to compiling *An History of England in a series of Letters from a Nobleman to his Son*, a form suggested by Lord Chesterfield's *Letters* and designed to whet the public appetite. William Cooke records that Goldsmith would spend his mornings in reading Carte, Hume and Rapin-Thoyras, then stroll in the fields while digesting the material; take dinner; then, as we may surmise from other records, play with Christopher Smart's children who were living in another apartment of Canonbury House; and finally write up what he had in mind. As he wrote with great facility, the work may not have occupied more than six months. The research had been done by serious historians; yet there was some merit in co-ordinating and recasting the material in a form which people found attractive. The book

[1] Boswell, *Life of Johnson*, ed G. Birkbeck Hill, vol I, pp 423–6.
[2] For a calculation of the equivalent values of money between the decade 1760–70 and the year 1970, see Appendix III.

was published anonymously in June 1764 and enjoyed considerable success, especially when translated into French. The £21 he received from Newbery was no doubt as much as the work deserved. It appears that Newbery paid him a further £21 'for translating the Life of Christ and the Lives of the Fathers', which Goldsmith acknowledged in a receipt dated 11 October 1763. It has been shown, however, that these were simply abridgements of rather obscure and unimportant works.[1]

Chronically short of money, he had planned an edition of Pope, with a biographical preface and notes on the text. This he could only offer to a bookseller in the Strand named Tonson, who owned the copyright. The letter mooting the project did not impress Tonson, who sent a printer to Goldsmith's rooms to decline the offer. This today would be considered a perfectly courteous, even considerate, thing to do; but Goldsmith, who had a high notion of his importance, apparently struck the man.[2] They came to grips, and were separated – by whom we do not know, but possibly in the street. The story went round, and it was later rumoured that the printer had pushed Goldsmith into the kennel.

In spite of this lamentable affair, one doubts whether in 1763 Goldsmith's life was very strenuous. He was composing *The Traveller*, expanding and adding to what he had begun in Switzerland.

Early in 1764 Joshua Reynolds, whom he had first met in 1762, proposed to Johnson that they should form a club. Johnson assented and took over the lead in the matter, inviting Goldsmith to be a member, and also two young men whom he had met in Oxford – Bennet Langton, son of an old Lincolnshire family, and the Honourable Topham Beauclerk, a grandson of the first Duke of St Albans. Beauclerk was a man of great wealth but also of personal distinction, keenly interested

---

[1] R. W. Seitz, 'Goldsmith's Lives of the Fathers', in *Modern Philology*, vol XXVI, pp 295–305. Cited by Wardle, pp 150, 310.

[2] Johnson frequently struck people who displeased him; on one occasion he knocked a man down. Goldsmith was far less violent, and much better mannered.

in science and literature, well-informed and witty. To these members were added Anthony Chamier, a civil servant, Edmund Burke, Dr Nugent, Burke's father-in-law, and Sir John Hawkins. The Club was to meet once a week at the Turk's Head, dine and talk – dining and talking being Johnson's means of escape from 'the vile melancholy' which was exacerbated by his dread of insanity and fear of death.

In the course of 1764 Goldsmith composed an oratorio, *The Captivity*, based on the story of the Israelites in Babylon, and apparently suggested by Christopher Smart's *Hannah* which the King's Theatre had produced on 3 April. If Smart could write an oratorio, Goldsmith could compose a better one; yet apart from a few verses on Hope, *The Captivity* was neither produced nor even printed during his lifetime, although Dodsley had paid him ten guineas for it. For Dodsley he also wrote a *Chronological History*, which was sold to Newbery, and a *Concise History of England*, abridged from the so-called 'Letters from a Nobleman', but cast in language markedly different. These two potboilers brought him thirty-eight guineas. He had not overworked himself, and there is no evidence that he earned more than £70 in 1764, which explains why, according to Prior, he was in default for the rent of his room. Richard Cumberland says that Mrs Fleming offered him the choice between arrest and marriage. He preferred the lesser of these evils. How he escaped from both, we do not know. Perhaps John Newbery again proved his guardian angel; his son Francis relates that Goldsmith read him parts of *The Traveller* on which he was then engaged, and the publisher foresaw that this would make money.

It is curious that a man who had written about opera and musicians and who had been a keen flautist, says nothing about the great musical event of the years 1764–65. On 20 April Leopold Mozart had brought Wolfgang Amadeus, then eight years old, to London, after a triumphal reception in Paris. The boy was received at Court where he accompanied on the clavichord a song by the Queen. He gave recitals in London, and lodged with his parents in Soho, where Goldsmith could easily have gone to hear him.[1] One wonders if any members of Goldsmith's circle were interested in music. The Turk's Head was in Gerrard Street.

Goldsmith must somehow, in spite of appearances to the contrary, have been in funds by October, because he took rooms at 2 Garden Court in the Temple, and in November often met Percy and Johnson for dinner or tea. Boswell had left for Holland in August and was not to return until 1766.

The Traveller: a Prospect of Society appeared on 19 December, commended by Johnson who had written the concluding lines, and warmly eulogised by the Press. Goldsmith had spent months revising the style, and he continued to revise and improve it in successive editions. If *The Citizen of the World* had established him in the eyes of the *cognoscenti*, *The Traveller* won him the favour of the public. 'He was sought after with greediness,' according to Reynolds.[2] Other members of the Club could hardly believe this poem to be the work of a man whose conversational efforts were usually pitiful. Chamier, who was especially incredulous, at last admitted that he believed Goldsmith had written the poem himself, 'and, let me tell you, that is believing a great deal'.

Popularity now brought him many invitations to dine with distinguished people, and also the acquaintance of Robert Nugent, an Irishman of good family with whom he felt more at home than with the Chamiers and Beauclerks. Nugent, who later became Lord Clare, had turned Anglican, probably with an eye to the main chance. He now had a house in London and a mansion in Essex, and was Goldsmith's first friend who was in a position to afford him material assistance. He presented him to the Earl of Northumberland who had just been

[1] He interpreted Bach and Handel and, during this long stay in England, which he did not leave until 1 August, 1765, composed his first symphony.
[2] *Portraits by Sir Joshua Reynolds,* ed F. W. Hilles, New York, 1952, p 48.

appointed Lord Lieutenant of Ireland and who, having been impressed by *The Traveller*, invited its author to call on him. Goldsmith afterwards told Hawkins, who had also that day been at Northumberland House, that the Earl had said "he should be glad to do me any kindness'. The poet had replied that he had a brother in Ireland 'who stood in need of help', but he had asked nothing for himself. And the Earl probably forgot the distant brother, who could be little more than an abstraction for him. 'As for myself,' Goldsmith explained to Hawkins, 'I have no dependence on the promises of great men: I look to the booksellers for support; . . . and I am not inclined to forsake them for others.' Prior, who found this story in Sir John Hawkins' narrative, commends Goldsmith's 'disin-terestedness and affection'. But since the Earl had made a clear and unsolicited offer of help, Goldsmith could easily have asked if he might be able to find him some part-time appoint-ment in London, to supplement his literary earnings. Hawkins considered Goldsmith 'an idiot in the affairs of this world'. It is certainly strange that he did not later seek the Earl's help or advice, since his friend Percy, the Earl's kinsman, became his chaplain, and also since, in this same year, Goldsmith com-posed *The Hermit*, a ballad which he caused to be printed as *Edwin and Angelina* 'for the amusement of the Countess'. Prior considered it 'the most beautiful ballad in our own or perhaps in any language'. Today it seems artificial and senti-mental, far removed from the wild and natural feeling of a genuine ballad. But Goldsmith, who inserted it in *The Vicar of Wakefield*, said he thought it could 'hardly be amended', and most people probably agreed with him at the time. It was translated into French by four writers, including Léonard; like many other of Goldsmith's writings, which enjoyed an immense vogue beyond the Channel.

Having no compilation in hand, he next collected some twenty-nine pieces which had appeared in various magazines, and these were published on 3 June 1765 by Newbery and

Griffin as *Essays by Dr Goldsmith*. A number of them having been pirated, he observed in his preface that 'as these entertainers of the public [the pirates] . . . have partly lived upon me for some years, let me now try if I cannot live a little upon myself.' They could easily have retorted '*Et tu, quoque*', since he himself had partly lived upon French writers for some years. The volume was, however, well received by the Press, one paper declaring that the essays showed that 'one of the first poets in the English language' was 'one of the first essayists too'. The critics were no more exacting in those days than the public. A number of these pieces were not essays in any strict sense of the term. 'Asem' is an Eastern Tale, treated as an allegory, the 'Reverie at the Boar's Head Tavern', an imaginary dream-talk with Dame Quickly who relates the metamorphoses which the building had experienced – long and decidedly boring. 'Alcander and Septimius' is a short story translated from Boccaccio; and 'The Adventures of a Strolling Player' is also a short story, most of it translated from Marivaux. Goldsmith must have been gratified by the volume's success. Several new editions were called for. In 1787 Prince Boris de Galitzin published a French translation, and three other French versions were to appear.

Was Goldsmith now growing a little weary of dependence on the booksellers? One wonders; because Reynolds, who realised that he was a man of genius and must have supposed that he had some kind of medical licence,[1] advised him to practise once more as a physician. To inspire proper respect he bought a wig and cane, 'purple silk small clothes' and 'a scarlet roquelaure buttoned to the chin'. He also moved to better rooms at 3 King's Bench Walk and even engaged a servant. All this proved a costly misadventure. A prescription which he wrote for a Mrs Sidebotham was declared by the apothecary to be unsafe, and the lady took fright. Goldsmith

---

[1] This seems possible, but no record exists of any kind of medical diploma that might have been awarded him. See pp 63, 67, and note on p 125.

then said he would prescribe no more for his friends. Beauclerk agreed with him: 'My dear Doctor, whenever you undertake to kill, let it be only your enemies.'

The year 1765 had brought him little work and less money. Yet he had spent a great deal, having ordered three suits in addition to the physician's outfit. It is impossible to know how he contrived to make ends meet or even to live. Robert Nugent sometimes entertained him in London or at Gosfield, and may have helped him with funds; but this is only a guess.

Chapter 10

Novelist and Dramatist

❧ 1766-68 ❧

1766 was to prove a year of exceptional importance in Gold-smith's life. *The Vicar of Wakefield* appeared in April, and in the autumn Reynolds introduced its author to Mrs Horneck and her family.

Johnson had been ill in January, suffering from the 'vile melancholy' which has been ascribed to his neurosis but which was equally caused by over-eating and lack of exercise. His 'illness' alarmed some of his friends. Goldsmith and Murphy tried to cheer him, but Mrs Thrale, the young wife of a wealthy brewer, was the only person who knew how to deal with his attacks of depression and terror. To her attentions, according to Goldsmith, Johnson 'owed his recovery'. But he was still unwell when, about mid-February, Boswell returned from his Grand Tour and called to see him. A few days later Boswell and Goldsmith arranged to sup together at the Mitre, and went first to invite Johnson to join them, Thomas Davies being also expected. But the Great Cham still felt out of sorts and, while he offered the visitors port, his conversation was sententious (and apparently slightly indecent). When the others suggested that he should write something,[1] he complained that 'a man is to have a part of his life to himself. . . . The good I can do by my conversation bears the same proportion to the good I can do by my writings, that the practice of a physician retired to a

[1] The best possible advice. Regular work on a literary project, such as his later *Lives of the Poets,* might have cured him.

small town, does to his practice in a great city.' Small wonder if, after they had left him, Goldsmith asked if Johnson was not failing in his head. The other thought he was more impatient if contradicted, and Goldsmith pointed out that 'no man is proof against continual adulation'.[1]

Goldsmith then invited Boswell to his rooms in the Temple where Boswell probably described his meetings with J.-J. Rousseau and Voltaire and his visit to Corsica – a long and ambitious tour, all at his father's expense. Goldsmith would have been less than human, if he had not envied such good fortune. Envious by nature, he envied Johnson, who had accepted a pension of £300 a year and was bone idle. Goldsmith, however, in spite of his depleted finances, did not deny himself many luxuries, in clothes, meals and entertaining.

In February and March he completed for Newbery a translation of J.-H.-S. Formey's *Histoire abrégée de la Philosophie*, and some minor works; and on 27 March Francis Newbery published *The Vicar of Wakefield*.

The public was not impressed: it seems doubtful if more than two thousand copies were sold in Goldsmith's lifetime. He himself, in the 'Advertisement', apologised for its defects, adding other remarks which today sound equally disingenuous. One can hardly be surprised if readers were puzzled by the book. *The Monthly Review* praised its 'beauties' but regarded its faults as putting readers 'out of all patience with the author capable of so strangely underwriting himself'. *The Critical Review* was more indulgent and more amused: '. . . was it necessary to bring the concluding calamities so thick upon your old venerable friend?' The reviewer suggested that Goldsmith had hurried the catastrophe because impatient to get to the end of his task – an unlikely conjecture. To readers then and for a century and a half since, the book has appeared at once humorous, pathetic and romantic. Few people saw how much Goldsmith had put of himself into the characters, and

[1] See Boswell, *Life of Johnson*, vol II, pp 14–15.

none realised that the story was an attempt to defend himself and also an ironical parody of romantic fiction. If Goldsmith intended to mystify his readers, he succeeded beyond any possible expectation.[1]

Sociable by nature, he was frequenting several circles at this time, in addition to attending the Club meetings on Mondays. A gay and noisy group foregathered on Wednesdays at the Globe Tavern in Fleet Street, and here Goldsmith was in his element, among men who appreciated him and his songs. Another member of the circle, equally entertaining, was Gordon who sang 'Nottingham Ale' and looked like a tun of it. As parodies are said to have contributed to the fun, it is possible that Samuel Foote was sometimes there: no one could have succeeded better in that vein. Tom King, who played Lord Ogleby in Colman's *The Clandestine Marriage*, was certainly a member of the group. Garrick naturally avoided such company; but Johnson deigned to put in an appearance, and on one of these occasions Hugh Kelly was presented to him and also, it would seem, to Goldsmith.

He had been born at Killarney in 1739 and had come to London in 1760. A hack-writer, like Goldsmith, he had, in his *Thespis*, drawn satirical portraits of the principal actors of the day, some of them extremely cruel, while taking care to laud Garrick to the skies. This was to pay off most handsomely in years to come, for Garrick rewarded adulation as much as he neglected the absence of it. Apart from this, Kelly had considerable fluency as a writer and knew how to flatter the taste of the age. Johnson thought nothing of him, but he himself was overawed by the Great Cham. On the day when he was presented he seems to have sat listening to Johnson's talk and then, rising from his seat, said that he feared lest by staying longer, he might be troublesome. 'Not in the least, Sir,' came the reply, 'I had forgotten you were in the room.' Goldsmith may by now have come to regard this kind of rejoinder as natural:

---

[1] For a study of *The Vicar of Wakefield,* see chs 21 and 22.

the society of Johnson certainly encouraged him in self-conceit and disregard for other people's feelings. But as Kelly was a fellow-countryman, he seems to have got on well with him, and is even said to have thought of suggesting marriage with his sister-in-law.

He continued to spend as much time as ever with Reynolds, especially in the second half of the year, and he was among the many people who often dined at his home in Leicester Fields – now Leicester Square. The artist was about four years older than he; about the same height, five feet six inches; and marked like him with smallpox, but of an appearance more agreeable. Having settled in London in 1753, he had quickly made his name as the most popular of English portraitists and was now a well-to-do man with a wide circle of friends. For Goldsmith he was the best of friends. Some mysterious affinity appears to have bound them together. No one, except Lord Clare and the Hornecks, understood Goldsmith as well as Reynolds. He saw into his weaknesses and limitations, and understood that something of what people regarded in Goldsmith's behaviour as absurd, was really intended as humour: this also may explain why he tolerated in Goldsmith what others would have strongly resented. His so-called *Portrait* of the writer tells us much that was essential about him. Through Reynolds, Goldsmith became a friend of Mrs Horneck, of her son and of her daughters, Catherine and Mary – an intimate friend, since he afterwards accompanied the ladies on a visit to Paris.

Socially, then, the year 1766 was pleasant enough. From the material point of view he appears to have received £127 in June for various pieces of work, a sum which included £21 for *The Traveller* and £20 for translating Formey's book. In December he was paid five guineas for an English Grammar. He also produced an anthology of *Poems for Young Ladies*, which was reprinted twice but met with no critical approval, and a more serious selection entitled *The Beauties of English Poesy*, published in 1767. This was even less well received, and commercially less successful; yet Griffin is said to have paid £200 for it. Now £200 in the 1760s was worth well over £2,000 in terms of purchasing power today.

Already in 1766 Goldsmith had begun to try his hand at drama. He knew Mr and Mrs Yates, the actors, and through them probably met Woodward and Shuter who were to play the comic parts in *The Good-Natured Man*; possibly also John Quick who, in March 1773, was to make his name in the role of Tony Lumpkin. It may have been they who encouraged him to write a comic comedy by way of reaction against the 'sentimental' sort. However that may be, *The Good-Natured Man* was completed by the spring of 1767, and Reynolds thoughtfully invited Garrick to his house to meet Goldsmith. Garrick took the manuscript, considered it and temporised. It has been thought that if the author had now flattered and cajoled him, he would have staged the play. As it was, he suggested William Whitehead, the Poet Laureate, as an independent referee, a proposal which was rejected. Goldsmith then offered the play to Colman, the manager of the Covent Garden theatre. Colman is said to have thought well of it, though he must have advised some alterations because, on 19 July, Goldsmith wrote to thank him for 'your kind partiality in my favour', and for replying so promptly, and also to agree to Colman's putting 'the piece in such a state as it may be acted. . . .' There was now hope of its being presented in November, but in the event the performance was delayed until January 1768.

It is evident that for the past year or two Sir Joshua Reynolds and Robert Nugent, now Viscount Clare, but known familiarly as 'Squire Gawky', had been doing what they could to introduce Goldsmith to a wider and more respectable circle, to entertain him personally, and generally to spare him the expense of meals. With these men, who made allowances for his eccentricity, he got on very well. With others he was less at ease, or involuntarily awkward. When Dr George Baker,

Reynolds' physician, invited him to dinner to meet Angelica Kaufman, a talented portraitist from Chur in the Grisons, the invitation came at such short notice – possibly only two hours or so before the meal – that Goldsmith, being still unshaven, declined in an extraordinary verse-letter:

> Your mandate I got –
> You may all go to pot;
> Had your senses been right,
> You'd have sent before night. . . .

He names each member of the party, and says they are to be told that he could not shave in cold water; also

> Tell each other to rue
> Your Devonshire crew,
> For sending so late
> To one of my state. . . .

What Dr Baker and Miss Kaufman thought of this reply, we do not know. Perhaps Reynolds explained that Goldsmith now expected to be treated as a person of quite exceptional distinction.

At some time in the spring Lord Clare invited him to Bath, where he had taken a house next door to the Earl of Northumberland's. It was probably similar, if not identical, in appearance. So, early one morning, Goldsmith, having gone out for a stroll, mistook the house on his return, walked into the Northumberlands', where the Earl and Countess were about to breakfast, and made himself comfortable on a settee. The Northumberlands, suspecting the error, started a conversation and invited him to join them at breakfast; whereupon he realised his blunder and withdrew with an apology.

Little is known of his doings in the summer of 1767, or even where he was living. His letter of 19 July to Colman was written from Garden Court in the Temple; but he had previously had rooms in King's Bench Walk and in December he moved to Brick Court.

Amazing as are the stories of his fecklessness and gullibility, many of them appear to be true, and the biographer feels obliged to recall them, even at the risk of suggesting a rather low opinion of his character. Yet there was something in his personality that endeared him to men of distinction and to quite ordinary men. There have been one or two brilliant and entertaining writers whose death has left the world indifferent, because they were never loved. The grief, even the tears, inspired by Goldsmith's death, among those who had liked him, among those who had laughed at him, even in Hugh Kelly who had been at odds with him, were extraordinary. People were not lamenting the loss of one who 'wrote like an angel and talked like poor Poll'; they were grieving for someone truly beloved.

His faults were well known. He dressed extravagantly. He gambled, probably for large sums. One evening, after taking a 'coach' to the Devil's Tavern to play cards, he is said to have given the driver a guinea instead of a shilling. He ruefully discovered the mistake and mentioned it to the other players. Later in the evening a man whom he took to be the driver, called, expressed regret, and handed over what looked like a guinea; Goldsmith began to hold forth on this rare example of honesty when he discovered that the coin was counterfeit. The bogus driver had been sent by the company to play this trick on Goldsmith.

The story, related by Prior, is probably true. That he was induced to part with seven and a half guineas for a new history of England in French, for which a certain 'Colonel Chevalier de Champigny' alleged that he was collecting subscriptions from distinguished people, sounds plausible. Similar appeals are made today. But it is a feature of many of the anecdotes related by Boswell and by Prior, that the months, even the years, when they are said to have occurred are unknown – which throws some doubt on their authenticity.

Throughout the second half of 1767 money remained Goldsmith's great preoccupation. The hope that the play would be staged in November, with the prospect of a long and profitable run, was disappointed. Goldsmith signed a contract with Davies to write a history of Rome for two hundred and fifty guineas, but this was cold comfort at the time, and December must have been a dreary month in all senses of the word. He raised money by one means or another because in January 1768 one finds him entertaining some fellow Irishmen to a dinner in his rooms. One has the impression that in these days London was full of Irishmen, many calling themselves 'Doctor', and most of them scraping a bare living with their pens. Edward Purdon who had died in 1767, probably of starvation, was one of these, and Goldsmith wrote his epitaph:

> Here lies poor Ned Purdon, from misery freed.
>   Who long was a bookseller's hack;
> He led such a damnable life in this world,
>   I don't think he'll wish to come back.

On the occasion of the January dinner-party, the guests seem to have been literary men, because Goldsmith is reported as expressing opinions on the older dramatists and on some contemporary poets. He thought Otway the greatest dramatic genius since Shakespeare, regarded the dialogue in Congreve's plays as too witty to be *vraisemblable*, and ascribed to Farquhar 'a better spirit of comedy' than to any other modern dramatist. Gray and Shenstone as poets he admired, with reservations.

On 23 January Garrick produced *False Delicacy*, Hugh Kelly's play, to enthusiastic applause, and this cannot have raised Goldsmith's spirits since he had been aiming at a kind of play in which the comic should arise from faults of character and which should not aim ostensibly at inspiring sentiment or a feeling of pathos. He held that the delineation of character was essential to a comedy; and for anyone who understands his own character, which was somewhat schizophrenic, the most curious thing about *The Good-Natured Man* is the way in which he stands apart from himself, watches, judges and ridicules himself, in the person of young Honeywood. Molière had done this sort of thing, if far more poignantly, in at least two of his greatest pieces. But classical comedy, or anything that looked like it, was now less fashionable than the 'sentimental' kind – the word 'sentimental' being then taken in good part. (One would say 'romantic' today.) Hence, on 29 January, when *The Good-Natured Man* was to come on at Covent Garden, its author was in great trepidation.

Johnson's Prologue did nothing to help. What was the audience to think when, on the curtain's rising, an actor stepped forward and began:

> Press'd by the load of life, the weary mind
> Surveys the general toil of human kind?

or again, when he spoke of 'our anxious bard'; and when, near the end, he continued:

> 'This night, our wit,' the pert apprentice cries,
> 'Lies at my feet – I hiss him, and he dies'?

The mood of a first-night audience is usually decisive, and a play should be presented with an air of polite confidence. Johnson, when writing the Prologue, must have taken leave of his senses; for he firmly believed in comedy of manners and he had encouraged Goldsmith in his venture to depict nature and delineate character. For some time indeed the fate of the play lay in the balance. In fact, sentiment rather than character was depicted in young Honeywood, but neither his heedless benevolence nor his mute and timid adoration of Miss Richland produced much effect. Croaker, suggested by Johnson's 'Suspirius', and Lofty, imitated from Brueys' *L'Important*, caused amusement as they well might. But the scene at the beginning of Act III when Twitch and Flannigan, the bailiffs, take possession of Honeywood's house, where Miss Richland finds them, was too much for the public's sense of propriety. True, the scene had been suggested by a real episode in the life of Steele (as related in Johnson's *Lives*[1]); but Goldsmith had unfortunately overdone the vulgarity of the bailiffs; and Twitch's rejoinder to a remark of Miss Richland: 'That's all my eye. . . .' was hissed. By this time Goldsmith was in the depths of depression. He sat out the rest of the play. Shuter, who played the part of Croaker, made the most successful hit of the night in Act IV, when reading the now famous 'incendiary' letter which, he thought, threatened to blow him up, with his house and family – in the speech beginning: 'Death and destruction! Are all the horrors of air, fire and water to be levelled only at me?' From this moment the play went well, but its author thought it had failed. After thanking Shuter and rewarding him with ten guineas, he joined the members of the Club at the Turk's Head. Here he joked, laughed and sang to prevent himself from crying; it was only when alone with Johnson that he gave way in a flood of tears.

He had become the plaything of nerves and imagination. The play was a success. On 1 February, when 'the bailiffs' scene' had been omitted, a run of nine more nights brought him from £350 to £400; while the edition published by Griffin went through four impressions by the end of the month, and for this he received £50. £450 in 1768 was worth what £4,685 would purchase today. He should have been content.

But *False Delicacy*, with its ingenious plot and agreeable characters, was proving one of the box-office triumphs of the century, and it is difficult to discount the suspicion that Goldsmith's play had been deliberately held up so as to give Kelly's

---

[1] I am indebted to I. Lytton Sells for pointing this out.

a better start. Ten thousand copies of the printed version were sold in the course of the year, and Kelly was entertained at a public breakfast and presented with a piece of plate. It was not in Goldsmith's character to practise the saintly indifference of the sceptics. He disparaged *False Delicacy*, and charitable souls repeated and probably distorted his remarks. The result was an unpleasant rift between men who had been on friendly terms; Kelly was unwilling to overlook the slight. When Goldsmith brought himself to congratulate his rival, the latter replied: 'I cannot thank you, because I cannot believe you.'

Goldsmith could not hope to revolutionise the theatre overnight or even for many years to come. Public and critics recognised his merit but still on the whole preferred the genre to which they were now growing accustomed: hence the success of Cumberland's *The Brothers* in 1769, of his excellent *West Indian* in 1771, and of the *Fashionable Lover* in 1772; hence also the continued applause which greeted in 1773 Kelly's *The School for Wives*. This last won a resounding triumph which, according to Beauclerk, 'almost killed Goldsmith with envy'. Today these plays, which are contained in the many volumes of *The British Theatre*, are unjustly neglected. Some are poor, others, like *The West Indian*, remarkably original and dramatic. Goldsmith's are chiefly valued for the style. *The Good-Natured Man* has been acted privately from time to time, and was successfully revived on the public stage in the late autumn of 1971. It has since been adapted for television.

Not only was literary London full of Irishmen, the stage was dominated by them. Apart from Kelly's triumphs, and Mrs Sheridan's success, Murphy's tragedy of *Zenobia* and Bickerstaffe's opera, *Lionel and Clarissa*, won popular acclaim; so much so that Kenrick, while ignoring Murphy, ridiculed the three others by parodying Dryden's 'Three Poets in three distant Ages born' in verses too wretched to be worth quoting.

Goldsmith consoled himself for Kelly's success by buying a Wilton carpet, a sofa, chairs and curtains for the three rooms he now occupied in Brick Court; and by entertaining on a generous scale. The outlook after all was brighter than in the previous year. One successful play might be followed by others, and in any event he could now command a higher price for his compilations. At some moment in the spring he paid a visit to Ilam, just west of Dovedale, possibly because Johnson occasionally stayed with Dr Taylor at Ashbourne nearby. But on his return to London, he received a shock in the news of his brother Henry's unexpected death at Athlone. He had been more attached to Henry than to any other members of the family, and this bereavement may have inspired him to write *The Deserted Village*, which was his next serious venture. In the meantime he and a lawyer named Edward Bott, who was a neighbour in Brick Court, had arranged to spend the summer at a cottage near Edgware. It had been reconditioned by a prosperous shoemaker and, with its attractive garden, was known as 'the Shoemaker's Paradise'. Here Goldsmith worked at the history of Rome and, when in the garden or strolling in the fields, meditated *The Deserted Village*. Occasionally the two drove into town in Bott's gig, and returned after dinner – and after drinking more heavily than was wise, since night would have fallen long before they got back. On one occasion Bott drove into a wayside post,[1] while obstinately maintaining that he was in the middle of the highway: an episode to which only Surtees could have done justice.

Goldsmith was back in London by 20 August, because on the twenty-first he met H. B. de Saussure, the famous Genevese scientist[2] – an important meeting which Goldsmith's biographers have overlooked. De Saussure and his wife had reached England earlier in the month and had been received in London by Dr Turton, whom they already knew (and who, incidentally, was to be one of the doctors to attend Goldsmith

---

[1] Prior, vol II, pp 190–91.
[2] For this information I am indebted to I. Lytton Sells, to whom it was communicated by C.-E. Engel, the well-known Alpinist.

during his last illness). Turton introduced them to the Beau-clerks, and on the twenty-first took them to see a brother[1] of John Wilkes, who lived a few miles out of town. Here, says De Saussure, they found a 'famous painter' [perhaps Reynolds] and 'an author named Goldsmith – "un homme fort original, fort singulier, naturel, gai, vraiment comique dans ses idées et dans ses expressions" '. From Wilkes's house they all went to a mansion which De Saussure describes as 'full of the most beautiful pictures and marbles', and which Dr Freshfield, De Saussure's biographer, identifies with Kenwood House, be-tween Hampstead and Highgate.[2] From De Saussure Gold-smith might have gleaned useful information for his *Animated Nature*. If the scientist noted Goldsmith's singularity and spontaneity, he had been a great deal more impressed by the Beauclerks. Thus, on the eighteenth, he writes:

'Drove with Turton into the country with Lady Diana Boling-broke, wife of Mr Beauclerk[3]. . . . The estate Mr Beauclerk inhabits is very pretty, there is a fine collection of exotic trees with a pleasant path winding among them. . . . Dined with My Lady, who knows and understands French. . . . After dinner looked at some instruments with Mr Beauclerk. He studies mathematics with his wife and is a man of great attainments.'[4]

Later in the year Goldsmith seems to have entertained Mr and Mrs Seguin, an Irish couple, to a dinner to which Percy, Bickerstaffe and Kelly – of all people! – were invited. He also introduced a Mr and Mrs Pollard to Johnson, after warning

[1] Probably Heaton, a Distiller. The eldest brother, Israel Wilkes, had gone to America.

[2] D. W. Freshfield, with the collaboration of H. F. Montagnier, *Horace-Bénédict de Saussure,* London, 1920, pp 108–9. The scientist was 28 at this time, but already professor of natural philosophy in the Academy of Geneva. In London he met Lord Palmerston who had visited Chamonix the year before.

[3] They had been married earlier in the summer, after her divorce from Viscount Bolingbroke. The estate was near Richmond.

[4] Freshfield, p 107.

them that they must never interrupt the flow of the great man's wisdom. These and other soirées and entertainments proved very costly, though it seems that Bott, who had money, contributed a good deal to the expenses. Great was the amusement one evening when Goldsmith, attired in one of his brightly coloured silk coats, 'walked a minuet' with Mrs Seguin, moving in so quaint a fashion that she was nearly convulsed with hilarity. She and her husband had a house in the country where they sometimes entertained Goldsmith.

But the Irish, if one excepts the Seguins, Arthur Murphy and of course the Burkes and Lord Clare, were a constant drain on his resources; and also, one suspects, an incitement to buy popularity. According to an anonymous writer, 'Our Doctor, as Goldsmith was now universally called, had a constant levée of his distressed countrymen whose wants, as far as he was able, he constantly relieved; and he has been often known to leave himself even without a guinea. . . .' All of them were not distressed. Bickerstaffe seems to have been a criminal type, Glover an expert at cadging meals and at amusing the company by his gift for mimicry. His story of how, when he and Goldsmith were returning one afternoon from Hampstead, he introduced his friend into a house where they were perfect strangers and obtained an invitation to tea, sounds circumstantial and may even be true.[1]

One major event of 1768 has been passed over in silence by Goldsmith's biographers. On 18 March Laurence Sterne died in his lodgings in Old Bond Street. A nurse had been engaged to tend him, but otherwise he was alone. A party of noblemen, including Grafton, who greatly admired him, had just sent to enquire how he was, not realising that the end was so near. They at least lamented poor 'Yorick', and Garrick, who was one of the party, had been a friend of his; though Johnson and Goldsmith always disapproved of him.

---

[1] Prior, vol II, pp 185–7.

Chapter 11

The Professor of Ancient History

❧ 1769 ☙

In the course of 1769 Goldsmith undertook more work than ever, appears to have received more money than ever, and spent more than ever. His activities were multifarious. He composed an epilogue for Charlotte Lennox's *The Sister*, a play which failed, although sponsored by Colman. On 29 February he signed a contract with Griffin for 'a new Natural History of Animals, &c. in 8 octavo volumes, each to contain from 25 to 27 sheets of pica print' for 800 guineas, that is, the equivalent of £8,745 in the currency of today.[1] In March he and Johnson, who went to receive his doctorate, paid a visit to Oxford, but there is no evidence that Goldsmith there received a degree of any kind.[2] For the past eight or nine months he must have worked exceptionally hard, for in May the *Roman History* was published in two octavo volumes, each containing about five hundred pages. He had become expert in digesting material from standard histories such as, in this instance, Vertot's, and casting it into readable English. But he did not pretend to be an historian, and while the present compilation, like the others, proved useful and popular, it was hardly deserving of Johnson's eulogy. This indeed astonished Boswell, who records a con-

[1] See Appendix III.
[2] It is possible. There is a gap in the Register from 14 March to 18 March. A contemporary paper seems to have reported the conferring of a degree on Goldsmith also.

versation which took place at Beauclerk's house in April 1773. Johnson had just declared that 'whether we take Goldsmith as a poet, as a comic writer, or as an historian, he stands in the first class'. – Boswell: 'An historian! . . .' – Johnson: 'Why, who are before him?' – Boswell: 'Hume, Robertson, Lord Lyttleton.' Johnson replied that he had not read Hume, but that Goldsmith's work was 'better than the verbiage of Robertson', and that the latter's work was not history but imagination. 'He who describes what he never saw draws from fancy. . . . You must look upon Robertson's work as romance.' An extraordinary view! If this were to be the criterion, all but historians of their own times would be romancers. Johnson continued in a similar vein before returning to his praise of Goldsmith: 'I will venture to say, that if you compare him with Vertot in the same places of the Roman History, you will find that he excels Vertot.'

He excelled most people as a stylist. Johnson was arguing, as so often, not for the sake of truth but to silence opposition. William Robertson (1721–93) was one of three principal historians in eighteenth-century Britain, a friend of Gibbon, who regarded him as 'a master-artist'. Johnson may well have been envious of his financial success. René Aubert, abbé de Vertot (1655–1735) had published a number of historical works of which the *Histoire des révolutions de la République romaine* (1719) was the most famous. He was not a profound analyst like Montesquieu, nor an historian as careful and scholarly as Voltaire, but neither was he a simple compiler. We must be content to class Goldsmith in this field as an admirable populariser. He had no other pretensions in publishing the *Roman History*; nor had he when on 13 June he undertook to write for Davies, within two years, and for a fee of £500, 'an History of England from the birth of the British empire to the death of George the second, in four volumes octavo'.

It was probably now that he began to work on the Natural History, a more ambitious and difficult undertaking than histories of Rome or England; and one which would involve the use of a large number of primary and secondary sources. It is certain that he devoted what leisure he could to the *Deserted Village*; but did not for these reasons withdraw from public life or social intercourse. His name indeed was commonly coupled about this time with Johnson's: they were 'the literary Castor and Pollux', and also 'Holofernes and Goodman Dull'; though 'Dull' was the last word to describe Goldsmith. One night when he and Johnson were dining at Jack's Coffee House in Dean Street, on rumpsteaks and kidneys, Johnson said that these were pretty little things, 'but then a man must eat a great many of them before he fills his belly'. – 'Aye, but how many of these would reach to the moon?' asked Goldsmith. – 'To the moon! Sir, I fear that exceeds your calculation.' – 'Not at all, Sir . . . one, if it were long enough.' Johnson was not amused. 'Well, Sir,' he admitted, 'I have deserved it. I should not have provoked so foolish an answer by so foolish a question.'[1]

In October Goldsmith was called on to give evidence in favour of Giuseppe Baretti, the distinguished man of letters who was a friend of Johnson's and whom he himself had known, though perhaps not for so long. It appears that on the sixth 'he had been assailed in the grossest manner possible by a woman of the town and, driving her off with a blow, was set upon by three bullies. He thereupon ran away in great fear, for he was a timid man, and being pursued, had stabbed two of the men with a small knife he carried in his pocket.'[2] One of the ruffians died, and Baretti was imprisoned in Newgate, where Johnson and Burke went to see him: they, with Reynolds and Garrick, also offered bail. At his trial for murder on 20 October in the Old Bailey, it transpired that the weapon had been nothing more fearsome than a fruit knife, such as everyone carried on the Continent. Garrick and Beauclerk

[1] Prior, vol II, p 481.
[2] *Dr Johnson: his Friends and his Critics*, p 288.

assured the Court that this was so, and they, with Reynolds, Johnson, Burke and Goldsmith, testified to his peaceable character. Reynolds explained that he had known the prisoner for fifteen or sixteen years and that on the evening of the sixth he had been expected at the Royal Academy, where he was Secretary for foreign correspondence. Johnson had known Baretti since about 1754 and regarded him as peaceable and rather timorous. Burke and Garrick gave similar evidence. Goldsmith said: 'I have had the honour of Mr Baretti's company at my chambers in the Temple. He is a most humane, benevolent, peaceable man. He is a man of as great humanity as any in the world.' No further witnesses were called, and Baretti was acquitted.

Boswell, who hated Baretti, had hoped that he would be hanged; Davies later spoke to Mrs Thrale of Baretti's 'ferocious temper', but she demurred to this. He had been a friend of Thrale since 1752; in 1768 he had accompanied Thrale on a visit to France, and he had taught Italian to one of the Thrales's daughters. So too, when Davies in his *Memoirs of David Garrick* writes that Goldsmith 'considered [Baretti] as an insolent, over-bearing foreigner', one is inclined to be doubtful. He was impressive in conversation, like Johnson, who admired his powers in that direction. In Italy, prior to 1751, he had been a vigorous satirist, and an attack on Professor Bartoli of Turin had led to his exile; but in England he must have learned prudence. One cannot ignore the testimony of six men as important and intelligent as those we have mentioned. Of his literary brilliance, as displayed in the *Frusta letteraria* (1763–65), and of his knowledge, as evidenced by his *Italian and English Dictionary*, there can be no doubt.

Goldsmith's recent entry into high society had, in the meantime, increased his old sense of physical unimportance and also a desire to amend it. He was of middle height, stockily built, with a low forehead, slightly bulbous, and features rather badly pock-marked. To mitigate these disadvantages he spent

2. Trinity College, Dublin (see p. 31 *et seq.*)

3. Edinburgh, *c.* 1750 (see p. 43)

4. Temple Bar, looking west, c. 1760. In 1757 Goldsmith used to write his letters from the Temple Exchange Coffee House

very large sums on clothes: some £52 in 1767; at least £32 in 1768; and £33 13s 5d in 1769. The details are revealing. In 1767 he had received a 'superfine suit', a 'superfine frock-suit' and cloth breeches, and a 'suit of state mourning', – for what occasion is unknown. In 1768 he blossomed out with a 'Tyrian bloom satin grain' suit and 'blue silk breeches', two other suits, and a suit of mourning, probably for Henry. He was content with two suits and a half-dress suit in 1769; but in 1770 he was to buy a dress suit, two other suits, and a suit of half mourning – for his mother; in addition to the coat he bought in Paris. The shabby hack-writer had turned into the peacock of Brick Court.

Not understanding that a man is judged rather by the propriety than by the showiness of his clothes, he boasted of them. Boswell records that at the dinner which he gave several friends on 16 October – when the Baretti trial was pending – Garrick teased him about this, and Goldsmith defended himself. 'Well, let me tell you, when my tailor brought home my bloom-coloured coat [this, with the blue silk breeches, had cost £8 2s 7d], he said, "Sir, I have a favour to beg of you, when any body asks you who made your clothes, be pleased to mention John Filby, at the Harrow in Water Lane."' Johnson here intervened to ridicule 'a coat of so absurd a colour'.

Yet Johnson, whose clothes were slovenly and his wig in constant need of replacement, could hardly pose as an arbiter of the elegances, and Goldsmith was not easily to be suppressed. He continued to wear a bag-wig and a sword like any man of fashion. Something odd in his appearance one day attracted the notice of two men in the Strand. Raising his voice, one of them said: 'Look at that fly with a long pin stuck through it.' Goldsmith warned the onlookers to beware of 'that brace of disguised pickpockets', then stepped out into the street and half drawing his sword, motioned to the man who had insulted him to do the same. But the fellow slunk away amid the jeers of the crowd.

E

Garrick and Johnson might mock at Goldsmith, but people like Sir Joshua and the Hornecks understood him better. It was through Sir Joshua's influence that in December the King appointed Goldsmith Professor of Ancient History in the Royal Academy. The post was honorary and there were no duties, but it carried the privilege of attending the annual dinner and also the title, which seems to have been the only one to which he could rightfully lay claim.

Chapter 12

An Offer from Lord North: a Visit to Paris

✣ 1770 ✣

In January 1770 he sent news of the professorship to his brother Maurice who, having failed to obtain a post of any sort, was living with the Lawders. The best that Oliver felt he could do was to make over to him a sum of £15 which he had inherited from Contarine. He asked for news of his mother, of Charles, of Hodson and his son; but curiously not of Catherine. If out of sight was not out of mind, it was so for practical purposes. A fraction of the money which he squandered on beggars and cadgers would have proved a godsend to Mrs Goldsmith. And yet, in order to make still more money, he was now collecting material for the Natural History and starting to write it up. Richard Cumberland, a dramatist then as popular as Kelly, called on him one day at Brick Court: what he tells us suggests that they were already acquainted. 'Distress drove Goldsmith,' he writes, 'upon undertakings neither congenial with his studies nor worthy of his talents. I remember him when, in his chambers in the Temple, he showed me the beginning of his "Animated Nature", it was with a sigh, such as genius draws when hard necessity diverts it from its bent to drudge for bread, and talk of birds and beasts and creeping things, which Pidock's showman would have done as well. Poor fellow, he hardly knows an ass from a mule, nor a turkey from a goose. . . .'

It is questionable whether Goldsmith deserved as much sympathy or, on the other hand, was quite as ignorant as Cumberland thought; although he did make some surprising mistakes.

It was about this time that two young Irishmen, Robert Day and Grattan, who had come to study law and were living in Essex Court, were introduced to him by Sir John Day – not a relation of Robert. To the latter we owe many details of Goldsmith's life and habits, and of his cheerfulness and sometimes boisterous manners. He ordinarily frequented the Grecian Coffee House, a rendezvous of law students from Ireland and Lancashire. If he had much money in hand, he would spend it at Vauxhall or Ranelagh Gardens, or gamble heedlessly with it. Even so, these reminiscences of Day's, who later became a judge, are favourable to Goldsmith.

At some date which has not been established, but which cannot have been much earlier than the summer of 1770, Goldsmith received an offer that could have assured him of a comfortable future. According to Prior, Dr James Scott was sent to Goldsmith's rooms by the Ministry, 'which was then hard-pressed by the opposition in Parliament and by Junius, Wilkes and . . . other political writers. . . .' Scott had told the story to Basil Montagu, Keats's friend, who passed it on to Prior. 'A few months,' wrote Montagu, 'before the death of Dr Scott, author of Anti-Sejanus[1] and other political tracts in support of Lord North's administration, I happened to dine with him. . . . Dr Scott mentioned . . . that he was once sent with a *carte blanche* from the ministry to Oliver Goldsmith to induce him to write in favour of the administration. "I found him," said the Doctor, "in a miserable set of chambers in the Temple; I told him my authority; I told him that I was empowered to pay most liberally for his exertions, and, would you believe it! he was so absurd as to say – '*I can earn as much as will supply*

---

[1] There is confusion on this point. The *Anti-Sejanus* had been an attack on Lord Bute's government: it belonged to an earlier period.

*my wants without writing for any party; the assistance therefore
you offer, is unnecessary to me,'* and so I left him . . . in his
garret." [1]

The Rev. James Scott, a former Fellow of Trinity College,
Cambridge, was chaplain to Lord Sandwich. It is clear
from Scott's story that he was supporting the government,
and Prior assumed that this was Lord North's, as Montagu
had implied, and as other circumstances confirm. But Scott
died in 1814, and the experience he related had taken place
at least forty-three years earlier, so that his memory may
have misled him in some point of detail, for example as to the
'garret'.

In any event, Prior believed that Scott had come as an
emissary of Lord North. He placed the episode after Goldsmith's first banquet at the Royal Academy (December 1769)
and before his visit to Paris. This accords with the fact that in
1769 and 1770 Wilkes was attacking the Duke of Grafton's
ministry and that of North, who succeeded him early in 1770;
and that Junius was supporting Wilkes.

Other writers on Goldsmith, however, disagree as to the
date. John Forster (1855), William Black (1878) and Austin
Dobson (1888) all place Scott's visit towards the end of 1767;
and Professor Wardle also dates it at 'about this time' (end of
1767). He says that Scott offered Goldsmith 'a handsome
stipend, if he would write in defence of Lord North's ministry,
then under attack by John Wilkes and the mysterious Junius'.[2]
But North did not become First Lord of the Treasury until
March 1770, after Grafton's resignation. Moreover Wilkes had
gone into exile in 1763, and apart from brief visits to London,
did not return until February 1768. Scott could not therefore
have visited Goldsmith in 1767. Again, since the uproar created
by Wilkes centred round 1769 and 1770, when the London
mob attacked North in person and overturned his carriage, it

---

[1] Prior, vol II, pp 277–8.
[2] *Oliver Goldsmith,* London, 1957, p 180.

seems most probable that it was in 1770 that Scott was sent to enlist Goldsmith's aid.

Frederick North had inherited an extraordinarily difficult situation, owing to the enormous National Debt and the problem of persuading the Americans to bear a trifling part of a burden incurred on their behalf. Wilkes, however, was the principal gadfly, and North had no capable publicist to carry the war into the enemy's camp. Hence the mission entrusted to Scott.

Was the interview as brief and Goldsmith's response as curt as the story implies? Or did Scott's irritation colour and distort his memory of a distant event? Goldsmith was generally averse from becoming involved in political controversy, and he may have feared that any pamphlets in support of the Government might provoke the kind of venomous reprisal from which Thomas Gray had suffered in 1769.[1] But while Gray was indifferent to such virulence, Goldsmith would have felt it keenly.

He could on the other hand have accepted Scott's offer with a good conscience. His sympathies were Tory, and he was a convinced monarchist. Furthermore, the character of George III and the history of the North administration have been grossly misrepresented by the Whig historians, who have taken their views from C. J. Fox and neglected the State Archives. George III was at this time, as Mr John Brooke has

[1] For the Duke of Grafton's installation as Chancellor of Cambridge University, Gray had agreed to write the Installation Ode, because it seemed a public duty and also because he owed his professorship to Grafton. He could hardly have refused; and nothing he wrote merited the parody of the Epitaph in the famous *Elegy*:

> '. . . Fair science frown'd not on his humble birth,
> And smooth-tongued flatt'ry marked him for her own.
> No further seek his deeds to bring to light,
> For ah! he offer'd at Corruption's shrine;
> And basely strove to wash an Ethiop white,
> While Truth and Honour bled in ev'ry line.'

This had appeared in the *London Chronicle* where Goldsmith may have read it.

just shown,[1] perfectly sane and normal. He was not ill-disposed to the Americans. The Stamp Act had been repealed in 1766, and further concessions were granted in 1770. Lord North's weakness lay in hesitating between a desire to conciliate the Americans and the need to repress rebellion; but it is doubtful if appeasement is ever wise or effective. And in any case neither the King nor his minister could disregard the wishes of Parliament and of the nation as a whole. Independent opinion soon grew tired of Wilkes's violence and began to veer over to the side of the Government. Goldsmith would have performed a public service by writing in support of the ministry.

From the negative standpoint, he disliked Wilkes, an unscrupulous demagogue, to such an extent that in 1773 he actually wrote in support of James Townsend who had put up against Wilkes for election as Lord Mayor of London. Other men of distinction supported North's ministry, including Johnson who published three pamphlets in its favour. Gibbon, who was to enter Parliament in 1774, voted steadily on its side. There was nothing dishonourable in a man of letters' defending or voting for the North administration.

It was not true that Goldsmith could 'earn as much as would supply [his] wants'. Periodically in debt, he continued to depend for his livelihood on the compiling of works of popularisation – a drudgery so painful that it was impairing his health and shortening his life. Had he consented to write for the Government, he could have bargained for substantial remuneration and he would certainly have been given a pension.[2] He could then have discontinued the compilations, earned the rest which he needed and devoted more time to the kind of

[1] John Brooke, *King George III*, with a Foreword by the Prince of Wales, London, 1972. Mr Brooke has examined the Royal Archives at Windsor, and discovered how George spent his personal income, on his library, on Science and on private charity. He was personally quiet and modest. It has been remarked that it makes as much sense to blame George III for the loss of America as it would be to reproach George VI for the loss of India.

[2] It is true that he might have squandered the down payment, but he would not have been allowed to anticipate the annual pension.

work for which his gifts fitted him. He might have continued to live for years, as well as enriching our literature with further comedies and humorous verses.

He must still have attended meetings of the Club from time to time, but dinners or suppers with Johnson seem to have been less frequent. His great friends now, apart from Lord Clare, were Reynolds and the Horneck family. For them he felt real affection, with them he was at ease and in no fear of being overawed or shouted down. On literary matters indeed Johnson advised and supported him staunchly; Goldsmith was grateful; but affection and ease of mind do not always go with gratitude.

The Deserted Village was published on 26 May, and proved an immediate success, four re-impressions appearing by 16 August. Five separate translations into French succeeded each other. For the London edition he received about an hundred guineas – a very large sum. He would have preferred a pension. Yet when one reckons up what he had got for the *Vicar of Wakefield* – £63, equivalent to about £650 in the currency of today – ; £450 or more for the *Good-Natured Man*; and especially what the publishers gave for his many compilations – £525 for one, £840 for another – one sees that he was exceptionally well paid, and, had he known how to manage his budget, could have lived in comfort and freedom from anxiety.

The Deserted Village had been dedicated to Sir Joshua and he, significantly, was the only person to whom Goldsmith is known to have written during his visit to France. For this journey he had been invited to accompany Mrs Horneck and her daughters, Catherine whom he called 'Little Comedy', and Mary, the 'Jessamy Bride'. One wonders why he, and not a clearly eligible bachelor, was asked to escort these girls and their mother. Was he considered eligible? If so, the arrangement was natural; if not, it seems strange, even unkind. Here lies the principal mystery of Goldsmith's life – of an inner life, too, of which we know nothing.

The travellers set out about the middle of July, staying a night at Canterbury on their way to Dover. An undated letter to Reynolds which was begun at Lille tells the story of their tribulations:

'My dear Friend,

'We had a very quick passage from Dover to Calais, which we performed in three hours and twenty minutes, all of us extremely sea-sick, which must necessarily have happened, as my machine to prevent sea-sickness was not completed. We were glad to leave Dover, because we hated to be imposed upon; so were in high spirits at coming to Calais, where we were told that a little money would go a great way. Upon landing two little trunks . . . we were surprised to see fourteen or fifteen fellows all running down to the ship to lay their hands upon them; four got under each trunk, the rest surrounded and held the hasps; and in this manner our little baggage was conducted, with a kind of funeral solemnity, till it was safely lodged at the custom-house. We were well enough pleased with the people's civility, till they came to be paid; every creature that had the happiness of but touching our trunks . . . expected six-pence, and they had so pretty, civil a manner of demanding it that there was no refusing them.'

At the Hotel d'Angleterre where they put up, a valet offered his service. They had no occasion for it, 'so we gave him a little money because he spoke English and because he wanted it'. Mary Horneck relates how she and the others, on the balcony of the hotel at Lille, were watching a part of the garrison on parade, when some of the officers who saw her and her sister outdid each other in compliments. Goldsmith listened for a time before observing that he too had his admirers. Boswell afterwards cited this story as an example of his envious disposition, whereas it was understood by the ladies as a piece of mock-serious humour.

The parrots which he heard here and in other French cities provided material for the 'Natural History' which he had undertaken. In the course of an extraordinarily funny passage in the *History of the Earth and Animated Nature*, in which he says that, according to 'a grave writer', a parrot had been taught to recite a whole sonnet of Petrarch's, he writes:

'In going through the towns of France sometime since, I could not help observing how much plainer their parrots spoke than ours, and how very distinctly I understood their parrots speak French, when I could not understand our own, though they spoke my native language. I was at first for ascribing it to the different qualities of the two languages, and was for entering into an elaborate discussion on the vowels and consonants; but a friend that was with me "assured" me that the French women scarce did anything else the whole day than sit and instruct their feathered pupils. . . .'

Possibly; but Goldsmith's first idea was better.

Reaching Paris towards 28 July the visitors put up at the Hotel du Danemark in the rue Jacob. This is an old quarter which has scarcely changed in the course of two centuries. The hotel, which stood at the angle of the rue Jacob and the rue Saint-Benoît, was thus called because in October 1768 Christian VII, King of Denmark and Norway, who had recently married a sister of George III, stayed there with his wife. It had formerly been the 'Hotel d'York'. The quarter seems to have attracted English visitors. Readers will recall how Sterne tried on gloves in a shop nearby and after essaying a number, asked the glover's wife if he might feel her pulse; and how her husband entered a moment later and was told of Sterne's 'kindness'. Goldsmith had no such humorous experience to relate when, on the twenty-ninth, he wrote at some length to Sir Joshua.

Paris no longer delights him as it had fifteen years before:

'I set out with all my confirmed habits about me, and can find nothing on the Continent so good as when I formerly left it. One of our chief amusements here is scolding at everything we meet with, and praising everything and every person we left at home. You may judge, therefore, whether your name is not frequently bandied at table among us. . . . I never thought I could regret your absence so much as our various mortifications on the road have often taught me to do. . . .' They had trouble with postillions and landladies, and with food.

But one guesses that the hotel was comfortable and that they expected to enjoy their stay, which was to last for a month. Meanwhile Goldsmith begs Reynolds to send news of himself and all the members of the Club. He has been meditating 'the plot of a comedy, which shall be entitled "A Journey to Paris", in which a family shall be introduced with a full intention of going to France to save money'. After again urging his friend to write, he asks whether he can do anything for him in Paris. He himself has bought a silk coat which, however, makes him 'look like a fool'. But 'I must say, that if anything could make France pleasant, the very good women with whom I am at present would certainly do it. . . . I have one thing only more to say, and of that I think every hour of the day, namely, that I am your most sincere and affectionate friend, Oliver Goldsmith.'

The month in Paris may not have been as disagreeable as he had feared; although there seems to have been one fly in the ointment, a lawyer named Hickey whom they met and who, being well acquainted with Paris, seems to have acted as guide. He apparently took them to Versailles on a day when the great fountains were playing;[1] but apart from this, we know nothing of Goldsmith's doings. If he preferred not to look up any of the acquaintances he had made in 1755, probably Irish priests, one might have expected him at least to have called at the Embassy. Here he would have been put in touch with some of

[1] A ridiculous story which he afterwards related about this excursion is probably as apocryphal as a similar story about Goldsmith at Barton.

the distinguished anglophiles of Paris, men like Suard, Garat, Diderot and the Duc de Choiseul; and since *The Citizen of the World* had met with great success, he would certainly have been fêted. This is clear from Sterne's experience in 1761 and from that of Dr Burney who had spent nearly a fortnight in Paris less than two months before Goldsmith's visit. Burney had met a number of people including Suard, but also Choiseul and Lacombe (Garrick's bookseller); he was of course mainly anxious to meet musicians.[1] Goldsmith may not have heard about this, but everyone knew of Laurence Sterne's first visit. He had come to Paris while the Seven Years War was still being fought, and D'Holbach had guaranteed his good conduct. The author of *Tristram Shandy* had been showered with invitations, received by great noblemen and generally lionised. To cap it all, he had preached a sermon at the Embassy before a select congregation of free-thinkers, including Diderot, D'Holbach – and David Hume.[2] No such glory came Goldsmith's way, and it is likely that he suffered from a sense of inferiority. After all, he had been a cosmopolitan only on paper. In 1770 he was more Anglo–Irish than ever, and not even at home in Paris.

After landing at Dover about 7 September, Mrs Horneck and the girls went to Devonshire, while Goldsmith returned to work, and especially to make up arrears. But almost immediately he received news of his mother's death. Even before going to Edinburgh he had been estranged from her, and this, and the lack of natural feeling which most men have for their mothers, are the saddest things about him. He ordered a kind of half-mourning, 'a grey suit trimmed with black', and told Miss Reynolds that this was for 'a distant relation'. She

---

[1] *Music, Men and Manners in France and Italy: 1770; being the Journal written by Charles Burney. . . .* Edited by H. E. Poole, London, 1969, pp 9–23.
[2] H. D. Traill, *Sterne*, London, 1882, pp 67–86.

herself thought him unfeeling; Sir Joshua can hardly have
approved.

But he was probably indulgent, and may have reflected that
Goldsmith was harrassed as usual for want of money. He had
received something for a short life of Parnell, published with an
edition of the latter's poems, and he now undertook an abridgment of the *Roman History* for the use of schools; for this
Thomas Davies contracted to pay fifty guineas. As Davies was
planning to republish Bolingbroke's *Dissertation on Parties*
which he thought would be apposite at a time when Wilkes
and others were attacking Lord North, he asked Goldsmith to
write also a sketch of Bolingbroke's life to serve as preface.
Here was more than enough to occupy him for some weeks.
But he had scarcely begun the memoir of Bolingbroke before
he heard that Colonel Nugent, Lord Clare's son, had fallen
very ill. It has been said that he took him to Bath where Lord
Clare was staying at the time, and there Nugent died. His
father was so grief-stricken that he asked Goldsmith to stay
with him at Gosford Park. Goldsmith took his work with him.
Although most of it seems to have been done, Davies was
greatly perturbed. 'Dr Goldsmith,' he wrote, 'has gone with
Lord Clare into the country, and I am plagued to get the proofs
from him of the "Life of Lord Bolingbroke."' He need not
have worried. Goldsmith could work at great speed when he
wished, and the book appeared before the end of the year.

He probably spent a month or more at Gosford and certainly did much to divert his host's mind and even perhaps to
entertain him. His very vanity was amusing. Lord Camden
who was a guest at Gosford, did not appear to realise how great
a man he had the opportunity of meeting; or so Goldsmith
explained to Johnson after he had returned to town. 'I met him
at Lord Clare's house in the country; and he took no more
notice of me than if I had been an ordinary man.' Boswell and
the others could hardly refrain from laughing. It was not that
Goldsmith was more vain than many a talented and successful

writer; but that he displayed his vanity with the ingenuousness of a child. He had never acquired one of the first arts of social behaviour – the art of dissembling.

It was the same with his jealousy of literary rivals and his envy of success which seemed a challenge to his own. This attitude had begun to appear after the staging of *The Good-Natured Man*, and in the years that followed it turned into a habit which more than once involved him in ridicule. At the moment, however, in the December of 1770, Lord Camden's neglect was forgotten in the delight he received when a present of venison and possibly other gifts from Gosford Park reached him in the Temple. He acknowledged the game in a humorous poem entitled 'The Haunch of Venison'.

> Thanks, my lord, for your venison; for finer or fatter
> Never rang'd in a forest, or smok'd in a platter. . . .

The haunch looked so beautiful, that he thought of sending it to Sir Joshua to be painted; and he was pondering how the rest could be cooked when a high-handed acquaintance called on him (or so he says), declared that his wife would make a pasty of it and that he would invite Johnson, Burke and of course Goldsmith to a supper party. In the event, neither Johnson nor Burke was free; a Jew and a Scot took their place, and the supper consisted of tripe and bacon – the pasty having been ruined by the cook.

This fiction, which would not have amused Boswell, must have enchanted Lord Clare. Although Goldsmith had borrowed the main idea from Boileau, he was becoming an adept at humorous verse and good-natured satire. This vein, still largely derivative, he developed until, in 'Retaliation', it became entirely original.

Chapter 13

Summers in the Country: Winters in Town

✘ 1771-72 ✘

As a consequence of his refusal to write for the Ministry, there was no prospect of a respite from hard labour. He devoted the first months of 1771 to the *History of the Earth and Animated Nature*. This was an arduous task, and more difficult than the 'Histories', since a great many works by recent scientists had to be consulted. True, there was charm as well as novelty in the subject. He was able to insert his own observations, for example, of the habits of spiders, and of the rooks he had watched from his windows in the Temple; and of French parrots. Even so, he would rather have been composing a comedy he had in mind. He was more witty and alert than usual. In a company which included Reynolds and Johnson he complained that the animals in Fables rarely talk in character. 'For example,' he continued, 'the fable of the little fishes who saw birds fly over their heads and, envying them, petitioned Jupiter to be changed into birds. The skill consists in making them talk like little fishes.' Johnson began to shake with laughter, and Goldsmith retorted: 'Why, Dr Johnson, this is not so easy as you seem to think; for, if you were to make little fishes talk, they would talk like whales.'

In the early spring he went with Lord Clare to Bath for a month or so, and on his return began work on *The Mistakes of a Night*, as he thought of calling the new comedy. Then came an invitation to Johnson and himself to attend the annual banquet of the Royal Academy which was to be held on 23 April in the Exhibition Room. Here the year's paintings were on view; Goldsmith's mind, however, was then occupied not with paintings, but with the much talked of poems which young Chatterton had presented as the work of a mythical Rowley. This Rowley, he asserted, had been a fourteenth-century monk of Bristol. Chatterton, though no more than an office-boy of sixteen, had written the poems himself. Goldsmith like many others regarded them as genuine; they were certainly brilliant and impressive on any count; and he spoke of them with admiration. Johnson who believed them to be forgeries, laughed at him, and Horace Walpole, who was sitting near Goldsmith, referred ironically to Chatterton's 'trouvaille'. He said: 'I might, had I pleased, have had the honour of ushering the great discovery to the learned world.' For a time indeed he had believed not only the poems to be authentic, but also a history of English painting, ascribed to Rowley, which Chatterton had sent him. But having discovered that they were forgeries, he was amused by Goldsmith's enthusiasm. Some of the people present must have known that Chatterton had come to London early in 1770 and that his opera, *The Revenge*, had been produced; but perhaps no more; and when Walpole asked Goldsmith what had become of the young poet, he was told that 'he had destroyed himself'. He had in fact taken arsenic and died on 24 August. Walpole felt dashed by the news. Yet had it been his duty to support and finance Chatterton when Gray and Mason had convinced him that the Rowley works were a hoax? The question is not easy to answer. In any event, Goldsmith continued to believe the poems to be authentic, and argued very warmly to that effect with Dr Percy. It was not until after Goldsmith's death that Tyrwhitt furnished definite proof of their being spurious.

After spending the rest of the spring and early summer with

Lord Clare,[1] Goldsmith took lodgings in the house of a farmer named Selby. It stood on rising ground near the village of Hyde, by 'the six-mile stone on the Edgware Road'. Here he occupied a room on the first floor, but used the room below to entertain visitors. Boswell called on him, as did Sir Joshua Reynolds and Sir William Chambers, designer of Chinese gardens. The strain of work, however, was telling on him, and he suffered from insomnia. Lying in bed when his candle was still alight, he would sometimes aim a slipper at it to extinguish it: a risky habit, though less spectacular than that of a French nobleman of the previous century who extinguished the candles with bolts from his arquebus.

Goldsmith appears to have returned occasionally to Brick Court, but most of his time was given to the journeyman work which was so wearisome, such as correcting the proofs of a new *History of England* which appeared in August in two volumes; and steadily building up the *Animated Nature*. He also completed the comedy, as we learn from a letter to Bennet Langton, written from Brick Court on 7 September, in reply to Langton's invitation to Reynolds and himself to visit his place near Spilsby:

'My Dear Sir,

'Since I had the pleasure of seeing you last I have been almost wholly in the country at a farmer's house quite alone trying to write a Comedy. It is now finished but when or how it will be acted, or whether it will be acted at all are questions I cannot resolve. I am therefore so much employed upon that that I am under a necessity of putting off my intended visit to Lincolnshire for this season. Reynolds is just returned from Paris and finds himself now in the case of a truant that must make up for his idle time by diligence. We have therefore agreed to postpone the affair till next summer when we hope

---

[1] In a letter to Smollett, of 9 July 1771, John Gray wrote: 'I am told he now generally lives with his countryman, Lord Clare . . . . '

to have the honour of waiting upon her Ladyship[1] and you and staying double the time of our late intended visit. We often meet, and never without remembering you. I see Mr Beauclerc very often both in town and country. He is now going directly forward to becoming a second Boyle. Deep in Chymistry and Physics. Johnson has been down upon a visit to a country parson Doctor Taylor's and is returned to his old haunts at Mrs Thrale's. Burke is a farmer . . . but visiting about too. Every soul is visiting about and merry but myself. And that is hard too as I have been trying these three months to do something to make people laugh. There have I been strolling about the hedges studying jests with a most tragical countenance. The natural History is about half finished. . . . God knows I'm tired of this kind of finishing, which is but bungling work, and that not so much my fault as the fault of my scurvy circumstances. . . . the cry of Liberty is still as loud as ever. . . . Davis (sic) has published for me an Abridgement of the History of England for which I have been a good deal abused in the newspapers for betraying the liberties of the people. God knows I had no thoughts for or against liberty in my head. . . . However, they set me down as an arrant Tory and consequently no honest man. When you come to look at any part of it you'll say that I am a soure Whig. God bless you, and with my most respectful compliments to her Ladyship I remain dear sir

Your most affectionate
humble servant,
Oliver Goldsmith.'

If we know how Goldsmith passed the spring and summer, what happened after early September is matter for guesswork. He may have remained another month at the Selbys. Back in London he was always welcome in Leicester Square, where

[1] Lady Rothes, Langton's wife.

Reynolds and his sister entertained in an informal atmosphere, and so generously that they sometimes ran short of dishes and cutlery, and the cooking occasionally suffered. One evening when the peas were served yellow, a guest called the servant and asked him to send them to Hammersmith. 'Yes, Sir, but why to Hammersmith, Sir?' – 'Because that's the way to Turnham Green.' Goldsmith was so delighted with this that when, some time afterwards, he was dining in other company and the peas were yellow, he too called the waiter, pointed to the peas and said 'Take them to Hammersmith.' – 'To Hammersmith, Sir?' – 'Yes, because that's the way to make 'em green.' Everyone stared, which only increased his confusion. He tried to explain: 'I mean, that's the road to Turnham Green.' For Goldsmith to bungle a good story was in character; but was it unintentional? One can imagine in any case, that he contributed much to the mirth of the company.

In November he was in touch with Joseph Cradock, a young squire with literary tastes, to whom the actor Yates had introduced him a year or two before. Mutual sympathy and a common admiration for Voltaire seem to have drawn them together, and Cradock was to prove one of Goldsmith's kindest and most hospitable friends. On the present occasion, Cradock had adapted for the English stage three acts of Voltaire's *Les Scythes*, under the title of *Zobeide*, and he asked Goldsmith for a prologue. It is interesting to observe that whereas Goldsmith experienced great difficulty in persuading Colman to stage his comedies, Cradock had none, and *Zobeide* appeared at Covent Garden on 11 December. Perhaps Yates and his wife – who played the heroine and received the profits – arranged the performance. The prologue which Goldsmith provided, was one of his most brilliant pieces, full of verve and wit, and perfectly adapted to the subject of the tragedy. It was spoken by Quick, who was to play Tony Lumpkin in *She Stoops to Conquer*. Cradock afterwards sent a copy of the printed version to Voltaire, who replied as follows in October 1773:

'9.8^bre, 1773. a ferney.

'Sr,
    'Thanks to yr muse a foreign copper shines,
    Turn'd in to gold, and coin'd in sterling lines.
'You have done to much honour to an old sick man of eighty.
I am vith the most sincere esteem and gratitude
                    'Sr.   Yr obdt. Servt. Voltaire
'A Monsieur Monsieur J. Cradock.'[1]

In 1772 Goldsmith's health was beginning to deteriorate. Work on the *Animated Nature* remained his principal care. In February, Mrs Cornelys who owned a hall of entertainment in Soho, was planning a concert with verses, singers and orchestra, in lament for the late Dowager Princess of Wales; and a printer named Woodfall was commissioned to ask Goldsmith to write the verses. Goldsmith knew that he had as little talent for this sort of thing as he had great for humorous rhyming, but he agreed on condition that his name should not be divulged. Woodfall then, on 10 February, explained the arrangements Mrs Cornelys had in mind. The younger Bach was to be asked to adapt some of Purcell's and Handel's music for the purpose, and Goldsmith might adapt his verses to the music. The letter concludes: 'If it appears to Dr G. that more or less [presumably of words] may be proper for the occasion, and his opinion does not occasion an Expence inadequate to the ultimate view of Profit on the side of Mrs Cornelys, it will be adopted. Secrecy as to the name of the Author shall be inviolably preserved.'

Goldsmith wrote the 'poem' in just under three days. His verses were facile, well-rhymed and artificial. A trio, followed

---

[1] Printed by Austin Dobson in *The Complete Poetical Works of Oliver Goldsmith*, London, 1907, pp 215–6.

by a chorus, begins on a note of woe, while at the end, somewhat comforted, the chorus lays a garland of cowslips and
primroses on the grave of Augusta. Such was the *Threnodia
Augustalis*, as it was afterwards called.

But obtaining the verses was the least of Woodfall's woes.
His next letter, dated 14 February, reveals that, as Bach had
evidently declined to help, Matteo Vento had agreed to compose the music. He, however, needed to confer with Goldsmith
in order to understand the sense and meaning of the words, and
so he would send his carriage to call for the poet if a man of
Goldsmith's 'Merit and Consequence' would consent to go to
Vento's rooms. Furthermore, Goldsmith was on no account
to mention the name of Mrs Cornelys. '. . . the Story now
stands that I am directed by some Persons of Consequence to
secure the performance at some great Room in Westminster
at the instance of several of the 1st Nobility. . . .'

Though this was news to him, he was trapped and he agreed
to go to Vento's on the Sunday, having forgotten that he had
arranged for Cradock, a connoisseur of music, to go with him
to the rehearsal, which he had expected to take place on the
same day. So he sent a message to Cradock, and in an atmosphere now quaintly conspiratorial, went off to explain to the
Italian composer 'the sense and meaning' of the words. The
rehearsal was held next day and the concert was performed on
Thursday the twentieth. An affair which should have been
grave and elegiac had turned into a comedy of mystifications.
One feels sorry for Vento who had been treated as a stop-gap
and had apparently composed the music for what was quite a
long piece in less than twenty-four hours, staying up the whole
night to complete it. The book of words, which was sold as a
programme at the concert for a shilling, contained a short
preface in which the anonymous author explained how little
time he had had, and said that the work should 'more properly
be termed a compilation than a poem'. A similar criticism was
also probably true of the music.

To pursue work on the *Animated Nature* in some kind of tranquillity, he sent all the books he needed, enough to fill two post-chaises, to Selby's farm at Hyde and again took up residence there. This must have been about the middle of March. The farmer's son afterwards related how he would sometimes come down to the kitchen to think over the work, then rush back to write what had occurred to him; or he would take a walk, probably a better way of composing in his head. On the twenty-second, a number of friends, including Reynolds, came to see him, and on the thirty-first the Percys. Once, when he had paid a visit to a neighbour named Hugh Boyd, and returned after nightfall, it was found that his shoes had stuck in the mud and remained behind! So far from being the complete hermit, he played with the farmer's children and even took the family to see a theatrical show at Hendon. It was largely owing to his popularity with children, whom he had a genius for amusing, that young Robert Selby was able to recall so many of his doings to Prior.

He had seen little of Johnson in the past two years, a period during which Johnson spent much of his time with the Thrales, and Goldsmith with Lord Clare or at the Selbys's. We know, however, from Boswell that they met at General Oglethorpe's on the occasion of a dinner party which he gave in London on 10 April.

Born in 1698, James Oglethorpe had served on the Continent against the Turks and had been a Major-General in the British Army at the time of the '45. Although a Jacobite in sympathy and accused of favouring the rebels, he was exonerated. After this, however, he had resigned from the Army, had been elected to Parliament and was famous at this time for his part in founding the colony of Georgia. He was an excellent raconteur and, owing to his varied experiences, extremely interesting. On the present occasion he related stories of his service as a subaltern under Prince Eugène. At dinner one night the Prince of Würtemberg, probably disdaining him as a junior, had flicked his wine glass in such a way that several drops spurted in Oglethorpe's face. The latter felt that while the affair was not serious enough for a young man to challenge a senior to a duel, it was too serious to be overlooked. 'Prince, that is an excellent joke,' he said, 'but we do it much better in England.' Whereupon he threw the contents of his own glass in Würtemberg's face. The outcome might have been tragic if an old general officer had not intervened by saying: 'Il a bien fait, mon prince; vous l'avez commencé.'

This led Boswell to raise 'the question whether duelling is consistent with moral duty'. Oglethorpe was emphatic: 'Undoubtedly a man has a right to defend his honour.' Goldsmith then asked Boswell: 'What would you do if you were affronted?' Boswell replied that he should 'think it necessary to fight'. – 'Why then, that solves the question,' Goldsmith concluded. Johnson denied this with his usual vehemence: 'No, Sir, it does not follow that what a man would do is therefore right.' But he went on to concede that, as society blackballs a man who refuses to fight when insulted, he 'may lawfully fight a duel out of self-defence, to avert the stigma of the world, and to prevent himself from being driven out of society'.

But did this solve the question? And why had Johnson contradicted Goldsmith so roughly? If it was 'lawful' to fight a duel when affronted, was it, or was it not, 'consistent with moral duty?' Are the rules of society inconsistent with Christian morals? Evidently, the Great Cham evaded this problem.

The next question that was raised – 'how far people who disagree in any capital point can live in friendship together' – proved equally contentious. Johnson affirmed that they might. Goldsmith thought it difficult, if not impossible, since they had not the *idem velle atque idem nolle*. Johnson replied that they must 'shun the subject as to which [they] disagree'. Goldsmith argued that this would be difficult: 'But, Sir, when people live together who have something as to which they disagree and

which they want to shun, they will be in the situation mentioned in the story of Blue Beard: "You may look into all the
chambers but one." But we should have the greatest inclination to look into that chamber, to talk of that subject.'

'Sir,' shouted Johnson, 'I am not saying that *you* could live
in friendship with a man from [sic] whom you differ as to some
point; I am only saying that *I* could do it.'

Could he? It was evident that he could not have lived peace-
ably with Goldsmith, nor indeed with anyone who did not
consistently defer to him, like Boswell. He saw little of Goldsmith throughout this year, and yet could not refrain from
discourtesy when they did meet. He seems to have objected to
Goldsmith's joining in any discussion. He was 'so much afraid
of being unnoticed', Johnson told Boswell, 'that he often talks
merely lest you should forget' his presence. If he wanted to
argue, 'he should wish to do it not in an awkward posture, not
in rags . . . he should not like to hear himself'. One would wish
to have evidence that Goldsmith's conversation was so awkward, or that he intervened in a manner so unreasonable as to
justify Johnson's frequent criticisms. On the present occasion
his remarks had been harmless and good-humoured, and yet he
had been shouted down. Goldsmith admitted on one occasion
that there was no arguing with Johnson, 'for when his pistol
misses fire, he knocks you down with the butt-end of it'. Yet
he maintained that 'no man alive has a better heart. He has
nothing of the bear but his skin.' That this was far from true is
evident from passages in the *Life of Johnson* and in the *Tour of
the Hebrides*: one recalls in particular his kind reception by
Lord Auchinleck, when he quarrelled violently with his host
and would have provoked further unpleasantness but for
Auchinleck's adroitness.

Apart from an occasional visit to London, Goldsmith spent
the whole of the spring and most of the summer at Hyde. One
attraction, however, drew him to London. The new Assembly
Rooms known as the Pantheon had recently been opened in the

Oxford Road (now Oxford Street) and the charge of half-a-guinea for entrance assured an upper-class clientèle. A grand masquerade was held here on 30 April. The Horneck girls and their brother appeared as French dancers, Reynolds in domino dress. Great ladies and actresses were present, and, not least, Goldsmith and Cradock in medieval costume. Goldsmith thoroughly enjoyed such jollifications, and this one continued until daybreak. Back at Selby's farm in May he worked hard on the *Animated Nature*, sometimes scrawling on the wall of his room descriptions, if not pictures, of the creatures he had to describe, much to the amusement of Boswell who brought William Mickle, the translator of the *Lusiad*, to see him. The book was still in its early stages; it was far more difficult than anything else he had attempted; and since, on 27 June, Griffin paid him the £340 outstanding, after the earlier payment of £500, he probably felt seriously impelled to put his back into it. Whether from overwork, lack of exercise or some other reason, he contracted an inflammation of the bladder. Early in August a surgeon named Percival Pott operated on him, and the result seems to have proved the treatment had been necessary. It is probable that the operation permanently weakened him; but the immediate effect and the rest enforced by convalescence must have been beneficial, and one may suppose that he returned to work with renewed zest. Although he was now not more than forty-three, it would have been wise to live a quieter life than in recent years. He needed some distraction in the evenings, and being now the literary lion of London, he was in great demand with society hostesses, like Mrs Montagu, 'the Queen of the Blues', and others. *The Deserted Village*, more than any other of his works, brought him celebrity. Reynolds had produced a picture named 'Resignation' to illustrate the *Deserted Village*, and he made a portrait of Goldsmith, extremely sympathetic, presenting him wearing one of those loose-fitting robes, vaguely classical but more or less timeless in character. Such renown brings demands on a man's time, if not obligations, which are usually impossible to escape. It would have been difficult in any case to decline invitations to Sir Joshua's and to Burke's.

For the past year or two Edmund Burke had been assiduous in his invitations. Not that Burke was as considerate a friend as the Hornecks, but he no more than others detected premonitory signs. Goldsmith was usually in high spirits, apart from anxiety for his play which Colman was considering, and none of them saw that incessant toil, followed by a strenuous round of pleasures and entertainments, was hastening the end. On one occasion, probably in 1771, when Goldsmith was at Burke's house, a lady, said to be an Irish poetess and a widow, had been shown in. She had written a book of verse and was collecting subscriptions to enable her to publish it. She spoke with an Irish accent, appeared perfectly genuine, and she naturally expressed the highest admiration for Goldsmith. She then asked his opinion of her poems, some of which she recited. Incapable of answering unkindly, he made a few polite comments and gave her a subscription; but after she had left, he said the verses were execrable. No wonder; for it soon transpired that the 'poetess' was not an Irish widow at all, but a friend whom Burke had engaged to play this trick on Goldsmith.

The latter was probably amused. Yet it says much for his good humour that he bore no grudge against Burke, although Burke continued to tease him. Thus one day, possibly in the latter part of 1772, when both he and Goldsmith had been invited to dine with Sir Joshua, Goldsmith came alone on foot while Burke and Colonel O'More happened to be following him. On reaching Leicester Square they found a number of people, including Goldsmith, gazing at some foreign ladies who were at the upper window of an hotel, and whose appearance excited admiration. 'Observe Goldsmith,' said Burke, 'and mark what passes between us at Sir Joshua's.' When after a short time Goldsmith joined them for dinner, Burke adopted an air of cold disapproval. Asked what was the matter, he replied: 'Really, I am ashamed to keep company with a person who could act as you have just done in the Square.' Goldsmith being at a loss to understand, the other continued: 'Did you not exclaim as you were looking up at those women, "What stupid beasts the crowd must be, for staring with such admiration at those *painted Jezebels*", while a man of your talents is passed by unnoticed?' – 'Surely, surely I did not say so?' – 'Nay, if you had not said so, how should I have noticed it?' – 'That's true,' replied Goldsmith. 'I am very sorry. . . . I do recollect that something of the kind passed through my mind, but I did not think I had uttered it.' Nor did anyone. Burke had invented the words, and taken advantage of Goldsmith's credulity.

She Stoops to Conquer was probably not the only major work which the latter completed in 1772. From a story communicated to Prior by a Mr Harris, who had succeeded to Francis Newbery's business, it appears that Goldsmith had contracted with the latter to write a novel; on the strength of which Newbery advanced 'two or three hundred pounds' in 1771 and 1772. The book, when submitted, 'proved to be in great measure the plot of . . . *The Good-Natured Man*. . . .' Objecting to this, Newbery returned the manuscript. Goldsmith felt unable to produce another, but in settlement of the debt offered to cede the copyright 'of a play coming forward at Covent Garden', although he was not sanguine of its success. Newbery, however, agreed, and in the event profited from the bargain.

Prior assumed (II, 417–18) that this was the same novel a part of which was read to the Horneck ladies after Catherine's marriage to Bunbury (1771); although Mary thought it had never been finished. Quoting the remarks of Southey in his *Omniana*, Prior thought it 'just possible' that this may have been the *Histoire de François Wills, ou le Triomphe de la Bienfaisance: par l'Auteur du Ministre de Wakefield*. But neither Southey nor Prior seems to have read the latter –

evidently a translation – and one wonders indeed who has read it, except Robert Browning (who described it, inaccurately, twenty years after reading it). It is now known that it was in fact an English novel and that the first edition had been published by Vernor and Chater in 1772, but anonymously. As the story bears so many resemblances to *The Good-Natured Man* and especially to *The Vicar of Wakefield*, it is quite conceivable that Goldsmith sold it, perhaps through an intermediary, to these other publishers; and, to preclude any complaint from Newbery who had rejected it, specified that his authorship should not be acknowledged. The problem is so complex that I have discussed it in detail in Appendix I.

Chapter 14

'She Stoops to Conquer'

℀ 1773 ℀

Life was hard, apart from his failing health. He had submitted the manuscript of his new comedy to Colman in the hope that it would be staged at the beginning of the season and enjoy a long run. But in 1768, just after Garrick had produced *False Delicacy* and Colman, *The Good-Natured Man*, Goldsmith had been reported as complaining 'that the stage was ruled by blockheads', which had gone far to alienate both the theatre-managers. And now, despite the success of the earlier play and the fact that his friends regarded the new one as more brilliant, Colman was not impressed by it. To say he could not believe that a comic piece, unless written by himself, would be accepted by the public, seems an exaggeration. He must, on the other hand, have seen that the strange improbabilities in the action, and also the character of Marlow, were serious defects. Colman objected, probably with reason, to a number of passages, and finally returned the copy with notes on the back of the pages to indicate the alterations he wanted. Goldsmith's friends disagreed with these suggestions, and the play was then withdrawn from Colman and offered to Garrick.

But Garrick had probably been quite as much irritated as Colman by Goldsmith's foolish outburst; he too temporised; and the author was left in a state of wretched uncertainty. Would his play ever see the footlights? If it did not, there appeared no means of repaying the debt to Newbery. In this impasse, the manuscript was returned to Colman, and Goldsmith, now in a state bordering on despair, implored him to accept it:

'Dear Sir,

'I entreat you'll relieve me from that state of suspense in which I have been kept for a long time. Whatever objections you have made or shall make to my play, I will endeavour to remove and not argue about them. To bring in any new judges either of its merits or faults I can never submit to. . . . I have, as you know, a large sum of money to make up shortly; by accepting my play I can readily satisfy my creditor that way. . . . For God's sake take the play and let us make the best of it, and let me have the same measure at least as you have given as bad plays as mine.

'I am your friend and servant,
'Oliver Goldsmith.'[1]

The tone of the letter and the syntax are evidence of the state of his nerves. Rarely has a man of such talent been reduced to such self-abasement. What would have happened next is hard to guess, if friends had not put the strongest pressure on Colman and, according to Johnson, virtually compelled him 'to bring it on'. However that may be, the play was being rehearsed by 4 March and Goldsmith could assume that it would enjoy at least a short run in that season and perhaps a longer in the following. His friends, meanwhile, were rallying to his support in a way that must have heartened him. Reynolds and his sister, as well as Johnson, attended some of the rehearsals, and – what especially cheered him – the whole Horneck family including Mary, of whom he continued to be very fond, came up to London to be present.

He had not, however, reckoned with the caprice of actors and actresses. Smith excused himself from playing Marlow on the ground that he was committed to learning a role in another

<hr>

[1] *Collected Letters*, pp 116–17.

piece;[1] while Woodward declined to play Tony Lumpkin, possibly because Colman may have foretold that the comedy would not survive the first night. In this situation Lee Lewes agreed to take the part of Marlow, and young Quick that of Tony. Further difficulties, however, arose in connexion with the Prologue and especially with the Epilogue, great importance being then attached to these pieces. Joseph Cradock sent an Epilogue which was not accepted, it is not known why. At the beginning of March Arthur Murphy submitted an Epilogue 'which was to be sung by Mrs Catley, and which she approved'. But then 'Mrs Bulkley . . . insisted on throwing up her part [that of Kate Hardcastle] unless, according to the custom of the theatre, she was permitted to speak the Epilogue' – as she could not sing. In this juncture, Goldsmith conceived the clever notion of composing a dialogue between the two actresses, who were supposed to be quarrelling, as indeed they had been. This has been preserved and is very good. But Mrs Catley refused. Goldsmith then wrote an Epilogue for Mrs Bulkley to speak: Colman rejected it. He then wrote another, which is now printed with the play, as it had at last been accepted by the actress. The Prologue was by Garrick; it is a clever satire of the sentimental genre, and one wonders why he had at last agreed to support the play. And now, to add to the oddity of the whole business, this Prologue was spoken by Woodward, who had refused to play Tony Lumpkin and who now came on the stage 'dressed in black, and holding a handkerchief to his eyes'. 'The Comic Muse,' he declares, 'long sick, is now a-dying!' But

> One hope remains:—hearing the maid was ill,
> A Doctor comes this night to show his skill:
> To cheer her heart, and give your muscles motion,
> He, in Five Draughts prepar'd, presents a potion –
> A kind of magic charm – for, be assur'd,
> If you will swallow it, the maid is cur'd. . . .

[1] But Marlow's is a thankless role, and it would be natural to demur to it.

Finally the question of a title, like that of an Epilogue, was settled only at the last moment. The first title, *The Old House a New Inn* (reminiscent of Dancourt's play) was replaced by *The Mistakes of a Night*; but, since this may have sounded ambiguous, Goldsmith made a further effort and proposed 'She Stoops to Conquer', though *The Mistakes of a Night* was retained as subtitle.

Whether or not the text of the play was altered to meet Colman's objections is not known; but the *Morning Chronicle* for 22 March observed that Colman had provided no new costumes for the actors and no appropriate scenery. He himself, during the rehearsals and even on the first night, continued to be a wet blanket, which was incomprehensible. It was generally felt that the new play was quite as amusing as *The Good-Natured Man*. Besides, having once agreed to produce it, Colman should in his own interest have promoted it by every possible means, and by believing in it himself.

Goldsmith had done what he could. In the *Westminster Magazine* of 1 January he had published an 'Essay on the Theatre: a comparison between Sentimental Comedy and Laughing Comedy'. This was inspired by Boileau's insistence on the separation of the genres and by Voltaire's attack on the 'Comédie larmoyante', to which Goldsmith added observations and witticisms of his own, quite inaccurate but plausible and effective.[1] This manifesto must have encouraged those who were ready to welcome a 'laughing comedy'. But nothing apparently did as much to prepare the public for Goldsmith's play as Samuel Foote's Puppet-Show. This famous actor,[2] manager and playwright, was an irrepressible comedian. For many years he had not been allowed to put on a regular play at the Haymarket, in the season, this being a monopoly of Drury Lane and Covent Garden. Inspired now by the success of the Italian Fantoccini, he had devised a puppet-play of his own,

[1] See pp 344-6.
[2] See p 91, and note 1 on p 163.

5. Charing Cross, *c.* 1760

6. Goldsmith behind the scenes at Covent Garden on the first night of *She Stoops to Conquer* (from a picture by A. Forestier in *The Jessamy Bride*). Colman to Goldsmith: 'Psha! Doctor, don't be fearful of *squibs*, when we have been sitting almost these three hours upon a barrel of gunpowder.' (see p. 162)

entitled *The Handsome Housemaid, or Piety in Pattens*, which provoked explosions of mirth at the Haymarket. This had been on 15 February, and on 19 March, four days after the first night of Goldsmith's play, the *Morning Chronicle* felt no doubt that 'the ridicule aimed by Foote at what has for some time been received as comedy . . . aided in establishing . . . *She Stoops to Conquer*'. Even so, prior to the fifteenth, Foote's success did not reassure Goldsmith or his friends. On 4 March Johnson had written to Mr White, an American: 'Dr Goldsmith has a new comedy in rehearsal at Covent Garden, to which the manager predicts ill success. But I think it deserves a kinder reception.'

Goldsmith's supporters were prepared to do all they could to belie Colman's forecast, and on 15 March, when the theatre was packed, Johnson, Burke, Reynolds and his sister, and probably the Cradocks and the Hornecks, were in their boxes, ready to laugh heartily. Cumberland relates that he and his friends had taken up positions in various parts of the theatre, so as to applaud whenever possible – a generous move, since Cumberland was one of the principal dramatists in the genre which Goldsmith was trying to displace. But this statement, written years after the event, has been seriously discounted. More probable is the story that the audience watched Dr Johnson for their cue, and that when he roared, they roared in unison. Kelly was in his box, perhaps out of curiosity. There is no evidence of any concerted hostility.

Colman's pessimism, however, had filled Goldsmith with apprehension. Not daring to witness the performance, he wandered disconsolately in St James's Park, a prey to alternations of hope and despair. Moved at last by the impulse which leads a man sometimes to seek pain rather than endure uncertainty, he made his way to the theatre and arrived while the last act was being played. From behind the scenes he heard someone hiss Mrs Hardcastle at the moment when she imagines she sees a highwayman. Goldsmith turned to Colman. 'Psha! Doctor,'

F

said the manager, 'don't be fearful of *squibs*, when we have been sitting almost these three hours upon a barrel of gunpowder.' That this was absurd is evident from the review which appeared next day in *The Morning Chronicle*. Lee Lewes had succeeded in interpreting Marlow; Quick, as Tony Lumpkin, had brought the house down; all the others had done well. The play had been applauded from the moment when the audience saw that Johnson was guffawing; and on the four following nights its success was further assured.

Praise was not, however, general. Horace Walpole described it as the lowest kind of farce. The *London Magazine* criticised the artificial way in which incidents were manipulated 'in order to make things meet',[1] and also pointed to the farcical elements. The *Monthly Review* drew attention to the striking improbabilities in the plot, and argued that Sentimental Comedy afforded a more appropriate picture of contemporary manners and morals than a play like Goldsmith's. It would seem that the kind of people and doings presented in *She Stoops to Conquer* belonged to an earlier period in English social life.

The notice in the *Morning Chronicle* had mentioned the serious handicaps under which Goldsmith had laboured, such as the behaviour of Smith and Woodward and the rumour that the piece would be damned; and had feared that 'at the fag end of the season' the author would reap small benefit financially. The review, fairly detailed and very friendly, described the plot as 'probable and fertile', noted the wealth of wit and humour, approved the character-drawing and complimented the actors. Eulogy could have gone no further. On the eighteenth, *The Public Advertiser* reported that the second performance was more clamorously applauded than the first, and that on the night of 'the Author's Benefit the theatre was filled with the loudest acclamations that ever rung within its walls'.

Since the character-drawing was approved, the language

---

[1] Exactly as in *The Vicar of Wakefield*.

must have appeared to the *Morning Chronicle* as up-to-date and appropriate. Whether it did to the *Monthly Review* is another matter. Be that as it may, it has not occurred to anyone to wonder how Goldsmith, a city-dweller and not, until recent years, admitted to good society, had conceivably learned the language of country gentlewomen. He had recently met Mrs Cradock and Mrs Thrale; but there was no one of the class in question whom he frequented except the Horneck ladies. He had been on friendly terms with them since about 1768, and it seems likely, if not certain, that Kate, Constance and Mrs Hardcastle spoke the language of Mrs Horneck and her daughters, and that this was not identical with that of London women of a similar rank.

Twelve performances of the play were given between 16 March and 31 May, the night of 5 May being a Royal Command; and seven, also at Covent Garden, from October to December. For his benefit nights, in the Spring, Goldsmith received £502 18s 6d, a very handsome sum. He got nothing for the six performances given by Samuel Foote at the Haymarket Theatre;[1] nor for the performances in Dublin, in a number of English towns, and even in New York which was a very loyal city at a time when Massachusetts and Virginia were in a rebellious mood.

The success of the play had in the meantime been hailed not only in the Press, but in verses and prose-pieces by private individuals who ridiculed Goldsmith's detractors, and

[1] Foote, born in 1720, was the son of a former MP for Tiverton. A brilliant caricaturist and mimic, he was dreaded by nearly everyone in London. He had managed the Haymarket Theatre, as a place of entertainment only, on and off since 1747. In 1766 when at Lord Mexborough's place, the Duke of York had induced him to mount a vicious horse, which threw him and fractured his leg. This was amputated, and the Duke persuaded George III to grant him permission to produce regular plays in a theatre in Westminster from 14 May to 14 September annually. He then, in 1767, bought the Haymarket Theatre, and called it a Theatre Royal. At the present time therefore he was one-legged. He exploited this handicap, turned it to advantage, and continued to caricature well-known people, though not always with impunity. Garrick was compelled to endure it. Few people dared quarrel with him.

especially Colman. Of the eulogies one of the most pointed began:

> Long has the Comic Muse, seduc'd to town,
> Shone with false charm, in fin'ry not her own;
> And strove by affectation's flimsy arts,
> And sickly sentiments to conquer hearts;
> But now . . .
> With sweet simplicity she smiles again,
> And *Stoops to Conquer* with her Goldsmith's pen.

But it was easier to satirise the 'Sentimentalists' than to eulogise Goldsmith. Colman above all was pilloried without mercy in the verses 'On the Success of Doctor Goldsmith's New Comedy':

> Come, Coley, doff those mourning weeds,
>   Nor thus with jokes be flamm'd;
> Tho' Goldsmith's present play succeeds,
>   His next may still be damn'd.
>
> As this has 'scap'd without a fall
>   To sink his next prepare;
> New actors hire from Wapping Wall,
>   And dresses from Rag Fair.
>
> For scenes let tatter'd blankets fly,
>   The prologue Kelly write,
> Then swear again the piece must die
>   Before the author's night.
>
> Should these tricks fail, the lucky elf
>   To bring to lasting shame,
> E'en write *the best you can yourself*
>   And print it in *his name*.[1]

---

[1] Prior printed about nine such pieces (vol II, pp 398–406).

From such and similar raillery Colman sought escape by going to stay quietly in Bath – a circumstance likely to provoke further merriment. He seems to have feared that in the preface or dedication to the printed version, Goldsmith too might ridicule him; so he wrote to 'beseech' him

'... to put me out of my pain one way or other. Either take me off the rack of the newspapers or give me the *Coup de Grace*. In a word ... I beg if you think I was vile enough to *wish* ill of your play (whatever I thought of it) e'en say so in your preface to it – but if you acquit me of this in your own mind, absolve me in the face of the World....'

But Goldsmith was not vindictive. In the letter of dedication to Johnson, he pays him a graceful compliment and adds: 'I have, particularly, reason to thank you for your partiality. . . . The undertaking a comedy, not merely sentimental, was very dangerous; and Mr Colman, who saw this piece in its various stages, always thought it so. However, I ventured to trust it to the public; and, though it was necessarily delayed till late in the season, I have every reason to be grateful.'

Nothing, in the circumstances, could have been more tactful. The use of the word 'necessarily' and the ambiguity of 'grateful' cannot but have soothed Colman's feelings. He became a genuine admirer of Goldsmith and some years after the latter's death paid him a warm tribute.

Meanwhile, on 25 March, Francis Newbery had published the play. It appears that no new piece had ever sold so many copies during its whole run, that is, until the end of May.[1] Sales continued as successive reprints were called for. Four thousand copies had been disposed of in the first three days, and at least two thousand more by the end of the year. New editions appeared in Dublin and in Philadelphia.[2]

[1] Prior, vol II, p 392.
[2] For many of the above details of performances and editions the writer is indebted to Professor Friedman's edition of *The Collected Works,* vol V, pp 89–93.

The increasing profits from the play and from the printed edition enabled Goldsmith to repay Francis Newbery and to settle the bills with Filby (£50) and with Dr Hawes, and of course to have money in hand. But the relief and satisfaction were short-lived. An open letter in *The London Packet* for 24 March threw him into a state little short of frenzy. Goldsmith had not, said the anonymous writer,

'. . . been the editor of newspapers and magazines, not to discover the trick of literary *humbug*. But the gauze is so thin, that the very foolish part of the world see through it, and discover the Doctor's monkey face and cloven foot. Your poetic vanity is as unpardonable as your personal; would man believe it, and will woman bear it, to be told that for hours the *great* Goldsmith will stand surveying his grotesque orang-outang figure in a pier glass. Was but the lovely H-----k as much enamoured, you would not sigh, my gentle swain, in vain.'

Freedom of the Press could scarcely be carried further. No one could have been insensitive to the personal insults, but it was the allusion to Mary Horneck that goaded him to action. The reference may have been well founded, but this would only make it worse. Looking cooly at the situation, one cannot blame him for going with a friend to the office of the *Packet*, which was published by Thomas Evans, and complaining of the allusion. Evans disclaimed knowledge of the letter, and while he was stooping to find a copy of the paper, Goldsmith foolishly struck him over the back. Evans grappled with him and an oil-lamp was overturned, spattering Goldsmith's coat with oil. Kenrick, who had probably written the offending letter, rushed in; the combatants were separated, and Goldsmith, bruised and dishevelled, went home.

Few troubles come singly. The Club was to meet that evening, and Beauclerk and Garrick called for him on their way to the Turk's Head. He would have preferred not to go; but, according to Percy, they induced him to attend in order 'to show the world how little he was affected by the late Rencounter'. Perhaps it was as well. Chatterton's poems were read by Lord Charlemont, and Goldsmith's interest in them may have diverted his mind; but not for long. A few days later the *Packet* returned to the attack with a garbled account of his fight with Evans and further ridicule of his play, his person and occupation. Small wonder if he wrote to *The London Chronicle*, a friendly paper, and to others, protesting that he was not a 'newspaper scribbler' and questioning whether freedom of the Press should be allowed such license. The letter was reasonable, but he had better have let the matter drop. Evans had threatened to sue him for assault, and to keep the man quiet, he had parted with £50 for a Welsh charity.

Meanwhile, an imprudent reference in the play had involved him in another kind of trouble. Marlow, while boasting to Kate of his popularity at 'the Ladies Club' – or the Female Coterie, as it was more commonly called – speaks of 'old Miss Biddy Buckskin' among others. From a letter of 27 March from Walpole to Lady Ossory one gathers that this was aimed at Miss Loyd[1] and was naturally resented. 'Miss Loyd,' he wrote, 'is in the new play by the name of Rachael Buckskin, though he [Goldsmith] has altered it in the printed copies. Somebody wrote for her a very sensible reproof to him, only it ended in an indecent *grossièreté*. However, the fool took it seriously, and wrote a most dull and scurrilous answer; but, luckily for him, Mr Beauclerk and Mr Garrick intercepted it.'

Goldsmith had felt so much indebted to Quick for ensuring the success of *She Stoops to Conquer* that for Quick's benefit-performance he adapted a three-act farce by Brueys and

---

[1] Her real name was Lloyd, although Walpole spelled it with one *l*. Both he and Miss Lloyd were members of the club in Albemarle Street.

Palaprat, *Le Grondeur* (1693), under the title of *The Grumbler*; or, to be exact, he adapted Sir Charles Sedley's translation of it, which had been produced in 1702. But he reduced this version from three acts to one and renamed some of the characters. Thus Grichard (the Grumbler) becomes Sourby, Terignan (the young hero) Octavio, and Jasmin, Scamper; but Clarice (the heroine) remains Clarissa, while the notary and the dancing-master retain their French names. The comedy turns on the manner in which Sourby's son Octavio, and Clarissa, with whom Octavio is in love, overcome the obstacles which Sourby raises to their marriage. Especially farcical is Sourby's perverse decision to marry Clarissa himself. The girl invents various stratagems for disgusting him with her character; for example, she sends a dancing-master who insists on his dancing until he is absolutely worn out. This scene is almost identical in Brueys, Sedley and Goldsmith; but the immediate sequel is abridged; while the last Act, in which Grichard still opposes every suggestion and which again provides excellent fun, is omitted in Goldsmith's version.[1] *The Grumbler* was performed once only, on 8 May, probably because the manners were those of the seventeenth century and no characters or behaviour of the kind were conceivable in the 1770s.

Curiously enough, James Boswell, who had received news in Edinburgh of Goldsmith's success, had conceived the warmest admiration for a man whom he had hitherto regarded with mixed feelings. So strong was his emotion that on 29 March he wrote:

'I sincerely wish you joy on the great success of your new comedy . . ., the English nation was just falling into a lethargy. Their blood was thickened and their minds *creamed and mantled like a standing pool*; and no wonder; – when their comedies, which should enliven them like sparkling Cham-

---

[1] For a fuller description, with quotations, see *Les Sources françaises*, pp 165–7.

pagne, were become mere syrup of poppies, gentle, soporifick draughts. . . .'

He added that, by a happy coincidence, his wife had given birth to a daughter on the very night of the first performance of *She Stoops to Conquer*. She was

'. . . a healthy, lively child, and I flatter myself shall be blest with the cheerfullness of your Comick Muse. She has nothing of that wretched whining and crying which we see children so often have; nothing of the *comédie larmoyante*. . . . I beg the favour of hearing from you. . . . You have not a warmer friend or steadier admirer . . . while all the great and the gay in the British metropolis are literally hanging upon *your smiles*, let me see that you can *stoop to* write to me.'

And he begged him to write 'as if in repartee'.[1]

Amid the sea of troubles in which he was struggling, Goldsmith was touched by a letter so kindly. On 4 April he wrote to thank Boswell, while confessing that he had lost all taste for the theatre and intended to cease writing for it. A successful play was 'great cry and little wool' – an Italian expression which Florio had cited as the equivalent of 'Much Ado about Nothing'. He congratulated Boswell on being a father; acknowledged that he himself had behaved like a fool in the affair with Evans, but doubted whether the latter's threat of prosecution would be followed up; and ended by urging Boswell to join him in London. 'We shall laugh it off, whether it goes for or against me.'[2]

Boswell, however, had already arrived.

---

[1] *Letters of James Boswell,* ed C. B. Tinker, Oxford, 1924, vol I, pp 192–3.
[2] *Boswell Papers,* vol IX, pp 112–13. (Cited by Wardle, p 245.)

Chapter 15

Falling Shadows

🙥 1773 🙣

They were delighted to see each other, Goldsmith having been touched by the warmth of Boswell's letter, and Boswell having realised as never before that Goldsmith's talent amounted to genius. Goldsmith was still in bed. They talked for some time about the play; then Goldsmith got up and dressed, while the other, who had observed a letter of thanks for the loan of £15, reflected that his friend was as generous as ever. 'Now that he has a huge supply of gold by his Comedy all the needy draw upon him.'[1] He also probably reflected that it would be worth recording everything possible about Goldsmith, much as he had done about other men of genius like Rousseau and Voltaire, and perhaps as deservedly. It is thanks to Boswell that we have so many details of what Goldsmith said and did in the spring of 1773. Many were what Boswell heard or saw himself, others were what Beauclerk or Johnson told him. Goldsmith had confessed to Boswell that 'As I take my shoes from the shoemaker, and my coat from the taylor, so I take my religion from the priest'; and when this was repeated to Johnson, the latter declared: 'He knows nothing; he has made up his mind about nothing.'

It is true that Goldsmith was deficient in general knowledge and that, after collecting material and writing it up in his compilations, he forgot most of it – to judge from what Reynolds

---

[1] *Boswell Papers*, vol IX, pp 92–3.

tells us. But his knowledge of English and recent French literature, and of the Greek and Latin classics, was extensive.

On 13 April General Oglethorpe entertained him to dinner, together with Johnson and Boswell, and Goldsmith raised the question of luxury. Here was a topic on which he had definitely made up his mind. In the *Citizen of the World* he had not condemned it, but in the *Deserted Village* he had inveighed passionately against it; and he now argued that the race had grown smaller from its effects. Johnson retorted that the growth of commerce and industry might have been bad for people's physique, but '*that* is not luxury'. No one seems to have hinted that Goldsmith himself indulged in luxuries beyond his means, though the thought must have crossed their minds. Later in the evening when Mrs Oglethorpe was dispensing tea Goldsmith regaled the company with Tony Lumpkin's song, and Kate Hardcastle's, from *She Stoops to Conquer*, and his virtuosity in rendering two pieces so diverse in subject and feeling was a great success.

More interesting was a conversation at General Paoli's on the fifteenth. Boswell had met the General in Corsica when the latter was in revolt against the Genoese Republic, as a consequence of which he had sought refuge in London. On the present occasion he had invited Vincenzo Martinelli, as well as Johnson and his friends. Martinelli having published a history of England, Goldsmith urged him to add a section that would bring it up to date. Johnson objected that a great number of notables would be offended. Goldsmith admitted that this might be dangerous for an Englishman, but argued that a foreigner, visiting us 'without prejudice', could 'speak his mind freely'. This Johnson would not accept. A foreigner would be well advised to cross to Calais 'before he publishes his history of the present age'. But Goldsmith stood his ground. 'For my part, I'd tell the truth and shame the devil', he said; and when Johnson replied that he would 'choose to be out of reach of his claws', Goldsmith retorted: 'His claws can do you no harm, when you have the shield of truth.'

The question came up of a possible Royal Command performance of *She Stoops to Conquer*. Goldsmith hoped that the King would attend, though he did not think it would do him, personally, any good. He did, however, wish to please the King and, citing Dryden's 'And every poet is the monarch's friend', thought it ought to read: 'And every monarch is the poet's friend'. He went on to deprecate rebellion and to assert that our revolutions had damaged the Constitution. Here was Toryism with a vengeance! All these views, including the opinion that one should speak the truth without fear, lead one to speculate once again as to why he had declined to write in support of Lord North. It would not have been violating his principles, and it would certainly have brought him a pension. He was now resenting the fact that while Johnson enjoyed a pension, the King gave no sign of being ready to confer one on him. Had George III been offended by what Hastings says to Constance Neville in Act II, which was clearly an allusion to George's objection to the Duke of Gloucester's marrying Lady Waldegrave: 'We shall soon be landed in France, where even among slaves the laws of marriage are respected'? It was in reference to this that Paoli who had seen the play now observed of Goldsmith: 'Il a fait un compliment très gracieux à une certaine grande dame'. Boswell wondered if Goldsmith had intended to refer to Lady Waldegrave, and as Goldsmith hesitated, Paoli tactfully intervened: 'Monsieur Goldsmith', he said, 'est comme la mer qui jette des perles et beaucoup d'autres belles choses, sans s'en apercevoir.' The observation was not only kind, it was rather profound, and the author was charmed. 'Très bien dit, et très élégamment', he replied. He was more accustomed to being laughed at than complimented.

Relations with Johnson were not what they had been. If Goldsmith was sometimes captious, the other could rarely resist the desire to have the last word. A few days later, on the twenty-first, a recent suicide gave Boswell the chance to start a discussion. Did Johnson think that those who commit suicide are mad? Johnson replied that 'one passion presses so upon them that they yield to it'. He had often thought that when a man has resolved 'to kill himself, it is not courage in him to do anything . . . because he has nothing to fear'.

Goldsmith demurred to this: 'It is for fear of something that he has resolved to kill himself; and will not that timid disposition restrain him?'

The company may not have known that he spoke with knowledge: he had once been seriously tempted to end his life. Johnson of course persisted in his view. But can anyone be sure, or even generalise with confidence? This discussion took place in the Thrales' country-house at Streatham, where Johnson now spent long periods of ease, with Mrs Thrale waiting on him like a servant. Although Goldsmith was sometimes invited, Mrs Thrale complained that in her absence, she had been told, he had wandered into her boudoir and turned over her articles of toilet – a statement rather difficult to credit. However that may be, Goldsmith and his eccentricities were being increasingly discussed. Boswell being particularly curious, spoke of him one day towards the end of April to Beauclerk and Johnson, and recorded the latter as saying:

'Goldsmith should not be for ever attempting to shine in conversation: he has not temper for it, he is so much mortified when he fails. . . . When he contends, if he gets the better, it is very little addition to a man of his literary reputation: if he does not get the better he is miserably vexed.'[1]

But could anyone expect a man of Goldsmith's standing and intelligence to sit quietly, night after night, while others were

---

[1] *Life of Johnson*, vol II, p 231. It appears from the *Boswell Papers*, vol VI, p 124, that these were not his exact words. He had used 'hurt' instead of 'vexed'; and he had not said 'to shine in conversation'. (Wardle, p 252.)

discussing topics of great interest? Was he to be reduced to praising the food or deprecating the weather? More sensible than Johnson's criticism was Thomas Percy's offer to write a life or at least a memoir of Goldsmith. The poet had breakfasted with him on 21 April and a week later he brought him some manuscripts that might assist, and related circumstances of his early life which Percy took down at the time.

Goldsmith was again being discussed on 30 April when Beauclerk gave a dinner party for Boswell and several members of the Club, because Boswell had been nominated for membership. Why Johnson began to disparage Goldsmith is not apparent, unless it were because everyone was thinking of him. Johnson said: 'It is amazing how little Goldsmith knows. He seldom comes where he is not more ignorant than anyone else.'

'Yet,' Reynolds interjected, 'there is no man whose company is more liked.'

'To be sure, Sir. When people find a man of the most distinguished abilities as a writer, their inferiour while he is with them, it must be highly gratifying to them. What Goldsmith comically says of himself is very true, – he always gets the better when he argues alone....' Attempting to be more just, he added that *The Traveller* was 'a very fine performance', as was *The Deserted Village*, 'were it not sometimes too much the echo' of *The Traveller*. A strange criticism indeed! After which, he delivered the famous eulogy: 'Whether ... we take him as a poet, – as a comick writer, – or as an historian, he stands in the first class.'

Boswell's objection to Goldsmith's being considered a first-class historian has already been commented on. Johnson was right however in maintaining: 'Sir, he has the art of compiling, and of saying every thing he has to say in a pleasing manner. He is now writing a Natural History and will make it as entertaining as a Persian Tale.' Goldsmith could be witty, too, in conversation. 'I remember once,' Johnson added, 'being with Goldsmith in Westminster Abbey. While we surveyed the

Poets' Corner, I said to him, "*Forsitan et nostrum nomen miscebitur istis*". When we got to Temple Bar [on the top of which were displayed the heads of decapitated rebels] he stopped me, pointed to the heads upon it, and slily whispered me, '*Forsitan et nostrum nomen miscebitur ISTIS.*'

Later that evening, at the Turk's Head, after Boswell had been elected, Goldsmith who was now present began to discuss equality, which led Burke to tease him by saying: 'Here's our monarchy man growing Republican'. Goldsmith was amused. 'I'm for Monarchy,' he said, 'to keep us all equal.'

But all the Club meetings and dinner parties were not as agreeable as this, and it seems that Johnson frequently humiliated him. 'Sir,' he once complained, 'you are for making a monarchy of what should be a republick.' The most painful of his experiences with the Great Cham was at dinner with the Dilly Brothers on 7 May. Boswell, hoping to record some important pronouncements by his hero, raised the question of religious toleration. It seems to have been beside the point for Johnson to say that 'the only method by which religious truth can be established is by martyrdom'. Goldsmith, however, accepted the change of subject, as well as the statement:

'But how is a man to act, Sir? . . . may he not think it wrong to expose himself to persecution? Has he a right to do so? Is it not, as it were committing voluntary suicide?'

Johnson replied that 'twenty thousand men in an army do much the same'.

'But have they a moral right to do this?' Goldsmith asked, referring to martyrs, not to soldiers.

Johnson conceded that if a man doubted whether it would be better to 'expose himself to martyrdom or not, he should not do it. He must be convinced that he has a delegation from heaven.'

'I would consider,' Goldsmith rejoined, 'where there is the greater chance of good or evil upon the whole'; and he gave examples of what a sensible man would do in circumstances that might well arise. As Johnson simply repeated that one must be sure that one 'has a delegation from heaven', Goldsmith asked how this was to be known. The discussion was now pursued by others, while Goldsmith held his peace; but when at last he tried to put in a word, it was drowned in a torrent of verbosity. A clergyman in the company was hoping to join in the argument, and there being no apparent sign that Johnson would give him a chance, Goldsmith intervened: 'Sir, . . . the gentleman has heard you patiently for an hour; pray allow us now to hear him'.

Johnson said that he 'was only giving him [the clergyman] a signal of my attention', and added: 'Sir, you are impertinent'; but he apologised later that evening.

When, on another occasion, Goldsmith was allowed to speak for a few minutes, a foreigner, apparently some German, stopped him with the words: 'Stay, stay, Toctor Shonson is going to say something'. It is certain that by the 1770s the Great Bear could not refrain from domineering over everyone. To shine in conversation, to triumph in argument, had become as necessary for him as food and drink – which is saying a great deal. For many years past people had deferred to him, and some like Edward Gibbon, whom Goldsmith met about this time, took care never to argue with him.

Meanwhile a considerable amount of drudgery was occupying Goldsmith, while his habit of promising a manuscript by a certain date and of obtaining part payment on account – tempting as all this was – put a strain on his nerves and kept him for long hours at his desk. He had undertaken to make an abridgment of the *History of England*, for which after all the material was in hand. But to write a *Grecian History from the Earliest State to the Death of Alexander the Great*, in two volumes, was too ambitious an enterprise to embark on; especially while the Natural History was still on the stocks. At the end of May he had not yet finished the first volume of the *Grecian History*. He did, however, complete it by 22 June, and the publishers –

for it was a joint enterprise – paid him £250, half of which was on account.

Although he informed the Selbys that he intended to keep on his room at the farm, he did not in 1773 take advantage of the quietness and the country air which would have done him so much good. To have been staying with the Selbys would also have spared him, at least in part, a humiliation such as he had never yet experienced.

It chanced that towards the end of May a certain James Beattie, still remembered as author of *The Minstrel*, had come to London. Born in 1735, he had been a schoolmaster for some years before an influential friend got him appointed as professor of moral philosophy and logic at Marischal College in Aberdeen. He probably learned something about these sciences while teaching them. But he had a genuine feeling for nature and scenery, and his poem gives a certain foretaste of Wordsworth. He had formerly met Johnson when visiting London in 1771; but already in 1770 he had completed an *Essay on Truth* in which he attacked Hume in language hardly suited to learned controversy. As a counterblast to scepticism the book was valueless, and no publisher would take it until Sir William Forbes and another friend of Beattie's had it printed at their own expense.

Goldsmith met Beattie and his wife at Reynolds's London home on 9 June when Mary Horneck and the Bunburys were among the guests. Reynolds arranged further meetings including one at his Richmond villa on the fourteenth. It was rumoured that Beattie might receive a pension, and Goldsmith was understandably mortified. 'Why,' he asked, 'should he receive a pension? For writing *The Minstrel*? Then surely I have a better claim.' Someone passed this on to Beattie. The probability that the pension was to be granted in recognition of the *Essay* only made matters worse. Beattie was granted an audience with the King, who complimented him on the *Essay*; on 9 July Oxford conferred on him and on Reynolds the degree of LL.D. *honoris causa*; and it looked certain, as the summer wore on, that a pension would follow. This was more than Goldsmith could bear with equanimity; and when at every party he had to listen to fulsome praise of the Aberdonian, it was hard not to express his vexation. One day when he and Johnson were at Mrs Thrale's, he exclaimed: 'They talk of Beattie for an author; and what has Beattie done compared to me, who have written so many volumes?'

'Ah, Doctor,' Johnson replied, 'there go many sixpences to make one guinea.'

This story we owe to Mrs Thrale, who little realised the effect it would have on Johnson's reputation for common sense. Unhappily Goldsmith put himself in the wrong by reproving Reynolds for his allegorical picture of Beattie. In this painting the Professor is portrayed in his doctor's gown, with the *Essay on Truth* under his arm. Truth, an allegorical figure, stands beside him, holding in one hand a pair of scales and with the other overthrowing three persons who represent Prejudice, Scepticism and Folly. Of these, two were portraits of Hume and Voltaire. Sir Joshua had no knowledge of philosophy. But Goldsmith naturally felt outraged:

'It very ill becomes a man of your eminence and character, Sir Joshua, to condescend to be a mean flatterer, or to wish to degrade so high a genius as Voltaire before so mean a writer as Dr Beattie; for Dr Beattie and his book together will, in the space of ten years, not be known ever to have been in existence, but your allegorical picture and the fame of Voltaire will live for ever to your disgrace as a flatterer.'

Such was the outburst recorded by James Northcote in his *Life* of Reynolds; and it says much for the gentleness of Reynolds' character that he did not resent the reproof, but continued to be kind and hospitable to Goldsmith. In a letter of 7 August, Gibbon speaks of recently meeting them both at parties. Johnson's departure on the sixth for Edinburgh, where Boswell was awaiting him, removed one source of irritation, and Goldsmith could forget his troubles in the work that was absorbing him, on the *Animated Nature* and the *Grecian History*. He had a friend in Edward Gibbon who probably saw a good deal of him during this autumn, and who, a sceptic himself, must have appreciated the defence of Voltaire. Calling one day at Goldsmith's rooms in the Temple, Gibbon found him nearing the end of Volume II of the *Grecian History*. 'What,' Goldsmith asked him, 'was the name of the Indian king who gave Alexander so much trouble?' Gibbon mischievously replied: 'Montezuma'; and Montezuma would have been written if the historian, in alarm, had not told him that it was Porus.

Some weeks before this, Goldsmith had invited a number of his friends to contribute articles to a new *Dictionary of Arts and Sciences* which he was planning to edit. The idea was excellent and they undertook to collaborate: Reynolds to write on painting, Garrick on acting, Burney on music, Burke on the Sublime and the Beautiful, and so on. Goldsmith wrote an introduction, which has been lost, though it appears to have been one of his best compositions; and also circulated a prospectus. Unfortunately the publishers felt unwilling to commit themselves to producing a work so ambitious and involving the collaboration of a number of specialists, especially when the editor himself was so often in arrears with copy he had promised.

In October *She Stoops to Conquer* returned to the boards at Covent Garden and performances were repeated in November and December. Apart from these circumstances and the story of a 'Poetical Exordium' which he composed for Mrs Yates, who was to recite it on 20 November, it seems impossible to reconstruct the life of Goldsmith during the latter part of 1773 and the first few weeks of 1774 in much detail. He had no Boswell, and references by his contemporaries are rarely dated.

From a letter of Horace Walpole we know that Goldsmith had dinner with the Beauclerks on 11 December, that he and Garrick played the fool, and that this was the first night of Kelly's *School for Wives*, 'which was exceedingly applauded'. Here are definite facts; but since Walpole says nothing about Goldsmith's being sick and unable to take anything but hot milk, how are we to reconcile this with the story of the extravagant dinners which he offered Johnson, Reynolds and others in his own rooms, when he himself could take nothing else? Nor do we know exactly what work he was engaged on. He is said to have written something in support of James Townsend who was opposing Wilkes in the election for the Lord Mayoralty; and he composed the abridgment for the use of schools of his *History of England* – an undertaking already mentioned. Now, or early in 1774, he was asked to make a new translation of Scarron's *Roman comique*, but, as will be shown later, he can only have done a little of this. The success of Hugh Kelly's play, which good judges considered very bad and the public very delightful, 'has almost killed Goldsmith with envy' – so Beauclerk wrote to Lord Charlemont. It is known for a fact that Garrick lent him £40 at the end of the year; and that he had been paid over £800 for the *Animated Nature* which was now nearly finished.

It is certain that he was unhappy. This was probably due to the state of his health and to financial worry; but if he was giving lavish dinner-parties – and we have the Rev. Andrew Kippis's evidence to show that he gave some and that his friends were worried by his extravagance – this served only to sink him further into debt; and it explains his appeal to Garrick. There was a vicious circle here. That he needed company and distraction was natural, but he could have had both at far less cost. Judgement, common sense, self-control – all seem to have left him.

Chapter 16
The End

❧ 1774 ❧

I

Prospects for Christmas and the New Year would have been dismal, if friends had not been thinking of him. Cradock indeed could be relied on for company and entertainment, but not for money, since he knew, and said, that as soon as Goldsmith had £30 in his pocket, he would take it into the country to gamble and return penniless. Garrick not only lent him £40, but offered to revive *The Good-Natured Man* as an author's benefit at Drury Lane; and Goldsmith, in acknowledging this, said he would make such alterations as would satisfy his friend.[1] Although nothing came of this, Garrick – who was unwell at the time – promised a further loan of £60 which Goldsmith had asked for, in view of a New Year party to which he had been invited.

On Christmas Day he gratefully acknowledged the promise:

'My dear Friend

'I thank you! I wish I could do something to serve you. I shall have a comedy for you in a season or two at farthest that I believe will be worth your acceptance, for I fancy I will make it a fine thing. You shall have the refusal.... I'm sorry you are ill. I will draw upon you in one month after date for £60, and your acceptance will be ready money part of which I want to go down to Barton with....'[2]

[1] *Collected Letters*, pp 125–6.
[2] Ibid., pp 127–8. He enclosed a bill of exchange, by the terms of which he could draw £60 on 28 January. Garrick endorsed this.

Catherine Horneck – 'Little Comedy' as Goldsmith called her – who had married W. H. Bunbury, a country gentleman with some talent as a portraitist, had invited Goldsmith to join a house-party for the New Year. It was to be held at Sir Charles Bunbury's, her brother-in-law's place, at Barton in Suffolk. The Jessamy Bride – no small attraction – would be there, and this holiday among cheerful people would be an escape from the drudgery and obsessions of London. While pretending to hesitate, he accepted in a letter which begins in prose, then passes into humorous verse to describe, in advance, a game of loo into which they will inveigle him. They will advise him so badly that he will lose money, and so he asks whether he ought not to sue them at Bow Street, before Sir John Fielding,

> For giving advice that is not worth a straw
> May well be called picking of pockets in law.

He greatly enjoyed himself at Barton, played with the children who were among the guests, and entertained the company with his songs. Many of these were of his own composition, according to Mary Horneck to whom we owe an account of his doings at Barton. As she makes no reference to sickness or to his being unable to eat a normal meal, it looks as if his health had improved for the time being. He was in high spirits. 'Come now, and let us play the fool', he would say, and this together with his eccentricity tempted people to play very heartless tricks on him. 'Being at all times gay in dress,' Mary[1] afterwards told Sir James Prior, 'he made his appearance at the breakfast table in a smart black silk coat with an expensive pair of ruffles; the coat someone contrived to soil, and it was sent to be cleansed; but either by accident or probably design the day after it came home the sleeves became daubed with paint, which was not discovered until the ruffles also to his great mortification, were irretrievably disfigured.' Someone also

---

[1] She married Colonel Gwynne.

damaged his wig beyond repair. Yet he appears to have remained good-humoured. There is no reason to accuse Mary Horneck of undue partiality when she writes:

'His benevolence was unquestionable, and his countenance bore every trace of it. He was a very plain man, but . . . it was impossible not to love and respect his goodness of heart . . . nobody that knew him intimately could avoid admiring and loving his good qualities. They accused him of envy, but it certainly was not envy in the usual sense of the word. . . . I am sure that on many occasions, from the peculiar manner of his humour and assumed frown . . . what was often uttered in jest, was mistaken by those who did not know him for earnest.'[1]

This testimony from one who knew and understood him probably as well as did Reynolds, disposes of some of the stories which represent him as morbidly jealous of success in others; but envious of literary rivals he certainly was.

The visit to Barton had not removed the craving for distraction, still less had it reconciled him to the need for steady work. Later in the month he spent some time as the guest of a friend named Purefroy at Windsor, and while there heard that certain proofs of the section on Birds in the *Animated Nature* were awaiting him at the Temple. Instead of sending for them, he wrote to ask Cradock if he and Percy would correct them for him. Neither of them knew anything about birds, but they read

---

[1] Prior, vol II, pp 377-9. These souvenirs as communicated by Mrs Gwynne, sound as though they relate to one holiday at Barton; but it is possible, perhaps likely, that Goldsmith was invited there more than once after Catherine had married Bunbury. It is not improbable that he stayed there at least once in 1772, and that on that occasion he read to Mary and Catherine the first chapter or chapters of the novel he was writing for Newbery. Since Prior's statement about this novel shows that it must have been finished – and rejected – at a time when Goldsmith was still uncertain whether *She Stoops to Conquer* would be a success, it follows that the 'reading' of the novel took place in 1772, possibly before the summer; and not necessarily at Barton. See Chapter XIII above, and Appendix I.

and apparently passed the proofs in question.[1] This we can believe; but are we fully to accept what Beauclerk implied in a letter to Charlemont of 12 February? 'Our Club has dwindled away to nothing,' he reported. 'Sir Joshua and Goldsmith have got into such a round of pleasures that they have no time.' Washington Irving, one of the very few writers who have contrived to make Goldsmith live again, believed that the 'round of pleasures' was no more than 'a joyless dissipation'.

His health was fluctuating. One day when dining with the Cradocks, he took only some wine and biscuits, and his attempts at conversation were not spontaneous. With the loss of appetite went the loss of any energy for work. Cradock's idea that a new and annotated edition of the two long poems would be generously subscribed to, met with little response. He roused himself enough to revise the old *Enquiry into the Present State of Polite Learning* and to correct the final proofs of the *Animated Nature*. He even, on 20 February (when he must have been feeling better) wrote to Nourse who had acquired the rights of publication from Griffin, to ask if Griffin could buy back a share in these rights. 'As I have thought of extending the work into the *vegetable* and *fossil* kingdoms, you shall share with him in any such engagement as may happen to ensue.' Nourse, however, did not take up the suggestion.

By the end of February he seems to have been eating normally, and he was dressing as showily as ever, 'the *bon ton* . . . breaking out in Dr G. under the form of many a waistcoat', according to George Stevens, a friend of Garrick's. But no one perceived that the sands were running out. The Club being less attractive than before, since his proposal of Gibbon for membership had been turned down, he spent much, if not most, of his leisure at the St James's Coffee House in the West End, a district more agreeable than Gerrard Street. It is not fanciful to picture him leaving the Temple and the dirt and

---

[1] Joseph Cradock, *Literary and Miscellaneous Memoirs*, London, 1826–28, 4 vols, vol IV, pp 285–6.

murk of Fleet Street, making his way to Leicester Fields and
thence along Piccadilly, which began with what is now
Coventry Street; then past the White Bear Inn (Regent Street
did not then exist) and Alton's bookshop, St James's Church,
looking much as it does now; and Fortnum and Mason's (not
the modern building) which supplied the Court with groceries
and oriental delicacies. In this noble thoroughfare, with its
mansions and coaching inns, one was in aristocratic London
and had a sense of the high fitness of things. At the Coffee
House, too, the company was very much to his liking; he met
friends like Reynolds, Garrick and the Burkes, but also Cumberland, Dean Barnard, Canon Douglas, Whiteford, Hickey
and Samuel Foote, whose presence Johnson would never have
tolerated. Neither Johnson nor Beauclerk frequented this
place. But Garrick amused the company with his wit and
talent for mimicry, and Foote, unscrupulous but irresistibly
funny, stumped in on his wooden leg and out-mimicked
Garrick.

The tone in short was gay and informal, so much so that
Goldsmith and Garrick agreed to write epitaphs for each other,
an idea suggested perhaps by the epitaph which Dr Primrose
had composed for his wife, which might confirm the subject
in his virtues while correcting his faults. Garrick immediately
produced the following:

> Here lies Nolly Goldsmith, for shortness call'd Noll,
> Who wrote like an angel, but talk'd like poor Poll.

There was tragic irony in this, and still more tragic was Goldsmith's response, which was to plan a series of epitaphs on the
principal members of the circle, though not on Foote, whom
no one dared offend. These portraits – for such they were –
would show them that while they could applaud Garrick's
epitaph on Goldsmith, Goldsmith could, in retaliation, be just
as witty, and also more just and more urbane. His penetration

into character was as keen as ever and his style had never been more brilliant. Feeling a need for the solitude that would enable him to think and write without social distractions, he moved, probably at the beginning of March, to his old quarters in Selby's farm, and here he nearly completed 'Retaliation'. A practice of Scarron's in holding parties to which each guest brought his own food, suggested the opening lines; each member of the St James's circle being characterised by the dish most appropriate to his character. Thus 'Burke shall be tongue, with a garnish of brains'; Cumberland, sweetbread; Reynolds, lamb; and 'Magnanimous Goldsmith a gooseberry fool'. After this came the epigrams, still in the anapaestic metre so suited to good-natured satire.

Unhappily a renewed attack of kidney trouble brought him back, about 23 March, to his chambers in Brick Court. On the 25th he took an emetic, but as he was suffering from severe headache and running a temperature, he sent for Dr Hawes. He himself wished to take Dr James's 'Fever Powders', a popular remedy which many people, including Horace Walpole, swore by. They had previously given him relief. Hawes advised against them in the present instance, and Dr Fordyce who was called in for consultation took the same view. Goldsmith, however, took three of the powders, and on the Saturday morning, when Hawes called, he appeared to be dozing. But before nightfall diarrhoea and vomiting had set in, and by Sunday morning this had greatly weakened him. Fordyce called in Dr Turton, while Hawes withdrew from the case. It has been argued that the fever powders could hardly have made him worse. What appears most likely is that the malady was simply taking its course, that his constitution had been undermined by irregular habits and lack of exercise, and that he was tormented by the fear that he could never repay his debts, which he knew to be mountainous. 'All was inwardly disturbed', wrote Cradock.

During the following week his condition seems to have

fluctuated. According to Prior, he was calm and even cheerful at times; but he slept little and could hardly eat anything. Fordyce and Turton came every day, without apparently realising that their patient was doomed. On Sunday 3 April Percy called. It is strange that Goldsmith, who was a believer, did not ask to take communion: Percy could have arranged it. And it is equally strange that no other of Goldsmith's friends came to see him during the ten days of his sickness. After Percy's visit, Dr Turton took his patient's pulse, and said: 'Your pulse is in greater disorder than it should be from the state of fever which you have. Is your mind at ease?' – 'No, it is not' was the reply. That night, however, he fell into a sound sleep, but was awake before 4 a.m., with violent convulsions. At about 4.30 he was dead.

II

Three days later, on 7 April, Horace Walpole wrote to the Reverend William Mason:

'The republic of Parnassus has lost a member: Dr Goldsmith is dead of a purple fever, and I think might have been saved if he had continued James's powder, which had had much effect, but his physician interposed. His numerous friends neglected him shamefully at last, as if they had no business with him when it was too serious to laugh. He had lately written Epitaphs for them all, some of which hurt, and perhaps made them not sorry that his own was the first necessary. The poor soul had sometimes parts, though never common sense. . . .'

One can only assume that Goldsmith's friends had not been warned by Dr Turton of the gravity of his condition. Burke and Reynolds in particular felt shattered by the news of his death. Boswell, who was in Edinburgh, wrote to Garrick: 'I have not been so much affected with any event that has happened for a long time'. A young doctor named McDonnell whom Goldsmith had employed as an amanuensis when he, McDonnell, was in financial straits, was still more moved. 'I was abroad at the time of his death,' he wrote, 'and I wept bitterly when the intelligence first reached me. A blank came over my heart as if I had lost one of my nearest relatives. . . .' Few deaths of notable men have provoked such widespread grief. It was of course conspicuous among the many poor folk whom he had assisted, and as much, it seems, from gratitude as from self-interest. Two milliners whom the poet had employed told Cradock that they would rather work for Goldsmith than let him apply elsewhere.

Dr Hawes, Sir Joshua and others were planning a funeral in the Abbey, with six distinguished men as pall-bearers; but the expense would be considerable, and when it was discovered that Goldsmith's debts amounted to over £2,000 – equivalent to perhaps £20,000 in the currency of today – it was decided to invite inscriptions for a simple monument. On 9 April the body was interred in the Temple Burying Ground, a little way west of the Master's House. For some reason only six or seven people attended, including Hugh Kelly, who was so deeply affected as to weep. And just before the coffin was lowered, Mary Horneck asked for it to be opened so that she might take a lock of his hair. The relations between these two remain a mystery. It is at least curious that of all Goldsmith's friends Mary Horneck was the only one to attend the burial. Years later, when she was seventy but still handsome, Hazlitt met her in Northcote's studio. When she had left them Northcote remarked: 'I do not know why she is so kind as to come and see me, except that I am the last link in the chain that connects her with all those she most esteemed when young – Johnson, Reynolds, Goldsmith – and remind her of the most delightful period of her life.'

In the days following the burial many tributes to Goldsmith were published in prose and verse. The best is an epigram in

Greek Elegiacs by Johnson, imitated from the sepulchral epigrams of the Hellenistic Age. For the monument in the Abbey the medallion-portrait was executed by Nollekens, while the Latin inscription, by Johnson, was dedicated to the memory of

Olivarii Goldsmith,
Poetae, Physici, Historici,
Qui nullum fere scribendi genus
Non tetigit,
Nullum quod tetigit non ornavit.

And it went on to praise one who was powerful yet gentle in moving the emotions and to foretell that his memory would last as long as reading is held in esteem.

But why '*Physicus*' and '*Historicus*', when he was neither? There had been dramatists and novelists in the Roman world. And why an inscription in Latin? Goldsmith was not being presented at Cambridge for an honorary degree. Goldsmith's friends felt so strongly that the epitaph should be in English that in 1776 Burke drew up a memorial requesting Johnson to rewrite it in the vernacular, as 'we think', he explained, that 'the memory of so eminent an English writer ought to be perpetuated in the language to which his works are likely to be so lasting an ornament, which we also know to have been the opinion of the late Doctor himself.' Twelve people, including Gibbon and Sheridan, signed the appeal and Reynolds summoned up enough courage to take it to Johnson. The latter was as intractable as ever. Never would he 'consent to disgrace the walls of Westminster Abbey with an inscription in English'. There was no more to be said.

The estate was quickly dealt with. Dr Hawes was given a few mementoes, but most of the furniture and the very large library, full of scholarly works, were sold by auction on 11 July. Goldsmith's debt to Newbery had been settled by the latter's acquiring the copyright of *She Stoops to Conquer*; the debt to Garrick had also been liquidated. But the poet's lawyer friend, Edward Bott, seems to have lent him substantial sums, possibly as much as £1,000, and it is not clear that he received anything. The publishers, however, were amply covered. The *Animated Nature* proved a gold-mine, as did the 'Histories'.

The posthumous works appeared in rapid succession, 'Retaliation' on 19 April being the first. The wit and geniality of the portraits, and their kindness, must have given intense pleasure. *The Grecian History* came out on 15 June; *An History of the Earth and Animated Nature*, in eight volumes, on 1 July, and the abridged *History of England* on 2 July. More interesting to us today was the publication by Kearsley in 1776 of 'The Haunch of Venison'. All these, and the many translations into French, will be discussed in Part II of the present work.

Amid the various reprints and editions of *Select Poems*, *Miscellaneous Works*, and so on, which appeared in the twenty-five years after Goldsmith's death, most curious is the absence of any serious biography. Glover's *Life of Dr Goldsmith* (July 1774) was not a Life, but a selection of anecdotes and extracts. Percy who had undertaken to write a biography, seems to have felt that the notes he had collected hardly sufficed for such a work – and this was true. He handed over the task to Johnson, and Johnson produced nothing. It was not until 1801 that Percy published his *Memoir* as preface to an edition of the *Miscellaneous Works*. And ever since then critics have been trying to understand a man whose character so often appears in contradiction with his writings.

Conclusion

Goldsmith was a puzzle to his contemporaries. Walpole regarded him as 'a man who had sometimes parts, though never common sense', and many, like Garrick and Beauclerk, probably agreed with him. It seems to have been thought that Goldsmith the writer was a different being from Goldsmith the man. And a recent biographer has described him as an anomaly. One might make a parallel between Goldsmith and the subject of Henry James's short story: *The Private Life*.

If Sainte-Beuve, with his vast knowledge and unique gift for 'penetrating to the man behind the poet', had analysed the Goldsmith case, a convincing portrait might have been drawn long ago. As it is, most biographers have been content with recording his sayings and doings and contriving to whitewash his character. A few – literary men rather than academic writers – have inspired the reader with a desire to know and read him, which should be a prime motive of the critic.

On one point everyone is agreed. Acutely conscious of his physical disadvantages, Goldsmith tried to make up for them by dressing extravagantly. He liked brightly coloured coats and waistcoats, and this also caused unfavourable comment. His character had been formed, for better or worse, before ever he set foot in London. His social habits, his behaviour, his accent, were unadapted to English standards. To many Englishmen he seemed a fool, because they did not understand his sense of humour, as the Irish did. It seems to have been appreciated by Mary Horneck, and also by Reynolds whose 'Portrait' of Goldsmith is most sympathetic. Goldsmith probably became aware that people regarded him as silly, and decided to play up to them. After all, as La Rochefoucauld had observed, 'Qui vit sans folie n'est pas si sage qu'il croit'.

Two features of his character appear both in his life and in his writings. Although Johnson exaggerated when he said that Goldsmith knew nothing, he was in fact surprisingly deficient in general information. Even more strangely, he had none of the cultural interests, except in Natural History, which were shared by most educated men at that time, as for example by Dr Burney, who was no writer, but immensely curious about everything he saw on the Continent. Goldsmith appears to have been quite indifferent to music apart from the simple songs and airs he could manage on his flute, to painting, to sculpture, to architecture, even to the monuments of classical antiquity. While well equipped with a knowledge of the Latin classics, he passed through or near Mantua without apparently thinking of Virgil, he stayed in Padua, yet never mentions Livy in that connexion; he must have passed by Lake Garda, which should have revived memories of Catullus.

One may conclude that the contradictions between his life and his writings were more apparent than real. While there was in him, as in most people, a tendency to schizophrenia, the man and the writer were not two different beings. How many authors have been wiser – or more righteous – in their books than in their conduct! Goldsmith was no more an anomaly than La Fontaine or Verlaine. No great poet has displayed more good sense, a wider knowledge of human nature and a truer feeling for justice than La Fontaine in his *Fables*; yet in his life he was irresponsible, neglectful of his wife, a sponger, and so naïve that Racine could easily deceive him into thinking he had been worsted in argument. Verlaine in his poems was an exquisite artist, naïvely pious and with the soul of a child; in his life he sank into vice and corruption. Of La Fontaine, Goldsmith and Verlaine it can be said that they had never really grown up. They had put so much of themselves into their art that little aptitude was left for the practical conduct of life.

Finally, it should be pointed out, Goldsmith's absurdities have been exaggerated. He by no means always 'talked like poor Poll'. He could sometimes be as witty as in his books, and also as quick-witted. We know from the records of Boswell, who came to like and admire him, that he sometimes talked as sensibly as anyone, and could display more intelligence than Johnson and a deeper knowledge of human nature; for example, in the argument about suicide. It seems to be true, however, that he was often ineffective or incoherent as a talker. Even so, one suspects that Burke and Beauclerk exaggerated his blunders, if they did not fabricate an anecdote and father it on him. One is thinking of Goldsmith's alleged effort to re-tell the story of the yellow peas which should be sent to Hammersmith. Are we to suppose that he had a favourable opportunity to attempt this witticism? and if so, that he bungled it out of all recognition? The anecdote comes from Beauclerk and bears the marks of having been added to, and perfected, by that remarkable raconteur. He was capable of inventing a story *de toutes pièces*, as witness the following: 'Johnson has been confined for some weeks in the Isle of Skye; we hear that he was obliged to swim over to the mainland, taking hold of a cow's tail. Be that as it may,' he added thoughtfully, 'Lady Di has promised to make a drawing of it.' Even so, the story of Goldsmith and the yellow peas may be literally true, and it is so good that one hopes it is.

Goldsmith was often *étourdi*; and often misunderstood. But whatever view one takes of his absurdities,[1] he certainly had serious faults. He was so irascible that on two occasions he assaulted men who had irritated him. He gambled, at times recklessly. He gave away money which did not always belong

---

[1] He was a great deal less eccentric, less violent and better-mannered than Johnson. The latter astonished observers by his strange grimaces, by the habit of rolling his body, and by the animal-like voracity with which he fell upon his food. He frequently struck those who annoyed him.

G

to him; he bought popularity at the expense of his creditors. His extravagance in offering lavish dinner parties can be palliated only by the need he felt for distraction and making merry with friends. In matters literary he pushed plagiarism to the point of dishonesty. But perhaps his worst fault was the neglect of his mother.

As a young man his fecklessness had caused her to lose all heart, and he seems to have been oblivious of the distress he was causing. In the end he forced her to despair; the natural and right course would have been to strive to win her back. Perhaps he did. It seems certain, however, that, while he knew she was in greatly reduced circumstances, he made no move to assist her. After about 1765 he was earning more money than he needed for his own support; he could easily have sent her remittances, either direct or through the intermediary of Henry or of the Hodsons. It was probably a case of out of sight, out of mind.[1]

All this may be explained on the ground that he had been born irresponsible, impulsive and odd, and that his father failed to correct him in youth. How far can a man be censured for defects in nature?

Yet there was a different side to his character, and this should be dwelt on in conclusion. 'There is no man whose company is more sought,' Reynolds had said of him. A bad man would not have been so much loved by people as intelligent and diverse as Burke, Reynolds, the Hornecks and Boswell. The death of a simply brilliant writer is never mourned by such a multitude as grieved for Goldsmith.

Even so, our knowledge of him is fragmentary. He refused to give more than the most sparse information about his past life to Johnson and Percy, both of whom undertook to write his biography. He recorded here and there a few of his experiences on the Grand Tour, but at least two of his statements

---

[1] He ordered only half-mourning for her death, but suits of mourning for three other occasions.

were untrue. There remain great gaps in the records left by others. To consider a few of the questions which arise: what were his relations with Baretti, Samuel Foote, Hugh Kelly and Cumberland – all prominent figures in literary London? With regard to the Italian, the evidence is contradictory. Goldsmith spoke in high terms of his character and humanity; but he seems to have disliked him and to have been jealous of his influence with Johnson. Boswell and Johnson often discussed Foote, and such was the latter's gift for mimicry and habit of caricaturing people on the stage that nearly everyone dreaded him. Did he caricature Goldsmith? It would not have been difficult. Goldsmith appears to have met Kelly at the Wednesday Club in 1765, if not earlier, and they were on good terms. But by publicly disparaging *False Delicacy* in 1768, he made an enemy of Kelly. Were they reconciled before Goldsmith's death?

So far from ingratiating himself with Richard Cumberland, a quiet, inoffensive character, he ridiculed the kind of comedies which Cumberland was producing. Yet the latter says that he paid a friendly call on him at Brick Court in 1770, and there is no evidence that in 1773 he did anything to injure the prospects of *She Stoops to Conquer*. Did not Goldsmith see that 'sentimental' comedy and his own kind were not as different as he pretended, and that to call Cumberland's kind a 'bastard' genre was inexact? Both derived from the Greek 'New Comedy', the social kind, of which Menander had been the great practitioner. In any event, Goldsmith and Cumberland used afterwards to meet at the St James's Coffee House; and in 'Retaliation' the portrait of Cumberland is in some ways the most flattering of all: 'The Terence of England, the mender of hearts.' No other man of letters received such a compliment.

In respect of all these men Goldsmith's real feelings are not clear. A greater mystery surrounds his relations with women. Irregularities there may have been; Garrick referred to such.

But was there ever a serious attachment? Washington Irving hinted at a certain tenderness which he may have felt for Mary Horneck, and in our own days 'F. Frankfort Moore' (E. Littlemore) has built up a charming romance on the subject, in *The Jessamy Bride*. A recent biographer deprecates any such notion. Mary was only fourteen when they first met, he points out, and the poet's feelings were probably paternal. This is guesswork. In the years that followed, the disparity in age was less marked. Why did Mrs Horneck invite Goldsmith to escort her and her daughters on a long visit to Paris, when it was obvious that no man of his age could enjoy the company of such attractive girls without being seriously affected or disturbed? If she did not consider him as a possible suitor for Mary's hand, she was treating him inconsiderately. Why did the friendship continue, why was he invited to Barton for the New Year Party of 1774? And why did he call Mary his Jessamy (i.e. distinguished) Bride? If he had intimated that he was not in a position to marry and that he had no such intention, these questions would be answered; but such an *éclaircissement*, extremely embarrassing to both parties, is not easy to imagine. If Mary had not been very fond of him, she would not have had his coffin unnailed so that she might take a lock of his hair.

Between Goldsmith and Mary Horneck there existed some feeling quite out of the ordinary. That he was in love with her and that she, at least partly, reciprocated the feeling, is as likely a conjecture as any. But to assume, as most biographers do, that this was no more than a jolly sort of friendship, is to ignore the evidence.

Here then is one of the many blanks in our knowledge of Goldsmith. Renan once pointed out that when we attempt to bring to life the great spirits of the past, 'a share of divination and conjecture should be permitted. A great life is an organic whole which cannot be represented by the mere agglomeration of little facts.' He did not pretend that so to interpret and fill in the blanks would enable us to restore the original, but at least it would present 'one of the ways in which it may have existed'.[1]

There are occasions when the advantages of such a procedure are so manifest as to impose themselves. I have attempted to reconstruct Goldsmith's doings during the Grand Tour by presenting what, in the light of evidence, was likely and possible; while elsewhere I have compensated for 'the silence of the documents' by introducing an outline of the social and political conditions of the time and of the physical environment which affected Goldsmith as closely.

---

[1] *Origines du Christianisme* (ed 1925), Paris, vol I, pp c–cii.

Part Two

THE WORKS

Chapter 17

The Critic

I

Goldsmith had intended to become a physician, but he failed to study systematically and there is no evidence that he received a medical degree. It transpired that his vocation was for writing. Of this he became aware only at the age of twenty-eight when, in April 1757, he began to write book-notices for the *Monthly Review*. Even then he does not seem to have fully committed himself. Yet his education – for which his mother had been mainly responsible – had fitted him admirably for the purpose. He knew Greek, and Latin well, and was acquainted with the principal Latin Classics; he had read widely in English literature since the Restoration and in eighteenth-century French literature. His knowledge of modern English and French writers seems to have been the reason for Griffiths and others employing him; and, as I have shown elsewhere,[1] his familiarity with contemporary French literature explains much of his work as journalist, dramatist and writer on natural history.

He, however, matured late. He was not very well fitted to understand and explain writers from the inside. Much of his critical work is impressionistic, and in the course of time personal vanity rendered him prejudiced. But he was thoughtful, and from the critical notices he wrote, and more particularly from his *Enquiry into the Present State of Polite Learning in Europe*, one can see that he was working towards certain principles of criticism.

Taste was to be the touchstone of excellence in a writer. He defines taste as the power to perceive and enjoy beauty in the

[1] *Les Sources françaises de Goldsmith*, Paris, 1924.

objects of nature; and it is perhaps the only guide for the artist. 'Taste in writing is the exhibition of the greatest quantity of beauty and of use that may be admitted in any description without counteracting each other.' Criticism, he adds, cannot increase taste 'with regard to beauty', because our perceptions of it 'are most vivid in infancy'; but it can 'improve our taste in the useful'. But taste varies in time and space: in space because only in the temperate zones can a people produce works of the highest excellence; in time, because ages of barbarism are unfavourable to literary production. The state of society determines the quality of its literature; and there is a close connexion between literature and morals. Vice fosters stupidity and kills literature; good morals foster intelligence and encourage literature.[1] Goldsmith sees that the various national literatures vary because they express the sensibility and the habits of the peoples which produce them; and he also sees, though he does not of course use the word, that each of them undergoes an evolution from the age of original creation to the age of criticism and commentary, which stifles it. In these observations are implicit the idea of relativity which had been advanced by Saint-Evremond, the sensationalism which derived from Locke, and the vital part played by climate and geography which the Abbé Dubos had developed.

Goldsmith's critical articles vary greatly in value, according to his knowledge of the subject in question and according as they stimulated his interest. His review of Paul-Henri Mallet's *Remains of the Mythology and Poetry of the Celts*[2] does little more than describe the *Edda*, that is, the poem incorporating the Scandinavian and not the Celtic mythology. But his notice on Burke's *Philosophical Enquiry into the Origin of our Ideas of the Sublime and Beautiful*[3] is a close and interesting study. He analyses the book in detail, and, so as not to interrupt Burke's

[1] *Enquiry,* ch XIV, 1774 edition.
[2] *Monthly Review,* April 1757.
[3] Ibid., May 1757.

'chain of reasoning', adds his own reservations in lengthy foot-notes. Burke insists on the distinction between the sublime and the beautiful. Our perception of them derives from our passions or affections, and these originate in the instinct of self-preser-vation and in society. When danger or pain threaten us, they are terrible and give no pleasure, but when the *idea* of these things is excited, it may give delight. Now whatever inspires *ideas* of pain or danger, or, in other words, of the terrible, is the source of the sublime. Secondly, the affections inspired by social intercourse may occasion pleasure, and this gives rise to beauty. Burke associates the sublime with what we can see or hear. Magnitude inspires fear. A gloomy mountain appears more terrible than a verdant; a cloudy sky, than a clear. The roar of a cataract, a peal of thunder, inspire terror. On the contrary, 'the qualities of beauty . . . are comparative small-ness'. A sense of beauty is awakened by what is clear, smooth, delicate and proportioned to ourselves. 'As the sublime is founded on pain and terror . . .' whatever produces this tension must be productive also of the sublime. The idea of beauty, on the other hand, arises from a 'relaxation of the nervous system'.

Goldsmith points out that pleasure and pain may subsist without relation to each other, or may even produce each other. He holds that love and admiration can be sources of the sub-lime. We need not see an object to have an idea of its sublimity. The idea of God is sublime; even ideas can inspire an *idea* of the sublime.

As regards pleasure and pain he is right. One may experience pleasure, and even happiness, on a bed of pain. His real objec-tion to Burke's theory is his confining of the sublime to ideas of terror. He does not, however, question the bases of Burke's reasoning, which were usual at this time. Our ideas derive from sensations, and aesthetic perceptions are inspired, not by the reality of things but by our ideas of them. We do not know whether Burke had read the Abbé Dubos's *Réflexions critiques sur la poésie et la peinture* (1719 and 1733), or whether Goldsmith had, although he possessed a copy in later life. Dubos had explained more convincingly the difference between real emotions and aesthetic emotions, in respect of tragic drama. If, he argues, we saw a real Phèdre dying of poison, we should experience real terror; but as Racine's play is a *copy* of a real action, so the emotion it inspires is a *copy* of the real emotion, but one that gives pleasure.

In the same number of the *Monthly Review* Goldsmith devoted three or four pages to John Home's *Douglas: a Tragedy*. While recognising that it had been well received in an age when the theatre was in the doldrums, he could not refrain from damning it with faint praise.[1]

Of the many other notices which he contributed to the *Monthly* and to the *Critical Review*, in addition to innumerable shorter notices, one can make only a choice. They are usually well-balanced and conscientious. There is much to be said for his amplifying them with copious quotations. In his review of Smollett's *A Complete History of England* he states his own opinion of the qualities needed in an historian and appraises Smollett in a fair and discriminating manner. Dobson's translation of Cardinal de Polignac's Latin poem, *Anti-Lucretius*, inspired Goldsmith to write one of his liveliest reviews (July 1757); very favourable on the whole, though he regrets that the Cardinal had relied so much on Descartes and opposed Gassendi, Newton and Locke. To the *Monthly Review* of August 1757 he contributed a long article on Voltaire's *Essai sur les Moeurs* (Geneva, 1756); but most of this consists of a summary of Voltaire's account of the recent war and a long excerpt from the description of Charles Edward's rebellion. One misses a critical estimate of Voltaire as historian.

The review of Thomas Gray's *Odes* – on 'The Progress of Poesy' and 'The Bard' – is one of his most important. He had

---

[1] It had been welcomed in Edinburgh and at Covent Garden, where Mrs Woffington created the character of Lady Randolph. In later years, Mrs Siddons won applause in this role.

admired Gray's earlier work but now regretted that the imitator of Pindar had not, like Pindar, kept his public constantly in view. The present odes he regards as too remote from what English readers are used to; and the irregular rhymes as involving a 'natural imperfection'. While advising Gray to 'study the people', he tries to do justice to his work by quoting several passages. In Goldsmith's mind Dryden and Pope represented the norm of poetry and the rhymed couplet the verse form par excellence. His taste was reactionary rather than conservative, rational rather than imaginative. He would have admitted the distinction between poetry and versification, without realising the primacy of inspiration. It was precisely from the tyranny of rationalism and the rhymed couplet that Gray was freeing himself. What makes him the major poet of the mid-eighteenth century is not his great learning but his sense of the 'romantic' in nature, his sense of the tragic in human life, his homage to inspiration (in 'The Bard'), his experiments in new verse-forms – all those qualities which make him the great precursor of Romanticism. For this, Goldsmith had no feeling; but his treatment of Gray is always courteous.

It may seem surprising therefore that he should admire Spenser's *Faerie Queene*. He in fact warmly commends Ralph Church for establishing the original text of 'this ancient poet'. The pleasure inspired by allegory he regards as 'of a subordinate nature'; and yet, 'with all his faults, no poet enlarges the imagination more than Spenser'. In reading him, 'all the ages of primeval innocence and happiness rise to our view. Virgil, and even Homer, seem to be modern, upon the comparison.'[1]

Goldsmith positively amuses himself, and his reader, when he has a bad book to review. His notice of William Massey's translation of Ovid's *Fasti* begins with a remark of Madame de la Fayette, 'that a bad translator was like an ignorant footman, whose blundering messages disgraced his master . . .', which

_____
[1] *Critical Review*, February 1759.

sets the note for what follows.[1] Stephen Barrett, who had translated Ovid's *Epistolae*, fares no better than Massey. 'Ovid, as if born to misfortune, has undergone successive metamorphoses,' appearing now as a pedant, now as a rake. Several passages of rhymed couplets are cruelly quoted by Goldsmith, who, however, concedes that Mr Barrett 'may be an excellent schoolmaster'.[2] Very different is the impression he receives from Bion's Elegy on *The Death of Adonis* as translated by John Langhorne. This is a model of what an elegy should be, employing the language of nature and of passion; and he quotes Boileau's strictures on the forced and frigid in style, as showing what an elegy should avoid. He commends Langhorne's version, and hopes it will inspire other translations of minor poets.[3]

Arthur Murphy had adapted Voltaire's *Orphelin de la Chine* (1755) in *The Orphan of China*, which was produced at Drury Lane, Garrick playing Zamti and Mrs Yates Mandane. Goldsmith, in his notice of the printed version,[4] after referring to the current vogue for things Chinese, observes that Chinese novels are the most phlegmatic one can imagine. Voltaire has deviated from his model; Murphy deviates still further; and 'as the plot has become more European, it has become more perfect' (sic). The defect of the present tragedy is that the 'anguish' begins in Act II instead of being more gradually prepared. Preferring to dwell on 'beauties' rather than on faults, he quotes a long dialogue from Act II and the final scene between Zamti and Mandane in Act V. Murphy's play he considers superior to Voltaire's in action and in 'justness of sentiment'. Murphy is, however, gently chided for the letter to Voltaire which accompanies the printed version and which seems hardly courteous to a man to whom he is so greatly indebted.

A very long notice of the Reverend R. Kedington's *Critical*

---

[1] *Critical Review*, November 1757.
[2] Ibid., January 1759
[3] Ibid., March 1759
[4] Ibid., May 1759

Dissertations upon The Iliad of Homer has been ascribed to Goldsmith by Professor R. S. Crane, although neither Percy nor Gibbs identified it as by him. The reviewer, whoever he was, censures a number of typical passages, and concludes that we are not to regard Homer as a model for all epic poets. We have probably improved on Sophocles and Euripides, and why may we not improve on Homer and Virgil, by following 'nature in the dress she wears at present?'[1] Of equally uncertain authorship are 'A Poetical Scale' and its sequel, which appeared in the *Literary Magazine* in January and February 1758. Prior ascribed them to Goldsmith and gave good reasons for his view;[2] many of the opinions of the major English poets which are expressed in these articles are known to have been Goldsmith's. J. W. M. Gibbs published them in his edition,[3] and students of Goldsmith may find it difficult to agree with Professor Friedman's rejection of them. On the other hand, they do no great credit to the writer's judgement. To set Dryden, Addison and Pope above Shakespeare and Milton is not a view that any subsequent age would have endorsed.[4] The very system of classification seems to be defective, and, in

[1] *Critical Review,* 1760. The reviewer finds fault with such passages as the lying dream which Zeus sends to Agamemnon; a detail in Phoenix's description of Achilles' childhood; the taunts and sarcasms which a hero flings at his victim; and Achilles' barbarous treatment of Hector's body – episodes which Kedington defended as would critics of today. All this was a continuation of the 'Querelle d'Homère' in which Houdart de la Motte and Madame Dacier had been the principal protagonists. Although the critic of Kedington's book did not agree with La Motte's travesty of *The Iliad,* he still took eighteenth-century taste as the standard by which Homer should be judged. One reason for ascribing the review to Goldsmith is that certain passages in it are taken from vol V of the *Encyclopédie,* a well-known source of Goldsmith's. But the office of the *Critical Review* may have owned a copy, which was used by contributors. Be that as it may, no critical notice would do more damage to Goldsmith's reputation than this, and I regard his authorship of it as extremely doubtful.

[2] Vol I, pp 232–5.

[3] Vol IV, pp 417–28 and 513–5.

[4] The poets are assessed in respect of genius, judgement, learning and versification, twenty points being given for each of these qualities; but surely one should assign much more for genius than for learning, and certainly for judgement; judgement and versification are perhaps aspects of genius itself. 'Inspiration' might have been a better word to use.

short, admirers of Goldsmith would probably be as ready to see these articles discarded from an edition of his works as they must earnestly hope that he did not write the dreadful review of Kedington's book on *The Iliad*.

II

In the intervals of the above work, Goldsmith had made his one incursion into literary history: *An Enquiry into the Present State of Polite Learning in Europe*, which appeared in April 1759. Such a project would be hard enough for a critic of great learning and mature experience; Goldsmith had probably picked up a good deal of information during his tour of the Continent; in other ways he was scarcely equipped for the task. The book was badly composed. The four opening chapters were too long in proportion to the whole, and the salient points of the argument are not easy to disengage. He revised the work early in 1774 by discarding Chapter IV, the substantial Chapter VII and part of Chapter XII; and by running certain chapters together and renumbering them. But both editions are so defective that it matters little which we prefer.

Taking as his text the often repeated complaint that morals and literature are in decay, he compares the decline of learning and literature in the Greek and Roman world with their decline, real or alleged, in the eighteenth century. The growth of commentary and criticism is accompanied, he thinks, by the decay of art; and while criticism professes to improve taste, it in fact discourages spontaneity. In the original Chapter VII ('The Polite Learning of England and France incapable of comparison') he states his principles of criticism. To be able to receive pleasure 'may be called Taste in the objects of nature'. The arts are an imitation of nature, and for the artist 'Taste is perhaps his only director'. Goldsmith next (Chapter IV) begins to review the 'state of polite learning' in various countries. In Italy he sees swarms of critics, but few original writers, except

Metastasio and F.-G. Maffei. In Chapter VI, as a kind of after-thought, 'Apostolo Zeno, Algarotti, Goldoni, Muratori' are mentioned as deserving 'the highest applause'; but not Baretti, with whom Goldsmith was personally acquainted by 1770, and who was an influential figure both in Italy and in London. Goldsmith may not have heard of Giambattista Vico, whose *Scienza nuova*[1] remains one of the most original contributions ever made to the philosophy of history; but it is extraordinary that, having spent two months or more in Padua and having presumably visited Venice, he should not say more about Carlo Goldoni, who was producing his famous comedies in Venice in the 1750s, and was indeed at the height of his renown.

In Chapter V, on Germany, we read: 'If criticism could have improved the taste of a people, the Germans would have been the most polite nation alive.' But their works are solemn, voluminous and wearisome. The Academy of Berlin is a fine institution, but Goldsmith feels that to have adopted French as its language may have been a mistake. Again, as an after-thought, he mentions Haller, Klopstock and Rabener; (but von Haller was Swiss, not German). The Dutch exhibit the same faults as the Germans in devoting their time to criticism and neglecting their language. Spain is behind the rest of Europe, and polite learning in Denmark is confined to Holberg.

Chapter VII, on French Literature is more informative. Goldsmith rightly regards the age of Louis XIV as superior to that of Louis XV, but considers that contemporary writers 'have not fallen so far short of the merits of their ancestors, as ours have done'. For this he sees four reasons. Their belief in progress and their natural 'self-sufficiency' have given them confidence; noble patrons assist a writer enough to encourage him, but not so much as to induce indolence; ladies expect their admirers to be able to discuss Newton and Locke, and not

---

[1] Naples, 1725; a second edition, 1730; a final redaction, 1744. The work was not well known outside Naples, or indeed anywhere, until Michelet translated and praised it.

simply to sigh and ogle; while the prestige and universality of the language have led other nations to write in French rather than in their own tongue. Of the Frenchmen whose works 'do honour to the age', Voltaire and Montesquieu enjoy the primacy. J.-J. Rousseau, whose most famous writings had not yet appeared, is regarded with amusement. D'Alembert and Diderot are commended without much comment; but Piron and Gresset receive more attention. Goldsmith considers Piron's *La Métromanie* as 'incomparably the best theatrical production that has appeared of late in Europe'. The play is, in fact, exceptionally diverting. He quotes Piron's epitaph on himself :

> Cy-gît Piron qui ne fut rien,
> Pas même Académicien –

by mistakenly inserting 'jamais', to read 'qui ne fut jamais rien'. Of Gresset he names his comedy *Le Méchant* and his humorous poem, *Ver-Vert* – about a learned parrot – as works of merit, which they are; and agrees with Gray in admiring the younger Crébillon.

To this catalogue, he says, other names might be added 'such as Marivaux, Le Franc, Saint-Foix, Destouches and Modonville' by whom 'the character of the present age is tolerably supported'. Here he is associating men of quite unequal merit. Destouches is a delightful writer of social comedy, while Marivaux remains the most popular dramatist in the eighteenth-century repertory. There is something disobliging in Goldsmith's treatment of a writer to whom he was to be more indebted than to any other. He modifies his high opinion of contemporary French literature by deprecating the trend to irreligion, the habit of deriving all arts and sciences from simple principles, and the other habit of publishing dictionaries of all the arts and sciences – hence 'those monsters of learning, the Trévoux, Encyclopédies, and Bibliothèques of the age'. In contributing to such, Diderot and Desmarest 'are candidates for oblivion'!

The following chapters, which are devoted to Great Britain, are more diffuse and more confusing. He ascribes the decline, as he supposes, of our literature, partly to the fact that young writers of merit are neglected or despised, but still more to the influence of criticism. His advice is: 'Write what you think, regardless of the critics.' The stage offers no encouragement for original production; the dramatic poet can please neither managers nor critics. All the public can do is 'to admire even the absurdities of Shakespeare'. To revive his far-fetched conceits and hyperbole 'is rather gibbeting than raising a statue to his memory'.

Goldsmith has reservations in respect of the usefulness of a university education, and he also distinguishes between the various universities. 'There is more value to be acquired from one page of the volume of mankind . . . than in volumes of antiquity.' Mathematics are 'too much studied', being 'a science to which the meanest intellects are equal'.

No one will accuse Goldsmith of not saying what he thinks; one can only regret that he says so much. In respect of contemporary English literature, he mentions no writers by name; but is it true that our writers then fell as far short of their predecessors as he insists? And was not the era which produced Hume in history and philosophy, Richardson, Fielding, Smollett and Sterne in the novel, Thomson, Young, Collins and Gray in poetry, as distinguished as the age of Swift, Pope, Congreve, Addison and Steele? That drama had fallen on evil days will be admitted. Fielding and others had to have recourse to adapting Molière, Destouches and other French dramatists.

The argument that criticism is prejudicial to literature cannot be sustained. A century later, Matthew Arnold argued that English writers, and notably the Romantic poets, suffered from the absence of a body of sound critical writing, such as existed in France and Germany – criticism which would have remedied what is sometimes provincial and eccentric in their work. Goldsmith would have done better to confine his *Enquiry* to English and French literature; and to have cited specific examples of the former. The work as it stands, whether in the 1759 edition or in the 1774 revision, lacks the clear exposition and argument which a reader is entitled to expect. Its principal value is to inform the reader of his views on the authors he had read; but one learns a good deal more from remarks scattered through *The Bee*, the *Essays*, *The Citizen of the World* and the Biographies.

III

Of French writers he could not be expected to know much before Montaigne, whom he quotes more than once with approval. Cartesianism he at first misunderstood, simply repeating Voltaire's misrepresentation. 'The romantic system of Des Cartes was adapted to the taste of the superficial and the indolent'! But Descartes's psychology in the *Traité des Passions* is illuminating and valid, while his metaphysics continues to fascinate philosophers. Some of Descartes's views, on the 'Tourbillons' and the 'Animal Machine' have of course been discarded. Later in life, in his Introduction to *A Survey of Experimental Philosophy*, Goldsmith discusses Descartes at greater length and more dispassionately. He names a number of other scientists, including Pascal who 'improved philosophy by producing new objects of speculation' – and this is his only mention of the greatest and most versatile thinker of the seventeenth century. He alludes to various minor writers, and expresses a high opinion of the grammarian Vaugelas, and of Segrais, whom, in 'The Fame Machine', he puts in the same carriage with Cervantes; but he may have believed Segrais to be the author of Madame de la Fayette's novels. In a paper in *The Bee* on 'Happiness . . . dependent on Constitution' he praises the Cardinal de Retz as possessing a more happy and equable temper than anyone of whom he had ever read. Scarron was one of his favourites. He had probably read *Le*

Roman comique and seems to have translated the first few chapters before he died.[1] He nowhere names La Rochefoucauld and only once appears to be quoting him, and then in a watered-down version of one of the maxims. It may be that La Rochefoucauld's astringent dissection of our motives did not appeal to him. Corneille and Racine he places on the same level with Nicholas Rowe.[2] Like most eighteenth-century critics he speaks of Molière as an undoubted master, and quotes Boileau as an authority; he admires La Bruyère. But it is evident that his knowledge of seventeenth-century French literature was superficial.

Goldsmith's attitude to English literature[3] was somewhat different. For the Elizabethan and Jacobean Ages he felt no great enthusiasm. He naturally deplored the indecency of Restoration Comedy; but he admired Dryden and considered the age of Anne our true Augustan Age. Thus Farquhar, Pope, Addison and Steele appear as the best models, and it is from the standards they set that he regards his contemporaries as having fallen away. In Voltaire's view, poetry and drama were the noble genres: Goldsmith agreed. He set little store by the novel and none at all by the novels which were published in his own day. He thought nothing of Fielding. The story of Dick Whittington, '*were the cat left out*, might be more serviceable to the tender mind than either Tom Jones, Joseph Andrews,

---

[1] See pp 362-4.

[2] Among the many French works in his library at the time of his death, we find four volumes of Corneille, the *Mémoires* of Retz, Boileau's works, a selection of La Fontaine, but nothing of Racine.

[3] The four 'Letters' on 'The History of our own Language' which appeared in the *Literary Magazine* between February and May 1758 were printed by Gibbs (vol IV, pp 437–62) in the belief that they were by Goldsmith. Friedman excludes them from his edition; and the first 'Letter' is so ill-informed and strange that one would be glad to regard it as spurious. The second and third have no particular distinction; but most of the fourth was reprinted by Goldsmith in the last number of *The Bee* (24 November 1759) as 'An Account of the Augustan Age of England'. It is reasonable to conclude, either that he had written this fourth 'Letter', or that he agreed with the estimates expressed in it of the various writers of the age of Queen Anne. These views (of Dryden, Locke, Otway, Pope, Addison and the others) are in line with what we know to have been Goldsmith's opinion.

or a hundred others, where frugality is the only good quality the hero is not possessed of.'[1] Even more surprising is the eulogy of Smollett, who is implied though not named in 'The Fame Machine'.[2] The coachman admits this person on the ground that 'a well written romance is no such easy task as is generally imagined'. Could the heroes of *Roderick Random* and *Peregrine Pickle* be particularly 'serviceable to the tender mind'? But Smollett was shortly afterwards to employ Goldsmith on *The British Magazine*, and there may here be some explanation. If Smollett is eulogised but not named, Sterne is both named and attacked. Letter LIII in the 1762 edition of *The Citizen of the World* is headed: 'The absurd taste for obscene and pert novels, such as "Tristram Shandy," ridiculed.' In Letter LXXV, after disparaging French romances, Goldsmith adds: 'In England, if a bawdy blockhead thus breaks in on the community, he sets his whole fraternity in a roar.' Some years later, when he was talking with Johnson, the latter said: 'Sir, any man who has a name, or who has the power of pleasing, will be very generally invited in London. The man Sterne, I have been told, has had engagements for three months.'

> *Goldsmith:* 'And a very dull fellow.'
> *Johnson:* 'Why no, Sir.'

So much for *Tristram Shandy*, of which the first six volumes had appeared by 1762. Already in 1760 London hostesses were vying with one another to entertain Sterne. The *Sentimental Journey*, which has been more widely and more justly appreciated than *Tristram Shandy*, did not appear until 1768.

Taking Goldsmith's opinions as a whole, one feels obliged to concede that, in the role of a critic of English literature, he had no more insight than as a critic of French; and – what is even more surprising – that French critics understood the

[1] *The Bee,* 10 November 1759.
[2] Ibid., 27 October 1759.

novelty and importance of contemporary English literature better than Goldsmith did.

The inner trend of poetic feeling after about 1725 was drawing writers away from the so-called 'Augustan' ideal. Edward Young first expressed in memorable verse that sense of the tragic and irreparable which made the melancholy of Gray seem pleasant by comparison. Thomson and Collins were cultivating the poetry of nature; Gray was experimenting in his *Odes* on lines that would be developed later. Without the work of these pre-Romantics, Wordsworth and his contemporaries could never have written as they did. Now all these poets were known in France, translated and often imitated. Indeed, the literary production of Britain had been followed closely in Paris since the 1730s, and even more closely after 1754 by the *Journal étranger* and after 1764 by the *Gazette littéraire*, both of which reviewed English books.

The French also understood the significance of the English novel. Many of them, wearied of wit and laughter, greeted with enthusiasm the stories of Pamela and Clarissa, the more so as they read them in translations which abridged the *longueurs* and improved the style. From these novels, and also from the *Nouvelle Héloïse*,[1] arose a new ideal type, that of 'the sensitive soul', incarnate in a drawing of a young girl whose eyes are turned skyward on the verge of tears.[2]

With Fielding, not a sentimentalist, it was of course another matter. His three principal novels were translated between 1743 and 1762. The low jinks of which Parson Adams is the victim reminded French readers too much, as Joseph Texte observes,[3] of Scarron and Furetière, of whom they were tired; whereas the honest realism of *Tom Jones* was understood only by the

---

[1] Which owed something to Richardson, including the epistolary form.

[2] Daniel Mornet, *Le Romantisme en France au XVIIIᵉ siècle* (Paris, 1912) shows how after about 1725 a part of the public was as romantic-minded as the 'Romantics' of 1830.

[3] *Jean-Jacques Rousseau et les origines du cosmopolitisme littéraire*, Paris, 1895, pp 176–7.

discerning. Here, as Madame du Deffand saw, were truth and 'true lessons in morality'.[1] Most people indeed saw that *Tom Jones* possessed 'truth and gaiety', while failing to perceive its deeper significance. Only La Harpe declared frankly: 'Pour moi, *Tom Jones* est le premier roman du monde.' He recognised that, as distinct from the novel of analysis, in which the French were truly masters, the realistic novel, depicting a whole community and not two or three persons, had been launched by Fielding and that it was an event of exceptional significance.

Goldsmith, however, seems to have been insensitive to the significance of Fielding and Sterne; and also to what was original and forward-looking in the pre-Romantic poets; in brief, to the kinds of writing that prepared the way for the flowering of Romantic poetry and of the Romantic and Victorian novel.[2]

[1] Letters to Horace Walpole, 14 July and 8 August 1773.

[2] The seven papers 'On the Study of the Belles Lettres', which appeared in the *British Magazine* between July 1761 and January 1763, were ascribed by Percy to Goldsmith and reprinted by Gibbs in his edition of the *Works*. Cunningham, however, gave reasons for doubting Goldsmith's authorship of them; and Friedman has excluded them from his edition. They are carefully composed and are the work of a very learned writer. Collectively, they constitute a kind of *Ars Poetica*. It is not easy to see, however, during the period in question, how Goldsmith could have found time to compose so careful a series; and also whether, as Cunningham argued, he would have paid the attention to Scottish poets which appears in them. A great difficulty in determining the authorship of so many anonymous papers published between 1758 and 1763 is that, in critical writing, Goldsmith's style is not personal enough to enable one to distinguish it from that of other journalists. Nor are his critical writings and 'Essays' marked by anything that can be called 'genius', unless we accord that term to the 'Chinese Letters' as a whole. Although the writer is loth to believe that Goldsmith could have written the review of Kedington's book on the *Iliad*, it seems better to accept in regard to the 'Belles Lettres' series Professor Friedman's opinion (see his edition, Oxford, 1966, vol III, pp *vi–xiv*).

Chapter 18

The Journalist

Having made himself known as an incisive and readable book-reviewer, Goldsmith next embarked on literary journalism. His ventures consisted of *The Bee*, a weekly periodical; a large variety of papers, many of which he collected and published as *Essays* in 1765 and 1766; and especially the 'Chinese Letters' of 1760 and 1761 which were issued as *The Citizen of the World* in 1762. These writings enabled him to make a living, if a precarious one. They are very uneven in quality. In some the matter is decidedly mediocre; the best are humorous sketches of London life. All are marked by an improvement in his prose-style and a remarkable command of English. During the first two or three years he relies too often on translating or adapting passages from foreign writers, especially French; but in the course of time he writes more and more from his own observation, and his work becomes more personal and original.

On 6 October 1759 he launched *The Bee: being Essays on the most interesting subjects*, with, as epigraph from Lucretius:

> '*Floriferis ut Apes in saltibus omnia libant*
> *Omnia nos itidem.*'

A number appeared every Saturday until 24 November, when he abandoned the project. This periodical followed the tradition of *The Spectator* (1711–12), but derived more nearly from the Dutch and French magazines which the originality and success of that work had called into being. These were Justus van Effen's *Le Misanthrope* (1711) and especially Marivaux' three journals.

Of all contemporary French writers none was more popular nor more appreciated in England than Marivaux, less, paradoxically, for his plays, than for these journals of moral observation, and in a lesser degree, for his novels. Lesbros, in *L'Esprit de Marivaux* (1769), was to write: 'His *Spectateur français* won him the honour of being placed by the English above La Bruyère'; while D'Alembert declared that 'They [the English] are so favourable to Marivaux that they reproach us with not showing him enough esteem.' One can well believe this from the example of Thomas Gray, who said that his idea of Paradise was of a place where one could read perpetual novels by Marivaux and the younger Crébillon. Marivaux, after producing a number of very original plays for the Théâtre Italien, had ventured into journalism in May 1721 with *Le Spectateur français*; he resumed it in January 1722 and continued it at irregular intervals until 1724, having issued twenty-five 'feuilles' in all. In 1728 he launched *L'Indigent Philosophe* which had a shorter existence, with only seven numbers; and in 1734 *Le Cabinet du Philosophe*, which he discontinued after the eleventh. These journals contain some of the best of his writings.[1]

Marivaux, who was to be Goldsmith's great stand-by, had not been an imitator of Addison and Steele. The English *Spectator* had unity of design; it described the characters and doings of a circle of which 'Mr Spectator' was the centre. The observations were urbane and mildly ironical, and it owed its success to its novelty, its gentlemanliness, and above all to its style. Finally, it was business-like. A number appeared every day at tea-time, and there were in all 555 numbers, of which rather more than half were by Addison and most of the others by Steele.

[1] There is now a complete edition of Marivaux's *Journaux et Oeuvres diverses*, ed F. Deloffre and M. Gilot, Garnier, 1969.

Marivaux' design was different, and less systematic. His 'Spectateur' is a man rather advanced in years and in knowledge of the world. He relates his chance experiences, he makes the people he meets relate theirs, according to their characters and positions in life. He is preoccupied with problems of social life, education and morals, and he is a Christian observer. He pities the poor and unfortunate. Nourished on Pascal and La Rochefoucauld, he is more thoughtful and more profound than the English spectator. For the rest, he sometimes reviews a new book, or describes a current event, or invents a story. As in his plays, he is markedly original.[1] Finally, he is an artist, a man of good taste. In *L'Indigent Philosophe*, the narrator is a man who has wasted his substance, yet remains gay and observant; he is now the 'Spectateur'. The design here is more objective but the spirit is similar. Each 'feuille', or number, of these periodicals contains a single essay or story, there is no consecutive plan, but all are animated by the same spirit of sympathetic or amused observation.

Goldsmith's plan is different again. Each number of *The Bee* is a miscellany, containing four, five or even seven articles with no particular connexion; moral speculations, short stories, fragments of history, remarks on the theatre, and so on. He flits like a bee from one flower to the next, unexpectedly; and the reason is clear. He could not produce five original papers every week. Sometimes he records his own observations as in the striking 'Happiness in a large measure dependent on Constitution', in the paper on 'The Sagacity of some Insects', and in his remarks on the Stage; but for the greater number of papers, including most of the best, he simply lifts whole passages from Van Effen, and from Volume V of the *Encyclopédie*, or in four instances, takes the ideas and sometimes the words from *Le Spectateur français*. Thus 'A Letter from a

---

[1] Even so, he almost certainly had some knowledge of Shakespeare and more recent English dramatists. Madame Lucette Desvignes-Parent has studied this question for some years and published her findings in *Marivaux et l'Angleterre*, Paris, 1970.

Traveller', and 'The Sentiments of a Frenchman on the Temper of the English' are translated from Van Effen's *Le Misanthrope*. The 'Story of Alcander and Septimius' comes not, as he states, from a 'Byzantine Historian', but from the *Decamerone*. 'A City Night Piece' in No. IV is different, in that it is a skilful fusion of personal experience, and perhaps imagination, with an expression of a feeling of pity borrowed from Marivaux. Goldsmith has been reading and writing in his garret:

'The clock has struck two, the expiring taper rises and sinks in its socket, the watchman forgets the hour in slumber, the laborious and the happy are at rest, and nothing now wakes but guilt, revelry and despair. The drunkard once more fills the destroying bowl, the robber walks his midnight round, and the suicide lifts his guilty arm against his own sacred person.'

So he walks out into the deserted street:

'What a gloom hangs all around! The dying lamp feebly emits a yellow gleam; no sound is heard but of the chiming clock, or the distant watch-dog. . . .'

Perhaps this city, like others in the past, will one day be no more than a heap of ruins. Yet, even at this hour, the streets are not tenantless. Who are these sleeping at the doors of the opulent, from whom they will get neither pity nor redress? 'These poor shivering females' who 'have been prostituted to the gay luxurious villain, and are now turned out to meet the severity of winter. . . .'

'Why, Why was I born a man, and yet see the sufferings of wretches I cannot relieve! Poor, houseless creatures. . . .
'Why was this heart of mine formed with so much sensibility! or why was not my fortune adapted to its impulse!'

There is feeling here; probably observation; but certainly 'literature'. In the fourth 'feuille' of his *Spectateur*, Marivaux tells of the distress of a young girl whom he has encountered. Her father was dead, her mother in danger of losing a lawsuit against an influential adversary. In despair she has appealed to a 'riche bourgeois' who is very ready to assist her family on condition of her giving herself to him. Hitherto she has resisted. The 'Spectateur' has no means of helping her, and he reflects: 'Qu'il est triste de voir souffrir quelqu'un quand on n'est point en état de le secourir, et qu'on a reçu de la nature une âme sensible, qui pénètre toute l'affliction des malheureux. . . .'

Repeating these exclamations at greater length, Goldsmith has dramatised the episode and turned the virtuous French girl into a 'shivering female' who has been the victim of a 'luxurious villain'. 'A City Night Piece' is one of his most successful efforts. The essay 'Of Eloquence and Sermons' also derives from Marivaux. But, curiously, the articles which contain some original matter are less characteristic than the pieces translated without acknowledgement.[1] It is not that he was insincere or averse from expressing his opinions. In some of the questions discussed he was keenly interested. The theatre fascinated him. 'Upon Political Frugality', a long and closely reasoned article, raises the question of luxury, a topic dear to eighteenth-century economic thinkers. Should government encourage opulence and luxury, or provide only the necessities of life and promote simplicity of manners? Goldsmith commends 'a just mean between both extremes' – of prodigality and avarice. This subject continued to occupy him and he returned to it in *The Deserted Village*.

The Bee was not a commercial success, whether because a miscellany which contained no topical scandal and no political

---

[1] Professor Friedman, while admitting that no source has yet been found for the story of 'Sabinus and Olinda', suspects that it has been borrowed, like many of the other pieces.

commentary did not appeal to the public, or because readers ended by suspecting that most of it was not Goldsmith's original work at all.

II

In spite of this set-back he continued to write articles and stories, for the *Busy Body*, the *Royal Magazine*, the *British Magazine*, the *Lady's Magazine*, and *Lloyd's Evening Post*. The seven papers 'On the Study of the Belles Lettres' (*British Magazine*, between July 1761 and January 1763) have already been examined. The important 'Essay on the Theatre' (*Westminster Magazine*, 1 January 1773) will be considered later. In 1765, when *The Traveller* had won him a certain reputation, he collected over twenty of these papers and published them as *Essays by Mr Goldsmith*. To a further edition, in 1766, he added 'Alcander and Septimius' from *The Bee*, and five pieces from various periodicals. A few other anonymous articles, which have been ascribed to him only in recent years, were never collected, and Goldsmith's authorship must still be considered unproved.

It will be enough to examine five or six of the pieces contained in the so-called *Essays* to convey an idea of his ability in this kind of journalism.

One of the more ambitious is 'A Reverie at the Boar's Head Tavern in Eastcheap'. Sitting here one evening, the narrator has called for another bottle to 'toast the memory of Shakespear, Falstaff, and all the merry men of Eastcheap. . . . Here, by the pleasant fire, in the very room where old Sir John Falstaff cracked his jokes, in the very chair which was sometimes honoured by Prince Henry . . . I sat and ruminated on the follies of youth . . . and transported my imagination back to the times when [they] gave life to the revel.' While talking with the landlord, he dozes off and while the room remains the same, the landlord is transformed into Dame Quickly, who engages him in a lively conversation.

This is a promising start, and would be still better if we did not know that the old Boar's Head Tavern had been destroyed in the Great Fire. Even so, the sequel is disappointing. Dame Quickly, who has the gift of prophecy, describes how the old tavern was 'purified' by the Prior of a neighbouring convent and turned into a monastery, how it was 'filled with continual lewdness'; how Wycliffites were burned there, and then the Prior himself on a charge of witchcraft; how it was again used as a tavern and set apart for riot and debauchery; how monarchs themselves took part in such lewdness, and so on. And at intervals, Dame Quickly interrupts the narrative of debauchery and violence by exclaiming: 'Those, those were the times, Mr Rigmarole! You see how much more just our ancestors were than us!' The best one can say of this dull and sordid 'Reverie' is that readers may have been gratified with the reflexion that they were living in a 'politer' age.

Goldsmith was catering for a different class of reader in 'The History of Miss Stanton',[1] which, it is implied, is a true story. There resided in the north of England a clergyman, a widower named Stanton, who possessed a small fortune. Persistent in 'benevolence and his duty', he 'was esteemed by the rich and beloved by the poor'. For his only child, Fanny, his tenderness increased with the passing years. Every morning he gave her 'lessons in morality', and engaged the best masters to instruct her in music and dancing. But a gentleman whom we will call Dawson happened to pass that way and to cast his eyes on the lovely Fanny. Posing as a scholar, he ingratiated himself with the parson, who often entertained him. He in turn invited Stanton and Fanny to his own home, forty miles away, and impressed them with his wealth and 'grandeur'. He then set about seducing Fanny and at last 'succeeded in his villainous design'. The affair became known, and Mr Stanton, though

[1] *British Magazine,* July 1760.

reduced to agony and despair, determined that the betrayer should 'pay for it'. He called on Dawson and, 'with his eyes bathed in tears', fell at Dawson's feet and implored him 'to wipe away the infamy'. The other 'desired him to have done'; whereupon the old man, rising to his feet, produced two pistols, and gave one to Dawson. They withdrew to a proper distance and fired. Stanton fell. Fanny rushed up and 'in an agony of distress she fell lifeless upon the body'; but, recovering consciousness, displayed such extremity of affliction that Dawson himself was overcome with anguish, 'flew to the lovely mourner, and offered to repair his foul offences by matrimony'. At this, old Stanton (who, as Voltaire would say, had not been completely murdered) stood up and demanded fulfilment of the promise. Dawson 'had too much honour to refuse. They were immediately conducted to church . . . and now live exemplary instances of conjugal love and felicity'.

One wonders if any reader took this tissue of absurdities for anything but a parody of romantic fiction and a mark of Goldsmith's contempt of it. 'The History of Miss Stanton' clearly provides an outline of the story of Olivia and young Thornhill in *The Vicar of Wakefield.*

From this exercise in a rather heavy irony, Goldsmith passed to the opposite extreme of lively and full-blooded realism. The influence of Marivaux fills all this period of his life, as appears in his later 'Specimen of a Magazine' under the heading of *The Indigent Philosopher*, a title taken from Marivaux' second periodical, *L'Indigent Philosophe.* After a dedication to the Ambassador of Tripoli, Goldsmith invents 'a speech spoken by the Indigent Philosopher to persuade his Club at Cateaton not to declare War against Spain' – a mark of Tory opposition to Pitt's aggressive foreign policy. These pieces appeared in *Lloyd's Evening Post* in January and February 1762; but already in October 1760 he had turned his reading of Marivaux' second periodical to more substantial account. 'The Adventures of a Strolling Player,' one of his most popular short stories, is adapted and in large part translated (without acknowledgement) from an unfinished story in the second and third 'feuilles' of *L'Indigent Philosophe*. Marivaux' narrator has dissipated a large fortune, but in spite of his indigence leads a life of carefree gaiety. One day, in the house of a charitable gentleman, he meets a vagabond who invites him to the tavern. Wine is served and the vagabond begins with a lyrical rhapsody on the existence of beggars, then relates the story of his life. Goldsmith says he was strolling in St James's Park when he fell into conversation with a shabbily-dressed man, who had quarrelled with his employer and had come here to starve. Yet few people are merrier than he. Having some pence in his pocket, he invites his new acquaintance to 'a steak and a tankard' in a neighbouring alehouse. At this point Goldsmith begins to adapt and translate the story of Marivaux' vagabond, the account of his adventures in the army, as the servant of a country-priest and finally as a stage-player. Both the narrative and the vagabond's talk are marvellously vivid and picturesque. The conclusion of the story is of Goldsmith's invention, as are the local colour and the circumstantial details. It would be impossible, without quoting a substantial extract, to convey any real notion of the *verve* and, if one may say so, the 'actuality' of this narrative. It reveals Goldsmith in 1760 at the top of his form as a humourist and stylist. If Marivaux excelled in originating characters and inventing stories, Goldsmith was good at developing and adding picturesque details to other men's inventions.

In December 1759 he had tried his hand at another kind of fiction, very popular at the time, and characterised by the use of oriental magic for the purpose of edification. This was 'Asem: an Eastern Tale', or, as it was first entitled, 'The Proceedings of Providence vindicated'.

In a cavern of Mount Taurus dwells Asem the Man-hater. Having wasted his substance by ill-considered generosity, he has found, when reduced to poverty, that those whom he had

H

assisted have now turned their back on him. Disgusted by their ingratitude, he has come 'to brood over his resentment in solitude'. From his rocky shelter he gazes over the glassy lake below and the cloud-capped peak beyond. How fair is Nature! How just and reasonable! Man alone 'is a solecism. . . . Were men entirely free from vice, all would be uniformity, harmony and order.' How can it be that Allah is perfect and that his creatures are not?

He is about to plunge into the lake and so put an end to despair, when a majestic Genie appears. This envoy of Mahomet conducts him beneath the waters to a world which Allah has created to satisfy the ideas of the Prophet; for Mahomet had once shared Asem's doubts and dissatisfaction. It is the land of men without vice. At first he advances in a state of beatitude; but by and by he sees a man pursued by an army of squirrels, and another by a pack of savage dogs. These people are too indulgent to tyrannise over the beasts and too gentle to resist them. They have no cities, no fine houses, only dwellings just sufficient to afford shelter, for they are too good to indulge in the arts which minister to pride or inspire envy in others. There is no wisdom here, for wisdom is a sense of our duties and in this land everyone knows what he should do. There is no social organisation. All societies arise out of fear or friendship; and these people are too kind to fear each other and, being all equally good, have no motive for forming friendships. They have no occasion for communicating ideas, since this would lead to flattery and curiosity, which are vices. They possess only just enough for their needs, and so if one of them falls sick, no one can help him. Gratitude therefore is unknown in this country. Its inhabitants practise no virtues except temperance, and the virtues we esteem are unknown here.

Asem confesses 'that to be unacquainted with vice is not to know virtue', and he begs the Genie to take him back to the world which Allah had created without the advice of his Prophet. There he will abstain from vice and pity it in others.

Asem awakes on the rock where the divine vision had visited him. Returning to his native city, he applies himself to commerce and by practising frugality (a word dear to Goldsmith) soon grows opulent. His friends come to see him, nor does he disdain them; and an unhappy youth is 'concluded with an old age of elegance, affluence and ease'.

Knowing Goldsmith's habits as we do, it is difficult to suppose that all this is of his invention. The initial situation had indeed been set out by Marivaux in the thirteenth *feuille* of the *Spectateur français* with more economy and greater effect. Here he tells how one evening the sage Anacharsis asks hospitality of a misanthrope who lives alone in 'a house at the foot of a mountain'. The solitary, whose name is Hermocrates, relates the story of his life and the reason for his hatred of mankind. Sprung from a family, once senators of Athens, he had 'l'âme généreuse et sensible', and loved nothing so much as 'the pleasure of obliging others' (like Sir William Thornhill in *The Vicar of Wakefield*). His liberality caused everyone to love him, but he was imprudent to count on gratitude. When competing for 'an honourable post', no one supported him and a rival was appointed: a dangerous man whom people feared. Hermocrates consulted a philosopher who gave him a magic powder; when mixed with wine, it had the virtue of making men sincere. So he invited his friends to a banquet and by this means discovered the truth. They liked him, but were not sure of him. One of them explained that in certain men

'... their vices ... give them an importance which your virtue does not give you. ... I like you, because you will always be kind to me; but you weary me because you will never be unkind to anyone. ... Tell me! in what way do you incite us to serve you? ... it is not worth while putting one self out for a man whose kindness cannot be rebuffed and whom no one can provoke to resentment. ...'

Furious in face of such egoism, Hermocrates had got rid of his friends and come to live in the wilderness.

The fragment is one of Marivaux' original ideas which, as so often, he did not trouble to develop. Goldsmith knew this number of the *Spectateur français* because he translated the beginning of it in Letter LXVI of *The Citizen of the World*, in the essay on 'The Difference between Love and Gratitude'. Asem, however, apart from the initial situation, is not an imitation of it. The Genie and the visit to the country of men without vice may have been Goldsmith's invention; but the ideas on the wisdom of the Creator had been disseminated over the past half-century by such writers as William Derham, John Clarke and William King, and are in keeping with the optimism of Pope and his disciples. Marivaux, following La Rochefoucauld, was content with noting the facts; but Goldsmith probably felt that these would displease a public which preferred its illusions about human nature. The Genie's argument has the same object as that of the Angel (disguised as a hermit) in the later part of *Zadig* (1747), when he seeks to prove, by a series of practical demonstrations, in what a wonderful and mysterious way Providence works for our advantage; but there is this difference, that whereas Asem fully accepts the Genie's demonstration, Zadig still raises objections, even when the Hermit has changed into the Angel: 'Mais, s'il n'y avait que du bien, et point de mal?' – 'Mais . . .?' Even so, Asem is one of the most pleasing of the pieces published in the 1765 and 1766 collections.

If the paper entitled 'A Comparative View of Races and Nations' was by Goldsmith,[1] it shows him in a more than usual ironical mood. The writer describes the feelings of an imaginary Englishman who has returned home after an absence of fifteen years. He finds more pleasure 'in cultivating

---

[1] *Royal Magazine*, June 1760. Professor Crane believed this paper to be by Goldsmith, and Professor Friedman has reprinted it in the *Collected Works*, vol III, pp 66–77.

his little kitchen-garden . . . than when indolently stretched beneath the luxuriant shades of Pisa. . . .'

'Hail Britain, happiest of countries! happy in thy climate, fertility, situation, and commerce; but still happier in the peculiar nature of thy laws and government. . . . What constitutes the peculiar happiness of Britain is, that laws may be overlooked without endangering the state.'

He continues: 'England is not less happy with respect to climate: the almost continual spring of Italy does not indeed adorn our fields. . . .' and so on! Whoever wrote this was either very ignorant or very ironical.

More worthy of Goldsmith are the papers 'on National Prejudices' and 'Of the English Clergy, and Popular Preachers'. Being, as he alleges, one of those mortals who spend most of their time in taverns and coffee-houses, he was recently drawn into conversation with some men engaged in a political argument. One of them had raised the question of the various national characters of Europeans, when another declared that the Dutch were 'avaricious wretches', the French 'flattering sycophants', the Germans 'drunken sots and beastly gluttons', and the Spaniards 'haughty and surly tyrants'; whereas 'in bravery, generosity, clemency and in every other virtue, the English excelled all the rest of the world'. The speaker insisted on Goldsmith's giving his opinion; but Goldsmith suggested that, before speaking so peremptorily, one should visit the various countries and carefully study the natives; after which one might recognise 'that the Dutch were more frugal and industrious, the French more temperate and polite, the Germans more hardy and patient of labour . . . and the Spaniards more staid and sedate, than the English'. But his opinion gave so much offence that he paid his score and, retiring to his room, reflected on the absurdity of such prejudices as he had listened to. Among the famous sayings of antiquity none, he thinks, did more honour to its author than that of the philosopher who declared himself 'a citizen of the world.' If one may not love and serve one's country without hating the natives of others, he himself would prefer that title to the name of 'an Englishman, Frenchman, European, or any other appellation whatsoever'. Goldsmith was composing the *Chinese Letters* at this time. Naturally and rightly he had not forgotten his Irishness; he had probably appreciated his treatment in Paris; and generally he was in a cosmopolitan mood. Ten years later he had become a good deal Anglicised – so much so, as will be recalled, that when revisiting Paris, he had felt far less at home than most Englishmen of distinction who at once made friends with the Parisian anglophiles.

The Essay 'Of the English Clergy, and Popular Preachers'[1] is perhaps the best in the collection, both for the good sense of the argument and for the sincere expression of personal opinion. Although 'English divines receive a more liberal education . . .', in his view, 'than any others . . . they are nowhere so little thought of by the populace as here . . . the vulgar in general appearing no way impressed with a sense of religious duty'. The sermons we hear in England are usually 'dry . . . and unaffecting'. Reason is helpless when a preacher aims at curbing indulgence in strong passions; he must fight them by invoking another passion, if possible stronger. Goldsmith regards English preachers as too often bashful and afraid of offending their audience; whereas the French 'assume all that dignity which becomes men who are ambassadors of Christ'. As an example of their effectiveness, he translates a long passage from the beginning of the first sermon which Massillon preached. He had perceived that the members of his congregation were heedless or indifferent, but he completely changed their attitude by the striking images he evoked and by

---

[1] Entitled 'Some Remarks on the modern manner of Preaching' in *The Lady's Magazine*, December 1760.

the immediacy of his appeal to their emotions. Massillon was no stern theologian like Bossuet but rather a man of sensibility and popular appeal. The eighteenth-century preferred him to the great orators of the Age of Louis XIV, and in fact Goldsmith found this passage, not in Massillon's published works but in the *Encyclopédie*![1] Apart from the need of dignity and assurance, a preacher should remember that the talents needed for effective speech are quite different from those needed for effective writing; that 'a just and manly sincerity' will usually inspire respect; and that in controverting the deists, it is better to attack them than to defend. Goldsmith, who felt little sympathy for Methodism, still thought that young Anglican preachers might well take as their model the 'earnest manner of Whitfield'.

It will have been noticed that the collected *Essays* of 1765 and 1766 are as miscellaneous as the articles in *The Bee*; that three of them possibly deserved reprinting, but that most are hardly worthy of a serious writer. The essay is a reflective or speculative genre, even when its starting-point is a material experience, and many of these pieces are short stories. Even so, the collected editions were warmly praised by *The Critical Review* and by *Lloyd's Evening Post*; but not by *The Monthly Review*, with which Goldsmith had been at odds.

'It is easy (wrote the anonymous critic) to collect from books and conversations a sufficiency of superficial knowledge to enable a writer to flourish away with tolerable propriety; but when these his lucubrations assume the form of a book, it is also easy for the critical reader to discover whether they possess that consistency of sentiment which attends on real knowledge,

---

[1] *Works,* ed Friedman, vol III, p 153, note. Goldsmith had written 'The Bishop of Massillon', a curious blunder. Massillon (born at Hyères) was an Oratorian, and had lived and preached in Paris during the Regency before becoming Bishop of Clermont.

and distinguishes the author who writes from his own ideas, from the copyist of other men's thoughts.'

This criticism, though probably dictated by personal animosity, certainly pinpoints Goldsmith's literary vices, but it might have singled out for praise the three or four pieces which stand out above the rest, and also done more justice to the style. It is true, however, that the collection contains no 'consistency of sentiment', and also that Goldsmith did frequently copy 'other men's thoughts'.

III

After 1763 Goldsmith abandoned journalism of this kind in favour of ambitious compilations and occasionally an original work. In 1767 however he contributed to Hugh Kelly's periodical, *The Babler*, an 'Essay on Friendship', which was reprinted by the *Universal Magazine* in April 1774, the month of his death.[1] After deprecating the view of friendship as presented in novels and romances, Goldsmith argues that, rather than being sought for and cultivated, it should be allowed to spring up of itself. Similarity of temperament, community of interests, sometimes even a diversity of pursuits, may give rise to it. But it cannot be purchased by gifts or service. Men dislike being placed under an obligation and are disposed to be friends only when debts of gratitude are equally shared. Goldsmith illustrates this view by a perhaps imaginary story. The kind and wealthy Plautinus desired the friendship of Musidorus, and gave him many presents together with assurances of his friendliness. But while the other's circumstances obliged him to accept them, he was too proud to give his heart. People naturally regarded him as most ungrateful. But when Plautinus, having dissipated his fortune (like Asem, the Man in Black and Sir William Thornhill) had fallen into poverty, Musidorus at

[1] I owe these bibliographical details to Professor Friedman's edition, vol II, pp 199–200.

once came to his aid and helped to restore him to his former estate. Obligations being now evenly balanced, it was possible for them to become friends.

'The History of Cyrillo Padovano, the Sleep-Walker' appeared in *The Westminster Magazine* for February 1773, and was thus the last of Goldsmith's journalistic publications. As a schoolboy this Cyril displayed no ability. Having failed to solve a problem which his master had set for homework, he went to bed in a state of despondency; but on getting up next morning, he found the problem correctly worked out and in his own hand. He subsequently entered the Carthusian order, where during his waking life he was noted for piety and virtue. When sleep-walking, however, he not only shocked the other monks by unseemly mirth but actually rifled the altar of the church, concealed the vestments under his mattress and was as surprised as anyone on finding them there. Finally, after a wealthy benefactress had been buried in the conventual church, Cyrillo actually opened the grave and mutilated her fingers in order to remove the jewelled rings. He himself, when awake, was horrified by what he had done; but having been transferred to a convent where the Prior was empowered to confine the monks to their cells, he passed the rest of his life in a most exemplary manner.

One would have supposed that this Cyril was really a Paduan and that Goldsmith had heard of him when staying in Padua. That city may indeed have been the home of someone like him. But it appears that for the above paper the material was taken from the same sources as were used in the chapter on Sleep in Volume II of the *Animated Nature*, which Goldsmith was compiling at this time. The astonishing feat ascribed to Cyrillo as a schoolboy was really that of a student (perhaps German) described in the *Miscellanea curiosa medico-physica* . . ., a Leipzig publication (1670–1706);[1] while his exploits in a

---

[1] Winifred Lynskey, *Goldsmith's Interest in Natural History, 1759–74*, University of Chicago thesis, 1940.

Carthusian convent seem to be adapted from the story of an Italian Franciscan, named Arlotto.[1] To ascribe these separate stories to one and the same person was a mark of Goldsmith's occasional habit of mingling fact and fiction.

[1] I am again indebted to the Friedman edition, II, 215, for these details.

Chapter 19

The Biographer

It was characteristic of Goldsmith that his first essay in biography should have been the *Memoirs of Monsieur de Voltaire*. There was no writer, or at least no contemporary, whom he so greatly admired. The work had been announced in the *Public Advertiser* of 7 February 1759, as preceding a new translation of the *Henriade* and to be published by Griffiths. In a letter to his brother Henry he described it as a catch-penny, and said he had written it in a month and sold it for £20. It appeared, not with the *Henriade*, but as a serial in the *Ladies' Magazine* in 1761.

In a rapid outline of the principal events of his hero's life, Goldsmith concentrates on such episodes as the long dispute about *L'Oedipe* with Houdart de la Motte, and especially his sojourn in England; the friends he made there; the rapidity with which he learned English; his appreciation of Shakespeare; and how he popularised English poets on the Continent. There are good anecdotes, like the interview with the Duchess of Marlborough, whose memoirs he had offered to write, but who decided that he was merely 'a fool or a philosopher'. Congreve shocked him by his desire to be regarded rather as a country gentleman than as a poet. The narrative elsewhere is filled out by translations of Voltaire's 'Discours des Trois Unités', of the 'Discours sur la Tragédie' which had served as preface to *Brutus*, and of three letters of Voltaire's, which Goldsmith had probably found in the *Mercure* and the *Journal encyclopédique*. The best anecdote is of the joke which Piron once played on Voltaire. He had handed him a panegyric in verse, written supposedly by a young lady in a distant province, who had become enamoured of Voltaire's genius. The latter fell into the trap and engaged in correspondence with this imaginary adorer, dispatching letters so ardent that he actually in the end fell in love with her. Thereupon Piron promised to bring her to Paris. She is starting; she is on her way. Voltaire awaits her with all a lover's impatience. She arrives. Voltaire, in his best finery, rushes to the meeting-place, only to find Piron grotesquely attired as a woman, and Madame du Châtelet, Voltaire's mistress.

Goldsmith had singled out, from the first, one of Voltaire's leading qualities, the untiring activity which produced a stream of poems, tragedies, controversial writings, thousands of letters, and two so-called epics, the second of which, *La Pucelle*, exiled him from Paris until the year of his death. The last pages of the essay describe the company of wits and scientists which graced the court of Potsdam. Voltaire is represented as filling the most honourable role there and enjoying 'the strongest marks' of Frederick's friendship. And the essay ends before Voltaire's fall from favour and departure for Switzerland. It is curious, however, that Goldsmith says nothing of Voltaire's *Contes*. Their author set little store by them, yet they are the works of his that are now most generally read, and on which his literary reputation is most securely founded. *Micromégas* and *Zadig* had appeared by 1747, *Candide* in 1759, two years before the Memoir was published.

II

The Life of Richard Nash, Esq., Late Master of the Ceremonies at Bath is a more serious performance, even when one allows for the triviality of the subject. It was written in the summer and autumn of 1762, and the way in which Goldsmith collected information from John Wood's *Essay towards a description of Bath* and from other sources, and wove it into a readable narrative, testifies to the skill he had by now acquired. The book contained two hundred and fifty pages, though small ones, and the author received fourteen guineas from the publisher and £15 from the Corporation of Bath.

It is both the life of a curious personality whose fecklessness and self-confidence were counterbalanced by real merits; and a history of Bath as a fashionable resort. Born in 1674, Nash as a youth entered Jesus College, Oxford, but was sent down without a degree. After trying his fortune in the Army, he became a member of the Middle Temple, and distinguished himself, not as a man of law but as an *arbiter elegantiarum*. He was good-mannered and good-natured. Invited one day on board a warship, he was carried out to sea and wounded in action. At the age of thirty he found himself without fortune or occupation, save that of a gamester. He came to Bath about 1704 and was soon appointed master of the ceremonies.

Although Bath had been made fashionable by Queen Anne's coming to take the waters, the city had no amenities. The houses and streets were mean, the people unmannerly and the entertainments ill-organised. Gradually, all this was improved. Better houses and a new Assembly Room were built. Nash drew up rules for behaviour, not only at balls, but in the vicinity of the Pump-Room and the Assembly Room. Balls were to be held from 6 to 11 p.m. From 6 to 9 minuets were danced, from 9 to 11 country-dances. Nash enjoined the strictest decorum in dress and deportment, and in enforcing these rules he became known as 'the King'. He would suffer no lady to wear a white 'apron', and on one occasion, seeing a Duchess so attired, he tore it from her, saying that only 'Abigails' should wear one. Meanwhile, he amused himself at the gaming-table; playing honestly, he did well at the tables, but did not save anything for his old age, because he gave away large sums to relieve real or apparent distress. A famous and picturesque figure, he received as presents dozens of snuff-boxes, until he had enough to furnish a shop. But as old age gradually overtook him, a time came when he lacked strength to carry out his duties. In 1760 there was a question of replacing him. Yet he lingered in his old haunts, despised by the great and neglected by those whom he had formerly helped. Friendless now, and penniless, his health began to break down, and to save him from starving the corporation voted him a pension of £10 a month. He died in February 1761. Goldsmith concludes the book by printing some of the letters he had found and a number of epitaphs on Nash.

This was the best of Goldsmith's essays in biography, perhaps, Forster thought, because he had a fellow-feeling for the old gamester who gave away money as quickly as he made it. The book proved popular, without, however, impressing the critics. It was a pity, said one, that a man with Goldsmith's talents should waste them on a subject so trifling. Today, however, the work has some value as a document of social history.

III

The Life of Thomas Parnell, D.D., Archdeacon of Clogher, appeared in 1770 as preface to an edition of Parnell's verses. It is a very slight affair. Parnell was born in Dublin in 1679, was educated at Trinity College and died in 1717. He knew Greek and helped Pope in the translating of Homer. A good Latinist, he put part of *The Rape of the Lock* into Latin verse. Goldsmith expresses warm admiration for his verses, especially 'The Hermit' and the 'Night-piece on Death', which, he thinks, 'with very little amendment', could surpass 'all those night-pieces and church-yard scenes that have since appeared'. A little earlier he had remarked: 'It is indeed amazing, after what has been done by Dryden, Addison and Pope to improve and harmonize our native tongue, that their successors should have taken so much pains to involve it in pristine barbarity. ...' From this, and from what he says in detail of the faults of these 'innovators', it seems that he has Gray and Warton in mind.

'From these follies and affectations the poems of Parnell are entirely free.'

Henry St John, Viscount Bolingbroke, to whom Goldsmith in 1770 devoted the last of his biographies, is too well known to call for more than passing reference. The memoir served as a preface to a new edition of the *Dissertation on Parties*. Goldsmith had by now acquired great fluency in narrative style, his work is well-proportioned and gives a good impression of the subject and the author; but so far from being the outcome of patient research, it was mostly adapted from the *Biographia Britannica*.

Critics have studied Goldsmith in connexion with the so-called art of biography which was then coming into fashion. He has been praised for departing from the former habit of panegyric, and for recording the faults as well as the qualities of his subject. But Goldsmith did not take these 'biographies' as seriously as critics do, and he made no progress in the art, if it were one. *The Life of Parnell* shows him at his worst; both here and in the *Life of Bolingbroke* one misses the anecdotes which brighten the *Memoirs* of Voltaire. None of these works would have been remembered, if they had not been by Goldsmith.

Chapter 20

'The Citizen of the World'

By ascribing to a foreigner, usually a virtuous Oriental who is supposed to be visiting western Europe, a series of letters addressed to his friends in the East, a writer could satirise the customs and beliefs of his own people without incurring personal responsibility. Since most persons like to hear what others think of them, provided that the irony is not too pointed and that it corresponds with what they secretly suspect, the satire is not usually resented.

Goldsmith adopts the disguise of a mandarin from Pekin, Lien Chi Altangi. He writes from London, sometimes to his son Hingpo who replies with accounts of his own adventures and who rejoins Lien Chi at the end; but most often to 'Fum Hoam,[1] first President of the Ceremonial Academy of Pekin', who occasionally answers. The letters give more than a humorous picture of daily life in London; they contain a great variety of topics. Lien Chi begins by describing the people he encounters: the simpering fop; the lady who is furnishing her house in what she supposed to be the Chinese fashion; the follies and amusements of the populace. The best pages depict types of the lower and middle class: the Man in Black, the pawnbroker's widow, Beau Tibbs, a shabby and pretentious little man, and his boring wife. Here are portraits that would fit into a novel or a play. Elsewhere Lien Chi describes an 'Authors' Club', discusses the Republic of Letters, comments –

---

[1] The name was probably suggested by the *Aventures merveilleuses du mandarin Fum-Hoam, contes chinois,* by T.-S. Gueulette, Paris, 1723, as the writer points out in *Sources françaises,* p 98.

often effectively – on Anglo–French relations or on current events, such as a General Election. On the other hand, we hear something of oriental manners and beliefs. The writer uses Chinese expressions, alludes to the teachings of Confucius and invokes the enlightenment of his countrymen when he is disgusted by western ignorance and folly. He of course relates eastern tales, then much in vogue. These various themes are interspersed among the letters, but they recur in such a way that a general pattern is more or less preserved.

The pattern is a picture of middle-class life as seen, ostensibly, through Chinese eyes; but Goldsmith makes no great effort to maintain the illusion. His grave mandarin is apt to relax, even to forget himself and make frivolous remarks; and it is here that Goldsmith shows the tips of his ears. One wonders how far he was really trying to compete with Montesquieu and other authors of satirical letters. Perhaps he intended the work to mean whatever readers wished to see in it. For many, it would be a series of Chinese letters and nothing more; for the perceptive it would be a mischievous parody, the more successful as the author was employing the traditional devices and simulating the indignation of an upright Oriental in the presence of western depravity. The strange mixture of the disciple of Confucius, the enlightened cosmopolitan and the irresponsible Anglo–Irishman, can be explained by the supposition that Goldsmith was parodying his predecessors in this genre.[1]

They were numerous, especially in France. G.-P. Marana's *L'Espion du Grand Seigneur* (1684), which Goldsmith appears to have read in Ireland,[2] had initiated a kind of book which was to engage the most gifted writers. Montesquieu's *Lettres persanes* (1721) became the model for social and religious satire. The unity of tone, the brilliance of the style, the humour of the character-studies have never been surpassed, not even in

[1] See *Les Sources françaises,* pp 89–90.
[2] See p 34 and Chapter 3 on Edinburgh.

Voltaire's *Lettres d'Amabed* (1769). The *Lettres persanes* were imitated in English by Lord Lyttleton, and in French by the Marquis d'Argens in the *Lettres chinoises* (1739) and the *Lettres juives* (1736, 1742), both of which were translated into English. Finally in 1757 Horace Walpole had published a short *Letter from Xo Ho, a Chinese Philosopher in London to his friend Lien Chi in Pekin*, the book which obviously set the spark to Goldsmith's imagination and led him to try his hand in this genre.

Apart from the satirical letters, the *Thousand and One Nights*, translated into French by Galland (1704–17) and from French into English, had created a vogue for anything oriental. Dozens of 'Eastern Tales' were published in France. Voltaire contributed to the fashion with *Zadig* (1747) and the *Princesse de Babylone* (1768); but China enjoyed the greatest prestige of all eastern countries. Pierre Martino has shown that in France 'the kingdom of mandarins and tea had made a triumphal entry into public favour. For sixty years it inspired everything: the novel and the stage, satire and philosophy, painting and engraving. There were times when the craze was extraordinary, especially about 1760.'[1]

Much the same was true of England, at this time quick to follow French fashions. As early as 1710 people began to lay out gardens in the Chinese manner, with little temples, pagodas, porcelain dragons and squatting mandarins. Sir William Chambers, the apostle of these 'Chinoiseries', had just published his *Designs for Chinese Buildings* when Goldsmith was beginning his 'Letters'. According to Lien Chi, in Letter XIV, people were disfiguring their gardens and even furnishing their houses in what they supposed to be the fashion of Pekin. If then, in 1760, an editor thought of publishing 'Chinese Letters', he could feel fairly sure that they would be welcome. A mandarin was not only more oriental, so to speak, than a

---

[1] *L'Orient dans la littérature française au XVIIe et au XVIIIe siècle*, Paris, 1906, pp 178–9.

Turk or a Persian, but supposedly more philosophical and therefore better fitted to satirise European manners.

Goldsmith had begun to speak of his 'Chinese philosopher' in a letter of 1758 and he had reviewed Murphy's adaptation of *L'Orphelin de la Chine* in 1759. The idea therefore was not new to him, but the moment was well chosen, and he pursued and completed the project in a more consecutive manner than his previous habits might have led one to expect. The first of the Chinese Letters appeared in the *Public Ledger* on 24 January 1760, and others followed, twice weekly during 1760, and at longer intervals until August 1761. Collected and published in book-form as *The Citizen of the World*, the 'Letters' have been regarded as showing Goldsmith at the height of his powers as a humourist. What grounds are there for this view?

He had got up his information about China, partly from the standard works by the Jesuit missionaries, Louis Le Comte and J.-B. du Halde, but also, and more easily, from D'Argens's *Lettres chinoises*. He had adapted and even translated some of the most amusing episodes from the *Lettres persanes*, and two of the most effective from his favourite Marivaux. Without the help of Montesquieu, D'Argens and Marivaux, Goldsmith's work would have lost much of its savour. It is true that he commented, often effectively, on such current events as a General Election, and his letters often take the form of essays on some speculative theme, such as the luxury which he then thought might make a people happier and wiser; the wisdom which is said to increase our happiness; the influence of climate on national character; and the question whether the progress of the arts and sciences has been of benefit or of prejudice to society. The debate about luxury he pursued in later writings; in *The Deserted Village* he was to treat it as a curse. Three Eastern Tales, of which 'The Story of the Chinese Matron' is the best, added interest to the correspondence, while Lien Chi's reaction to a startling piece of news, in 'An Apostrophe on the supposed death of Voltaire', showed Goldsmith at the top of his form. But two features of the letters which probably appealed most to readers while publication was proceeding, were the doings of the Man in Black and his friends, and the adventures of Hingpo and 'the beautiful captive'. These are resumed at intervals and brought together in the conclusion.

Some, perhaps many, readers enjoyed the story of Hingpo and Zelis, the sensational changes in their fortunes and the mystery surrounding the heroine. These adventures occupy Letters XXII, XXXV, XXXVI, LIX, LX, XCIV and CXXIII and, except for the first, are related by Hingpo to his father. Hingpo had planned to join Lien Chi in London but, having been captured by savage Tartars, was sold as a slave in Persia. In the house of his master, a wealthy 'tyrant', he meets a captive Christian maiden 'whose beauty seemed the transparent covering of virtue'. Under pressure from the tyrant, she has agreed to turn Moslem and become one of his many wives; but the reader learns to his relief that she and Hingpo have contrived to escape from Persia just before the nuptials were to be solemnised, and have taken refuge in the Caucasus. Here Zelis, for such was the maiden's name, tells the story of her life. Born far in the West, the only daughter of an elderly officer, she had been attracted by a friend, a designing suitor, without knowing that he was already married. Her father, believing her guilty of dishonour, had challenged the 'friend' to a duel and had been killed. Zelis had then accompanied a lady of distinction, who was also under a cloud, to Italy, but had been captured by Barbary pirates and so finally become a slave. From a subsequent letter we hear that when Hingpo and Zelis are making their way across Russia and are near the Volga, Hingpo is separated from his companion and despairs of ever seeing her again. Before long, however, Zelis finds her way to London, where it transpires that she is the niece of the Man in Black. Hingpo also arrives, and they are married. The Man in Black endows them with 'a small estate in the country'; Lien Chi settles money on them; and their story could not have ended more happily than the Chinese Letters end at this point.

The romance had not been very difficult to construct, since Goldsmith gave himself time to imagine the adventures, and also inserted in it a variation of 'the History of Miss Stanton'. A further variation of the latter was to be used for *The Vicar of Wakefield*. Writers with no great inventive powers are often obliged to plagiarise themselves. All three narratives are marked by the same inconsequence, the same improbabilities, and the same irony. Goldsmith had no more feeling for the romantic than Voltaire.

The other recurrent narrative concerns the life and character of the Man in Black, his friendship with Lien Chi, and their doings in company with the pawnbroker's widow and with Beau Tibbs and his wife. These pages have been admired as revealing in Goldsmith a forerunner of Dickens in the study of character, as well as a born humourist and master of irony.[1] The Man in Black's father has been regarded as an arranged and glorified portrait of Goldsmith's; the story of his youth is similarly 'arranged', and with deliberate humour. It is in Westminster Abbey of all places that Lien Chi encounters the Man in Black, who then acts as his guide and becomes his friend. He is 'a humourist in a nation of humourists'; now professing himself a misanthrope and cynic, now revealing his true nature as generous and benevolent. In Letter XXVII he tells his life-story. Through him Lien Chi meets the odd little trifler, Beau Tibbs, with his shabby clothes, his sword and his noble acquaintances. 'I despise the great as much as you do,' he assures his friends; 'but there are a great many damn'd honest fellows among them. . . . If they were all such as my Lord Mudler . . . I should myself be among the number of their admirers. I was yesterday to dine at the Duchess of Piccadilly's. My Lord was there. "Ned," says he to me, "Ned," says he,

---

[1] Cf. Austin Dobson, *Life of Oliver Goldsmith*; and Ricardo Quintana, *Oliver Goldsmith*, London, 1969, p 71.

"I'll hold gold to silver I can tell where you were poaching last night. ...." ', and so on. The character is a variant of that of Brueys' *L'Important*, the self-styled Count who has so many friends among the great. The 'Count's' character and talk were to be imitated more closely by Goldsmith in the person of Lofty in *The Good-Natured Man*.

When Lien Chi and his friends visit the pleasure gardens, presumably Vauxhall, Mr and Mrs Tibbs insist on sitting for supper in 'a genteel box', where they can both see and be seen. Although the members of the party are all convinced of their 'gentility', the officials are less easy to convince of it. The pawnbroker's widow – whom the Man in Black is courting – finds the meal excellent, 'but Mrs Tibbs thought everything detestable'; it was not, of course, as good a supper as they had had at Lord Crump's. When it is decided to ask Mrs Tibbs to sing, she coyly declines, as she is 'not in voice to-day'; but as the others are imprudent enough to entreat her, she complies. Meanwhile, an official announces that the water-works are going to begin. The widow is particularly anxious to see them. Of course Mrs Tibbs continues to sing, the tension grows excruciating, and she is still singing when the water-works have stopped.

This is a pleasing touch and may have been original. Yet, apart from such passages, Goldsmith appears to greatest advantage in the pieces he adapts or translates, such as the story of the Chinese Matron, already retold by Voltaire in the chapter of *Zadig* entitled 'Le Nez'; the episode of the 'Great Man' who knows so much more about China than the mandarin himself (LXXIV); the 'History of a Philosophic Cobbler' (LXV); and the 'Apostrophe on the supposed death of Voltaire' (XLIII). Examples speak for themselves.

'I [Lien Chi] was yesterday invited by a gentleman to dinner, who promised that our entertainment should consist of a haunch of venison, a turtle and a great man. . . .[1] The venison was fine, the turtle good, but the great man insupportable. The moment I ventured to speak, I was at once contradicted with a snap. I attempted . . . to retrieve my lost reputation, but was still beat back with confusion. I was resolved to attack him once more from entrenchment, and turned the conversation upon the government of China: but even here he asserted, snapped and contradicted as before. "Heavens," thought I, "this man pretends to know China even better than myself!" I looked round to see who was on my side; but every eye was fixed in admiration on the great man. . . .'

This is adapted from the episode of the 'Décisionnaire universel' in the *Lettres persanes* (LXXII) who, without having been in Persia, 'knows the streets of Ispahan' better than Usbek whose home is there. But Goldsmith has added some picturesque details which are not in Montesquieu. Another and perhaps more striking son of the 'Universal Decider' who was encountered by Lien Chi in the house of 'a great lady', 'talked of our cities, mountains and animals, as familiarly as if he had been born in Quamsi, but as erroneously as if a native of the moon. He attempted to prove that I had nothing of the true Chinese cut in my visage. . . . In short, he almost reasoned me out of my country. . . .'[2] Some twelve other passages are inspired by the *Lettres persanes*, either directly or by way of Lord Lyttleton's adaptation.

In the excellent 'History of a Philosophic Cobbler', Lien Chi's encounter with him and the cobbler's long discourse are translated from the *Spectateur français* (5e feuille); though the relation of his life which follows is partly original. The story of Mencius and the Hermit, in Letter LXVI, also comes from the *Spectateur français* (3e feuille); but an equally striking

[1] Mr E. A. Freeman thought that the 'great man' was probably Samuel Johnson, and this seems likely. If so, it is evident that, if Johnson ever read this passage, he did not recognise his portrait.
[2] Letter XXXIII.

example of Goldsmith's dependence on Marivaux[1] occurs in Hingpo's letter (No. LXXVI) to his father in which he describes the beauty of Zelis as due to 'this resistless magic that attends even moderate charms'. This he illustrates with an allegory, 'The Preference of Grace to Beauty', which is simply an abbreviated version of several pages in the second 'feuille' of the *Cabinet du Philosophe*. He renders 'La demeure du *Je ne sais quoi*' by 'The Valley of the Graces'.

It would be tedious to speak of Goldsmith's many borrowings from D'Argens. The Chinese Letters are indeed a patchwork of imitations and plagiarisms.

At the beginning of June 1760 a rumour that Voltaire was dead inspired Lien Chi immediately to compose 'An Apostrophe' on this sad event:

'We have just received accounts here that Voltaire, the poet and philosopher of Europe, is dead! He is now beyond the reach of the thousand enemies who, while living, degraded his writings, and branded his character. Scarce a page of his latter productions, that does not betray the agonies of a heart bleeding under the scourge of unmerited reproach. Happy, therefore, at last in escaping from calumny! happy in leaving a world that was unworthy of him and his writings!'

In fact, his heart was not bleeding; on the contrary he greatly enjoyed ridiculing Rousseau; and he urged the government to suppress Fréron who had had the audacity to criticise him. Lien Chi continues:

'Whence, my friend, this malevolence, which has ever pursued the great, even to the tomb?

'When I cast my eye over the fates of several philosophers who have, at different periods, enlightened mankind, I must

[1] As the present writer discovered and published in 1924 (*Les Sources françaises*, pp 114–18).

confess it inspires me with the most degrading reflections on humanity. . . .

'Should you look for the character of Voltaire among the journalists and illiterate writers of the age, you will there find him characterised as a monster. . . . But seek for his character among writers like himself, and . . . you perceive him, in their accounts, possessed of good nature, humanity, greatness of soul, fortitude and almost every virtue. . . . The Royal Prussian, D'Argens, Diderot, D'Alembert and Fontenelle conspire in . . . describing the friend of man, and the patron of every rising genius.'

There follows a brief outline of Voltaire's career, concluding with his settling near Geneva, where he entertained 'the learned and polite of Europe. . . . The being an Englishman was to him a character that claimed admiration and respect.'

Why Goldsmith held Voltaire in such exceptional esteem is not clear, unless it was on account of some personal kindness he may have received, and also, perhaps, of a similarly ironical and anti-Romantic attitude to life. It was natural to admire his vast learning and incomparable wit, but not to ignore those faults of character and conduct which were well known to other contemporaries.

The *Chinese Letters* possessed, as noted earlier, certain unifying features, and were animated in particular by a profession of the cosmopolitanism which was then fashionable among French writers. In 1750 Fougeret de Monbron had published a little book entitled *Le Cosmopolite, ou le Citoyen du Monde*, with, for its epitaph: '*Patria est ubicunque est bene*'; and this may have suggested to Goldsmith the title[1] he chose for the 'Letters'. They were collected and, with the insertion of four pieces which had appeared elsewhere, were renumbered; titles were given to each; and the whole was published in May 1762, in two volumes, as *The Citizen of the World; or Letters*

[1] For a short account of this work, see *Les Sources françaises*, pp 95–6.

from a Chinese Philosopher residing in London to his friends in the East. The work, which remained anonymous, created no stir among the critics or the public: 'Light, agreeable summer reading, partly original, partly borrowed,' said the *British Magazine*. The description was accurate. A reprint came out in 1766 and nothing more until 1780. On the other hand, the French translation by M. Poivre, in 1763, was immediately successful and reached its fourth edition in 1767. Readers in Paris, always curious to hear about London life, must have learned from Goldsmith's book that all Englishmen were not the profound and melancholy thinkers that they had been led to suppose.

Although the 'Letters' in book form were not as successful as they had been in the *Public Ledger*, Newbery seems to have been fully satisfied that he had found a useful contributor in Goldsmith; and the work won the esteem of Johnson, which explains why he chose its author as one of the original members of the Club.

Chapter 21

'*The Vicar of Wakefield*' (I)

I

It is not known exactly when *The Vicar of Wakefield* was written or what were the conditions of sale. According to Boswell, Goldsmith who was lodging with a Mrs Carnan in Wine Office Court, had been put under arrest for failure to pay his rent. This was in the latter part of 1762. He had sent an urgent appeal for help to Johnson, who despatched a messenger with a guinea and arrived shortly afterwards to see what could be done. He asked Goldsmith whether he had any work in hand, whereupon the other produced the manuscript of a 'novel'. Johnson took it to Newbery and, again according to Boswell, sold it for £60 and brought back the money in cash. William Cooke, however, says that Newbery 'advanced him twenty guineas'; he believed that Goldsmith 'finished *The Vicar of Wakefield*' in Wine Office Court. Finally, in his *Memoir of Newbery* which was published only in 1885, Charles Welsh asserts that Goldsmith sold a third share of *The Vicar of Wakefield* to Benjamin Collins of Salisbury for twenty guineas. This can be proved from Collins's account books; but it appears that in October 1765 Goldsmith actually went to Salisbury to see Collins, and it may be that only then, in 1765, did he receive the twenty guineas.[1]

One may conclude that enough of the story had been written in 1762 for Newbery to feel that he could risk twenty guineas on it; and that he persuaded Collins, a printer, to join him in the venture; that at a subsequent date a publisher named

---

[1] For a full discussion of this question, see Austin Dobson, *Life of Oliver Goldsmith*, London, 1885, pp 110–16.

Strahan took up a further share; but that Goldsmith did not actually complete the work until 1765, when Collins contributed his share of the payment. The above evidence appears to dispose of any notion that *The Vicar of Wakefield*, in its present form, had been finished by the autumn of 1762, or that Goldsmith received sixty pounds (or guineas) at that time. It is unlikely that a publisher would have risked so much money on an incomplete work by an author hardly known to the public at large.

Other evidence, of a more literary kind, would also suggest that the book was in progress in 1761, but not finished before the latter part of 1764; and so the long-held view that, after Johnson's sale of the manuscript, publication was held up for nearly four years is entirely unfounded.

The 1766 collection of *Essays* contained two papers addressed 'to the Printer' and supposed to come from a common councilman named Grogan, who had written them 'at the time of the last coronation', which was in September 1761. In the second of these 'Mr Grogan' described how he had bought tickets for his wife, his daughter and himself at two guineas each. To be sure of a good position the wife insisted on occupying the seats from 7 o'clock on the previous evening. But ' "Grizzle," said I to her, "Grizzle my dear, consider that . . . you will never bear sitting out all night on the scaffold. . . . Besides, my dear, our daughter, Anna Amelia Wilhelmina Carolina, will look like a perfect fright if she sits up. . . ." ' But of course she overrules him, as Mrs Primrose in the novel always overrules the vicar. Mr Grogan falls asleep in the early morning, has a wonderful dream about a venison pasty and, despite his family's efforts to awaken him, returns to consciousness only when the ceremony is over.

This 'letter' which had evidently been written in the autumn of 1761 (as it purported to have been) contains two points which connect it with the novel. Dr Primrose had wished to name his elder daughter 'Grissel' (Chapter I); and one of the

'London ladies' is Miss Carolina Wilhelmina Amelia Skeggs (Chapter XI). From this one might infer that Goldsmith was already at work on his novel in 1761. But there is evidence to suggest that he had not actually finished it until 1764 at the earliest.

It would appear, as will be argued here, that the event which decided this contemner of novels to write a novel was the publication in January 1760 of *Tristram Shandy*. If this were so, it would be natural for Goldsmith not only to view with envy the social success which Sterne enjoyed in London in 1760 and 1761, but also to fasten on any news of his reception in Paris in 1762 and again in the spring of 1764. Now it is known that in May of that year, after his return north from a long sojourn in the Midi, Sterne was in company in Paris with a certain Mr Thornhill.[1] If Goldsmith had already chosen this name for the benevolent magnate and also for the wicked squire of the novel, the coincidence would be strange indeed; but if he finally selected the name only after hearing of Sterne's doings in May 1764, it might add to the evidence (*verb. sap.*) that in writing his own novel, he had had Sterne's very much in mind.[2]

II

Since *The Vicar of Wakefield* resembles no other 'novel' one has ever heard of, it is evidently a very personal as well as peculiar performance. Its enchanting humour, and also its oddities and innuendoes, reflect the character of its author. It is not that the bare outline of the story was invented: Goldsmith took this partly from a tale in numbers 21 to 25 of the *Spectateur français*, partly from 'The History of Miss Stanton' which he parodies.

With the latter we are already familiar. The former consists of the 'Aventures de l'Inconnu'. This 'unknown' young man relates how his father had been obliged by a long malady to

[1] H. D. Traill, *Sterne*, London, 1902, pp 84–5: see note on p 267.
[1] Suggested to me by I. Lytton Sells.

abandon a lucrative position, and had then lost two-thirds of his fortune by a sudden bankruptcy. Having now only a small property in the country, he had taken his wife, his son (the narrator) and his daughter, a girl of seventeen, to live there. All this resembles the first misfortunes of the Primrose family. The Vicar loses most of his £14,000 when the merchant with whom he had invested the money fled to Antwerp to escape an action for bankruptcy. To resume the story of the 'Inconnu': after the death of his parents, he and his sister continue to live on the farm, of which the income is meagre. A young financier who owns a neighbouring estate falls in love with the girl; but she finds that he wishes to seduce her and that, if she consents, he will use his influence on her brother's behalf. She refuses: '. . . all your riches are not worth the scorn you inspire for them. . . .' If we add to this the story of another girl, more unfortunate, who relates her adventures in No. 10 of the *Spectateur français*, we have an outline of the story of Olivia and young Thornhill; while the contemptuous rejection of the financier's proposal is matched by Dr Primrose's parting words to the squire in Chapter XXIV. There is, however, this difference, that while the 'Inconnu' and his sister continue to live honourable and unmolested lives, Olivia and the whole family are submerged under a cascade of misfortunes.

Here is the outline of a plot which could be developed feelingly and sympathetically, or with cynical irony. The merit of the story would depend on the study of character and the spirit or tone of the narrative. The tale is 'supposed to be told' by the Vicar himself; but it is Goldsmith who makes him relate it in such a way as to reveal a character as apparently simple and gullible as his own; and Goldsmith is also standing behind him, and mischievously manipulating the sequence of events.

The society he portrays is rural and clerical, the only kind of society which he had properly known. The 'novel' is autobiographical, full of personal reminiscences, interpreted in the light of his disappointments and resentments. Goldsmith is, as always throughout his life, on the defensive, prepared to ridicule, under an appearance of good nature, all those who had given him ground for grievance. The 'good' people are the Primroses, and such prosperous farmers as Flamborough and Williams; the 'bad' people are Squire Thornhill and his associates, and Lady Blarney and Miss Skeggs – people who owe their vices to the depravity of London. From a sordid garret off Fleet Street Goldsmith is looking back on his boyhood days in Ireland, a sort of Eden from which he had been excluded as the Primroses are excluded from Wakefield. Like them, he hopes for another turn of the wheel of fortune. Life, meanwhile, has taught him to be humorous and even cynical, and this will serve as a weapon against misfortunes which he knows to be due mostly to his own fecklessness.

The story is to wear the appearance of an idyll, and until recent times most readers have taken it for such. Dr Primrose never tires of celebrating the charms of a modest existence in the country, much as in 1761 the *Nouvelle Héloïse* had contrasted the corruption of Paris with the innocence of rural Switzerland. So far from agreeing here with Voltaire, whom he admired, Goldsmith adopts an attitude similar to that of J.-J. Rousseau whom he had derided. Allowing for the irony and cynicism, which are Voltairean, this aspect of the story is probably serious.

III

An outline of the story, as related by the Vicar, may explain why virtually all readers prior to the 1930s have taken it for an idyll.

Dr Primrose, the Vicar of Wakefield, has chosen his wife 'for such qualities as would wear well'. They have six children; George, Olivia, Sophia, Moses and two little boys; and a fortune so large that the Vicar has made over the stipend of his living, which is £35, to the widows and orphans of the clergy.

His favourite topic is the great doctrine of clerical monogamy. He had written several tracts on the subject and had completed another at the time when George, his eldest son, is about to marry Arabella Wilmot, the daughter of another wealthy cleric. He shows the tract to Mr Wilmot, only to discover that the latter is courting a fourth wife. There follows an acrimonious dispute and, while this is going on, a friend informs Dr Primrose that his merchant banker has fled the country with all the funds entrusted to him. The Vicar now realises that out of a fortune of £14,000, £400 is all that remains. Mr Wilmot cancels his daughter's marriage, and Dr Primrose accepts a modest cure of £15 a year, some seventy miles away, where he can supplement his stipend from the proceeds of a farm of twenty acres (like Charles Goldsmith and many other country parsons in Ireland and England).

George leaves to seek his fortune in London, and the family set out for their new home. At a village inn on the way they learn that their new landlord will be Squire Thornhill, celebrated for his successes in seducing the country girls. Meanwhile a poor gentleman who has been staying at the inn has given all his money to an old soldier and cannot pay the bill. The Vicar pays it; and the stranger, whose name is Burchell, accompanies them on their journey. He tells them about the great Sir William Thornhill, uncle of the young squire, of the follies of his past and the affluence of his present condition. While fording a stream Sophia is thrown from her horse and would have been drowned if Mr Burchell had not saved her.

The family settle into a thatched cottage two miles from the church. Dr Primrose and Moses work on the farm, and they all find pleasure in country occupations and simple amusements. One day Squire Thornhill calls on them, treats the ladies with gallantry, especially 'the blooming' Olivia, who responds to his advances. The Vicar warns her and Sophia of the dangers of fortune-hunting. A servant arrives with a 'side of venison' and a promise that the Squire will come and dine with them in a few days' time. Soon after this Mr Burchell pays them a visit. He entertains the children and stays so late that they feel obliged to offer him a bed. Next day he works with them on the farm and is assiduous in helping Sophia; the Vicar, however, has 'too good an opinion of [her] understanding . . . to be under any uneasiness from a man of broken fortune'.

After Mr Burchell's departure, the Squire arrives with 'his chaplain and feeder' and a number of servants. Mrs Primrose entertains them all, 'for which, by the bye, our family was pinched for three weeks after'. As Burchell had hinted that the Squire was proposing marriage to Miss Wilmot, this somewhat damps 'the heartiness of his reception'. But the Squire treats the story as absurd, Miss Wilmot being 'a perfect fright'. He engages Moses in argument and turns him to ridicule by means of questions and answers which Olivia mistakes for humour. Mrs Primrose exults; she confesses that she has instructed the girls to encourage him. 'Who knows how this may end?' she asks; but her husband says he would prefer a 'poor, but honest suitor'.

Next day, again as if by accident, Mr Burchell comes to see them. The Vicar is obliged to admit that he is growing more amiable and seemingly wiser. Burchell expounds his ideas about poetry and reads them a long ballad which impresses Sophia. This idyllic scene is, however, interrupted by the report of a gun and by the chaplain bursting through the hedge. Sophia in alarm throws herself into Burchell's arms and would have refused the chaplain's offer of a bird he has shot, if her mother had not insisted on her accepting it. Mrs Primrose feels sure that Sophia has made a conquest; and the Vicar himself is surprised that she should 'prefer a man of broken fortune' to one with greater expectations.

At a dance by moonlight on the grass, Thornhill introduces two women of fashion from London, Lady Blarney and Miss Skeggs. Their language and behaviour are coarse, yet they talk of high life, pictures and Shakespeare, and consider that the

I

Primrose girls would be greatly improved by a season in town. Thornhill lavishes compliments on Olivia and declares that 'if a settlement of half [his] estate' would give her pleasure, 'it should be hers'. Dr Primrose regards this as a disguise for 'the basest proposal' and expresses resentment; whereupon the Squire commends his prudence, deprecates his suspicions and confesses 'sorrow for his former excesses'.

Mrs Primrose and the girls are dazzled by their grand acquaintances; while a fortune-teller encourages them in their expectations. Mrs Primrose is visited by a succession of sinister dreams which she interprets by contraries. Towards the weekend, the two ladies propose to attend divine service. Mother and daughters therefore spend hours on their dress and toilet, and plan to ride to church on the two plough-horses; but they are not ready in time. The Vicar reads the service and on his way back meets his family who are somewhat late. After this mortifying experience they accept an invitation from Farmer Flamborough, whom Mrs Primrose had regarded as beneath her rank. They 'suffer themselves to be happy' and take part in noisy games with Mr Burchell and Flamborough's daughters; but great is their consternation when Lady Blarney and Miss Skeggs unexpectedly enter the room. 'Death! to be seen by ladies of such high breeding in such vulgar attitudes!'

The London women, however, make much of the Primrose girls. They themselves engage in a high-flown dialogue – interrupted at intervals by Burchell's crying: 'Fudge.' The Londoners intimate that they might, after enquiring into the girls' characters, find employment for them as companions to ladies of quality – a prospect which puts Mrs Primrose in high spirits. In order to make a better show it is decided to sell the colt and buy a decent horse. Moses therefore takes the colt to the Fair, sells it for £3 5s 2d and is then cheated into buying a gross of green spectacles 'with silver rims', alleged to be worth double the money. Unfortunately they are not silver but merely gilt. In the meantime, Mr Burchell who has heard that Olivia and

Sophia are to be offered employment in London, advises 'the utmost circumspection' and urges Mrs Primrose not to agree. This gives rise to an unseemly quarrel, and to his departure.

The Vicar reproaches his wife for her rudeness; he thinks they may have been mistaken in Burchell's character; and Sophia asserts that he has always treated her in the most gentlemanly manner. Even so, the girls are to go to London and Thornhill promises to keep a friendly eye on them. To meet the expenses that will be incurred, Dr Primrose resolves to dispose of their remaining horse, a one-eyed, broken-down old animal. At the Fair he encounters 'a venerable old man' who is overwhelmed by the honour of meeting 'the great Primrose, that courageous monogamist who had been the bulwark of the church'. He launches into a pseudo-learned discourse, interlarded with tags of Greek, and finally agrees to buy the horse. But he has only a note for £30, and no one can change so large a sum; so he gives the Vicar a draft on Mr Flamborough, which to the Vicar is 'the same as money' – until, on visiting the farmer, he discovers that he has been cheated, and by the very rogue, a certain Ephraim Jenkinson, who had swindled Moses. Worse still, on returning home, he finds the women in tears, Mr Thornhill having called to tell them that the journey to London has been cancelled. Some malicious person has evidently spoken ill of the Primrose girls.

And now, by one of those coincidences which occur in a romance, they discover the copy of a letter which Mr Burchell had addressed to the London ladies; and by another coincidence the wording is so ambiguous that the terms 'infamy and vice' are taken by the Primroses to refer to their daughters. Burchell is indeed an enemy; and when he next comes to see them, the altercation could hardly be more unedifying. Subsequently Mrs Primrose tries to frighten the Squire into offering marriage to Olivia by pointing out that Mr Williams, a prosperous young farmer, has been courting her. Thornhill declares that Williams is utterly unworthy of her, but his reasons for saying more 'lie too deep in his heart to be discovered'. Olivia regards these words 'as instances of the most exalted passion'. Her father is not so sure. He insists on her agreeing to marry the farmer, unless Thornhill openly declares himself; and next time the latter calls, a date – a month hence – is fixed for her marriage. Three weeks later the Squire discontinues his visits. The Vicar feels relieved; he had never, he says, entertained such lofty ambitions as his wife. And the family is happily entertaining itself with songs and ballads when little Dick (one of the small children) runs in to say that 'Sister Livy . . . is gone off with two gentlemen in a post-chaise.' Dr Primrose is beside himself. He breaks out into the wildest imprecations and has to be calmed by the children. He makes enquiries at Thornhill Castle, where the Squire professes complete ignorance of the affair. Suspicion falls on Mr Burchell. Someone having said that Burchell and Olivia might be found at the Races, seventy miles away, the unhappy father makes his way there on foot; but without finding them. Fatigue has brought on a fever, and he lies for three weeks in a wayside inn. His money is now all spent, but a philanthropic bookseller (Newbery, no doubt) lends him enough for the return journey. On the way back he falls in with the manager of some strolling players, who is to be entertained at a noble mansion in the vicinity. He invites the Vicar to a meal there. After a long discourse on politics, in which the Vicar points to the danger of extending the franchise to the rabble – who should come in but the lovely Miss Wilmot. The house belongs to the Arnolds, her uncle and aunt, and they invite Dr Primrose to stay for a few days. Arabella enquires after George, for whom she feels such tenderness that she has refused several offers; although she is to marry Thornhill before long. Nothing indeed has been heard of George for the past three years. At the play which they attend that evening – it is *The Fair Penitent* – the part of Horatio is to be acted by a young amateur. He turns out to be George. Invited to stay with the Arnolds, he relates his adventures in London and on a tour of the Continent.

Thornhill calls on the Arnolds, and appears relieved to hear from Dr Primrose that he has not told either George or Miss Wilmot of Olivia's misfortune. He has purchased for George a commission in a regiment which is to sail for the West Indies. George leaves next day to take it up; and Dr Primrose sets out for home. At nightfall he puts up in a wayside inn, and while talking with the landlord, hears an outcry upstairs where the man's wife is ill-treating a young woman who cannot pay for her room. This of course is Olivia. The Vicar rushes to her help. She explains that Thornhill is the villain. He had 'married' her, but he had already married other 'wives', and all these ceremonies had been hoaxes. Moreover, she has promised not to inform against him. After leaving her at an inn nearer home, Dr Primrose goes ahead to prepare the family; but no sooner does he open his cottage door than the place is seen bursting into flames. The family are saved, but the Vicar's arm is badly burned in the work of rescue. They take up their dwelling in an outhouse. Williams offers his friendship, but Olivia, in whom a sense of guilt has been replaced by envy and jealousy, makes no response. As news arrives that Thornhill is to marry Miss Wilmot in a few days' time, Moses is despatched with a letter to Mr Wilmot, apprising him of the Squire's conduct; but Moses finds it impossible to deliver the letter.

The next morning being warm and sunny, the family are breakfasting on the honeysuckle bank, when Thornhill arrives to enquire after the Vicar's health and to invite Olivia to attend his wedding. He will arrange a suitable marriage for her. Dr Primrose denounces his infamy and refuses to countenance any marriage except with Olivia. Thornhill replies with menaces so terrifying that the family beg Dr Primrose to comply. He refuses. Next morning the steward calls for the annual rent. He cannot pay. He still refuses to comply with the Squire's terms; and on the morrow, after a heavy snowfall, the Sheriff's officers arrive to hale him off to the county gaol. The weather, it is to be noted, has changed very spitefully, in order to aggravate the Vicar's miseries, and at the same time to bring out his courage in bearing them.

Quarters are found for Mrs Primrose and her daughters in cheap lodgings, while Moses and the little boys are allowed to sleep with their father in the cold prison. The first person who speaks to the Vicar when he enters this sinister abode is the learned humbug Jenkinson. The Vicar forgives him; and he in return says he may still prove a useful friend.

Dr Primrose is shocked, though not dismayed, by the prisoners who raise a clamour of profanity and merriment. He undertakes to reform them and, after some days, wins their respect. He teaches them to make useful articles. After he has been a fortnight in prison, Olivia comes and begs him to submit to the Squire, while Jenkinson also advises submission. The Vicar refuses. He writes to the Squire's uncle, Sir William Thornhill, but the letter elicits no reply. News next reaches him that Olivia is in a decline; finally, that she is dead. There is now no pride nor resentment in the Vicar's heart, and he writes a letter of submission. The Squire replies that it is too late. Next, Mrs Primrose rushes in with the news that Sophia has been carried off in a post-chaise by a well-dressed ruffian. One would suppose that the family has now reached the rock-bottom of misery, even though they receive a letter from George who has been doing well in the Army; but this letter is immediately followed by the appearance of George himself, covered with blood and in fetters. Having heard of Thornhill's villainy, he had challenged him to a duel; but he had been arrested and, being the aggressor, he will be liable to capital punishment.

The Vicar has now freed his heart from 'all earthly ties'. To the assembled prisoners he preaches a sermon to prove that religion offers comfort where philosophy is of no avail. Soon after this, Mr Burchell brings in Sophia whom he has rescued.

He had stopped the post-chaise, knocked out the postillion and put the abductor to flight. The Vicar offers Sophia as wife to her rescuer; and the latter orders dinner to be brought in from the inn with 'a dozen of the best wine'. When George is permitted to join the party, he gazes on Burchell 'with . . . astonishment and reverence'. Burchell considers him guilty of a grave offence, but admits palliating circumstances; his main object is to see justice done to the Vicar. Young Thornhill has just arrived, and the whole affair will be examined. It is only now that Dr and Mrs Primrose learn that the 'man of broken fortune' is really the illustrious Sir William Thornhill.

The Squire presents a good legal case against George and asserts his innocence regarding Olivia; but when Jenkinson brings in the ruffian who had abducted Sophia; when this man confesses that he had acted on instructions from the Squire; when the Squire's butler declares that Jenkinson was one of young Thornhill's assistants, the one who had gone to fetch the priest for Olivia's supposed marriage – in face of all these witnesses, Sir William is convinced of his nephew's infamy. He orders George to be released; and as Miss Wilmot enters at this moment, he reveals to her the character of the man she was about to marry.

George now reappears, cleansed of blood and splendidly attired in Captain's uniform, and Miss Wilmot declares that if she is not to be his, 'she shall never be another's'. Thornhill, however, defies them all. By the articles of marriage signed by Mr Wilmot, he is in possession of Arabella's fortune. Alarm and dismay for Mr Wilmot. George alone finds pleasure in proving that he loves Arabella for herself. Mr Wilmot agrees to the match provided that Dr Primrose will settle £6,000 on Arabella 'if he should ever come into his fortune'. As nothing appears less likely, the Vicar readily agrees, and the young couple 'fly into each other's arms'. The wicked Squire, however, would still have triumphed, if Jenkinson had not intervened to prove that he was already married, and to no other than to Olivia. The Squire had employed him on this, as on many previous occasions, to procure a false priest and a false licence; but this time he had procured genuine ones. He produces the licence, which is perfectly in order; and he also produces Olivia, who was not dead after all. So now Arabella retains her fortune, and Olivia is an 'honest woman'. Jenkinson had reported Olivia as dead, as this seemed to him the best means of inducing the Vicar to submit to Thornhill and obtain release from prison.

Thornhill falls on his knees and implores compassion. Sir William grants him a bare competence; he himself will marry Sophia. The party now leave the prison and move to the inn, where a sumptuous entertainment awaits them. Dr Primrose, somewhat weakened no doubt by a month in an unheated prison, then retires to bed. On his awaking next morning, George brings news that the merchant who had absconded with the Vicar's fortune has been arrested in Antwerp, in possession of an even larger amount. George offers to give up the promise of £6,000 for Arabella, and his offer is accepted. They then all repair to the Church, where the Vicar is to marry the happy couples. The company is in a state of merriment, and the reading of two homilies and a thesis still leaves them refractory. Dr Primrose is 'tempted to turn back in indignation', but thinks better of it.

The weddings are followed by 'a very genteel entertainment . . . dressed by Mr Thornhill's cook'. Thornhill himself, Dr Primrose informs us, by the way, is living as companion to a melancholy relative; but Olivia tells her father that when Mr Thornhill reforms, 'she may be brought to relent'; and it seems unlikely that her parents will make difficulties.

The Vicar now has nothing 'on this side of the grave to wish for. . . . My pleasure (he adds) was unspeakable. It now only remained that my gratitude in good fortune should exceed my former submission in adversity.'

IV

The foregoing analysis – from which the innuendoes, the mischievous twists and turns, and the ironical observations have been mostly omitted – may possibly explain why the *Vicar of Wakefield* has for so long been regarded as a good-natured novel. But it also supports the view that the whole story had been planned from the outset.

Chapters I and II describe the Primrose family in affluence. Chapters III to XVI present them in reduced but still happy circumstances. Misfortune suddenly strikes them at the end of XVI, and in Chapters XVII to XXX they are smitten by a succession of appalling disasters. Fortune suddenly smiles on them in Chapter XXXI; and in the Conclusion, happiness is not only restored but enhanced. The story is divided so neatly in the middle that this cannot have been due to chance. In what we may call Part I all the principal characters are introduced, including Jenkinson who is to play a key role in the *dénouement*. We are made aware that Mr Burchell may be other than what he appears. Thornhill's assiduous, but ambiguous, courting of Olivia forewarns us of what may ensue. Thus the thunderstroke of Olivia's disappearance has been prepared for. As Dr Primrose has acted with apparent moderation when prosperous, so he is represented as displaying constancy and firmness in adversity. The conclusion, however, when all the good people are crowned with happiness is as unexpected (and improbable) as the disasters which had gone before.

Small wonder if Goldsmith's contemporaries were not sure what to make of the story. The *Monthly Review* approved its 'moral tendency' but expressed surprise that the author had so strangely 'underwritten himself'. The *Critical Review* praised the 'genuine touches of nature' and 'easy strokes of humour', but asked why the author had brought 'the concluding calamities so thick upon [his] old venerable friend' (sic). Hugh Kelly's *The Babler* praised it unreservedly. Yet the public displayed no enthusiasm. Among the author's friends, Burke admired the pathos of the story; Johnson saw little of nature in it. No one prior to our own days seems to have understood Goldsmith's underlying intention. The story was welcomed in France, probably as a moral tale enlivened with humour. Six or seven separate translations, including an excellent one by Nodier, were published; and for many years *The Vicar of Wakefield* was used as a text-book in French *lycées*. One wonders what exactly the children made of it. Taine, steeped in German seriousness and lacking in a sense of humour, appreciated in it the feeling for the *home*, which he imagined to be peculiarly English. Meanwhile it had been adapted as a drama by Eugène Nus and Tisserant, who himself played the part of 'Primerose' at the Odéon. The reception of the *Vicar* in Germany was equally enthusiastic and even less critical. Germans liked the *gemütlichkeit* of family life, the naïveté of the young girls, the superiority of the paterfamilias, and the veneer of sentimentality which they took to be genuine. At Strasbourg Herder read a German translation to the young Goethe, and the latter, looking back on his youth from the age of eighty-one, declared it one of the best stories ever written, and the one which had most impressed him. He admired in Dr Primrose a mind that rose superior to fortune and adversity until it reached the height of a 'truly poetical world' – or, as one suspects, became Olympian. He admired the goodness and innocence of the young girls because they reminded him of the *innamorate* of his youth, who had taken him as seriously as Olivia takes Thornhill. How Goldsmith would have chuckled! In few novels are women more cruelly derided.

Sir Walter Scott read it several times and blessed 'the memory of an author who contrives so well to recommend us to human nature'. He was unable, apparently, to see any malicious purpose in the story. Sir James Prior saw its great charm 'in close adherence to nature.... We find little in incident or character overstrained, excepting perhaps the moral turpitude of Thornhill.' John Forster, however, conceded that heroism 'may coexist with many follies . . . many harmless vanities'. And in view of these encomiums one can understand why Henry James thought that the 'amenity' of the book had protected it from adverse criticism and that it was 'the spoiled child of our literature'; a phrase which perhaps conceals a hint about the reason for its popularity.

It has been translated into every European language, and into others, and was reprinted every year. Most readers seem to have regarded it as the story of the Christian hero and to have followed the fortunes of the Vicar with bated breath. But recent critics have seen more in it than a philosophic idyll and a pleasant picture of family life, spiced with sensational adventures.[1]

[1] *Addendum.* As regards the name Thornhill (see p 253), Goldsmith may have known that Thornhill is a small textile town, then probably a village, in the West Riding; or he may have been thinking of Sir James Thornhill who had decorated great houses and made portraits of Newton, Handel and others. But Sir James had died in 1734.

Chapter 22

'*The Vicar of Wakefield*' (II)

I

Professor E. A. Baker in his *History of the English Novel* was perhaps the first to insist that the tone of the story is one of irony and that the events in the first part are comical.[1] William Freeman regards *The Vicar of Wakefield* as, to a large extent, autobiographical. Goldsmith 'distributed his personality and experiences among several characters'. He points out that 'most of the time Goldsmith is writing with his tongue in his cheek. Plot and conversations are suffused with private irony, which he must have feared his readers might realise – and equally feared they would miss. It is, in short, a satire of the gentlest, subtlest type. . . .'[2] No better criticism has appeared. American scholars, though unaware apparently of Mr Freeman's work, have followed E. A. Baker in seeing *The Vicar* as full of both irony and satire. Ralph Wardle thinks 'it can be read as ironic or idyllic'; or in other ways.[3] Ricardo Quintana dwells rather on satire sustained 'by an irony which places in doubt the moral generated by a too fortunate turn of events'; and he develops the argument in more detail in his *Oliver Goldsmith*.[4] Finally, Robert Hopkins goes much further. In a detailed analysis he sees Goldsmith as convicting Dr Primrose of self-seeking hypocrisy and materialism. The frequent twists in the narrative serve to reveal the real motive behind the pretended. A touching or poetical scene is immediately followed by a ludicrous episode. The Vicar, he argues, equates happiness with material

---

[1] Vol V, London, 1934.
[2] *Oliver Goldsmith*, London, 1951, p 197.
[3] *Oliver Goldsmith*, Lawrence (Kansas), and London, 1957, p 171.
   London, 1967, pp 107–15.

prosperity (a good many people do). He regards his children, especially his daughters, as good investments: they are his 'treasures'. Particularly significant is the title of Chapter XXXI: 'Benevolence repaid with unexpected interest.' The book as a whole is a great work of art and a satire 'on shallow optimism'. Goldsmith created Dr Primrose 'to satirise the complacency and materialism of a type of clergy. In a very real sense the Primroses were a threat to their age, as Wesley and Blake well knew.'[1]

This is perhaps to attribute to Goldsmith too deadly an intention. However much we may laugh at the story, we can hardly see it as such a serious indictment. Dr Primrose has good qualities as well as faults and weaknesses; and Goldsmith had put so much of himself into his character that he cannot have wholly disliked him. He had known Dr Percy, a prosperous country rector, since 1759 and Percy had befriended him. To attack with such venom the Anglican clergy would, in the circumstances, have been unthinkable.

But one could slily poke fun at them, and at the same time at oneself. Like Goldsmith, the Vicar is benevolent and easily duped. He has Goldsmith's droll sense of humour, and his low opinion of women. He is not exempt from Goldsmith's follies and tactlessness. There is something of the author, too, in Sir William Thornhill, that embodiment of benevolence who, in his youth, had dissipated a fortune. Some of George's adventures on the Continent were probably Goldsmith's. George is what Goldsmith would like to have been, handsome, honest, and about to marry an heiress. Mrs Primrose, for whom one can hardly imagine a model, is the silliest woman in fiction, not excluding any of Jane Austen's characters. Few portraits in literature, if we except some of Flaubert's, are more cruel. Prior to her abduction, Olivia is as ignorant and silly as her mother; afterwards, she becomes jealous and entirely self-centred. Young Thornhill is the villain of melodrama, so

[1] *The True Genius of Oliver Goldsmith*, Baltimore, 1969, pp 166–235.

infamous that it is impossible to believe in him. How can we treat the story as serious, when we see this scoundrel punished merely by being reduced at the end to the 'bare necessities of life', occupied 'in keeping some relation in spirits and in learning to play the French horn' (but with a good prospect of the Vicar's blessing on his eventual union with Olivia!). He is a caricature. In Ephraim Jenkinson, however, we are given a comic invention surpassing any in Goldsmith's comedies.

Goldsmith is thus amusing himself from beginning to end. No one is spared, not even Sir William. There is hardly a situation which is not mocked at, or parodied. 'Our eldest son was named George, after his uncle, who left us ten thousand pounds. Our second child, a girl, I intended to call after her aunt Grissel;[1] but my wife who, during her pregnancy, had been reading romances, insisted upon her being called Olivia.' The Vicar poses throughout as lord and master, yet his wife invariably overrules him.[2] He poses as being simple, generous and disinterested; yet he is obviously delighted that George is to marry 'the daughter of a neighbouring clergyman, who was a dignitary in the church, and in circumstances *to give her a large fortune. . . .*'[3] 'Miss Arabella Wilmot was allowed by all (*except by my two daughters*)[4] to be completely pretty.' Here, as though innocently, he is slily and surely not inadvertently revealing his daughters' jealousy and vanity. If intended to be taken in a good-natured way, surely the Vicar would have turned this differently – 'Well, my dears, I except you, of course.' The family, he further tells us, 'had but one character, that of being all equally generous, credulous, simple and inoffensive.' This is hardly borne out when he continues on the same apparently innocent note: 'We were generally awaked in the morning by music, and on fine days rode a-hunting. The

---

[1] Cf the name of Grogan's wife in the second 'paper' on the Coronation of George III on 22 September 1761, and p 252.

[2] Again, as in the same paper.

[3] My italics.

[4] My italics.

hours between breakfast and dinner the ladies devoted to dress and study: *they usually read a page*[1] and then gazed at themselves in the glass. . . .' Again this is not said teasingly, but apparently in all seriousness. Further, the frequency of anticlimax might have hinted to readers that the whole story is a kind of joke, and not as good-natured as it sounds. Here is Dr Primrose on the great 'Whistonian' doctrine:

'Matrimony was always one of my favourite topics, and I wrote several sermons to prove its happiness; but there was a peculiar tenet which I made a point of supporting; for I maintained with Whiston, that it was unlawful for a priest of the church of England, after the death of his first wife, to take a second. . . .

'I was early initiated into this important dispute, on which so many laborious volumes have been written. I published some tracts upon the subject myself, which, as they never sold, I have the consolation of thinking are only read by the happy *few*. Some of my friends called this my weak side; but alas! they had not, like me, made it the subject of long contemplation. The more I reflected upon it, the more important it appeared. I even went a step beyond Whiston in displaying my principles: as he had engraven on his wife's tomb that she was the *only* wife of William Whiston; so I wrote a similar epitaph for my wife, though still living, in which I extolled her prudence, economy and obedience till death; and having got it copied fair, with an elegant frame, it was placed over the chimney-piece, where it answered several very useful purposes. . . .'

Did this seem harmlessly funny to Goldsmith, or is he poking fun at the Vicar's fatuity? It would perhaps be harmless if it were not the Vicar's chief topic of conversation with other clerics; and if, in particular, he had not urged it upon Mr

[1] My italics.

Wilmot at a most inopportune moment. Why, one asks – since Wilmot is described as 'my old friend' – did the Vicar only then discover that he was contemplating a *fourth* marriage? Why had he not protested against the *second* marriage, and the *third*?

Equally absurd is his farewell to George when the young man sets out to seek his fortune in London. For a horse, he gives him a staff (a reminiscence of Goldsmith's story of his return home from Cork, after missing the boat for America), – 'and take this book too, it will be your comfort on the way: these two lines in it are worth a million, "I have been young, and now am old; yet never saw I the righteous man forsaken, or his seed begging their bread."' Worth a million lines, or pounds? The ambiguity seems, as usual, to be designedly deliberate. Here, and throughout the book, the religion is Judaic. Nowhere (except for the great doctrine of monogamy) is there a question of Christian teaching. Righteousness, in the mind of this humorous eighteenth-century Job, is more often than not equated with an eye to the main chance.

Again, readers of the novel might have wondered why the eccentric Burchell, whom we know to be wealthy, should be unable to pay for his two nights at the inn, unless he was merely putting Dr Primrose's charity to the test; and also why, after being warned that Squire Thornhill has seduced nearly every 'farmer's daughter within ten miles round', the Primrose family should not merely welcome him as a guest, but strive to inveigle him into marrying Olivia. Of course, he was rich. As to Mr Burchell, the Vicar's wife 'liked him extremely . . . and if he had birth and fortune to entitle him to match into such a family as ours, she knew no man she would sooner fix upon.' And the Vicar indulgently concludes: 'I was never much displeased with those harmless delusions that tend to make us more happy' – leaving us to wonder what exactly were the delusions he had in mind. Certainly Thornhill's first visit leaves the Vicar in some doubt as to whether the acquaintance should be pursued. He was 'not prepossessed in his favour'.

He adds, 'Let us keep to companions of our own rank. There is no character more contemptible than . . . a fortune-hunter; and I can see no reason why fortune-hunting women should not be contemptible too.' Yet before long he is stating: 'I had too good an opinion of Sophia's understanding, and was too well convinced of her ambition, to be under any uneasiness from a man of broken fortune' – referring to Burchell. And subsequently he allows the women to encourage the Squire's advances, and even arranges for a marriage between Olivia and the honest Williams (Chapters XVI and XVII) as a means of bringing the desirable Thornhill up to the mark! Is Goldsmith here deliberately underlining the Vicar's duplicity? It is hard to say.

Meanwhile a curious controversy has arisen, when it is found that Thornhill is a free-thinker. Mrs Primrose, however, has known several free-thinkers who made very good husbands; Olivia will doubtless be able to convert him, since she 'is very well skilled in controversy'. When her father questions this: 'Indeed, Papa,' replies Olivia, '. . . I have read a great deal of controversy. I have read all the disputes between Thwackum and Square . . . and I am now employed in reading the controversy in Religious Courtship.' – 'Very well,' cried I, 'that's a good girl, I find you are perfectly qualified for making converts, and so go help your mother to make the gooseberry-pie.'

Next day the family dines in the hayfield, while two blackbirds are singing. 'I never sit thus,' says Sophia, 'but I think of the two lovers so sweetly described by Mr Gay, who were struck dead in each other's arms. There is something so pathetic in the description. . . .' Mr Burchell, however, criticises Gay for loading his lines with epithets, and begs leave to read a ballad which, he alleges, is free from this defect; and he reads 'Edwin and Angelina', a hundred and fifty-two verses, from beginning to end. Sophia has been listening tenderly to this sentimental rigmarole when the Squire's chaplain bursts through the hedge to pick up one of the blackbirds which he has shot. A fine sportsman, to shoot a sitting bird! He offers Sophia 'what he had killed that morning', and we are left to guess whether it is the blackbird.

A little later, after Burchell's departure, the Squire arrives with 'two young ladies richly dressed, whom he introduced as women of very great distinction and fashion from town'. As there are not enough chairs, the Squire proposes 'that every gentleman should sit in a lady's lap. This I positively objected to, notwithstanding a look of disapprobation from my wife.' The company then takes part in a dance by moonlight, Thornhill and Olivia 'leading up the ball' to the general delight. Olivia indeed moves so gracefully that Mrs Primrose explains that 'all the steps were stolen from herself'. After about an hour the town ladies wish to stop. 'One of them, *I thought*, expressed her sentiments in a very coarse manner, when she observed that by the living jingo she was all of a muck of sweat.' The Vicar is not sure. He only thinks so! And when the town ladies propose to find situations in London for Olivia and Sophia, he still more incredibly takes them for society women, and not for the procuresses which they obviously are!

His daughters are full of high expectations. A fortune-teller (in return for a shilling) has told Olivia that she is to be married to a squire, and Sophy that she is to have a lord. 'How,' cried I, 'is that all you are to have for your two shillings? Only a lord and a squire for two shillings! You fools, I could have promised you a prince and a nabob for half the money.' Mrs Primrose has the luckiest dreams. 'It was one night a coffin and cross-bones, the sign of an approaching wedding; at another time she imagined her daughter's pockets filled with farthings, a certain sign they would shortly be stuffed with gold. The girls themselves had their omens. They felt strange kisses on their lips; . . . true love-knots lurked in the bottom of every teacup.'

As the town ladies propose to attend church on the following Sunday, Mrs Primrose and her daughters decide not only that they must dress with more than usual care, but that, to avoid looking 'all blowzed and red', they should not take the footpath which was only two miles, but ride the five miles on the road, mounted on the plough-horses. They are not ready when it is time to start, so Dr Primrose goes ahead and, after waiting an hour (and perhaps keeping the congregation waiting) goes through the service. It is only on his way back home, by the road, that he sees a little 'procession marching slowly forward'. The horses had first refused to move, then Mrs Primrose's pillion-straps had broken, and when they were repaired, a horse had decided to stand still, and nothing 'could prevail with him to proceed!'

At a game of blind man's buff on Michaelmas Eve, we learn more about the London women, Lady Blarney, undoubtedly a peeress ('our peeress', as Dr Primrose calls her), 'and Miss Carolina Wilhelmina Amelia Skeggs (I love to give the whole name)';[1] and we hear them engage in the fatuous dialogue which Mr Burchell periodically interrupts with cries of 'Fudge!' – 'an expression which displeased us all. . . .'

This farcical scene is followed by Moses being cheated into selling the colt in exchange for the green spectacles; then by the news that the London project has been cancelled; next by the 'discovery' that 'Mr Burchell is found to be an enemy'; next, by the Vicar's being cheated even more grossly than Moses had been; and finally by the open breach with Mr Burchell, when the latter's 'unexpected insolence' (for he had warned them that he could have them punished for breaking open the lock of his pocket-book) so enrages the Vicar that he cries: 'Ungrateful wretch! begone, and no longer pollute my dwelling with thy baseness. . . . Go from my door: and the only punishment I wish thee is an alarmed conscience, which will be a sufficient tormentor!' Later, when Dr Primrose discovers that

---

[1] In the second 'paper', ostensibly by 'a common council-man' about the last coronation, Grogan's daughter is named Anna Amelia Wilhelmina Carolina. This is supposed to be funny. The paper seems contemporary with *The Vicar* (see p 252).

Mr Burchell has been their vigilant protector, he is in no way abashed by the memory of this baseless and unseemly explosion.

The following chapter contains the episode of the travelling 'limner' who makes 'likenesses for fifteen shillings a head'. The Primroses decide to be 'drawn together, in one large historical family-piece' in the open air, since this will be cheaper and more genteel than the way in which the Flamboroughs had been painted. Mrs Primrose poses as Venus, while her husband, in gown and bands, is presenting her with his works on the Whistonian controversy. The others pose in attitudes equally absurd. When the picture is finished, it proves too large to get into the house, so that it is left to lean, 'in a most mortifying manner, against the kitchen wall'.

But the crowning absurdity is reserved for the moment of Olivia's abduction. The Vicar has asked the 'babe' Dick to sing the 'Elegy on the Death of a Mad Dog', (which turns out to have been adapted partly from the same French comic song, which Goldsmith imitates in the 'Elegy on Mrs Mary Blaize' and elsewhere; and partly from Voltaire's malicious epigram on Fréron). This is followed by a solemn disquisition on elegies and ballads, and a discussion as to which country has the best market for wives. Dr Primrose calls for 'one bottle more. . . . Yes, Deborah, we are now growing old; but the evening of our life is likely to be happy. . . .' Whereupon Dick rushes in with the news that Olivia has been carried off.

'Now then (cries the Vicar) my children, go and be miserable, for we shall never enjoy one hour more. And O may heaven's everlasting fury light upon him and his! . . . Go, my children, go, and be miserable, and infamous. . . .' – 'Father,' cried my son, 'is this your fortitude?' – 'Fortitude, child! . . . Bring me my pistols. I'll pursue the traitor. Old as I am, he shall find I can sting him yet. . . .' His wife tells him that 'the Bible is the only weapon' fit for his old hands; then proceeds to talk even more wildly than he. Olivia 'never had the least constraint put upon her affections', she declares, forgetting that she had insisted on Olivia's encouraging the Squire. 'The vile strumpet has basely deserted her parents . . . thus to bring your grey hairs to the grave, *and I must shortly follow*' (my italics).

This is the family which Goethe found so charming. It is true that Germans are not apt to recognise irony when confronted with it; but how so many other readers seem to have been taken in is more difficult to understand.

In the narrative of a father's journey in pursuit of a lost child, the tone becomes more sober; the irony turns rather from persons to events; and with the discovery of Olivia whom the innkeeper's wife is dragging along by her hair, we return to the mock-sentimental and a series of ludicrous misunderstandings. How inopportune, also, that, on the Vicar's return home, the house should burst into flames as soon as he opens the door! Perhaps the fire had been smouldering, and the Vicar's hasty action lets in the blast of air which sets it off?

After his arrest, although his arm is severely burned and he has fallen into a fever, he manages, despite his grey hairs, to walk eleven miles through deep snow to the county gaol. Here in a cold, stone-paved cell, he sleeps on a bed of straw 'with the utmost tranquility till morning'. And he remains in prison for a month, the arm having miraculously recovered and the fever abated. He even organises the other prisoners and preaches a long sermon – the only one we are privileged to hear. The arrival of Mr Burchell, who reveals himself as Sir William Thornhill, throws Mrs Primrose into a panic, remembering as she does the wicked jokes which she had made at his expense. His nephew Thornhill's entrance is the prelude to a sort of trial scene of comic informality. 'Heavens!' cries Sir William, 'what a viper have I been fostering in my bosom! . . . Secure him, Mr Gaoler – yet hold, I fear there is not legal evidence to detain him' – all this, as though he has only just discovered his nephew's evil character. Can he have forgotten that three years before, when George had called on him in London with a letter from the Squire, Sir William had indignantly repelled him as an 'instrument' of the Squire's vices? Not only Jenkinson but the Squire's butler now give conclusive evidence against young Thornhill, evidence which concerns his persecution of George as well as of the Vicar. 'Good heavens!' exclaims the Baronet, 'how every new discovery of his villainy alarms me . . . at my request, Mr Gaoler, set this young officer, now your prisoner, free, and trust to me for the consequences. . . .' (Apparently he can ignore the normal procedure of justice.) 'Who should' now 'make her appearance but Miss Arabella Wilmot, who was *next day* to have been married to Mr Thornhill.' The reader may recall that well over a month before this, they were to have been married 'in a few days'. Providence has been thoughtful enough to defer the wedding.

'O goodness!' cries the lovely girl, 'how have I been deceived! Mr Thornhill informed me . . . that Captain Primrose was gone off to America with his new married lady.' And after a further revelation of the Squire's debaucheries: 'Good heavens! . . . how very near have I been to the brink of ruin! but how great is my pleasure to have escaped it!'

One pictures Goldsmith writing this story very much as Thomas Gray pictured Sterne in the pulpit, 'tottering on the verge of laughter and ready to throw his periwig in the face of the audience.'

In 1766 readers were understandably puzzled by the 'Advertisement', in which the author admits that 'there are an hundred faults in this thing'. He is supposedly excusing himself for the improbabilities and contradictions in the narrative. Sir William is stated to be only thirty; his nephew must be at least twenty-five. Sir William is the great landowner of the district, a well-known baronet and MP; yet he wanders about under an assumed name without anyone recognising him. Both he and his nephew frequently visit the Primrose family, but always contrive to miss each other. When Dr Primrose meets a fellow-clergyman at the Fair, they discourse on the various turns of fortune they have experienced, Primrose speaking of 'the Whistonian controversy, my last pamphlet; the archdeacon's reply; and the hard measure that was dealt me.' But this is the first we have heard of this episode, or of any archdeacon. Mrs Primrose reminds her husband that he is old; he has told *her* that they both are; yet they have two small children who are described as 'babes'. Had anyone reminded Goldsmith of these discrepancies, he would have been amused. Of most of them he must have been perfectly conscious. He was not a novelist, but a *mystificateur*. In his 'Advertisement' to the story he observes, with an assumed air of old-fashioned piety, "The hero of this piece . . . is drawn . . . *as simple in affluence* (my italics), and majestic in adversity. . . . Such as have been taught to deride religion, will laugh at one [the Vicar] whose chief stores of comfort are drawn from futurity.' The only ground for this is in the last words of the sermon in prison; everywhere else his chief hopes lie in wealthy marriages for his children and in their general affluence.

The 'Advertisement' is simply part of a calculated ambiguity. By making the Vicar *appear* generous, good-humoured and disinterested in prosperity, and courageous, constant (and superhumanly robust) in prison, – the whole retailed in a cleverly smooth style – Goldsmith has contrived that for a hundred and fifty years readers have overlooked the inconsistencies and even, on occasion, the hypocrisy. The ambiguity was a kind of *gageure* against the public, and extraordinarily successful.

One must suppose that the book has been pre-judged on the basis of Goldsmith's winning style and mannerisms, and the beginnings of that elegance of composition which distinguishes his best period. The Vicar's 'dada' becomes amusing under his pen. The girls are indeed arrant minxes, yet deemed worthy to wed into the best family in the neighbourhood; George is a rash youth, but has a noble heart; even sly digs at Mrs Primrose may be intended more to stress the Vicar's forbearance and simplicity than her foolishness; whilst Moses, at least, shows up very well as the obedient, if precocious child of his parents; he is perhaps the family's redeemer. And, however one views them, one must admire the master-touches which hit off this admirable family's idiosyncrasies; and so relieved poor Goldsmith of his smarting sense of his injuries.

II

Goldsmith always entertained a low opinion of the novel as a *genre*. In January 1759 he had advised his brother not to allow the latter's son to read romances or novels, since they depict a happiness which has never existed.[1] In an article on Education in *The Bee*[2] he had disparaged *Tom Jones* and *Joseph Andrews*. In a 'Chinese Letter' of 30 June 1760 he had made Lien Chi ridicule bawdiness and 'pertness' in modern writing, and describe some people's attempts at humour as not humour at all. No one was named; but when the 'Letters' were republished in 1762 as *The Citizen of the World*, this one was headed: 'The absurd taste for obscene and pert novels, such as *Tristram Shandy*, ridiculed'. And we know that at 'a white-bait dinner' at Blackwall, probably in the spring of 1761, he had inveighed against *Tristram Shandy* as obscene and 'derogatory to public taste'. And he had so persisted in disparagement of Fielding and Smollett, as well as of Sterne, that he actually became involved in a brawl.

It could be argued that while composing the Chinese Letters he had discovered in fiction the most satisfying vehicle for self-expression; but this hardly explains a volte-face so complete as that of actually writing a novel himself. This could be accounted for only by an irresistible impulse. The facts appear to be, first that *The Vicar of Wakefield* was not intended to be

[1] To Henry Goldsmith, 1 January 1759. *Collected Letters*, p 60.
[2] 10 November 1759.

a novel, but a parody; and – what lies much deeper – that it was a *riposte* to *Tristram Shandy*.

Goldsmith seems to have regarded himself as the supreme exponent of humour and irony in Britain, and here was the 'Reverend' Laurence Sterne taking London by storm with two volumes full of irony and humour. Though it is unlikely that Goldsmith was as shocked by the caricature of Yorkshire worthies as were Yorkshire people, who recognised the portraits, one may agree with his disapproval of a certain indecency (and not merely a Rabelaisian 'broadness') in Volume I. Yet he can hardly have failed to see that the characters of Captain Toby and Corporal Trim in Volume II were extraordinarily vivid and life-like, and that he was faced in Sterne with a formidable literary rival. Sterne was a declared sentimentalist, who mixed sentiment with pathos in a way that exasperated Goldsmith as much as it enchanted other people. Anything bordering on the sentimental was to be mercilessly ridiculed in *The Vicar of Wakefield*.

Another source of vexation was that Sterne belonged to a clerical family as did Goldsmith, but to a family far more distinguished. His great grandfather had been Master of Jesus College, Cambridge, before becoming successively Bishop of Carlisle and Archbishop of York; while Sterne's uncle and benefactor was a powerful ecclesiastic who had accumulated six important offices in the Church, not to speak of two Rectories – surely a record even in that age of pluralists. Sterne himself had already acquired two benefices; and within two months of the appearance of *Tristram Shandy* he had installed himself in Pall Mall and was being 'waited upon' by admiring peers and by the world of fashion and literature – a social success such as Goldsmith was far from experiencing. He had probably heard that Garrick had become a personal friend of Sterne and had sponsored him in London, and that the reverend novelist had had the effrontery to publish a number of his pulpit orations as *The Sermons of Mr. Yorick*. He may have been spared the bitter knowledge that Bishop Warburton had actually given Sterne a purse full of gold; and that when, in January 1761, Volumes III and IV of *Tristram Shandy* had been published, Sterne had sold the copyright for these to Dodsley for £380. But even without this knowledge, Sterne's success must have been unendurable to a man so envious by nature, above all of literary rivals.

To prove, if only to himself, that he could write a story more humorous than Sterne's, but morally 'pure', was a natural and perhaps irresistible temptation. If it were not, how is one to explain Goldsmith's situating the scene of his story in Yorkshire and choosing as the narrator a Yorkshire vicar, except by regarding it as a counter-blast to Sterne's Yorkshire novel? Naturally, *The Vicar of Wakefield* contains no reference to *Tristram Shandy*; anything of the kind would have exposed Goldsmith to ridicule. No one in fact appears to have seen the connexion between the two works, so different were their subjects and their tone; and yet it seems that, but for Sterne, Goldsmith would never have thought of writing *The Vicar*.[1]

[1] He did begin a novel much later, probably in 1772; and read at least a chapter to Mary Horneck and her sister, when visiting the Bunburys at Barton. See Chapter 16 and Appendix I.

Chapter 23

The Poet (I)

Goldsmith considered the writing of verse as the most digni-
fied, if the least lucrative, of his occupations. He was characterised as 'poet Goldsmith', and it is certain that *The Traveller*
and *The Deserted Village* did far more than any other of his
productions to secure his reputation. He for his part devoted
more time to working over, and improving them than he gave
to either *The Citizen* or *The Vicar of Wakefield*, or indeed to
the comedies. In his own eyes, as in those of the public, he was
primarily a poet.

I

He had begun his career as a poet by publishing occasional
verse, mostly humorous, in *The Bee* in 1759; and he continued
with rather longer pieces to the end of his life. One would
better appreciate the early pieces if they were original, if they
sprang from observation of life or expressed a personal
experience. But they are nearly all adroit adaptations of
French poems. Here, even more than in *The Citizen* and in the
comedies, he was exploiting other men's inventions. 'The Gift:
to Iris, in Bow Street, Covent Garden' is taken from Bernard
de la Monnoye's 'Etrenne à Iris' (1715) and does little credit to
either. On the other hand, 'An Elegy on that glory of her sex,
Mrs Mary Blaize', 'An Elegy on the death of a Mad Dog', and
the 'Elegy on the death of the Right Honourable ***', are at
least amusing, but all use the same humorous trick which he

found in La Monnoye's edition of the *Ménagiana*. Mrs Blaize
had been a pawnbroker.

> Good people all, with one accord
> Lament for Madam Blaize,
> Who never wanted a good word –
> From those who spoke her praise
>
> The needy seldom pass'd her door,
> And always found her kind;
> She freely lent to all the poor –
> Who left a pledge behind.
>
> *   *   *   *   *
>
> Her love was sought, I do aver,
> By twenty beaux and more;
> The king himself has followed her –
> When she has walk'd before . . . etc.

So too with the dog that went mad.

> In Isling town there was a man,
> Of whom the world might say
> That still a godly race he ran, –
> When e'er he went to pray.

The dog bit him and everyone swore he would die, but

> The man recover'd of the bite –
> The dog it was that died.

which is merely imitated from Voltaire's epigram on his enemy
Fréron.[1]

The elegy on the Mad Dog was inserted in the *Vicar of*

---

[1] Itself imitated from a Greek epigram by Demodocus.

Wakefield; the elegy on the politician in the *Citizen of the World*:

> Ye Muses, pour the pitying tear
> For Pollio snatch'd away;
> Oh, had he lived another year!
> – He had not died to-day.
>
> O, were he born to bless mankind
> In virtuous times of yore,
> Heroes themselves had fall'n behind!
> – When e'er he went before.
>
> *   *   *   *   *
>
> His bounty in exalted strain
> Each bard may well display;
> Since none implor'd relief in vain!
> – That went reliev'd away.

These three elegies all owe their character to the old French song of 'Monsieur de la Palice'. Jacques de Chabannes, seigneur de la Palice, who had died at the battle of Pavia, had become the hero of a military song in which each of the many quatrains ends in a truism. It was not hard to invent them, and La Monnoye had added others before publishing it in 1729. Here are typical quatrains:

> Monsieur d' la Palice est mort,
> Mort devant Pavie;
> Un quart d'heure avant sa mort,
> Il était encore en vie.
>
> *   *   *   *   *
>
> On dit que dans ses amours
> Il fut caressé des belles,
> Qui le suivirent toujours
> Tant qu'il marcha devant elles.

Goldsmith could be excused for imitating this, once. Three times was twice too many. Even the epitaph on Edward Purdon, a journalist who like him had been at Trinity College and who died about 1767, is not in the least original.

> Here lies poor Ned Purdon, from misery freed,
> Who long was a bookseller's hack;
> He led such a damnable life in this world,
> I don't think he'll wish to come back.

This comes from 'La Mort du Sieur Etienne':[1]

> Il est au bout de ses travaux,
> Il a passé, le Sieur Etienne;
> En ce monde il eut tant de maux
> Qu'on ne croit pas qu'il revienne.

Olivia's song: 'When lovely woman stoops to folly' in the *Vicar of Wakefield* is effective in its kind of pathos and may be original.

II

In the whole of Goldsmith's work, *The Deserted Village* stands out as a rare, if not accidental, achievement. His natural bent was not for the elegiac, but for humorous narrative and witty portraiture. For years he had suffered from miserable lodgings, and of this the facetious 'Description of an Author's Bed-Chamber' (1759) is a reflexion. But at least he had only himself to care for. His ill-favoured face and person held women at bay and preserved him from what he feigned to believe the dangers of matrimony. Better be wedded to his books than become the neglected husband of an empty-headed coquette. Such were the

---

[1] This borrowing was noted by Forster, ed 1871, vol II, p 60, note, The imitations of 'Monsieur de la Palice' and of Voltaire's epigram were detected by Austin Dobson.

reflexions that inspired, also in 1759, 'The Double Transformation: a Tale' (*Weekly Magazine*, 5 January 1760.)

> Secluded from domestic strife,
> Jack Book-worm led a college life;
> A fellowship at twenty-five
> Made him the happiest man alive;
> He drank his glass, and crack'd his joke,
> And freshmen wonder'd as he spoke.

And all would have gone well if 'Flavia' (evidently a shop-girl) had been content with ogling the customers and had not cast her eyes on poor Jack. The honeymoon was bliss. A year later Jack had found that half her charms

> Arose from powder, shreds or lace;
> But still the worst remain'd behind –
> That very face had robb'd her mind. . . .
>
> By day, 'twas gadding or coquetting.
> Fond to be seen, she kept a bevy
> Of powder'd coxcombs at her levy;
> The squire and captain took their stations,
> And twenty other near relations. . . .

So, what with 'repartee and spleen' between the couple, they drifted apart, until smallpox, robbing Flavia of 'every youthful grace, left but the remnant of a face'. Her beaux now 'flew off by dozens' and

> Poor madam, now condemn'd to hack
> The rest of life with anxious Jack,
> Perceiving others fairly flown,
> Attempted pleasing him alone. . . .

No more presuming on her sway,
She learns good nature every day:
Serenely gay, and strict in duty
Jack finds his wife – a perfect beauty.

III

The Traveller was his first attempt at a poem of any length and
serious intention. He had begun it in Switzerland in 1755, and
resumed and composed it at Canonbury House in 1763 and
1764, with, according to Percy's *Memoir*, 'the greatest care,
and finishing it in his highest and best manner'. In the dedication to his brother Henry he writes: 'I have attempted to show,
that there may be equal happiness in states, that are differently
governed from our own; that every state has a particular principle of happiness, and that this principle in each may be carried
to a mischievous excess.' A plan of this sort he may have had in
mind during his tour of the Continent. He seems at all events
to have been thinking it out, especially towards 1760, when
four papers on 'A Comparative View of Races and Nations'
which are ascribed to him, appeared in the *Royal Magazine*.
Many of the observations appear to be personal, others come
from Buffon's *Histoire naturelle*, but the most important were
taken from Montesquieu's *Esprit des Lois* (Geneva, 1748). *The
Traveller* was not to be a descriptive poem, but a study of the
governments and peoples of the countries which he had
visited, a work of political and moral observation in which the
question of happiness predominated. In all this he was guided
by Montesquieu. The latter had made a systematic tour of most
of the European countries with a view to studying their laws
and governments and, thanks to his intelligence and insight,
had composed a work of lasting importance. In Book III he
had written that there is 'this difference between the *nature* and
the *principle* of a government that the first is its particular
structure and the second the human passions that make it work'.

7. 'The Battle of Temple Bar', showing the heads of decapitated rebels. Goldsmith to Johnson: 'Forsitan et nostrum nomen miscebitur ISTIS.' (see p. 175)

8. A Masquerade at Ranelagh

Laws must be relative to the geographical conditions in which
a people lives, and must respond to its manners, customs and
occupations; all these factors working together. 'If', he writes,
'I could so contrive that everyone should have new reasons for
loving his duties, his ruler, his country, his laws, *and could
better feel his happiness in every country, under every government,*
. . . I should think myself the *happiest* of men.'[1]
  This is Goldsmith's argument; and it is evident that he had
not thought it out for himself. It is also clear that Johnson had
helped him. Johnson had actually written eight out of the ten
concluding lines of the poem:

> How small, of all that human hearts endure,
> That part which laws or kings can cause or cure.
> Still to ourselves in every place consign'd,
> Our own felicity we make or find –

which again is a versification of Montesquieu.
  Goldsmith begins with a rapid survey of the regions he had
visited – some apparently in imagination only – from the banks
of the 'lazy Scheld, or wandering Po', from Carinthia in the
north-east to 'Campania', that is, presumably, the Roman
Campagna, in the south. But his heart turns fondly to his boyhood home, 'And drags at each remove a lengthening chain'.
  Next comes a brief vision of Switzerland, where 'I sit me
down a pensive hour to spend.' He is doomed to wander in
quest of happiness and to discover in every state a different
notion of it:

> Hence every state, to one lov'd blessing prone,
> Conforms and models life to that alone.
> Each to the favourite happiness attends,
> And spurns the plan that aims at other ends;
> 'Till, carried to excess in each domain,
> This favourite good begets peculiar pain.

[1] My italics.

K

A survey of each people in turn is found to confirm this observation.

> Could Nature's bounty satisfy the breast,
> The sons of Italy were surely blest. . . .

But

> . . . sensual bliss is all the nation knows.
> In florid beauty groves and fields appear,
> Man seems the only growth that dwindles here.

The Italians are at once poor and luxurious, submissive and
vain, grave and trifling, zealous and untrue.

> All evils here contaminate the mind,
> That opulence departed leaves behind . . .
> Yet still the loss of wealth is here supplied
> By arts, the splendid wrecks of former pride.

The people find compensation in pretentious shows:

> Processions form'd for piety and love,
> A mistress or a saint in every grove.
> By sports like these are all their cares beguil'd;
> The sports of children satisfy the child.

His last picture is of a peasant who has built his shed in some
palace 'where Caesars once bore sway' and who now 'Exults,
and owns his cottage with a smile'.

Much of this is superficial, with perhaps enough of partial
truth to commend it to the uninformed. It is evident that
Goldsmith had not got on well with the Italians and that he had
not met any Italian of distinction. He twice refers to the Italians
as a nation, when they were as yet nothing of the kind. In
passing through Italy, he had traversed five different states,
each with a different government and where the population,

apart from a small educated minority, thought itself different.
The Piedmontese, subjects of an independent kingdom, were
in fact different in character and outlook from the Lombards,
who were under Austrian rule, and from the Tuscans and
Venetians. Even the languages were not the same. But Goldsmith sums up these populations as a 'nation'.

> My soul, turn from them! turn we to survey
> Where rougher climes a nobler race display,
> Where the bleak Swiss their stormy mansions tread,
> And force a churlish soil for scanty bread. . . .

The conditions of the Switzer's life develop in him the manly
virtues of industry, self-reliance, frugality, contentment, and
patriotism.

> Thus every good his native wilds impart
> Imprints the patriot passion on his heart;
> And e'en those ills that round his mansion rise
> Enhance the bliss his scanty fund supplies. . . .
> And as a child, when searing sounds molest,
> Clings close and closer to his mother's breast,
> So the loud torrent, and the whirlwind's roar,
> But bind him to his native mountains more.

Here, however, are no powers 'that raise the soul to flame',
and so 'Their level life is but a smould'ring fire', except
when, on some yearly festival,

> In wild excess the vulgar breast takes fire
> Till, buried in debauch, the bliss expire.

Finally 'their morals . . . are but low', by which he probably
means that their manners lack charm and refinement.
   He had not apparently heard of Bodmer of Zürich, or
Gesner, or of De Saussure whom he was to meet in London a

few years later; yet all were leading figures in the intellectual life of Europe. He sees no charm in Switzerland, and so

> To kinder skies, where gentler manners reign,
> I turn; and France displays her bright domain,
> Gay, sprightly land of mirth and social ease,
> Pleas'd with thyself, whom all the world can please. . . .
> Theirs are those arts that mind to mind endear,
> For honour forms the social temper here:
> Honour, that praise which real merit gains,
> Or ev'n imaginary worth obtains,
> Here passes current. . . .
> They please, are pleas'd; they give to get esteem;
> 'Till, seeming blest, they grow to what they seem.

But these advantages give rise to such follies as ostentation, vanity and 'beggar pride' – a remark which reflects Johnson's view that in every nation virtues are counterbalanced by vices.

We next visit Holland. To win their land from the sea the Dutch have all acquired 'industrious habits',

> And industry begets a love of gain.
> . . . Their much lov'd wealth imparts
> Convenience, plenty, elegance, and arts;
> But view them closer, craft and fraud appear;
> Even liberty itself is barter'd here. . . .

Holland is 'a land of tyrants and a den of slaves'. The portrait of the Dutch is even more disobliging than that of the Italians. How unlike the latter to their nobler forbears! How unlike the Dutch to 'their Belgic sires of old!'

> Fired at the sound, my genius spreads her wing,
> And flies where Britain courts the western spring. . . .
> Stern o'er each bosom Reason holds her state.
> With daring aims irregularly great,

Pride in their port, defiance in their eye,
I see the lords of human kind pass by. . . .

The British are 'true to imagin'd right, above control'; but
freedom brings its own evils, independence 'breaks the social
tie', factions arise and threaten to stop 'the general system' – by
which he seems to fear that the Englishman's obstinate attachment to 'rights' and liberties will end in anarchy and destroy
the state.

As duty, love and honour fail to sway,
Fictitious bonds, the bonds of wealth and law,
Still gather strength and force unwilling awe.
Hence all obedience bows to these alone,
And talent sinks, and merit weeps unknown;
'Till time may come, when, stript of all her charms,
The land of scholars, and the nurse of arms. . . .
One sink of level avarice shall lie,
And scholars, soldiers, kings unhonour'd die.

All this part is a personal contribution of Goldsmith's, a
diagnosis of what he believes to be a national malady. The
humble Tory regrets the rise of a wealthy middle-class which
will infect the whole nation with materialism and greed. He
deplores the decline of royal power which provides some safe-
guard to the poor; he deplores the increase of commerce and
wealth and has

Seen Opulence, her grandeur to maintain,
Lead stern Depopulation in her train,

as a rich man, by his enclosures, has destroyed a whole village
and forced its dwellers to emigrate 'beyond the western main',

Where wild Oswego spreads her swamps around
And Niagara stuns with thund'ring sound.

Thus, if we exclude the last fifteen verses, *The Traveller* ends with what is to be the theme of *The Deserted Village*. Goldsmith lays claim, implicitly, to the title of political philosopher, and not in vain. If he knew too little of foreign countries to say much of value about them, he had lived long enough in England to see which way the wind was blowing, to put his finger on two of our outstanding faults, and to foresee the dangers which they threaten.

It is usual to appraise *The Traveller* more as a poem than as a 'Prospect of Society'; and while readers were doubtless gratified to think of themselves as 'the lords of human kind' and inclined to disregard the warnings, it seems certain that the poem's popular appeal was due mainly to the smoothness and harmony of the verses and the neatness of the aphorisms. The diction differs little from Pope's, nor is there anything novel in the rhymes, which are adequate for their purpose. *Enjambement*, such as Gray had ventured on, is avoided. From time to time an unexpected repetition of a word serves for emphasis or contrast, as in:

> When I behold a factious band agree
> To call it freedom, when themselves are free.

The antitheses are sometimes striking, but astonish less than the sudden shock of words or ideas which Racine and Pope had employed:

> This favourite good begets peculiar pain.

In brief, in an age of prose, critics and readers welcomed a work which did nothing to conflict with their general view of what 'poetry' should be. When the critic of *The Gentleman's Magazine* hailed 'a new poet, so able to afford refined pleasure to true taste', he meant by 'true taste' the norm of verse as written by Pope; and when he spoke of 'the crude and virulent rhapsodies . . . [which], if known to any future time, will disgrace the present', he was probably referring to Gray's 'The Progress of Poesy' and 'The Bard'.

The Traveller was published on 19 December 1764, as by Oliver Goldsmith, M.B. In reviewing it in *The Critical Review* for the same month, Johnson wrote that the author 'appears by his numbers to be a versifier; and by his scenery, to be a poet', and concluded that 'since the death of Pope, it will not be easy to find anything equal'. In *The Monthly Review* for January, Langhorne considered that the author 'makes no great figure in political philosophy . . . *The Traveller* is one of those delightful poems which allure by the beauty of their scenery, a refined elegance of sentiment, and a corresponding happiness of expression'.

This reads rather strangely today. There is in *The Traveller*, in the accepted meaning of the word, no sentiment for nature, no landscape depicted with its local colour, indeed little that appears to have been observed and experienced. To the Switzer in his 'shed', all around him is dear –

> So the loud torrent, and the whirlwind's roar
> But bind him to his native mountains more.

The landscape is suggested, not described. The interest is not in places, but in men. The versification is certainly elegant, but one can hardly accept the view that nothing equal to it could easily be found 'since the death of Pope'.

According to William Cooke, who had observed Goldsmith composing *The Deserted Village*, he was 'quick enough at prose, but rather slow in his poetry. . . His manner of writing poetry was this: he first sketched a part of his design in prose, in which he threw out his ideas as they occurred to him; he then sat carefully down to versify them, and correct them. . . .'[1]
We may infer that *The Traveller* was written in this manner.

[1] *European Magazine*, vol XXIV, 1793.

In a poem truly inspired, thoughts, words, rhythm or metre, fused into a living thing, spring from the outset from the poet's imagination. What pleased Johnson and other readers was the absence of anything novel or adventurous in the verse-form. In his early *Odes*, and in the *Hymn to Adversity*, Gray had shown what successful effects could be achieved by the use of 7-syllable and 8-syllable verses, by the alternation of 9-syllable and 6-syllable, and in *The Progress of Poesy* by free verse with irregular rhymes. To many readers *The Bard* seemed barbaric. How would they have described *The Fatal Sisters* and *The Descent of Odin?* This is not to imply that Gray's later poems were less finished. They were experiments which pointed the way to his successors: to Shelley, one suspects; and certainly to Arnold who was among the first of those who came to appreciate Gray. Arnold pointed out that, had Gray been born some seventy years later, he might have become one of our major poets. As it was, his genius flowered early, but not abundantly. There is an exquisitely delicate sensibility in the best, and best known, stanzas of the 'Elegy'. *Sunt lacrimae rerum*: he felt this as deeply as anyone, and the reader feels it too, even in the stanza[1] preceding the epitaph. The entire poem has an unique loveliness and moving quality not of his age.

Goldsmith, following Johnson, was a 'retardataire'. Neither he nor Johnson understood that the age was, if slowly, awakening to a feeling for nature and to a sense of wonder in face of the mystery of things. Dryden and Pope had had no such feeling. They belonged to a world where men's imagination had been stifled by Puritan repression. They naturally reacted against this, and hated it, but could not quite throw off the yoke. For them, Nature was external to man, it was not mysterious. Man alone mattered, and his 'nature' could be analysed and explained. He was what he ought to be! Years were to pass before men grew weary of this narrowly rational and inade-

---

1 This appears in the Pembroke College MS., but Gray omitted it in the editions of 1753 and 1768.

quate outlook; before they awoke to the sense of wonder – and to the sense of freedom. This new attitude appears in Christopher Smart; but Goldsmith could not have understood it.

One feels that he had little real inner life; that his outlook was positive and rational; and that his considerable talents could be exercised only within these narrow limits.

IV

Goldsmith thought highly of his ballad of 'Edwin and Angelina'. In 1765 a few copies were 'Printed for the Amusement of the Countess of Northumberland', as by 'Mr Goldsmith'. It reappeared in 1766, with some minor alterations, in Chapter VIII of *The Vicar of Wakefield*, where it is recited by Mr Burchell. Goldsmith reprinted it in his collection of *Poems for Young Ladies* in December 1766; and again in *A Collection of the most Esteemed Pieces of Poetry that have Appeared for Several Years*, in 1767; each time making small changes in the text until, as he told Cradock: 'As to my "Hermit", that poem . . . cannot be amended.' Finally, with the addition of a new stanza (though there were already too many), it was republished in the *Miscellaneous Works* of 1801.

A young pilgrim, overtaken by night in a lonely place, asks his way of a 'Saint-like tenant of the dale'. Far off, he has seen a fire whose 'hospitable ray' gives promise of shelter. But this, the hermit warns him, is 'a faithless phantom'; and he invites the pilgrim to spend the night in his cell. Seeing the stranger oppressed with grief and in tears, the hermit learns that he has come to scorn fortune, friendship and even love.

> 'And what is love? (asks the stranger) an empty sound,
>   The modern fair one's jest;
> On earth unseen, or only found
>   To warm the turtle's nest.'

But 'the bashful look, the rising breast' of 'the lovely stranger' now reveal him as a maiden. She tells her story. The only child, and heiress, of a nobleman who lived 'remote beside the Tyne', she had been courted by many suitors who desired her wealth, but also by Edwin 'who offer'd only love'. She had 'repaid his love with pride' until, in sore dejection, he had 'sought a solitude forlorn, And ne'er was heard of more'.

> 'Then since he perish'd by my fault,
>   This pilgrimage I pay;
> I'll seek the solitude he sought
>   And stretch me where he lay.

> 'And there in shelt'ring thicket hid,
>   I'll linger till I die;
> 'Twas thus for me my lover did,
>   And so for him will I.'

> 'Thou shalt not thus!' the hermit cried,
>   And clasp'd her to his breast –

revealing himself as her 'long-lost Edwin'. Never more will they part, but

> 'From lawn to woodland stray
> Blest as the songsters of the grove,
>   And innocent as they. . . .'

Goldsmith was accused in the *St James's Chronicle*, in July 1767, of having borrowed the subject from 'The Friar of Orders Grey', a 'literary' ballad which Thomas Percy included in his *Reliques of Ancient English Poetry*, the collection he had published in 1765. But it seems likely that both were adapted from a genuine ballad, 'The Gentle Heardsman', which had been printed in Volume II of the *Reliques*, and that 'Edwin and Angelina' actually dates from 1762. In the 'Gentle Heardsman',

the pilgrim is a girl disguised as a youth, the disguise is discovered, but the ending is tragic. Goldsmith turned the herds-
man into a hermit, devised the meeting of the two in the
opening stanzas, and invented the recognition-scene and the
happy ending. All this was very pleasing to the *Critical Review*
in its notice on *The Vicar of Wakefield* in June 1766: 'It is an
exquisite little piece, written in that measure which is perhaps
the most pleasing of any in our language, versified with
inimitable beauty, and breathing the very soul of love and
sentiment.'

The diction is conventional and at times unnatural. Could
anything contain more of artifice than stanzas xii, xiii and xiv?
The hermit has 'trim'd his pleasant fire, / And cheer'd his
pensive guest';

> And spread his vegetable store,
> And gaily prest[1] and smil'd,
> And, skill'd in legendary lore,
> The ling'ring hours beguil'd.

> While round, in sympathetic mirth,
> Its tricks the kitten tries,
> The cricket chirrups in the hearth,
> The crackling faggot flies.

Why 'tries' and 'flies'?[2] 'Plays' and 'faggots blaze' would be
more natural. There is nothing here of the spontaneous language, the words that come naturally and fit the feeling, such
as we expect of real poetry.

A genuine ballad is born of an unsophisticated society,
'primitive' in the sense of 'not advanced'; a society of which
poetry and not prose is the spontaneous expression. In such
ballads we recognise what Thornton Wilder has called 'the
signature of the heart', unspoiled by 'literary' conventions; we

---

[1] Pressed = urged to accept hospitality.
[2] Perhaps he liked the alliterative effect.

feel the untainted air of the uplands blowing through the verses. Of this kind are the medieval English ballads and those collected by Scott in the *Minstrelsy of the Scottish Border*. When in the later eighteenth century new ballads were composed, they were studied imitations. The poetry of Burns, a writer of natural genius, was an exception. But Goldsmith, living in a sophisticated and unpoetical age and milieu, could no more write a genuine ballad than any of his contemporaries. 'Edwin and Angelina', however, appealed to a society in which a taste for the pretty and the sentimental had killed the feeling for poetry and even for art. One has only to compare verses 125–40 of his poem with the four corresponding stanzas of 'The Gentle Heardsman', which he adapted, to feel the startling difference. In the old ballad, the maiden says:

> [I] grew soe coy and nice to please,
>   As women's lookes are often soe,
> He might not kisse, nor hand forsoothe,
>   Unless I willed him soe to doe.
>
> Thus being wearyed with delayes
>   To see I pittyed not his greeffe,
> He gott him to a secrett place,
>   And there he dyed without releeffe.
>
> And for his sake these weeds I weare,
>   And sacrifice my tender age;
> And every day I'll beg my bred,
>   To undergoe this pilgrimage.
>
> Thus every day I fast and pray,
>   And ever will doe till I dye;
> And get me to some secrett place,
>   For soe did hee, and soe will I.

This is poetry, it moves the reader. 'Edwin and Angelina' is not

THE POET (I) 301

of course without a certain skill, or even a few memorable lines,
as when the hermit says:

> No flocks, that range the valley free,
> To slaughter I condemn;
> Taught by that Power that pities me,
> I learn to pity them.

But, when he continues:

> Then trav'ller turn, thy cares forego,
> For earth-born cares are wrong;
> 'Man wants but little here below,
> Nor wants that little long' –

Goldsmith is quoting, or rather expanding, a verse in Young's
Night-Thoughts, 'Man wants but little, nor that little long'. And
by putting it between inverted commas, he supposedly thought
that no acknowledgement was needed.[1]

The time and trouble which Goldsmith gave to amending a
verse here and there, or even an epithet, show what importance
he attached to this effort. Forster considered that such care
should afford an example to be studied by young writers who
might profit by it. All a writer could learn from it is that it was
'Love's Labours Lost'.

---

[1] As pointed out by my wife, Goldsmith took also from Gray's *Alliance* . . . more
than a hint for *The Traveller*, according to Matthew Arnold; but dates are against this
view.

Chapter 24

The Poet (II)

The Captivity: an Oratorio was taken from Psalm 137: 'By the rivers of Babylon, there we sat down, yea, we wept, when we remembered Zion'; the conclusion comes from *II Chronicles*, Chapter 36 and *Ezra*, Chapter I. It contains three Acts; the speakers are two Jewish prophets, two Chaldean priests, a Jewish woman and a Chaldean woman. The chorus consists of Jewish youths and virgins. The prophets and priests speak mostly in rhymed couplets, but sometimes sing in a lyrical metre, as does the chorus. Act I begins in woe, by the waters of Babylon; and passages from the first five verses of the psalm are appropriately introduced; but the last two verses: 'O daughter of Babylon. . . . Happy shall he be, that taketh and dasheth thy little ones against the stones', are judiciously ignored. In Act II the Chaldean priest bids the Israelites acknowledge the gods of Babylon. They refuse, and their prophet foretells the fall of the city. In Act III comes news that the Chaldean army has been defeated by the Persians and that Cyrus, the deliverer, is approaching. The priests repent, since the Lord is stronger than the gods of Babylon; but the Prophet informs them that 'Too late you seek that power unsought before'; and the youths and virgins in chorus hail Cyrus and give praise to God.

It is not known when *The Captivity* was written. It may date from 1761, but Goldsmith probably revised it in 1764. The two manuscripts which exist show that he made many alterations in the text, which suggests that he hoped to get it performed. Professor Friedman has studied Goldsmith's emendations and changes of mind very carefully, perhaps too carefully. In spite of so much painstaking revision, no one set the Oratorio to music at the time, and although a score was composed later, and although the words were printed in 1820, the piece was never performed. The ten guineas which Dodsley and Newbery paid the author were generous in view of its lack of success. Two stanzas from Act II, however, deserve remembering:

> The wretch, condemn'd with life to part,
>   Still, still on hope relies;
> And ev'ry pang that rends the heart
>   Bids expectation rise.

> Hope, like the glim'ring taper's light,
>   Adorns and cheers the way,
> And still, as darker grows the night,
>   Emits a brighter ray.

These stanzas were published in 1776 together with 'The Haunch of Venison', for which they served as a kind of garnishing.

I

The Deserted Village has long been recognised as a minor classic. Goldsmith may have had the plan of it in mind when concluding *The Traveller*, since the picture in verses 401–412 of villagers uprooted by 'opulence' and compelled to emigrate becomes the theme of the later poem. In dedicating it to Sir Joshua Reynolds he writes: 'I know you will object . . . that the depopulation it [the poem] deplores is nowhere to be seen, and the disorders it laments are only to be found in the poet's own imagination. To this I can scarce make any other answer than that I sincerely believe what I have written; that I have taken all possible pains, in my country excursions, for these four or five years past, to be certain of what I alledge, and that all my views and enquiries have led me to believe those miseries real, which I here attempt to display.'

Whether or not he exaggerated the extent of the evil, *The Deserted Village* is a work of real sincerity, and this is one reason why it is superior to his other poems. It expresses a nostalgic regret for his childhood; a genuine love of country-life; a concern for the social effects of the enclosures; and a conviction that the growth of commerce and wealth are an unmitigated evil.

The poem begins with a vivid picture of 'Sweet Auburn, lov'liest village of the plain', and of its dwellers in the days of its happiness. 'These were thy charms – But all these charms are fled.' It is now deserted by all but 'the hollow-sounding bittern' and the lapwing. 'One only master' has seized the domain, and its children have left it.

The poet next strikes the keynote of his work:

> Ill fares the land, to hastening ills a prey,
> Where wealth accumulates, and men decay;
> Princes and lords may flourish or may fade,
>
> *   *   *   *
>
> But a bold peasantry, their country's pride,
> When once destroyed, can never be supplied.

The poet's grief is personal, too. In all his wanderings, he 'still had hopes, [his] long vexations past, / Here to return – and die at home at last'. But this was not to be. As he makes his way through the 'ruined grounds', and sees no living thing but an aged widow who strips water-cress for 'bread', the past rises vividly to remembrance: the 'sweet' sounds of men and girls, of children, noisy geese and watch-dogs, as night comes on, even 'the loud laugh that spoke the vacant mind' – all sounds mingle in what is for him a poetic symphony.

But three pictures, three groups of persons above all, dwell in the eye of memory, the 'village preacher' and the wanderers he befriended; the schoolmaster and his pupils; the alehouse and its inmates.

'Near yonder copse, where once the garden smiled. . . .
There, where a few torn shrubs the place disclose,
The village preacher's modest mansion rose,
A man he was to all the country dear
And passing rich on forty pounds a year. . . .

'Dear', for no one sought his hospitality in vain; and none, however wretched, but found comfort.

At church, with meek and unaffected grace,
His looks adorn'd the venerable place;
Truth from his lips prevail'd with double sway,
And fools who came to scoff, remain'd to pray.

Better still, or should one say, more believable, is the portrait of 'the village master'.

A man severe he was, and stern to view;
I knew him well, and every truant knew;
Well had the boding tremblers learn'd to trace
The day's disasters in his morning face;
Full well they laugh'd, with counterfeited glee,
At all his jokes, for many a joke had he. . . .

The village all declared how much he knew;
'Twas certain he could write, and cypher too. . . .
In arguing, too, the parson own'd his skill,
For ev'n though vanquish'd he could argue still. . . .

Good also is the picture of the inn,

Where village statesmen talk'd with looks profound. . . .
The white-wash'd wall, the nicely sanded floor,
The varnish'd clock that click'd behind the door. . . .
The pictures placed for ornament and use,
The Twelve Good Rules, the Royal Game of Goose; . . .
While broken teacups, wisely kept for show,
Ranged o'er the chimney, glisten'd in a row.
Vain, transitory splendours! . . .

For now 'the man of wealth and pride / Takes up a space that many poor supplied'. And where can the uprooted find refuge? Even 'the common's fenceless limits' are denied him. If he seeks work in the city, he sees only 'baneful arts' and luxuries he cannot share, while his daughter, once modest and virtuous, lies 'pinch'd with cold', near 'her betrayer's door'. But others, far more numerous, have sought a home in distant climes, on that 'horrid shore' where they toil under

Those blazing suns that dart a downward ray,
And fiercely shed intolerable day. . . .
Where at each step the stranger fears to wake
The rattling terrors of the vengeful snake;
Where crouching tigers wait their hapless prey,
And savage men, more murd'rous still than they. . . .

– a picture, heightened by other horrors, of the new colony of Georgia which had been founded largely by the efforts of General Oglethorpe – soon to be one of Goldsmith's acquaintances. The 'tigers', one might add here, were probably cougars (pumas), and not jaguars, which were found only in southern Texas.

After further laments for the lot of the poor exiles, the poet bursts into imprecations on 'these degenerate times of shame', that have followed the days of rural simplicity:

O luxury! thou curst by Heaven's decree,
How ill exchanged are things like these for thee!
How do thy potions, with insidious joy,
Diffuse their pleasures only to destroy!

And he ends with a farewell to Poetry,

Thou source of all my bliss and all my woe,
Thou found'st me poor at first, and keep'st me so. . . .

Poetry, which has fled with the exiles to other shores, 'O!
where'er thy voice be tried'

Still let thy voice, prevailing over time
Redress the rigours of th' inclement clime;
Aid slighted truth with thy persuasive strain;
Teach erring man to spurn the rage of gain;
Teach him, that states of native strength possess'd,
Though very poor, may still be very blessed. . . .

That the enclosure of common-lands and open fields in the
early eighteenth century had displaced a number of villagers,
is true. Most of them seem to have found employment in the
towns; emigration on a large scale was to come only in the
nineteenth century. Goldsmith had apparently seen a case of a
village being uprooted, within fifty miles of London; but the
picture he paints here is partly that of his own Lissoy, where
General Napier, the new proprietor, had refused to renew the
leases of his tenants. That, however, was in Ireland. Taking
England as a whole, research has shown that the suffering
affected very many fewer people than the poet suggests. As to
the larger question of economic policy, one should hesitate to
differ with him. He condemns without reserve all the ideals of
the modern world: the spread of industrialism, an expanding
economy, the increase of wealth and luxury for all. It is now

clear that this cannot continue indefinitely; that it is not even succeeding in its aim; that it is creating hideous towns and polluted rivers; and that, so far from promoting happiness, it is giving rise to envy, discontent and civil disorder. While admitting that, since Goldsmith's time, the industrial trend and its present appalling consequences have seemed inevitable, one must question whether men were not happier and more contented under an agricultural economy, in which industry depended more on hand-work than on machines, than in a complex industrial system, in which the whole community is dependent on the good will of each of the public services.

As poetry, *The Deserted Village* has less to offer. In Auburn Goldsmith was depicting Lissoy where much of his boyhood had been spent; he is also remembering the church of Kilkenny West, of which his father had held the cure. At the same time, he intended it to be taken as a generalised picture of an English village. But the portrait of the pastor is certainly drawn from memories of his father, whose easy-going benevolence, exercised at the expense of his wife and family, is here raised to the level of a virtue; it may also owe something to the character of Henry Goldsmith, who was probably of better stuff. But it is an ideal portrait: such paragons exist only in Plato's Heaven. Oliver's first schoolmaster, Thomas Byrne, may be the principal model for the village master, although some features possibly derive from memories of Griffin or Campbell. The portrait, in any case, is a masterpiece of humour, one of the best things Goldsmith ever wrote.

No other of his works has won him, in the Irish countryside, such affection as this. Lissoy has been renamed Auburn, and the village inn renamed 'The Three Jolly Pigeons' after the alehouse in *She Stoops to Conquer*.

The warmth of feeling that animates *The Deserted Village* finds fitting expression in the style. The rhymes come naturally, although they certainly result from thought and study. They are usually with words of one syllable, which is natural in

English, except in humorous verse and notably in anapaests. But despite the compliments received by Goldsmith for his freedom from poetic jargon, he could still write: 'No cheerful murmurs *fluctuate* in the *gale*', which is below his standard. The versification as a whole, however, is very superior to that of 'Edwin and Angelina'. Metaphors – the very soul of poetry – are adequate but not striking; for example:

> To husband out life's taper at the close,
> And keep the flame from wasting by repose.

A flame wastes more rapidly in a draught. Similes are more uneven:

> And, as an hare whom hounds and horn pursue,
> Pants to the place from whence at first he flew,
> I still had hopes, my long vexations past,
> Here to return – and die at home at last.

This appears to have been suggested by Honoré de Racan's *Stances sur la retraite*, which had first appeared in the *Délices de la poésie française* in 1630. Racan describes the retired nobleman as finding diversion in hunting:

> Aucunes fois des chiens il suit les voix confuses,
> Et voit enfin le lièvre, apres toutes ses ruses,
> Du lieu de sa naissance en faire son tombeau.

It might have been better not to imitate this time-worn, if touching image, but rather Metastasio's image of water drawn up in vapour from the sea, which then falls on the hills, forms rivers, and murmurs and moans 'until it returns to the sea, to the sea where it was born . . . and where, from its long wanderings it hopes to find repose'. Goldsmith's lot, in any case, was hardly as terrible as that of the hunted hare. Again, the comparison of the village pastor to some

> ... tall cliff that lifts its awful form,
> Swells from the vale, and midway leaves the storm,
> Tho' round its breast the rolling clouds are spread,
> Eternal sunshine settles on its head –

is forced and inappropriate. Neither is it original. The image may have been suggested by a like simile in Young's *Night Thoughts*, or have come direct from Chapelain's *Ode à Monseigneur le Cardinal Duc de Richelieu* (1633):

> ... Ainsi le haut Olympe, à son pied sablonneux,
> Laisse fumer la foudre et gronder le tonnerre,
> *Et garde son sommet tranquille et lumineux.*

Be that as it may, one would seek long and far for a peak of which the head is always sunlit.

Despite William Cooke's statement that Goldsmith 'first sketched a part of his design in prose' and then versified it, one may fairly imagine that, during his retreats in the farm off the Edgware Road, he often composed the verses in his head, while sauntering through the fields. He may have begun the poem in 1767. He finished it in 1769, and sold it to Griffin for a hundred guineas. As it was not published until 26 May 1770, Goldsmith probably revised and improved it while it was in proof. Six editions of this quarto booklet appeared in 1770; another in 1772, and an eighth in 1775. C.-M. Campion translated it into French in 1770,[1] and another French version appeared in 1772.

Though it is not known how many copies were printed in each edition, the poem proved immensely popular and set the seal on its author's reputation. Critics praised it warmly for its poetic qualities and congratulated Goldsmith on having freed

[1] As discovered by Professors Seeber and Remak of Indiana University.

himself from 'obsolete words' and 'forced constructions'. On the other hand, both the *Monthly Review* and the *Critical Review* dissented absolutely from his picture of a countryside ruined and depopulated. He had no doubt exaggerated, but he had some ground for anxiety. There probably were one or two instances of a village uprooted for the purpose of laying out 'pleasure grounds'; but in one of these cases the proprietor built a new model village to house the people who had been displaced. Most of the enclosures were effected in order to improve the methods of agriculture. The old system of multiple-strip tillage, without rotation of crops, was inadequate both for the needs of the villagers and for the general growth of population.

II

It is clear from the *Citizen of the World* that Goldsmith's Grub-street days had brought him in contact with very shabby milieux, consisting of folk half respectable, half pretentious, and usually aping their betters. It was only in the course of years that he drew away from them; but they had left their mark. The 'Verses in Reply to an Invitation to dinner at Dr Baker's' seem to date from 1768. Intended to be facetious, they were merely impertinent, and why they were tolerated it is impossible to know. One simply wonders if he was treated as a licensed jester, or if his literary fame in a society singularly devoid of great writers, was regarded as excusing anything. He evidently thought so, for his vanity was now passing all bounds; he was jealous of any rival and even maintained that he could literally do any one thing as well as anyone else. One wonders, in this context, what sort of people the Hornecks really were. One has been used to thinking of them as gentle-folk. They were certainly of the small country gentry, and, with Catherine's marriage to the brother of a baronet, were soon to be going up in the world. But they may at this time have been less than genteel; still perhaps rather provincial, and *mal décrottés*.

Lord Clare, the former Robert Nugent, with whom Goldsmith had become acquainted by 1767 and of whom he was soon to be a boon-companion, was certainly a rough kind of man, good-natured, hardly refined, but an amateur poet of sorts. When in December 1770 he sent Goldsmith a haunch of venison and possibly other gifts from his estate at Gosford, the recipient replied in 'A poetical epistle' – 'The Haunch of Venison' – which appeared posthumously in 1776.

The epistle begins with a eulogy of the venison:

> The Haunch was a picture for painters to study,
> The fat was so white, and the lean was so ruddy,
> Tho' my stomach was sharp, I could scarce help regretting
> To spoil such a delicate picture by eating. . . .

He even thought of keeping it as a show-piece in his chambers, but in the end sent most of it 'to Reynolds undrest / To paint it, or eat it, just as he lik'd best'. While debating what to do with the *neck* and the *breast*, he was surprised by the entry of an acquaintance, 'a Friend as he call'd himself', who insisted on taking the venison for his wife to cook in a pasty, for a dinner to which the poet is bidden next day:

> No words – I insist on't – precisely at three:
> We'll have *Johnson* and *Burke*, all the Wits will be there,
> My acquaintance is slight, or I'd ask my *Lord Clare*.

At this point Goldsmith begins to adapt the story in Boileau's Satire III, familiarly known as 'Le Repas ridicule.' In this satire, the narrator arrives exhausted at a friend's house, to recover from the effects of dining with a man whose importunate invitations he had previously managed to evade. On this occasion he had accepted only because his would-be host had promised good company:

Molière avec Tartuffe y doit jouer son rôle:
Et Lambert, qui plus est, m'a donné sa parole.

This was indeed tempting. Since any public performance of
Tartuffe had been banned by the Parlement, Molière was in
great demand to put on private shows for the nobility; while
Lambert, the musician, could practically never be prevailed on
to turn up to dinner, even though he was always accepting.
But now he had given his word.

To return to the 'poetical episode' – Goldsmith felt, despite
the high-handed way he had been treated:

Tho' I could not help thinking my gentleman hasty,
Yet *Johnson* and *Burke*, and a good venison pasty,
Were things that I never dislik'd in my life,
Tho' clogg'd with a coxcomb, and *Kitty* his wife.

He drives 'in due splendour' to the coxcomb's house, at Mile-
End, of all bourgeois localities!

When come to the place where we all were to dine,
(A chair-lumber'd closet just twelve feet by nine.)
My friend bade me welcome, but struck me quite dumb,
With tidings that *Johnson* and *Burke* would not come.

The same lot had befallen the narrator in Boileau's satire:

A peine estois-je entré, que ravi de me voir,
Mon homme, en m'embrassant, m'est venu recevoir,
Et montrant à mes yeux une allégresse entière,
Nous n'avons, m'a-t-il dit, ni Lambert ni Molière.

They have been replaced by two provincial nobles who con-
sole themselves for the indignity of eating with a low-class

bourgeois by adopting an air of proud self-sufficiency, twisting
up the ends of their moustaches and discoursing (stupidly, in
Boileau's opinion) on the many poets whom they have read.
In this poem, Boileau turns from the satire of bad food, in huge
quantities and uncomfortably served on a miniature table, to
the satire of bad books ('les sots livres'), which was his
favourite topic. It is a very long satire, the most popular of
Boileau's, though not the best.

Goldsmith's is prudently brief. Burke and Johnson are
replaced by 'a Scotchman' and a Jew, and the feast begins:

> At the top, a fried liver and bacon were seen;
> At the bottom was tripe, in a swinging tureen;
> At the sides there was spinnage, and pudding made hot;
> In the middle, a place where the pasty – was not.

It had gone out to the baker's; and while awaiting it, the Scot
and the Jew fall upon the tripe and the liver, while poor Goldsmith sits 'stuck like a horse in a pound'.

> But what vex'd me most was that d---'d Scottish rogue,
> With his long-winded speeches, his smiles and his brogue.

The Jew declares:

> 'I could dine on this tripe seven days in the week:
> I like these here dinners, so pretty and small;
> But your friend there, the Doctor, eats nothing at all.

The host explains that 'He's keeping a corner for something
that's nice: /

> 'There's a pasty.' – 'A pasty!' repeated the Jew,
> 'I don't care if I keep a corner for 't too.'
> 'What a deil, mon, a pasty!' re-echo'd the Scot,
> 'Though splitting, I'll still keep a corner for thot.'

So will the others, and they are still waiting when the maid
enters with the news that the baker

Had shut out the pasty on shutting his oven.

The first thirty-four verses of the poem are wittily invented
and contain topical allusions; the rest is an adaptation from
Boileau, and the key points, as already shown, are mere
imitations. The conversation in Boileau turns mainly and in
detail on books, for all Frenchmen, from the noble to the
waiter on a pavement restaurant, can talk intelligently about
literature. In Goldsmith the company speaks only of filling its
stomach, because he knew that in lower middle-class houses,
food, prices, relatives and their doings, are the main topics of
interest and are discussed *ad nauseam*.

'The Haunch of Venison' is one of Goldsmith's successes.
He felt at home in a setting decidedly low, like Tony Lumpkin
in the 'Three Jolly Pigeons' – and one is reminded here that
nowhere does he give us a conversation among gentlefolk,
except in *The Vicar of Wakefield* and *She Stoops to Conquer*; and
the latter was composed after he had known Reynolds and the
Hornecks, and some noblemen friends of Lord Clare, for some
years past.

The mockery of the Scotsman is impossible to explain.
Prior's belief that it was aimed at Dr James Scott who, about
this time, offered to pay Goldsmith a handsome fee if he would
write in support of the government – an offer which Goldsmith rudely and foolishly rejected – seems incredible. People
have bitten the hand that feeds them, but not usually until they
have been fed. As for the Scottish brogue and the pronunci-
ation of 'that' by 'thot', even if it were the Scottish pronun-
ciation, it would still be a case of the pot calling the kettle
black. Goldsmith three times at least rhymes 'creature' with
'nature,' and his own brogue must have been incredibly
broad.

III

While Goldsmith gave much time and trouble to the long poems, some of his most pleasing effects were dashed off at short notice, in prologues or epilogues. These are wonderfully apt – always adapted to the tone or topic of the play in question, whether his own, or a play by Mrs Lennox, or Murphy, or Cradock. And in these the rhymes are often more original than in the serious poems. The Epilogue to the *Good-Natured Man* is an example; its concluding couplet is almost Shakespearian:

> Blame where you must, be candid where you can,
> And be each critic the *Good-Natured Man*.

He composed three Epilogues for *She Stoops to Conquer* because not only had 'gentleman' Smith declined to play Marlow, but the two principal actresses, Mrs Bulkley who was to play Kate and Mrs Catley who took the part of Mrs Hardcastle, both made difficulties. Murphy had sent an epilogue which was intended to be sung, and Mrs Catley agreed to sing this; but Mrs Bulkley who could not sing, threatened to withdraw from the play unless she could speak it. Goldsmith then conceived the amusing plan of a 'quarrelling Epilogue' in which the two actresses should debate 'who should speak the Epilogue'. Now it was Mrs Catley who refused. But it was very well contrived, with brilliant rhymes, and included an old Irish song 'The Humours of Balamagairy', of which Boswell tells us he himself could sing the tune. Goldsmith next wrote an Epilogue for Mrs Bulkley to speak. It was original and well fitted to defend his plea for a realistic kind of middle-class comedy:

> Of all the tribes here wanting an Adviser
> Our Author's the least likely to grow wiser,
> Has he not seen how you your favours place
> On Sentimental Queens, and Lords in lace;

Without a Star, a coronet or Garter,
How can the piece expect, or hope for Quarter,
No high-life scenes, no sentiment, the creature
Still stoops among the low to copy Nature.

It was not brilliant, but 'Colman thought it too bad to be
spoken'; and this in the end proved fortunate, because the third
and last Epilogue which Goldsmith produced was far more
appropriate and better inspired. Mrs Buklley as Kate Hardcastle
begins:

Well, having stoop'd to conquer with success,
And gain'd a husband without aid of dress,
Still as a Bar-maid, I could wish it too,
As I have conquered him, to conquer you. . . .

She then passes in review the five acts in the life of a pretty
barmaid: in the first, she is harmless and timid, and can say
little better than 'I hopes as how to give you satisfaction'; in
the next, she 'Talks loud, coquets the guests, and scolds the
waiters'; in the third she 'soars' in a City chop-house, 'And on
the gridiron broils her lover's hearts.'

The fourth act shews her wedded to the 'Squire,
And Madam now begins to hold it higher;
Pretends to taste, at Operas cries *caro*,
And quits her Nancy Dawson for *Che faro*.

It is a pity if he thought that *faro* rhymes with *caro*, when *caro*
is accented on the first syllable and *faro* on the second. (*Faro*,
accented on the first, means a lighthouse.) But as his audience
knew no better (unless Baretti and Algarotti were there) it
didn't matter, and the blemish was but slight.

The Prologue which he wrote for Cradock's *Zobeide* (1771),
with its changed evocations of climate and scenery to fit the

sailor Quick's addresses to upper gallery, pit, balconies and stage, – and the background suggested by Captain Cook's voyages – could not be more apt or more amusing. Goldsmith was much indebted to Quick, two years later, when this young actor played Tony Lumpkin; and he expressed his gratitude by adapting Brueys' *Le Grondeur* for Quick's Benefit on 8 May 1773. Meanwhile, he acknowledged Lee Lewes' daring but successful venture at a serious part when he undertook to play Marlow, by an Epilogue for his benefit on 7 May 1773, when he spoke it in his more familiar role as Harlequin. This is a very literary piece. Lewes feigns to scorn his comic turns and the pantomime tricks that accompany them, demons rising from trap-doors and deities dangling from the ceiling:

> No – I will act – I'll vindicate the stage:
> Shakespeare himself shall feel my tragic rage.
> Off! off! vile trappings! a new passion reigns!
> The madd'ning monarch revels in my veins,
> Oh! for a Richard's voice to catch the theme, –
> 'Give me another horse! bind up my wounds! –
> soft – 'twas but a dream.'
> Ay, 'twas but a dream, for now there's no retreating,
> If I cease Harlequin, I cease from eating.

And he then likens himself to the stag in Aesop who, while scorning his 'drumstick shanks' as he sees them mirrored in a pool, suddenly hears hounds and huntsmen on his track and finds that the same shanks will carry him to safety, will save him – as the comedian jumps through the stage door.

IV

'Retaliation' was the last of Goldsmith's poems, not quite finished before he was taken ill; it was published about a fortnight after his death. Three or four people left accounts of the circumstance which gave rise to it, but Garrick being most closely concerned, his statement is probably the most accurate:

'At a meeting of a company of gentlemen who were well known to each other, diverting themselves, among many other things, with the peculiar oddities of Dr Goldsmith, who never would allow a superior in any art, from writing poetry down to dancing a hornpipe, the Doctor, with great eagerness, insisted on trying his epigrammatic powers with Mr Garrick, and each of them was to write the other's epitaph. Mr Garrick immediately said that his epitaph was finished, and he spoke the following distich extempore:

' "Here lies Nolly Goldsmith, for shortness call'd Noll,
Who wrote like an angel, but talk'd like poor Poll." '

'Goldsmith, upon the company's laughing very heartily, grew very thoughtful, and either would not, or could not, write anything at that time: however, he went to work and some weeks after he produced the following printed poem called "Retaliation", which has been much admired, and gone through several editions.'

This MS was found among Garrick's papers and was signed by him. He presumably had a copy of the poem, and there may have been others. Kearsley printed the first edition (18 April 1774), and the seven that followed down to 1777. Some alterations were made, probably from other MS versions; and explanatory notes were added. Garrick's extempore epitaph is usually taken to read: 'Here lies *poet* Goldsmith, etc.,' and this must have been due to revision. The original scene of the challenge was almost certainly the St James's Coffee House, and since the names of those who frequented it are known, one only wonders why Samuel Foote, a character so conspicuous in literary and theatrical London, is not included in the poem.

The reason for Johnson's exclusion is clear: he was not a member of the circle.

The full title was: *Retaliation: a Poem. By Doctor Goldsmith. Including Epitaphs on the most Distinguished Wits of this Metropolis*, and the poem was preceded by an anonymous letter to Kearsley, in which the writer describes how the epitaphs came to be written, without, however, mentioning Garrick. It seems that this person supplied a copy of the poem from which the first edition was printed. An autograph copy by Goldsmith may have reached Kearsley later, and if so, it would account for any revisions.[1]

Goldsmith had recently undertaken to translate the *Roman comique*, and an edition of the latter, in two volumes, figures in the catalogue of his library. It is evident that his interest in Scarron inspired the happy and original picture which occupies the first sixteen verses of 'Retaliation'. His copy of the novel must have contained the memoir which appears in the *Oeuvres de Monsieur Scarron*, as republished at Amsterdam in 1752,[2] for it is here he found the anecdote of Scarron's dinner parties to which he alludes at the beginning of the poem. In this memoir one reads that in the days when Scarron was still a bachelor 'il se faisoit chez lui de jolis soupers, où l'on se divertissoit parfaitement. Les gens de qualité qui étoient charmés de s'y trouver, à cause de la joye qui y dominoit, avoit (sic) soin sans-doute qu'ils ne fussent pas tout-à-fait aux dépens de l'hôte.'[3]

Since it was not customary for the 'persons of quality' who dined at the St James's Coffee House to bring their own food, then

[1] Friedman (vol IV, pp 345–6) thinks that Goldsmith did not intend to write epitaphs on any but the men initially mentioned in the poem; and that the flattering epitaph on Whitefoord was probably composed by Whitefoord himself. It was sent after an explanatory letter to the publisher, who printed it as a postscript in the second issue of the fourth edition.

[2] This edition is cited by Professor Friedman in vol IV of the *Collected Works*, p 352, note 2. Friedman cites in extenso the anonymous letter mentioned above.

[3] Vol I, p 115. I am indebted to Friedman for this citation.

9. 'The Comforts of Bath': a Concert

10. 'The Comforts of Bath': an Evening Reception (see p. 237)

11. Mr Shuter, Mr Quick and Mrs Green in *She Stoops to Conquer*. Tony Lumpkin (Quick) has played a trick on his mother by bringing her back at dead of night to the garden of her own home, where she takes her husband

If our landlord supplies us with beef and with fish,
Let each guest bring himself – and he brings the best dish:
Our Dean shall be venison, just fresh from the plains;
Our Burke shall be tongue, with a garnish of brains. . . .

After Dean Barnard and Edmund Burke, come William Burke, an M.P., Richard Burke, a brother of Edmund, and Richard Cumberland:

Our Cumberland's sweetbread its place shall obtain;

Canon John Douglas, Dean of Windsor; David Garrick; John Ridge, a member of the Irish Bar; Reynolds (who is lamb); Hickey, the attorney whose presence in Paris in 1770 had not been welcome to Goldsmith; 'and by the same rule,

Magnanimous Goldsmith a gooseberry fool.

One notices that it was not a literary circle. Two members only could be considered men of letters, while there were exactly two ecclesiastics, two politicians, two lawyers, one artist and one actor – a well-balanced company, if ever there was one. On all the men named, except Ridge and of course Goldsmith himself, there follow epitaphs which show him at the top of his form in witty portraiture.

For some members of the circle, for Barnard and Douglas, 'The scourge of impostors, the terror of quacks,' and for Reynolds, he has nothing but praise. Other portraits are *nuancés*, and may not have entirely pleased their subjects, but they were not ill-natured. The first is on Dean Barnard:

If he had any faults he has left us in doubt,
At least, in six weeks, I could not find 'em out;
Yet some have declar'd, and it can't be denied 'em,
That sly-boots was cursedly cunning to hide 'em.

L

This passage suggests that Goldsmith, and perhaps also Barnard, had been members of the circle since January, if we suppose that the poem was begun before mid-March. When the circle was first formed, and by whom, it is not known; perhaps about the turn of the year and on the initiative of Edmund and William Burke. Both were members of Parliament and St James's was within easy reach of the Palace of Westminster. The epitaph on Edmund Burke is among the most complimentary, though he is gently reproached with confining his great gifts to politics, and notably to party politics; and is reminded that he did not even there entirely fit in: a man

> Who, too deep for his hearers, still went on refining,
> And thought of convincing, while they thought of dining.

Burke's speeches were too serious, too studied and too long for the taste of the House, and when he rose to address it his fellow-members often trooped out to dinner: hence his sobriquet, the 'Dinner Bell'.

Cumberland is hailed as 'The Terence of England, the mender of hearts' – an extraordinary compliment; but then amusingly reproved for drawing 'men as they ought to be, not as they are.' The following verses summarise what Goldsmith had written in his 'Essay on the Theatre; or, a Comparison between Laughing and Sentimental Comedy':

> Say, where has our poet this malady caught,
> Or wherefore his characters thus without fault?

Was it that,

> Quite sick of pursuing each troublesome elf,
> He grew lazy at last and drew from himself?

He had never been on bad terms with Cumberland, as he was with Kelly, and Cumberland can hardly have resented the

criticism, since he continued to produce plays of the sentimental kind, as well as an occasional farce and tragedy until
1797, and with success.

The epitaph on Garrick is the longest and perhaps the
cleverest. Garrick's supremacy as an actor is stressed, but his
faults great and small are not ignored.

On the stage he was natural, simple, affecting,
'Twas only that, when he was off, he was acting. . . .
He cast off his friends, as a huntsman his pack;
For he knew when he pleased he could whistle them back,
Of praise, a mere glutton, he swallowed what came,
And the puff of a dunce, he mistook it for fame.

'The puff of a dunce' may be a reference to Hugh Kelly who
had dedicated *False Delicacy* to Garrick. If so, it was an ill-
judged remark, because Kelly had a real flair for the theatre,
and was moving in the direction of the comedy of manners.

The last epitaph is a warm and well deserved eulogy of
Reynolds:

To coxcombs averse, yet most civilly staring,
When they judged without skill, he was still hard of hearing:
When they talk'd of their Raphaels, Correggios, and stuff,
He shifted his trumpet, and only took snuff.

Here the poem ends, unfinished; but it appears from an MS
which Prior had before him, and which contained several
erasures, that one half-line would have been included: 'By
flattery unspoiled – '

With its pleasant prejudices, 'Retaliation' remains a little masterpiece of humour and goes to prove that here lay Goldsmith's

talent as a versifier. He lacked the habit, even the instinct for reverie, that makes a poet in any true sense of the word; and he lacked a sense of the tragic nature of life which makes a great poet. But he occupies a high place among our writers of good verse.

Chapter 25

The Dramatist (I)

I

There has been a tradition among writers, particularly in France but also since the eighteenth century in England, that no one has fully established himself until he has staged a successful play. Thus Goldsmith had some justification, and other reasons also, in trying his luck in the theatre. The *Chinese Letters* had shown that he had a sense of the dramatic; that he could compose effective dialogue; and that his bent was for the comic rather than the serious. Apart from these considerations a popular play would bring in far more money than the most brilliant poem. He would get the receipts for the four benefit nights, and would be paid for the rights of publication.

The London public adored the theatre. Throughout the season, which extended from September to May, Drury Lane and Covent Garden drew full houses; while in the early Summer the 'Little Theatre' in the Haymarket was allowed to stage regular plays. A high standard of acting prevailed. This was the age of Garrick and of such famous actresses as Mrs Abington, Mrs Baddeley and Mrs Bulkley. But the quality of new plays fell below the excellence of the interpretation. Since the time of Colley Cibber, no comic dramatist of outstanding ability had arisen. Lillo in *The London Merchant* and Moore in *The Gamester* had struck out a new line, that of the domestic drama or 'tragédie bourgeoise' as Voltaire called it, which impressed and influenced the French, but won no following at home. It was neither genteel nor funny; whereas the public desired fun and applauded every kind of comedy that was not 'low', from the Elizabethan kind and Molière's kind, to the high social comedy of Congreve and the farces of Samuel Foote. Hence writers for the stage either adapted Elizabethan, Jacobean and Restoration comedies (taking care to purge the latter of their indecencies), or they translated or imitated French pieces, both the best known of the Classical Age or the least known of their own. Such adaptations could be numbered by the score;[1] they were not as good as the originals, but they pleased the public. It is not easy today to imagine the prestige which French comedy enjoyed in eighteenth-century London. The successors of Molière maintained it intact; and if the public did not always realise how much of its pleasure was furnished by scenes of French inspiration, the truth was familiar enough to the playwrights themselves. Arthur Murphy, in the course of a career which counted numerous successes at Drury Lane and Covent Garden, showed how very many plots and themes could be adapted from Molière, Destouches and others, without the public's being fully aware of it. Goldsmith, with a lighter touch, but with little more regard for the distinction between *meum* and *tuum*, followed his example, as will be seen.

The comedy of manners, of which Menander had been the first great practitioner, has had a history of well over two thousand years, during which it has never fundamentally changed. Its background is that of a sophisticated middle class, and it has never been merely 'laughing comedy', to use Goldsmith's term. Menander's plays usually contained a love-interest which inspired sympathy, and they often posed serious social problems, although the moral intention was always subordinated to a feeling for art. They often provoked laughter, but as often only smiles; for the humour arose from a subtle insight into character and from the skill with which persons with different characters were placed in novel and unexpected situations; and also from witty dialogue.[2] All this was difficult,

---

[1] J. R. Allardyce Nicoll, *A History of Late Eighteenth-Century Drama: 1750–1800*, Cambridge, 1927, pp 117–22.
[2] See T. B. L. Webster, *Studies in Menander*, Manchester, 1960.

often impossible, to render in another language. Julius Caesar said that Terence's adaptations of Menander were not as funny as the originals; similarly Arthur Murphy, Goldsmith's friend, could not hope to make his imitations of Molière and Destouches as amusing as his models.[1] England in this age produced no great original writer of comedy, no one of the stature of Destouches, and no brilliant and prolific innovator like Marivaux.

But in the late 1760s the element of sensibility, which had been implicit in the comedy of manners from the beginning, received a new and vigorous lease of life from Hugh Kelly and Richard Cumberland; these men became the great box-office successes of the age. But their plays were to prove abhorrent to Goldsmith. He agreed with Boileau that comedy should provoke laughter by exposing vice and folly to ridicule. However, when he began to write *The Good-Natured Man* he was thinking of Kelly's immediate predecessors in the 'sentimental' genre, such as the playwrights Whitehead, Mrs Sheridan and Mrs Griffiths; and especially, according to him, of the cult of the kind of drama which the French had imitated from Lillo and Moore. In the Preface to *The Good-Natured Man*, composed at least two years after he had begun the play, he writes:

'When I undertook to write a comedy, I confess I was strongly prepossessed in favour of the poets of the last age, and strove to imitate them. The term *genteel comedy* was then unknown amongst us, and little more was desired by an audience than nature and humour, in whatever walks of life they were conspicuous. The author of the following scenes never imagined that more would be expected of him, and therefore to delineate character has been his principal aim. . . .'

It is not clear, as some might imagine, that the 'last age' refers to the age of Anne; he may mean the age of Shakespeare.

[1] Allardyce Nicoll, op. cit., p 124.

Goldsmith is thinking of a comedy such as *As you like it*.[1] His
Croaker is a 'humour' character, intended to be on the model
of the melancholy Jaques. He adds that

'. . . in deference to the public taste – grown of late, perhaps, too
delicate – the scene of the bailiffs was retrenched in the representation . . . [it] is here restored. The author submits it to the
reader . . . and hopes that too much refinement will not banish
humour and character from ours, as it has already done from
the French theatre. Indeed the French comedy is now become
so very elevated and sentimental, that it has not only banished
humour and Molière from the stage, but it has banished all
spectators too.'

It does not appear that he was aiming at reviving French
classical comedy, still less anything as true to life – to 'nature' –
as ancient comedy. He will not bring on the stage any wicked
or even unpleasant person; no one like the 'Leno' or the cruel
courtesan who figure in Menander. The former existed in the
London of Goldsmith's time; Hogarth had portrayed him; but
the audience would not have tolerated his appearance on the
stage. In fact the more closely one looks into Goldsmith's plays,
the more one sees him departing from his explicit aim; their
resemblance to the 'sentimental' pieces he decries, and also to
the farces which he does not mention, is obvious. He presents
two pairs of lovers just as the sentimental comedies do; a
'humour' character, as in these; and a genial atmosphere.

Again, Goldsmith suggests that the English stage was
dominated by the sentimental plays and that 'humour' and
'character' were in danger of banishment. Actually, there was
no lack of either in the comedies of his time, nor had audiences
forgotten how to laugh. For years past, the public had been
regaled by the satirical plays of Samuel Foote, 'the English
Aristophanes', and by the amusing farces of Arthur Murphy

[1] Allardyce Nicoll, op. cit., pp 158ff.

THE DRAMATIST (I) 329

and George Colman. It is true that all three relied largely on French models. Goldsmith writes as if no such dramatists existed and as if the delineation of character was to be something new. There were in fact some novelties in *The Good-Natured Man*: the invention of comic situations and absurd misunderstandings, such as Croaker mistaking Olivia for his daughter; Leontine and Olivia imagining that Croaker has understood the situation; young Honeywood trying to conceal from Miss Richland the character of the bailiffs, whom he presents as officers 'in the Fleet'; the episode of the 'Incendiary Letter'; Leontine flying into a rage with Honeywood and challenging him to a duel, because Honeywood had given him 'a bill on the city' – which had been protested; finally, and most absurd of all, Honeywood pleading with Miss Richland on behalf of Lofty (not the only reminiscence of *Twelfth Night*). The vivacity of the dialogue was also in large measure new; and above all, as will be shown later, the personal inspiration. *The Good-Natured Man* is, as it were, a dramatic variation of *The Vicar of Wakefield*. An analysis of the play will bring out these and other peculiarities.

II

The scene of Act I is an apartment in the house of young Honeywood, the 'good-natured man'. Sir William Honeywood who, since his return from Italy, has been an unseen observer of his nephew's heedless benevolence, is speaking to Jarvis, the young man's valet, of disinheriting him. He then leaves the room – for he is never, until the very end, on the stage at the same time as his nephew – and young Honeywood enters. Jarvis, a voluble but just censor of his master's follies, reproaches him with giving away money when he is himself deep in debt, and with encouraging, by his kindness, 'a pack of drunken servants' to plunder and exploit him. Honeywood justifies his indulgence in a passage imitated from *Le Philan-*

thrope, ou l'Ami de tout le monde, by Marc-Antoine Le Grand a play about a similar character.[1] He then speaks of his love for Miss Richland, of his resolve never to reveal it but 'to secure her happiness, though it destroys my own'. He is now joined by Croaker, a well-to-do tradesman and professional pessimist, who is Miss Richland's guardian. The terms of her father's will require her to marry Croaker's son Leontine; but Croaker admits to Honeywood that the match is not much relished by either party. After another scene, between Miss Richland, young Honeywood and Mrs Croaker – an irrepressibly cheerful woman – they leave the stage open for Leontine and Olivia.

Leontine had been sent to France to bring back his sister who has been living since childhood with an aunt in Lyon. But he had gone no further than Paris, where he had met and fallen in love with Olivia. She has entrusted herself to his honour in order to escape being forced into a convent 'by a mercenary guardian'. Leontine has presented her to Croaker as his sister; and he is now faced with the problem of continuing to deceive his father on the one hand, and of avoiding marriage with Miss Richland on the other. He seeks to dispel Olivia's alarm by assuring her that Miss Richland will refuse him. He is confident that 'her affections are fixed upon Mr Honeywood'. Croaker, however, is bent on hastening his marriage with the heiress. To Leontine's objection that she may have no inclination for the match, he replies that 'one half of [her large fortune] she is to forfeit by her father's will, in case she refuses to marry you. So, if she rejects you, we seize half her fortune; if she accepts you, we seize the whole, and a fine girl into the bargain'.

This completes Act I, a well-contrived exposition of a complicated plot. We have been introduced to the two pairs of lovers whose future prospects turn on a legacy, a situation

---

[1] 1724; published in 1731. Philandre ('lover of man') is excusing himself to Duraminte (the 'hard') for his indulgence to the servants. (A borrowing discovered by B. Gassman, in *Philological Quarterly,* vol XXXIX, 1960, pp 57–8.)

which is closely copied from Marivaux' *Le Legs*.[1] In this play, Hortense and the Chevalier correspond to Miss Richland and Honeywood, while the Marquis and the Comtesse correspond to Leontine and Olivia. Hortense is co-heiress with the Marquis to a considerable fortune. If she refuses to marry him, the Marquis will get it all. The Chevalier has no money and Hortense would naturally wish to bring him some; she knows, moreover, that if the Marquis refuses her, he will be obliged by the terms of the will to yield her a third of the fortune. How can she provoke a refusal? She will pretend to be ready to marry him, being sure that he loves the Comtesse. The Marquis on his side adopts similar tactics. He knows that Hortense loves the Chevalier and he has no desire to separate them. He need only therefore pretend to desire marriage with Hortense: she will refuse him, and he will then seize the whole of the heritage. Hence a war of nerves between Hortense and the Marquis, who proceed to throw dust in each other's eyes (if one may mix metaphors). But Hortense has the stronger character. She urges him to send for a notary to draw up the contract and insists that she will sign. In the end he takes fright and draws out. So she keeps her part of the fortune and marries the Chevalier.

It will be evident from Act II of *The Good-Natured Man*, of which the scene is in Croaker's house, that Goldsmith has adopted the whole of this plot, with a few minor alterations to suit his purpose. There are even, in the dialogue, textual borrowings.[2] The introduction of Croaker, and other features discussed above, give, however, a farcical character to Goldsmith's attempt to write a psychological play. In fact the first scene, full of 'double entente', contains a series of comic misunderstandings between Croaker on one side and, on the other, Leontine and Olivia who come near to letting the cat out of the

---

[1] Paris, 1736. First produced at the Théâtre français on 11 January 1736. See *Les Sources françaises de Goldsmith*, pp 150–2.
[2] For a comparison of the texts, ibid., pp 152–4.

bag. Despite his assertion that he is nobody, 'a mere article of family lumber', he orders Leontine to prepare for his marriage.

Miss Richland, in the meantime, has learned from her maid the truth about Leontine and Olivia, 'a young lady . . . of a prodigious family'; and that if Croaker does not 'consent to their marriage, they talk of trying what a Scotch parson can do'. She realises how far the two have tried to deceive her. Her guardian and his son are now about 'to open the affair in form . . . they shall find me prepared to receive them: I'm resolved to accept their proposal with seeming pleasure, to mortify them by compliance, and so throw the refusal at last upon them'. In the next scene, when Croaker brings in Leontine and obliges him to make an absurd declaration, she observes to Croaker: 'Why indeed, Sir, his uncommon ardour almost compels me . . . to comply. And yet I'm afraid he'll despise a conquest gained with too much ease; *won't you, Mr Leontine?*' The poor fellow assures her that he will avoid compulsion. 'No, Madam, I will still be generous and leave you at liberty to refuse' – which, as it transpires, she will have no need to do.

In Act III the scene returns to Honeywood's house, where the two bailiffs, Flannigan and Twitch, have taken possession. In vain the young man assures them that his debts will be discharged in two or three days, and his embarrassment is further increased by a visit from Miss Richland. He presents the bailiffs as 'officers'; she presumes they are 'in the marine service', but is quickly undeceived by the extreme vulgarity of their talk. And Honeywood is saved from further mortification only by a message that Leontine has called and wishes to speak with him.

The idea for this scene had come from a real episode in the life of Richard Steele. Once when bailiffs were in his house and he had invited to dinner 'a great number of persons of the first quality', he dressed the men in livery and had them wait at table.[1] This could have produced some really amusing

---

[1] Johnson relates this story in his *Life of Savage*.

effects. Goldsmith's adaptation is funny, but incredibly low; and it was the disgusting language of Flannigan and Twitch rather than the fact of their being bailiffs that shocked the audience and compelled him to withdraw the scene from subsequent performances. He would have been well advised to rewrite it for the printed version. Molière had introduced peasants and servants into his comedies, 'popular' and 'natural' in their way, but never disgusting: and in any case, the whole character of the scene is out of keeping in a comedy of manners where a certain unity of tone should be preserved.

Miss Richland, left alone on the stage with her maid Garnet, confesses that young Honeywood is being justly punished for his fecklessness; but she also reveals that she has arranged with her lawyer to pay his debts. Sir William who, since his return from Italy, has remained incognito, now enters and engages in conversation with her. While ignorant of his identity, although he knows hers and suspects that she is fond of his nephew, she makes excuses for the latter. Sir William points out that men pretending to 'universal benevolence are either deceivers or dupes'. She adopts a haughty tone until her interlocutor reveals who he is – to her confusion. She even learns that he has been acting on her behalf in the matter of her claims on the Treasury. Sir William, on his part, has been charmed by her generosity to his nephew. 'Thou amiable woman! I can no longer contain the expressions of my gratitude – my pleasure.' They are in an ecstasy of mutual admiration. Sir William then warns her that Mr Lofty, whom Croaker has employed as her business-manager, is perfectly 'contemptible among men in power' and, as we should say, bogus.

This Lofty had been introduced at the end of Act II, but his only real purpose is to furnish a comic element in a piece of which the main plot contained too little material for a five-act play. Announced by his French valet, Dubardieu, he had begun by instructing the latter:

'And if the Venetian ambassador, or that teazing thing the Marquis, should call, I'm not at home. Dam'me, I'll be pack-horse to none of them.' – [To Mrs Croaker]: 'My dear Madam, I have just snatched a moment' – [To Dubardieu]: 'And if the expresses to his Grace be ready, let them be sent off. ...'

Mrs Croaker believes that 'the world is no stranger to Mr Lofty's eminence. ...'

Lofty: I vow to God, Madam, you make me *blush*. I'm nothing ... a mere obscure gentleman. ...
Mrs Croaker: What importance, and yet what modesty!
Lofty: Oh, if you talk of *modesty*, Madam! There I own, I'm accessible to praise.... It was so, the Duke of Brentford used to say to me. I love Jack Lofty, he used to say ...; when he speaks upon his legs, by the Lord, he's *prodigious* ...; and yet all men have their faults; too much modesty is his, says his Grace.

The character comes straight out of Brueys's *L'Important* (1694);[1] even the first part of the dialogue is imitated from the 'Count's' instructions to his lackey, while his remarks to the lady he is visiting are adapted from Brueys. Lofty's pretended modesty, on the other hand, as well as his vanity, were suggested by Marivaux' story of the Strolling Player,[2] which Goldsmith had already adapted:[3]

'Je n'aîme pas à me vanter, moi (says the Player); je suis naturellement modeste, comme vous avez pu voir; cela n'empêchera pas que je ne vous dise que je parus comme un astre.... On ne parlait plus de moi dans la ville que comme d'un

---

[1] See B. Gassman in *Philological Quarterly*, vol XXXIX, 1960, pp 59–62.
[2] *L'Indigent Philosophe*, 3ᵉ feuille.
[3] *Les Sources françaises*, p 149.

petit *prodige*. . . . Mais passons cela, car je ne saurais le raconter sans *rougir*.'

One notices even the repetition of such words as 'blush', 'modesty' and 'prodigious'.

Just after Sir William's revelation of Lofty's character, the man himself comes in and, being unaware of Sir William's identity, speaks of him with disdain and tells Miss Richland that 'it was I procured him his place', and that 'no man had a better head – at a bottle'. A scene of not very subtle dramatic irony.

Act IV, in which we return to Croaker's house, opens with a conversation between Lofty and young Honeywood who regards this impostor as an influential friend. Lofty confesses himself in love – and with no other than with Miss Richland! 'Between ourselves, I think she loves me.' Will Honeywood 'open the affair to her'? And the good-natured man, like any hero of a sentimental comedy, resolves to plead Lofty's suit with the young lady, to 'be the instrument of their happiness, and then quit a country where I must for ever despair of finding my own'.

Lofty's assurance of being loved is a reminiscence of Malvolio's illusions regarding Olivia; while Honeywood's pleading of Lofty's case is a parody of Viola's pleading with the Duke for Olivia. *Twelfth Night*, as well as three French plays, was very much in Goldsmith's mind when composing *The Good-Natured Man*.

In the next two scenes Garnet and Jarvis are assisting 'Olivia' in her planned elopement with Leontine. Jarvis has gone into the City to cash a bill which Honeywood has made out for Leontine, only to discover that it 'is not worth a rush'. To Olivia's anguished outcry: 'How could Honeywood serve us so! What shall we do? Can't we go without it?' Jarvis replies: 'Go to Scotland without money! . . . We might as well set sail for Patagonia upon a cork-jacket.' Garnet however remembers that Leontine had obtained forty guineas from Croaker and advises Olivia to write to the inn where Leontine is waiting for the post-chaise, and ask him to send her half the money. Olivia is beside herself with anxiety, and so Garnet scribbles down a garbled letter, asking for 'twenty guineas [to be deposited] at the bar of the Talbot till called for, [with] expedition [or all] will be blown up [that is, the expedition will have to be abandoned] – All of a flame – Quick dispatch – Cupid, the little god of love'.

Honeywood's butler is entrusted with this missive, but being drunk he drops it. As it is addressed to 'Mr Croaker', that is, Leontine, old Croaker happens to pick it up, and completely misunderstands it. This supposedly 'Incendiary Letter' prepares the way for the hilarious scene in which the comedian Shuter assured the success of the Comedy. He bursts in now with a cry of 'Death and destruction!', reads broken extracts of the letter, including 'or yowe and yower experation will be al blown up' and 'make quick dispatch', and exclaims 'Inhuman monsters! blow us up and then burn us. The earthquake at Lisbon was but a bonfire to it.' Miss Richland, who comes in, refuses to take seriously a man who alarms the house almost daily. If the Jesuits are not swarming in the city, some other dire peril is menacing the kingdom. Young Honeywood enters next with the object of pleading Lofty's suit. She recalls that she had first met Honeywood at the French Ambassador's; and as he now opens in vague language, she supposes he is making a declaration for himself. They talk at cross purposes until she realises that he is speaking for Lofty, and tries to stop him with a cry of 'No more of this!' He still fails to understand, and when she has made it plain to anyone but an idiot that she has been prejudiced in his favour, he still thinks she is speaking of Lofty; and she leaves the room.

Croaker now comes back with the incendiary letter in his hand. Honeywood takes it seriously and proposes that they both go to the 'Talbot' and seize the blackmailer; but not treat him too severely, for 'universal benevolence is the first law of nature'.

The scene of Act V is the Talbot Inn where Olivia has been waiting for the post-chaise to take her to Leontine's inn and thence to Gretna Green. Leontine, however, has joined her and now learns that Honeywood's bill has been protested. Croaker, who enters at the back with Honeywood, asks where on earth his son and supposed daughter are going; and when Leontine discovers that Honeywood has brought Croaker here and so ruined the plan of elopement as well as revealing that Olivia is not his sister, he loads Honeywood with reproaches and insults, whips out his sword and cries: 'Draw, villain!' After a further scene of farce, Miss Richland and Sir William arrive. The latter explains to Croaker that Olivia is really the daughter of Sir James Woodville and therefore at least his son's equal.

Miss Richland asks Honeywood whether he still intends to leave the country. He assures her that he does, leaving her 'to one who loves you, and deserves your love' – that is Lofty. And of course Lofty now enters with his usual boasts of serving his friends by paying 'court to men in favour, such as Sir William Honeywood, and the rest of the gang.' But Sir William exposes his impostures, and declares his own identity, 'discovering his ensigns of the Bath'.

'*Honeywood* (aside):   Astonishment! my uncle!'

Croaker, equally amazed, gladly agrees to Leontine's marrying Olivia. Mrs Croaker, Olivia and Leontine now enter, and Sir William delivers a homily to his humiliated nephew, stigmatising his pretended virtues as contemptible faults. Young Honeywood admits everything and repeats his resolution of going into exile. But his uncle then explains that it is Miss Richland and not Lofty who has been working actively on his behalf and declares that if she will make the man she has befriended happy in her love, he will 'then forget all'. And she has actually to give her hand to Honeywood before he understands his good fortune, and concludes the play with the expected 'moral':

'Henceforth, therefore, it shall be my study to reserve my pity for real distress, my friendship for true merit, and my love for her who first taught me what it is to be happy.'

III

The Good-Natured Man is a patchwork of imitations, many of which Goldsmith must have known that his audience would recognise. He probably supposed that they would amuse them, as they amused him. It was observed, for example, that Croaker was a variation on Johnson's Suspirius. None of this really mattered to him. It is clear from the absurdity of the situations and the theatricality of the language that he not merely aimed at making his audience laugh, but that he himself was laughing at his audience. He was not really presenting a comedy, but the farcical parody of a sentimental play.

But there is far more than this in *The Good-Natured Man*. As in *The Vicar of Wakefield*, Goldsmith has projected himself into his hero, and into the whole bearing of the piece. Nothing is more striking than the way in which he stands apart from young Honeywood, laughs at him, sympathises with him and rewards him in the end. For Goldsmith is still on the defensive. The resemblances with *The Vicar*, of which some are only on the surface, are intentional. Of the two heroines of the play, the only one whose Christian name we know is Olivia – a 'romantic' name taken from *Twelfth Night* and from *The Vicar*. We can be sure that Miss Richland's name will be Sophia. In both pieces the powerful and providential uncle, who remains incognito until the end, is a Sir William; and both pieces are ironical parodies.

Goldsmith's attitude to the world in 1767 remains much the same as in 1765. In a very real sense, *The Good-Natured Man* is a dramatic variation on the theme of *The Vicar of Wakefield*, and an '*Apologia pro vita sua*'. Had the world been just to Oliver Goldsmith, he would have been endowed with a wealthy uncle and been married to a lovely heiress.

IV

As no one penetrated Goldsmith's underlying intention, the critics took account only of the surface-meaning of the play, and even so their verdicts were sometimes diametrically opposed. The *St James's Chronicle* thought that *The Good-Natured Man* would become 'a favourite comedy', if the bailiffs' scene were shortened or omitted and if some of the characters were differently interpreted. *The Gentleman's Magazine* for February considered that the characters were 'admirably drawn, contrasted and sustained', and seemed to be amused by the bailiffs' scene. *The London Magazine* on the contrary regretted that Goldsmith's great abilities had been so 'meanly employed'. He seemed 'to have erred . . . through an accountable (sic) partiality for the humour of Molière, and other celebrated writers of the last century'. A far from well-informed judgement. One sees no particular influence of Molière in Goldsmith's farce. The reviewer was clearly a partisan of sentimental comedy.

'An agreeable play to read' was the verdict of the *Monthly Review*. The bailiffs had 'appeared intolerable on the stage, yet we are not disgusted with them in the perusal'! Goldsmith was actually complimented by the *Critical Review* for his 'delineation of character', though it pointed out that the 'fable' had been neglected, that is, one supposes, that there is no real continuity in the development of the principal plot. This was the most flattering of the notices, although not the most representative of general opinion. The critic of the *St James's Chronicle* in his review of the printed version, expressed pleasure at seeing the public 'at once in possession of two such comedies as *False*

Delicacy and *The Good-Natured Man*; each of which . . . must be allowed to be the production of genius'. After comparing the two, he added: 'The merit of both is great, and we are happy that the beauties of each piece are of a different complexion from that (sic) of the other. . . . The character of Cecil in *False Delicacy* is drawn to the true spirit of comedy, and many scenes of the *Good-Natured Man* abound with the most elegant sentiments.'[1]

The reviewer did not see that all these 'elegant sentiments' were ironical. On the other hand, his praise of Cecil's character – the only one in either play which he mentioned – was well founded. To have depicted an elderly man in love with a young girl, and yet extricating himself from a situation which would have exposed him to ridicule, was no mean achievement.

The Good-Natured Man was revived in 1773, but after that year was not again performed in a public theatre until the Old Vic staged it on 9 December 1971, with success and applause from the critics. Desmond McNamara, wearing spectacles, looking bright and suitably silly, played Honeywood, while Maureen Lipman, also bespectacled, interpreted Miss Richland. One concludes that the director had guessed at Goldsmith's intention. Not surprisingly the greatest success was achieved by Bill Fraser as Croaker.[2] The play has also appeared on television – surely the last word in posthumous glory.

v

Goldsmith had grounds to be annoyed by Colman's delay in producing his comedy, and perhaps to suspect that Colman

[1] *The Good-Natured Man* can be praised as the best *farce* of the age. As a comedy of manners, it is inferior in plot and character-study to George Colman's *The Jealous Wife* (1761), and to Colman's and Garrick's *The Clandestine Marriage* (1766), one of the very few really good comedies of the period 1750–1800. Both were translated into French and German; while the second furnished the libretto for Cimarosa's *Il Matrimonio segreto*, the comic opera which Stendhal never tired of hearing.

[2] Reviews by John Barber in the *Daily Telegraph*, 11 December; and by Frank Marcus in the *Sunday Telegraph*, 12 December.

had agreed with Garrick's wish to let *False Delicacy* go off to a flying start; but even had *The Good-Natured Man* appeared on 15 instead of 29 January, Kelly's play would have been equally popular. Goldsmith is said to have gone about openly disparaging *False Delicacy* and speaking of the stage as being ruled by blockheads, which of course did him no good whatever. But one can recognise that his idea of comedy differed radically from Kelly's.

This is not to say that *False Delicacy* is a bad play or that there are no analogies between it and *The Good-Natured Man*. The characters are afflicted with the exaggerated benevolence which characterises young Honeywood. Lady Betty Lambton, although she loves Lord Winworth, is persuading him to marry Miss Marchmont (Hortensia), an orphan whom she has rescued from penury. Miss Marchmont agrees, although she is in love with Sir Henry Newbury, an attractive rake. Thus three possibly desirable marriages will be frustrated by good intentions on the part of those promoting them, and by complacency on the part of most of the victims. Fortunately Mr Cecil, a reasonable middle-aged man, and Mrs Harley, a humorous character, see the absurdity of the situation and are anxious to mend matters. Meanwhile, Newbury persuades Miss Rivers to agree to elope with him; but she changes her mind; and Cecil intervenes to prevent Newbury from forcibly abducting her. Newbury draws his sword on Cecil who, however, refuses to be cowed and shames him into compliance. In the end, Cecil and Mrs Harley make fun of the victims of false delicacy and oblige them to recognise, and act on, their real inclinations.

The plot, which appears to be original, is well calculated to excite interest and expectation. The parallelism in the characters and their situations may have been suggested by Racine's *Andromaque*. It is not so much a sentimental play, as a satire on excessive refinement and benevolence, and a plea for frankness in matters of the heart; in short a thoughtful play, which deserved its success.[1] Riccoboni translated it into French and made £700 out of the venture.

[1] Kelly drew even further away from the 'sentimental' formula in his subsequent pieces. In *A Word to the Wise* (1770) Miss Dormer pokes fun at 'an elevated thought in a sentimental comedy'. *The School for Wives* (1773) contains really amusing scenes. According to Lady Rachel, managers 'alledge that the audiences are tired of crying at comedies.' (Cited by Allardyce Nicoll, op. cit., pp 155 and 165).

Chapter 26

The Dramatist (II)

I

The first night of *The Good-Natured Man*, when the success of the play hung in the balance, had proved such a trial for Goldsmith's nerves that he abandoned, at least for the time being, any idea of pursuing his success. Losing all sense of proportion, he indulged in absurd strictures on his fellow dramatists. Thus, to say in public that the stage was being ruled by blockheads was worse than a mere outbreak of childish petulance; it was to insult Garrick as well as Colman, and neither of them was likely to forget it. One is astonished that, at the age of thirty-nine, Goldsmith had still not learned that success comes as much by influence as by merit.

Despite his resolve to write no more for the stage, his subsequent visit to Paris suggested to him the subject of a new comedy, in the experiences of an English family who go to France to save money; at first he did not follow up the idea. When the plan of *The Mistakes of a Night* began to take shape is not known. He began it when staying with Lord Clare in the spring of 1771, wrote most of it at the Selby's farm in the summer, and in a letter of 7 September told Bennet Langton that it was finished. He then appears to have laid it aside for a time, since most of his working hours were devoted to the *Animated Nature*.

Between 1768 and 1771 he must have reflected that in any play the principal plot should be kept in the forefront, as it had not been in *The Good-Natured Man*; that the 'hero' of a comedy should have a more positive fault or weakness than young Honeywood's; and that no sharp contrast should be allowed between serious scenes and farcical, but a certain unity of tone maintained throughout. It is not that the two plays differ greatly in any but the first of these defects, but the second play shows a slight improvement in its structure.

To Goldsmith's biographers the behaviour of Colman is inexplicable, while Garrick's refusal of the play is put down to vanity or caprice; yet anyone at the time except Goldsmith could have foreseen that both theatre-managers would raise difficulties. Goldsmith had gone out of his way to disparage them, and they were in a position to make themselves awkward. Colman must have seen that the new play was a good deal better than the average comedy, but he probably felt no desire to do Goldsmith a good turn, and if he temporised for so long, it was due to a fear that Garrick might change his mind. That, at least, seems the likeliest explanation. Johnson and others finally induced him to accept the play, but not to change his attitude. For this, Goldsmith had no one but himself to blame. As weeks went by, the actors and actresses, infected by Colman's pessimism, created difficulties; 'Gentleman' Smith refusing to play Marlow (a rather contemptible role) and Woodward to act the part of Tony Lumpkin (which probably struck him as vulgar and absurd); while Mrs Bulkeley and Miss Catley quarrelled about the Epilogue.

Meanwhile, Garrick's rejection of the play and Colman's pessimism had so alarmed Goldsmith that, in order to prepare the public for an eventual performance, he composed a manifesto, entitled an 'Essay on the Theatre; or, a Comparison between Sentimental and Laughing Comedy', which appeared in the *Westminster Magazine* on 1 January 1773. He begins by citing Aristotle's definition of Comedy, and insisting on its separation from Tragedy. 'Boileau, one of the best modern critics, asserts that comedy will not admit of tragic distress:

Le comique, ennemi des soupirs et des pleurs,
N'admet point dans ses vers de tragiques douleurs';

and he illustrates the principle with examples. 'Distress, there-fore,' he adds, 'is the proper object of tragedy, since the great excite our pity by their fall; but not equally so of comedy, since the actors employed in it are originally so mean,[1] that they sink but little by their fall.' He now begins to follow and adapt Voltaire's article on 'Art dramatique' in the *Dictionnaire philosophique*, as shown elsewhere.[2]

'Since the first origin of the stage, tragedy and comedy have run in distinct channels, and never till of late encroached upon the provinces of each other. Terence, who seems to have made the nearest approaches, always . . . stops short before he comes to the downright pathetic. . . . All the other comic writers of antiquity aim only at rendering folly or vice ridiculous but never make what Voltaire humorously calls a *tradesman's tragedy*.'[3]

This is very well put, and Goldsmith is not to be reproached with being not quite accurate. No one then had any knowledge of Menander, except through the scattered fragments. Even so, he seems to ignore the success of the many French tragi-comedies since the time of Robert Garnier, and also of such Shakespearean plays as *Cymbeline* and *Winter's Tale*. He next begins to ridicule the new

'Sentimental comedy, in which the virtues of private life are exhibited, rather than the vices exposed; and the distresses rather than the faults of mankind make our interest in the piece. . . . In these plays almost all the characters are good, and exceedingly generous; they are lavish enough of their *tin* money on the stage; and though they want humour have abundance of sentiment and feeling. . . .

[1] One wonders if Goldsmith regarded young Honeywood as 'so mean' that his humiliation was of little account.
[2] In *Les Sources françaises*, pp 144-7.
[3] 'Tragédie bourgeoise.'

'But it will be said, that the theatre is formed to amuse mankind, and that it matters little, if this end be answered, by what means it is obtained. If mankind find delight in weeping at comedy, it would be cruel to abridge them in that . . . innocent pleasure. . . . [But] the question is whether a character supported throughout a piece with its ridicule still attending, would not give us more delight than this species of bastard tragedy?'

Voltaire had called it 'une espèce bâtarde.' A little further on in his article he had described the genesis of La Chaussée's *Préjugé à la mode*, the most famous of the 'comédies larmoyantes', and after criticising it, had observed:

'Ce n'est pas ainsi que Molière fait parler ses personnages. Dès lors le comique fut banni de la comédie. On y substitua le pathétique; on disait que c'était par bon goût, mais c'était par stérilité. . . . On ne travaille dans le goût de la comédie larmoyante que parce que ce genre est plus aisé; mais cette facilité même le dégrade: en un mot, les Français ne surent plus rire.'[1]

Goldsmith expands all this in a very lively fashion:

'Sentimental comedy (he writes) will continue a kind of *mulish* production, with all the defects of its opposite parents, and marked with sterility. . . .

'But there is one argument in favour of sentimental comedy, which will keep it on the stage. . . . It is, of all others, the most easily written. . . .

'Humour at present seems to be departing from the stage . . . and it will be but a just punishment that when, by our being too fastidious, we have banished humour from the stage, we should ourselves be deprived of the art of laughing.'

If we did not know that Goldsmith was simply repeating Voltaire, a glance at the new comedies and farces which had

[1] *Dictionnaire philosophique* (73 articles), Geneva, 1764; 6th edn (112 articles in 2 vol), 1769, *Oeuvres*, ed Moland, vol XVII, pp 419-20.

appeared since *The Good-Natured Man* would show that humour was by no means departing. Colman's *Man and Wife* (1769) had been a success, though it was not a very good adaptation of *La fausse Agnès* of Destouches (1736; published in 1759); while Foote continued to turn out amusing farces, such as *The Lame Lover* (1770) – Foote had lost a leg and was able to treat his infirmity as a joke; *The Maid of Bath* (1771) and *The Bankrupt* (1773). None of these were sentimental. Goldsmith, following Voltaire, also writes as if the choice lay between the extremes of laughing comedy and sentimental, which was to misrepresent the situation. One of the most delightful French pieces of the earlier period, Destouches's *Le Philosophe marié* (1727), contained features both amusing and 'sentimental', and was later to be imitated by Mrs Inchbald in *The Married Man* (1789). *Le Glorieux* (1732), reckoned as one of Destouches's best plays, had similar features, though this author seems then to have been moving in the direction of pure comedy, as *La fausse Agnès*, a masterpiece of humour, makes evident.

II

Whether or not *She Stoops to Conquer* is a better play than *The Good-Natured Man*, it has always been more popular at home and abroad, and has remained on the repertory. Even its critics admitted that it made one laugh. Unforeseen situations, practical jokes, heroic impulses frustrated by set-backs or down-to-earth considerations, comedy of character and sheer farce – the content of the play is very complex, as a brief analysis will show.

The main theme comes from *Le Jeu de l'Amour et du Hasard*,[1] as has long been observed.[2] But instead of introducing

---

[1] First performed in January 1730 by the Italian *Comédiens*, for whom Marivaux was the regular purveyor.

[2] By Jules Guiraud in his edition of the English text (Paris, Berlin, 1892); and by A. Barbeau in his edition (Poussielgue, 1908). See *Les Sources françaises*, pp 155–62.

Marlow direct into the Hardcastle's manor, as Dorante is introduced into M. Orgon's house, Goldsmith has grafted on to this
plot the story of his own real *or alleged* mistake in taking Squire
Featherstone's house for an inn. After the opening scenes
between Hardcastle and his wife, and between Hardcastle and
his daughter, the 'Alehouse Scene' introduces Tony Lumpkin,
who is to prove the heart and soul of the play; but who is here
used for the purpose of directing Marlow and Hastings to his
stepfather's manor. He tells them that the way to Mr Hardcastle's is far too difficult for them to find that night, 'damn'd
long, dark, boggy, dirty, dangerous'; and advises them to put
up at the 'Buck's Head', one of the best inns in the country.
They are taken in by this because, on reaching Hardcastle's
manor, they see a large pair of horns mounted over the door –
extraordinary as that must appear. The 'Alehouse Scene' then
affords a plausible transition to Act II, in which Hardcastle, in
expectation of his guests, is training four of his servants to wait
at table. One of them, Diggory, refers to the famous story of
Ould Grouse in the gun-room. The arrival of the two young
men is thus prepared, and their initial error explained. Marlow
learns that Miss Hardcastle is here – supposedly at this 'inn' –
but when he meets her he is so bashful that he dares not look
at her face, which is shaded by a large hat (another artifice, like
the horns) and instead of paying court stutters nonsense. This
timidity was almost certainly suggested by the scene between
Isabelle and the tongue-tied Philinte in Destouches' *Le
Glorieux*[1] (Act II, scene 5), while his earlier anxiety that
Hastings and Miss Neville should not leave them *en tête-à-tête*
recalls Philinte's desire for Lisette to remain in the room to
help out the conversation.

A little later (Act III) when Kate is in her 'housewife's
dress', as she calls it, his manner changes, he takes her for the
bar-maid and tries to kiss her. She then decides to maintain the

---

[1] As noted by the anonymous reviewer of the present writer's *Les Sources françaises*
in *Times Literary Supplement,* 7 August 1924.

disguise and see whether he will bring himself to offer marriage, without knowing that she is Kate Hardcastle. This affair proceeds exactly as in Marivaux's play, and the feelings involved and even the language in Acts IV and V are imitated from the scenes between Dorante and Silvia in Act III of *Le Jeu de l'Amour et du Hasard*.

A further complication has been invented by bringing in Marlow's friend, Hastings, and Constance Neville, the girl he loves, who are as much astonished at meeting each other so unexpectedly at the Hardcastle's, as the reader. Tony has been expected by his mother to court Constance on account of her money, much of which consists in valuable jewels which she has with her. They pretend to court by teasing each other; and as Tony no more cares for her than she for him, he is quite ready to thwart his mother's plans. In order to prevent Constance from eloping with Hastings and taking her jewels, Mrs Hardcastle has decided to take her that very evening to the house of an aunt who lives at some distance. With this in view, Tony is ordered to have the carriage and coachman ready and to accompany them on horseback, even though this will involve a difficult night-journey, with the risk of being waylaid by highwaymen. Tony agrees and, under cover of darkness, directs the coachman through by-roads round and round the Hardcastle's manor, without his mother's recognising the familiar country. He stops the carriage at last a few yards behind the garden; when Squire Hardcastle, roused by the noise and coming out to investigate, is taken by his wife for a highwayman.

Hardcastle, meanwhile, has been nearly 'distracted' by the way in which Marlow has ordered him about. He tells the young man to quit the house. Marlow flatly refuses; but he now discovers that his host is a friend of his father; and when Kate laughs heartily at his supposing the house to be an inn, his former arrogance turns into dismay. He still thinks that Kate is a servant, and regrets that she is the only member of the family with whom he will be reluctant to part: 'But, to be plain with you, the difference of our birth, fortune and education make an honourable connection impossible.' In Act V his father, Sir Charles Marlow, arrives unexpectedly – but conveniently – and when he learns of his son's blunder, he cannot refrain from laughter.

Hardcastle – And yet he might have seen something in me above a common innkeeper. . . .
Sir Charles – Yes, Dick, but he mistook you for an uncommon innkeeper; ha! ha! ha!

From Marlow and Kate, who come on and go off the stage as if on purpose to miss each other, the older men discover that young Marlow is still under a misapprehension regarding Kate. When he comes to take leave of her and finds her alone, he has difficulty in tearing himself away. She tells him he will feel easier in a day or two; but in the end he determines to offer marriage, and to atone for his past conduct by 'respectful assiduities'.

The intrigue therefore ends, as it had begun, exactly like the affair in *Le Jeu de l'Amour et du Hasard*. At the beginning of that comedy, Monsieur Orgon informs Silvia that he has received a letter announcing the arrival of Dorante, who is proposed as her future husband. He is the son of an old friend of Orgon's; but the proposal is made only on condition that it shall be mutually agreeable to the young people. Silvia is not to treat her father's suggestion with any complacent desire to please him (Act I, scene ii). Hardcastle makes an identical announcement to Kate (Act I, scene iii). In Marivaux's play, Silvia, the better to study Dorante's character without his knowing it, changes dress and place with her maid, Lisette. Dorante soon discovers that the supposed Lisette is far more attractive in character and education than the false Silvia; and in the end he offers marriage despite what he takes to be the disparity in rank. The feeling and behaviour, sometimes even the words, of Marlow in Act V are the same as those of Dorante in Act III, scene viii.[1]

In Marivaux's play Dorante's mistaking Silvia for the maid is natural and unavoidable. Marlow's error is not. A man of the world could not mistake a country manor-house for an inn, or a gentleman for an innkeeper, or a young lady for a barmaid. Marlow's not even daring to look at Kate while talking to her – a timidity ascribed to bashfulness in presence of a lady – is artificially contrived. When he meets her in her working clothes, he at once turns amorous and loquacious. He is a great favourite, he tells her, 'at the Ladies Club[2] in town. I'm called their agreeable Rattle.... My name is Solomons. Mr Solomons, my dear, at your service.' (Offering to salute her.)

Miss Hardcastle – Hold, sir.... And you're so great a favourite there, you say?
Marlow – Yes, my dear. There's Mrs Mantrap, Lady Betty Blackleg, the Countess of Sligo, Mrs Langhorns, old Miss Biddy Buckskin,[3] and your humble servant, keep up the spirit of the place.

Just as there are many more topical allusions in this play than in *The Good-Natured Man*, so the characters are more lifelike, but not always more likeable. Marlow's conversation with Kate in Act III, part of which is quoted above, gives one a poor idea of his morals. He had told his servants to make themselves at home and drink as much as they like. No gentleman would have treated a courteous innkeeper as insolently as he treats Hardcastle in Act IV. In Act IV, scene ii, he tells Hastings

---

[1] For textual proof, see *Les Sources françaises*, pp 157–62.
[2] It was a new Club for social amusements and 'gallantry', but '*no scandal*'; and was designed to be called 'The Paphian Society'.
[3] The reference, which was to Miss Rachael Lloyd, involved Goldsmith in trouble and a further imprudence, from which Beauclerk and Garrick extracted him. See p 167.

that the barmaid, as he thinks her, is his. 'She's mine, you rogue. . . .'

Hastings – But are you so sure, so very sure of her?
Marlow – Why man, she talk'd of shewing me her work above-stairs. . . .
Hastings – But how can *you*, Charles, go about to rob a woman of her honour?
Marlow – Pshaw! pshaw! we all know the honour of the bar-maid of an inn. I don't intend to *rob* her . . . there's nothing in this house, I shan't honestly *pay* for.
Hastings – I believe the girl has virtue.

A singular character for the hero of a comedy, and one who goes to explain why Horace Walpole thought this the lowest of farces. It was not, in any case, Marlow who made the success of the piece, but Tony. Allardyce Nicoll thinks that Goldsmith was here drawing from Shakespearean comedy – as he certainly had in the earlier play – and that Tony is in the tradition of Sir Toby Belch. This may well be so, although Goldsmith may also have had in mind the Irish squirelings whom he had known as a young man. Marlow, however, goes back not to Shake-speare, but to the rakes of Restoration comedy. Tony, in spite of his rough manner and practical jokes, is more of a gentleman at heart.

III

If, as we have seen,[1] public response to the play and to the printed version was enthusiastic, criticism was divided both as to its technical merits and as to the kind of comedy best suited to the age.

In the view of the *London Magazine* (March 1773), the play was badly constructed, the 'incidents not naturally rising from

[1] See p 162.

the subject', but twisted 'in order to make things meet'. Yet the author should perhaps be pardoned 'for taking the field against that monster called Sentimental Comedy. . . .' However, 'in aiming at this point, he seems to have stepped too far; and in lieu of comedy, he has sometimes presented us with farce'. The *Critical Review* surveyed the recent evolution of comedy in France and England, concluding that since the time of Vanbrugh, Farquhar and Steele, true comedy had entirely languished in both countries. It criticised both French and English dramatists for following the fashion set by La Chaussé (sic) in the *Comédie Larmoyant* (sic), and went on to commend Goldsmith's 'attempt to revive the dying art', and to speak of 'the uncommon merit of his performance'. This was little more than a summary of Goldsmith's article in *The Westminster Magazine*, including its inaccuracies. The critic[1] in the *Monthly Review* for April displayed more intelligence in his appraisal, and also a keen awareness of the changing manners and morals which comedy may be expected to take account of; since 'Comedy is a dramatic representation of the prevailing manners of people not in very high or very low life.' Few English writers of comedy had been original, he said, except for Vanbrugh, Congreve and Farquhar, whose merit lay in representing the manners of their times. Since then, however, a gradual alteration has taken place, 'arising from trade and the progress of the arts, which "has brought the nation as it were together" ', and reduced the differences in characters. Hence some writers have 'very judiciously had recourse to what is called *sentimental Comedy*, as better suited to the principles and manners of the age. A general politeness has given a sameness to our external appearances. . . .' Some writers, he admits, have gone too far; but 'they are right in their general principle'. Now the plot of *She Stoops to Conquer* 'is a series of blunders . . . such mistakes as never were made, and, we believe, never could have been committed. . . . In this light we are obliged to con-

---

[1] William Woodfall, to whom Goldsmith refers in 'Retaliation'.

M

sider Dr Goldsmith's play, as most of its incidents are offences against nature and probability. We are sorry for it, because he certainly has a great share of the *vis comica.*' The performance may make us laugh, but the printed version gives no pleasure. Goldsmith should 'employ his talents . . . by taking some story of a distant date, when the manners were generally such as he chuses to represent'.

The judgement is sound, although insensitive to the merits of Goldsmith's style. But it represents a well-reasoned defence of the 'sentimental' genre, and we know that at least half of the public agreed with it and continued to applaud sentimental plays for the next twenty-five years. One guesses that the critic had admired Richard Cumberland's *The West Indian* (1771) which was in fact 'better suited to the principles and manners of the age' than Goldsmith's comedy. As this was certainly one of the plays which Goldsmith had in view in his *Essay on the Theatre,* a glance at it will enable one better to judge of the validity of his attitude.

IV

The West Indian presents the doings of the well-to-do young Belcour, who has just arrived in London from Jamaica and is staying with his merchant banker, Mr Stockwell. He is the child of a secret marriage between the clerk of a rich planter and the latter's daughter. Dreading her father's wrath, she caused the baby to be left at his door; he had brought up the foundling and made him his heir. The planter and his daughter are now dead, and the erstwhile clerk is Mr Stockwell. He plans to see how his son, who is unaware of the relationship, will behave.

In this strange world of London, Belcour at once becomes involved in the affairs of two neighbouring families, that of Lady Rusport and her stepdaughter Charlotte, and that of Dudley, an elderly captain on half-pay, and his children,

Charles an ensign, and Louisa, the heroine of the play. Charles, who is Lady Rusport's nephew, is in love with Charlotte, but refrains from declaring himself because of his family's poverty; although Charlotte would accept him. The Dudleys are lodging with a bookseller named Fulmer and his unscrupulous wife. Belcour meets the fair Louisa and falls desperately in love: they doubtless have that way in the tropics. Mrs Fulmer agrees to arrange a meeting in her house, and gives Belcour to understand that Louisa is not Charles's sister but his mistress. Concluding that she is therefore 'a profest wanton', he tries to seduce her. She refuses; her brother intervenes, brands Belcour a villain, and they are beginning to fight, when they are separated by an Irish mercenary, Major O'Flaherty, who is courting Lady Dudley. The young men, however, are to meet for a formal duel at the London Tavern. O'Flaherty agrees to be Charles's second, and Stockwell, on hearing the news, agrees to be Belcour's. He gathers that the quarrel is due to a misunderstanding; he has also discovered that the Fulmers have stolen Charlotte's jewels which she had sent to Stockwell as security for a loan of £200 – to help Captain Dudley.

To make ends meet, the Captain can regain his commission, for service in Africa, on paying £200. Now Belcour, on hearing of his plight, had already given him the money – an early example of American generosity. But now, having received Charlotte's diamonds from Stockwell with instructions to return them, he had not resisted the temptation to win Louisa's compliance by giving them to her. He had then bought another set of diamonds, of greater value, which, in a state of trepidation, he brings to Charlotte. She sees that they are not hers, but more valuable, and instead of displaying the indignation he expects, is enormously amused. The Fulmers, meanwhile, have been arrested when the diamonds were recovered, and Fulmer has confessed that his wife had deceived Belcour as to Louisa's identity, and that she is really Charles's sister. So the two young men are reconciled.

Lady Rusport, a money-loving Puritan, had inherited a substantial fortune from her father and she assumes that she will also have inherited her late husband's money; even so, she has refused to help her nephew Charles or his father. But now Varland, the Estate Solicitor, arrives with the news that, in a will made just before his death, her husband had left half his fortune to Charlotte, half to his nephew Charles, and an annuity to herself. The delay in bringing this news has been caused by a journey to Scotland where Charles has been on service; Varland has still not traced him, but there is no doubt about the will. Lady Rusport offers him £5,000 for it, and he is tempted to accept when he is surprised by the ubiquitous O'Flaherty who, having access to Lady Rusport's house as her suitor, has overheard the conversation. He easily compels the solicitor to hand over the will, which he will give to Charles.

Thus Charles can now propose to Charlotte. But what is to happen to Belcour and Louisa? In a private interview, Belcour confesses his faults, but does not conceal his lasting adoration. She for her part has been attracted to this vigorous but simple-souled colonial. Stockwell commends him to her and a marriage is arranged. Lady Rusport departs in a rage and, after Stockwell has revealed himself as Belcour's father, all ends happily at a banquet in his house.

Belcour, in Allardyce Nicoll's view, is modelled on Tom Jones, and his behaviour is not unlike that of Fielding's hero. But he seems far more than this. He is the first example in literature of the innocent colonial or ex-colonial, arriving in London (or Paris) and either deceived or bewildered by the corruption of the Old World – a theme which has hitherto been associated with Henry James's novels. Lady Rusport is another credible and realistic character. Balzac would of course have studied her in greater detail, painted her in somewhat darker colours and shown her as actually obtaining and destroying the will, much as in *Ursule Mirouet* Minoret-Levrault destroys the doctor's will; Varland would of course have taken the £5,000. By dint of accumulated detail, Balzac would have made Lady Dudley sound more credible; but Cumberland has still painted her to the life.

Goldsmith, in 'Retaliation', gently reproaches Cumberland with painting people not as they are, but as they ought to be. In *The West Indian* the Fulmers are rogues who are planning to escape to France after leaving their creditors in the lurch. Varland is hesitating whether to accept £5,000 for the will – a strong inducement to which, but for O'Flaherty's intervention, he would have succumbed. Of Lady Rusport one can say, she knows that if one offers a bribe, it should be substantial. That, apart from these four people, the other characters can be described as 'good', is the sort of situation we should expect in real life. One is at a loss to understand why writers on Goldsmith have accepted without demur his extraordinary misrepresentation of Cumberland.

The West Indian is a kind of romantic play, containing more realistic than idealised characters; although the concluding scenes are too sentimental by contemporary standards. It presents a story more original and more intelligent than *She Stoops to Conquer*, and it is forward and not backward looking. It established its author's reputation for years to come and remained for a long time on the repertory. But Cumberland[1] lacked the verbal brilliance of Goldsmith; he had not made his name as novelist and poet; and he was not backed by such influential men as Johnson and Reynolds. And so *She Stoops to Conquer* has survived, while *The West Indian* has not. Further-

---

[1] Richard Cumberland (1732–1811) was a grandson of Bentley, the great classical scholar and Master of Trinity College. His father had been appointed Bishop of Clonfert, on the Shannon, and Richard composed *The West Indian* while visiting his parents there. The play was revised by Garrick and staged in a particularly spectacular manner. It ran for twenty-eight successive nights and was more successful than any recent comedy; 12,000 copies of the printed version were sold. A royal command performance was given in 1785. Cumberland was a good scholar, well and widely read, and a handsome man; but apparently, like Goldsmith, jealous of rival authors. His *Memoirs* are not regarded as reliable. (See S. T. Williams, *Richard Cumberland: His Life and Dramatic Works*, Yale University Press, 1917.)

more, Goldsmith's reputation on the Continent ensured a favourable reception for his play. Two French comedies were adapted from the principal plot: *La fausse Auberge* (1789) and *L'Hotel Godelot* (1876); while Tony Lumpkin's exploit furnished the idea for *Un Voyage à Dieppe* (1821), in which F.-J.-D. de Bury develops the joke in a manner far more psychologically amusing.[1]

[1] See Appendix II.

Chapter 27

The Translator

In the course of his career Goldsmith undertook three translations, though he did little towards the last one.

There had appeared at the Hague in 1757 the *Mémoires* of Jean Marteilhe of Bergerac, a Huguenot who had been condemned to work in the galleys, apparently between 1700 and 1713, but who had escaped and found refuge in Holland. In March 1758 a translation of this work was issued by Griffiths and Dilly under the title of *The Memoirs of a Protestant, condemned to the Galleys of France for his Religion. Written by himself.* . . . [Translated] by *James Willington*. The evidence, based partly on a receipt for £6 13s 4d to Goldsmith from Dilly, indicates that Goldsmith had translated the book, although it is possible that Willington, who had studied at Trinity College, Dublin, while Goldsmith was there, had taken a hand in it. Austin Dobson, who published a more accurate version of these *Memoirs* in 1895, thought, however, that Goldsmith had adopted Willington's name as a pseudonym.

Marteilhe's narrative was to win the admiration of Michelet; among its merits are sobriety and freedom from exaggeration. Goldsmith in the preface, which is certainly by him, observes that the merits of the work may be considered by some readers as defects. There is nothing artificial in these pages; no events to astonish . . . no 'high finished pictures', but 'the simple Exhibition of Truth'. The reader 'must be satisfied to see Vice triumphant and Virtue in distress; to see men punished or rewarded, not as he wishes, but as Providence has thought proper to direct. . . .' He continues for a time in this strain, then explains the Revocation of the Edict of Nantes and the sufferings of the French Protestants at greater length, stigmatising the cruelty of Louis XIV and appealing to English patriotism in language as vigorous as that of Marteilhe is moderate.[1] The translation is fairly free. Goldsmith was probably well advised in making it shorter and more spirited than the original, though by no means very accurate. As however he had had to work in haste on a two-volume book, this was perhaps excusable.

A verse translation of Marco Vida's *Scacchiae Ludus* – the Game of Chess – came into the possession of Bolton Corney and was first printed in Cunningham's edition of Goldsmith's Works in 1854. Both regarded the handwriting of the manuscript as Goldsmith's. J. W. M. Gibbs reprinted it in Volume II of his edition in 1885. Gibbs considered it belonged to the period following the appearance of *The Traveller*, because of the great care evident in the MS. and also of the effort to take up (in Forster's words) 'the manner of the great master of translation, Dryden'. The care is evident from the interlineations and erasures, such as occur in Goldsmith's acknowledged works. American critics, however, do not consider that the MS. is in Goldsmith's hand, and this view explains the exclusion of Vida's *Game of Chess* from the Friedman edition. Even if it could be proved that the MS. is not in Goldsmith's writing, the translation could still have been copied by one of the penurious Irishmen whom he sometimes employed.

The versification is clearly the work of a writer as skilled as Goldsmith in handling the rhymed couplet. The version contains several examples of triple-rhymes, which are not a habit of Goldsmith's, and one does not detect any Irish rhyme, such as creature–nature. Internal evidence is not therefore conclusive; but as the translation consists of 679 verses, a practised versifier like Goldsmith might well have indulged in the

[1] Marteilhe is said to have lived to the age of 93. His daughter married an English naval-officer, Vice-Admiral Douglas.

popular triple-rhyme scheme. It seems fair, all things considered, to give him the benefit of the doubt.

Prior to the mid-eighteenth century, chess had been most popular in Spain and Italy, and the great players belonged to those countries. But Philidor's *Analyse des Échecs* (1749), the most frequently printed work on the game, rendered it fashionable in England as well as in France. Philidor, equally well known as an operatic composer, excelled as a blindfold chessplayer, and when visiting London, sometimes played three games simultaneously at the Chess Club in St James's Street.[1] Goldsmith must have heard of these remarkable performances, and they may well have inspired the translation of Vida's poem.

Marco Vida of Cremona, one of the brilliant neo-Latinists of the Renaissance, had made his name with the *Scacchiae Ludus*, and been rewarded by Leo X with the Bishopric of Alba. After this he had written a *Christiad*, an epic on the life of Christ in the idiom, and even to some extent in the atmosphere, of the *Aeneid*; and also an *Ars Poetica*. In the *Scacchiae Ludus* he explains how the game originated; it was when Jupiter and the other gods were visiting Ethiopia, in order to celebrate the marriage of Neptune. On this occasion Neptune produced a chess-board, with the pieces, and explained the rules. These, with a trifling exception, are the rules still observed (verses 81–162). The nomenclature was the ancient one, as explained in a footnote by the translator. Thus 'Archer'= Bishop; 'Horse'= Knight; 'Elephant'= Rook.

Phoebus and Hermes were commanded to play, and the former had white. Before long the Black Queen took the White Rook, and Phoebus would have lost his Queen too, by moving the pawn which protected her, if Venus (who was sitting opposite) had not warned him with a wink, so that he drew back the pawn. Jove then ruled that once a move was made, it must stand; Hermes, however, was so furious that he nearly swept all the pieces from the board. Recovering himself,

[1] These details have been pointed out by my wife.

he made a Bishop leap like a Knight; but Phoebus detected the cheating and made him withdraw it. The gods laughed aloud. After a time Hermes put back a pawn and a Knight which he had lost. This misdeed was observed by Vulcan, and Jove compelled Hermes to remove the pieces. The numbers on each side were now equal, and Phoebus seemed to be doing better, while Hermes burst into tears. In the end, however, the White King was mated.

Jove rewarded Hermes by giving him the mysterious wand which can send, or deny, sleep. Soon after this, Hermes brought the game to Italy. Here he saw

> Scacchis, the loveliest Seriad of the place,
> And as she stray'd, took her to his embrace,
> Then, to reward her for her virtue lost,
> Gave her the men and chequer'd board. . . .
> And taught her how the game was to be play'd.

*   *   *

> E'en now 'tis honour'd with her happy name;
> And Rome and all the world admire the game,
> All which the Seriads told me heretofore,
> When my boy-notes amus'd the Serean shore.

One regrets to think that Goldsmith could not have written so clever a poem; to translate it was for him the next best thing.

To Goldsmith has also been ascribed a translation of Paul Scarron's *Roman comique*, but this version is of more than doubtful authenticity. He seems to have promised to undertake the task, and in 1776 Griffin issued a version under the title of *The Comic Romance of Monsieur Scarron. Translated by Oliver Goldsmith. In 2 volumes. . . . London, 1775* (sic) *in 12⁰*. The first two parts of the *Roman comique* were by Scarron himself, the sequel was by Offray. It was excellently written, both in the comic episodes and in the romantic stories which interrupt the main narrative. The publisher's foreword states that, except for a few sheets, the version was made by Goldsmith, and that it was needless to insist on the merit of a work bearing his name; that the natural ease and delicacy of his style . . . have made him particularly capable of such an enterprise. He has preserved Scarron's true spirit, and has taught him to relate his story with grace, in good English.

The most recent of Goldsmith's biographers believes that our author translated a fair part of the French novel; but a close scrutiny of the English version dispels any such illusion.[1] It is very badly drawn up. The table of Contents does not invariably correspond with the text. The translator began by numbering the chapters without regard to the division of the novel into Parts; then, in the middle of Part II, he suddenly resumed the numbering of the original. The translation itself is not always very faithful; but, what is worse, it lacks the savour of Scarron's style, and it contains expressions which are not even English.

One may concede that Goldsmith hurriedly wrote a version of the first few chapters out of the twenty-three contained in Part I. The text is at times abridged, or expanded; a passage in Chapter I (page 4 of the English version) has been very well handled. Chapter III is not so good. An amusing passage in Chapter IX is omitted, perhaps by an oversight. The English of Chapter X is so bad that Goldsmith could not have been responsible for it; and there are fearful blunders in Chapters XIV and XXIII. At the beginning of Part II, Scarron's excellent prose reads: '. . . le silence régnait sur la terre, si ce n'était dans les lieux où se rencontraient des grillons, des hiboux et des donneurs de sérénades' – and for 'grillons' the English version has 'critics' instead of 'crickets'.

The names of certain characters are not rendered uniformly. In the early chapters, the name of the old actress La Caverne is

---

[1] Gibbs regarded Goldsmith's authorship of this translation as doubtful.

rendered by 'Cave', who is at times *Miss*, at other times *Mrs*; but in Chapter XVIII we find 'Madame Cave', and in Chapter XXVI she again becomes 'Mrs Cave'. Similarly, the heroine Mlle. de l'Estoile is at first called 'Stella', and also 'Mrs Stella'. In Chapter XVIII she becomes 'Star'. In Part III she is 'Mrs Star' and 'Star'; but in Chapter IV of Part III she is first 'Star' and then 'Stella'. The name of 'Inézille' is rendered with three different spellings.

Goldsmith's borrowings from French writers in his various works make it clear that he was a competent and elegant translator. In the present instance, one must conclude that he had handled only a small fraction of Scarron's novel.

[1] The use of 'Mrs' for an unmarried actress was correct in the eighteenth century.

Chapter 28

The Compiler

From the beginning to the end of his career Goldsmith remained a hack-writer, so that the bulk of his works were of only ephemeral value and for the past century or so have not been reprinted. If in his own lifetime they were more profitable than his original writings, it was because he had the art of abridging and popularising the work of serious historians and scientists.

His 'Histories' comprise some early religious works, on 'The Life of Christ', and 'The Lives of the Fathers', which were for the most part abridgements of earlier works.[1] There followed *An History of England, in a series of Letters from a Nobleman to his Son,* (1764, 2 volumes); *A Concise History of England; or, the Revolution of the British Constitution* (1765), which is a shortened version of the above; *The History of England from the Earliest Times to the Death of George II* (1771, 4 volumes); *An Abridgement of the History of England* (1774); *The Roman History* (1769, 2 volumes); *Dr Goldsmith's Roman History abridged by himself for the use of Schools* (1762); and *The Grecian History* (June, 1774).[2]

For the *History of England in a series of Letters,* his principal source was Rapin-Thoyras's work, up to the time of Charles I; but he used David Hume's *History of England* for the later period, and Voltaire's *Essai sur les Moeurs.* In *The History of England . . . to the Death of George II* he used much of the same

---

[1] See p 105.

[2] In a novel by Susan Warner, one reads that 'Mr Goldsmith's History' was used as a text-book in the U.S.A. as late as 1850. It was also in use in England in the same period.

material, supplementing it by reference to Thomas Carte's *General History of England* (1747–55, 4 vols) and Smollett's *Complete History of England* (1757). Paul de Rapin-Thoyras's *Histoire d'Angleterre, jusqu'à la mort de Charles Ier*, with a continuation, had appeared at the Hague between 1724 and 1735, in 13 quarto volumes.[1] It is a vast work, methodically arranged, and devoted mainly to a study of political institutions, ecclesiastical history being treated in several sub-chapters. In his 1771 volume Goldsmith follows Rapin's general plan for the division of the material, though he does not treat church affairs apart. Resemblances between Rapin's narrative and Goldsmith's are more striking in the medieval period than in the more modern. Thus the parts treating of King Alfred's attempts to improve the system of education; the consequences of the Norman Conquest; the Scottish invasion of 1346 and the Battle of Neville's Cross, are definitely taken from Rapin and lead one to conclude that for the Middle Ages he was Goldsmith's principal source. In following Hume for the period of the Great Rebellion and more recent times, he deprecates Hume's scepticism and even remarks that he 'seems desirous of playing a double part' – a rather disobliging criticism of an author to whom he was so much indebted.

In the Preface to his *Roman History* he explains the need for a book more compendious and easy to handle than the standard works, apparently the only ones, then existing. Rollin's *Histoire romaine*, to the battle of Actium, was in 16 volumes (1739–50), while Crevier's continuation, on the Imperial Epoch, contained ten. Hooke's *Roman History* covered the same period as Rollin's in 4 volumes (1738–41). Echard's work had originally appeared between 1695 and 1698 in 2 volumes, but subsequent editions contained five. Goldsmith probably also consulted the *Histoire de Rome* by François Catrou and

---

[1] This was the first serious attempt ever made to write a general history of England. An English version of the part written by Rapin himself, that is, down to 1649, had appeared between 1725 and 1731 in 15 volumes.

P.-J. Rouille of which a translation had been issued between 1728 and 1737; but he regarded it as too expensive and 'too meanly written to please'. On the other hand, none of these works possessed much critical value. Charles Rollin, honest professor though he was, had no understanding of the past; by commending Livy and Plutarch to his students, he – as Lanson observes – was unconsciously giving them a course on Republican manners and morals and so preparing a way for the Revolution. Goldsmith, in short, had set himself, in the *Roman History*, to collate and summarise the work of mediocrities. The same may be said of his *Grecian History*. One is amused to learn that it was actually translated into Greek.

Goldsmith had certainly felt some interest in history from his boyhood days. Livy and Tacitus, possibly also Polybius, he had studied at Trinity College; and he had acquired some knowledge of Xenophon and Plutarch. The historian, he says, must understand the human heart and try 'to catch the imagination'. No other study affords us 'so much wisdom on such easy terms'. In the chapter on universities in the *Present State of Polite Learning*, he holds that 'a course of history should precede a course of ethics'; but when advising his brother on the education of the latter's son, he makes no mention of it. He merely says that a good understanding of 'Latin, French, arithmetic, and the principles of the civil law', and of course clear handwriting, constitute 'an education that may qualify him for any undertaking.' Goldsmith was hardly an authority on education.

He of course had no leisure or opportunity for the study of primary sources, which real historical writing requires. Even so, one would have supposed that, after reading so much, he would have been led to speculate on the inner mechanism of historical development or even on the philosophy of history as a whole. He had reviewed Voltaire's *Essai sur les Moeurs* and probably glanced over the *Siècle de Louis XIV*, and so must have observed the role which Voltaire ascribes to 'providential princes' in cultural history. He could have asked himself how far a great man may have turned the whole course of a nation's destiny. And if he had troubled to read Pascal's *Pensées*, he would have seen the astonishing part which contingency plays in diverting the course of history, since Pascal points to definite instances of this.

There is no sign that he felt any curiosity in regard to these matters. One even wonders how much he remembered, once he had finished a compilation. 'His mind was entirely unfurnished,' someone said of him. A knowledge of Latin was usual in men who had taken a university degree. Goldsmith's knowledge of French literature was exceptional; but most educated men and women knew French, many spoke it and some wrote it correctly. But of the general information which is needed in social converse and which in any case adorns the mind, he possessed very little. If he and, say, Topham Beauclerk, who had had decidedly less formal schooling, had been set an examination on English history, general science and general knowledge, Beauclerk would have come out far ahead.

Goldsmith's 'Histories', which are the most voluminous of his writings, are no more than well-written potboilers.

One may perhaps put in a *caveat* in favour of *An History of the Earth and Animated Nature*, because nothing so compendious then existed in English and also because Goldsmith was genuinely interested in the subject and had previously written a long introduction to Brookes's *Natural History*. The book was published posthumously in 1774, by J. Nourse, in eight octavo volumes,[1] with illustrations copied from Buffon's *Histoire naturelle*, but badly reproduced. The publisher must have supplied him with a bound proof, since the work is listed as 'imperfect' in the catalogue of his library.

In the general Preface he reproaches writers like Ray,

---

[1] Part I: general Preface and Description of the Earth (vol I). Part II: Quadrupeds (vols II – IV). Part III: Birds (vols V and VI). Part IV: Fishes (vols VI and VII). Part V: Reptiles (vol VII). Part VI: Insects (and Zoophytes) (vols VII and VIII). References are to the 1774 edition.

Linnaeus and Brisson with giving 'the dry . . . air of a dictionary to their systems'; whereas Buffon, the most talented of all naturalists 'has almost entirely rejected method in classing quadrupeds'. He himself has adopted a method intermediate between that of the 'system-makers' and Buffon's. 'In other respects, as far as this able philosopher has gone, I have taken him for my guide.'

In Part I he reviews recent theories regarding the formation of our planet, and passes on to a general description, geographical, geological and meteorological. This is, in both senses of the word, the least animated part of the work.

In reading the remaining seven volumes, one is impressed in the first instance by the great interest of many of the descriptions, an interest due not merely to the charm of the style. Many of them are detailed, even well-informed; some are justifiably amusing. Thus 'the Marmout (sic) is chiefly a native of the Alps; and when taken young is tamed more easily than any other wild animal. . . . It is readily taught to dance, to wield a cudgel, and to obey the voice of its master.' After speaking of its burrow and nest, Goldsmith describes how it hibernates in winter when its body-temperature falls very low. A long chapter in Volume IV, based on Buffon, is devoted to the Elephant. 'Nothing can be more formidable than a drove of Elephants as they appear . . . in an African landscape; wherever they march, the forest seems to fall before them; in their passage, they bear down the branches upon which they feed.' Further on, he relates how the African Elephant was used in war by the Carthaginians, and how in modern times the Indian Elephant is tamed and employed by Indian princes. Quotations could be multiplied, many of them of fascinating interest. The description of the Chameleon is particularly vivid.

One must recognise, on the other hand, that Goldsmith's method of classifying the various genera and species is wildly confused. This was partly, but not entirely, due to the imperfect state of knowledge then obtaining. Thus he places the Otter among 'Amphibious Quadrupeds' along with the Beaver, the Seal and the 'Morse' (Walrus), instead of classing it with the 'Weasel Kind', that is, the Mustelidae. The Rodents are even more widely scattered between Chapters I, II and VI of Volume IV. Worse still, he classes the Apes with the Eléphant, Rhinoceros, Giraffe, Camel, Lama, Bear, Badger, Tapir, Raccoon, Coati, Ant-Bear, Sloth, Jerboa and Kangaroo, one after the other. The Opossum is described immediately after the Orang-Outang. He understands that it is what we now call a marsupial; but he does not know that the Kangaroo, which is described (inadequately) over a hundred pages later, is also a marsupial, and more characteristic. So too the Cetaceans are classed with the Fishes, although he is aware that they breathe like other mammals. Not knowing where to place the Zoophytes such as the Starfish, he places them after the Insects, at the end of Volume VIII.

It would be unfair today to point out that the whole system of classification is wrong, and that he should have divided animals into Vertebrates and Invertebrates, and begun with the most primitive forms of the latter. Even so, the work contains errors of a more elementary kind and pages which are entirely fantastic. Buffon had observed that our upper-jaw is immovable; Goldsmith, on the contrary, says that both our jaws move and that this can be proved by experiment! In the first chapter of Volume III we read: 'At three years old, [the Cow] sheds its horns, and new ones arise in their place, which continue as long as it lives'. One cannot blame him for supposing that the Chamois is related to the Sheep and Goats, and for not knowing that it is an Antelope. But there is complete confusion in what he says about the Puma. On page 232 he calls it 'a very contemptible animal . . . extremely cowardly . . . inferior even to the American Tiger'. On page 244 we read of 'the Red Tiger. . . . Mr Buffon calls it the Cougar'. It is 'the most formidable and mischievous' of the New World animals. But the accompanying plate shows that this is the Puma, as one would expect, and that he did not know that the Puma and the Cougar are one and the same animal. Elsewhere he is imprudent enough to copy from the *Oeuvres de Regnard* the now famous story of migrating squirrels in Lapland. On reaching a lake, each member of the horde collects a piece of bark, launches and sits on it, 'fanning the air with its tail. . . . In this orderly manner they set forward. But . . . the slightest additional gust of wind oversets the little sailor and his vessel together. The whole navy, that but a few moments before, rode proudly and securely along, is now overturned, and a shipwreck of two or three thousand sail ensues. This . . . is generally the most lucky accident in the world for the Laplander on the shore; who gathers up the dead bodies as they are thrown in by the waves, eats the flesh, and sells the skins for about a shilling the dozen'.

Readers must have delighted in this fairy-tale,[1] as they would be suitably thrilled by the sensation of an African landscape at nightfall, when 'nothing can be more terrible' than the chorus of animal cries: 'the deep-toned roarings of the lion; the shriller yellings of the tiger' [brought from India for the purpose]; 'the jackal . . . barking like a dog; the hyena with a note peculiarly solitary and dreadful; but to crown all, the hissing of the various kinds of serpents, who at that time begin their call and, as I am assured, make a much louder symphony than the birds in our groves in a morning'.

Goldsmith had always been interested in Natural History, and his own reminiscences or observations about the Otter, the Bittern, the Rook, the Spider and the Dragonfly add a certain freshness to the narrative. Some of these have been mentioned in the survey of his life. Most of them are probably reliable and one or two may help us to fix the date of his reaching this or that place in the course of his continental journey. In speaking of the Ephemeridae, he writes: 'As they are not natives of England, he who would see them in their greatest abundance

---

[1] Based apparently on what travellers had related about the migration of Lemmings.

must walk, about sunset, along the banks of the Rhine, or the Seine near Paris; where, for about three days in the midst of the summer, he will be astonished at their numbers and assiduity'. If he had actually seen these swarms of insects in midsummer, then the passage implies that he had crossed the Rhine, probably near Strasbourg, in that season; and this would contradict his statement, in Volume I, that he had seen the Falls of the Rhine at Schaffhausen 'frozen quite across', which it has never been known to do. One may tentatively conclude from the first statement that he had crossed the Rhine from Strasbourg in April or in May (from his other remark it could be conjectured that he returned by the same route the following winter, and fancied from the appearance of the frozen spray that the falls themselves were frozen. See Part I, Chapter IV).

No one in Great Britain had attempted so vast a work of collation, a task which involved his consulting not merely the general works on Natural History, but especially the latest scientific authorities, as well as books of travel which contained scientific observations. Many of them, like some of the research monographs, he had had to buy. But a copy of the best known Natural History, that of Buffon, he apparently borrowed.

The *Histoire naturelle, générale et particulière* by G.-L. Leclerc, Comte de Buffon and L.-J.-M. Daubenton (Paris 1749–67, 15 vols.)[1] was his principal source. Much of the description of the Earth in Volume I is taken from Buffon, and the 'Histoire des Quadrupèdes', to which Daubenton, who was more of a practical scientist, contributed a great deal, furnishes most of the information for Goldsmith's detailed descriptions of the Quadrupeds in Volumes II, III and IV. He frequently translates or adapts Buffon and Daubenton and often acknowledges his indebtedness, either in the text or in a footnote. When he had to describe the Birds, Buffon had only just begun to publish the nine volumes he devoted to them (Volumes

---

[1] It was a magnificently and expensively produced work, a large quarto, bound in gilded calf.

XVI–XXIV. Paris, 1770–83); nevertheless Goldsmith translated a few passages about the Eagle from pages 79, 80, 81 and 84 of Volume XVI. But one must not suppose that all this, substantial as it was, accounted for his dependence on Buffon. The frequent allusions he makes to him, throughout the work, show that he had these volumes constantly before his eyes.

Linnaeus's *Systema Naturae per Regna Tria* (Leyden, 1735) was a textbook which he probably consulted throughout, as he had a copy of his own. It could have guided him to a better system of classification. Of other general works, the *Dictionnaire raisonné et universel des Animaux* and Pennant's *British Zoology* (1763) provided him with material here and there.

In Part I, he had recourse to the Abbé J.-A. Nollet's *Leçons de Physique expérimentale* (1743, six volumes), to J.-P. de Tournefort's *Herbaria* (1719) and to three or four travel books. For the study of Quadrupeds, he also supplemented Buffon with the aid of John Ray's *Synopsis methodica Animalium quadrupedum* (1793) and even Konrad von Gesner's *De quadrupedibus* (Zürich, 1551). For the Birds, he used Francis Willughby's *Ornithology* (1768) and Ray's *Synopsis Avium et Piscium* (1713); but relied mainly on the more advanced *Ornitholgie* of M.-J. Brisson (1760, six volumes). In Part IV (Fishes) A. Gouan's *Histoire des Poissons* (Strasbourg, 1770) seems to have been his principal authority. For the study of Insects he used a Latin translation of Jan Swammerdam's *Historia Insectorum generalis* (Amsterdam, 1685), the first scientific work of its kind; and the more up-to-date treatise by R. A. F. de Réaumur, *Mémoires pour servir à l'Histoire des Insectes* (1734–42, 6 volumes) and the French version of Charles de Geer's work, of the same title (Stockholm, 1771, 2 volumes); and of course Linnaeus. Le Père Louis Feuillée's observations on the east coast of South America (1714–25) and a French translation of C. Le Bruyn's *Voyage du Levant* (Delft, 1700; Paris, 1704) provided material for the description of Reptiles; while A. Trembley's *Mémoires pour servir à l'Histoire d'un genre de Polype d'eau douce* supplemented what he found elsewhere about the Zoophytes.

Finally, scattered but often important details were taken from books of travel, relating mainly to the Levant, as already mentioned, and to West Africa, South America and Greenland. Of these, J.-B. Labat's *Nouveau Voyage aux Iles d'Amérique* provided descriptions of the Pelican and the Humming-Bird. He had his own copies of Tournefort's *Voyage du Levant* (1718) and of Don Antonio de Ulloa's *Voyage to South America*. He also consulted a description of Greenland and a history of the same country. It will have been clear that he took an immense amount of trouble and that, for scientific works, he had recourse to the most recent. Finally, while composing all these volumes, he observed the animal and insect life of the countryside; and when in London, spent some hours watching the animals in the Zoo at the Tower, for example the Cougar; and those in the Queen's Menagerie at Buckingham Gate, where a Zebra tried to kick him! Even so, his book remains an amateurish production. One has an uneasy feeling that it catered for the same taste as that of the well-known 'Cabinets d'Histoire naturelle'. Most well-to-do people with any cultural pretensions had one of these Cabinets, in which they exhibited shells, butterflies and moths, stuffed birds and freaks of nature ('monstres') preserved in spirits, and so forth. Topham Beauclerk had a very splendid 'Cabinet' of this kind.

Buffon's influence on Goldsmith was not altogether fortunate. The French Naturalist was as much a literary man as a scientist,[1] and his desire to be readable and amusing accounts for an occasional lightness of manner which is out of keeping

---

[1] De Saussure who met him in the spring of 1768 in Paris formed no favourable opinion of his scientific attainments; the Botanist Jussieu impressed him as a far more serious investigator. In one of his letters he says that the members of the Academy 'think nothing of [Buffon] as a man of science: they look on him neither as a physicist, nor a geometrician, nor a naturalist'. (Douglas Freshfield, *H. B. de Saussure,* 1920, pp 92-3.).

with an objective treatise. It also explains the absence of any
systematic classification; and all this affected Goldsmith
adversely. On the other hand, Buffon had had some premoni-
tion of the evolutionary process; he had realised that species
are not unchangeable. Lamarck of course was to go much
further in postulating the principle of Transformism. It is a
pity that Goldsmith failed to see this possibility.

*

A disinterested study of animals for their own sake was
foreign to the eighteenth-century mind. To present a Natural
History required explanation, if not excuse. In the *Conclusion
upon Quadrupeds* at the end of Volume IV he writes: '. . . all
knowledge is pleasant only as the object of it contributes to
render man happy'; and that this is particularly true of the
Quadrupeds which provide him with food, clothing and
amusements. Domestic animals, he observes elsewhere, are 'the
most fortunate and commendable'. The horse and the dog are
most desirably submissive; but hardly the cat. Buffon had said
hard things about cats, and Goldsmith remarks that the cat 'has
only the appearance of attachment'; but he attempts nevertheless to explain and excuse it. Apart from such fierce animals
which have entered man's service, 'there is a still more numerous tribe that wages an unequal combat against him, and thus
calls forth his courage and his industry'; or, as he puts it in
other words, these powerful and ferocious animals are useful
to man since they 'at once exercise his virtues and call forth his
latent abilities'. Even the most terrible convulsions of Nature
can be seen as beneficial. Volcanoes put us in mind of the
punishment that awaits those who fail to amend their ways;
earthquakes also, no doubt. And all this is part of a divine
scheme. 'The Universe may be considered as the palace in
which the Deity presides,' we read in the *Conclusion* to
Volume I. 'God beholds, with pleasure, that being which he
has made . . . bringing all the headlong tribes of nature into

submission to his will and producing that order and uniformity upon earth, of which his own heavenly fabric is so bright an example.' True, man is not what he ought to be, but God has made him capable of becoming so.

Everything therefore fits neatly into the divine plan, and if one contemplates the whole design, one will recognise that it is for the best.

This view strikes us today as pathetically blind to observed realities. Mr J. H. Pitman, to whose monograph[1] the writer is indebted in this connexion, ascribes Goldsmith's explanations to the optimistic Deism which infected so much of eighteenth-century thinking. The veneer of sentimentality which covers them was exactly what appealed to readers and what Goldsmith probably knew that they expected. But if his general interpretation of Man and Nature was sincere – and it probably was – then his attitude to the world had undergone a considerable change in the past seven or eight years. Underlying an air of good nature and humour, there are in *The Vicar of Wakefield* a great deal of pessimism and cynical misanthropy. By the early 1770s literary and social success had gone far towards reconciling him with the world, and he was now sharing the optimism and belief in progress that characterise the age.

*

The *Animated Nature* was to be revised and reprinted again and again, for over a hundred years, and to prove a gold mine to publishers. On none of his works had Goldsmith lavished so much care; in his own day, it represented an extraordinary achievement. Yet it is now no more than one of the curiosities of literature.

[1] *Goldsmith's 'Animated Nature'*, New Haven, 1924, pp 116–132. See also Winifred Lynskey, 'The Scientific Sources of G.'s *Animated Nature*' in *Studies in Philology*, vol XI, 1943; and 'G. and the Chain of Being' in *Journal of the History of Ideas*, vol VI, 1945. According to Miss Lynskey, Goldsmith adopted the idea of a great Chain of Being, a theory which Naturalists were sensible enough to avoid.

Conclusion

Born and growing up in a country full of legends and fairy-lore, in a so-called 'Celtic' atmosphere, Goldsmith might have been expected to become a pre-Romantic, like Gray. In the event, his taste and practice were both English and reactionary. It seems that the Anglo–Irish community, which numbered so many distinguished men, was largely isolated from any feelings genuinely Irish. In spite of Bishop Berkeley's plea, Trinity College did not admit Catholics in Goldsmith's time. His own taste seems to have been formed by the study of Latin – which, however, is not necessarily anti-Romantic – of such English writers as Dryden and Pope; and of classical French Literature. He accepted Boileau and Voltaire as authorities in matters literary. Conversely, he appears to have ignored the Abbé Prévost's novels, and although J.-J. Rousseau may have influenced him indirectly, he never mentions the *Nouvelle Héloïse*, and none of Rousseau's works figured in his library. To have ignored the writings of Rousseau seems to mark a rather narrow provincialism. Johnson may have been partly responsible for this. Again, neither he nor Goldsmith cared for the Ossianic poems. However factitious these may have been, they indicated a trend, at least in France and Italy, that was to go on increasing. Goldsmith, in short, remained strangely behind the times. To be reactionary in an age of literary corruption is a good thing; but was the eighteenth century such an age? Its later years were to see the birth of some of our greatest poets.

On the other hand, a curious passage in Letter CI of *The Citizen of the World* suggests that Goldsmith had no feeling for antiquity, at least in its architecture. When the Prime Minister of Tipartala was put on trial, a witness who was

'. . . inspector of the city buildings . . . accused the disgraced favourite of having given orders for the demolition of an ancient ruin, which obstructed the passage through one of the principal streets. He observed that such buildings were noble monuments of barbarous antiquity; contributed finely to show how little their ancestors understood of architecture; and for that reason such monuments should be held sacred. . . .'

So much for the negative criticism of Goldsmith's work. On the positive side, one finds a conscientious but not very liberal-minded critic, a journalist of uneven merit but with the ability to write on a wide range of subjects in a vein usually ironical or humorous. *The Vicar of Wakefield* has been accounted the best of his works, although, as has been suggested, not for the usual reasons. *The Deserted Village* owes its place among our minor classics to the memorable portraits it contains, to the excellence of the diction and the neatness of the versification. It seems evident, however, that poetry did not come naturally to Goldsmith, and that the merit of the long poems is due more to study than to inspiration. Goldsmith was most at home in humorous verse. When Johnson wrote of him, for his monument in the Abbey, that he was a man

> *Qui nullum fere scribendi genus*
> *Non tetigit,*
> *Nullum quod tetigit non ornavit:*
> *Sive risus essent movendi,*
> *Sive lacrimae. . . .*

it is difficult to agree that he adorned everything he touched, or that he had a gift for the pathetic. To this indeed he never pretended.

Of the two comedies, *The Good-Natured Man* is the more pleasing, *She Stoops to Conquer* the better constructed. It is a pity, however, that in the latter the hero is represented as both silly and caddish. The play is very laughable, but it owes its popularity also to the fact that for many decades England produced no playwrights of any literary merit who produced more than one or at most three good pieces. Colman, assisted by Garrick, wrote one, Cumberland one, Sheridan two or three in the tradition of Congreve. Cumberland was the most prolific of the abler dramatists, but his gift lay in the invention of original and interesting plots, and he lacked Goldsmith's verbal brilliance. The pity is, that so much of Goldsmith's best work, in *The Citizen of the World*, the occasional verses, and the comedies, is vitiated by bare-faced plagiarism. Had he greatly improved on the material he took from Marivaux and others, these borrowings might have been easier to justify.

His name stands out, partly because he lived in an age which produced fewer great writers than the seventeenth century or the Romantic era; partly because he belonged to a very small group, the members of which greatly admired each other and conspired in perpetuating each other's fame. One may question whether, had they lived in the nineteenth century, any of them would have been accounted so highly. Goldsmith wrote in a very clear and pleasing style, less personal, however, than the style of Dickens, or of Ruskin, or of Pater. He is best remembered for the well-turned couplets of *The Deserted Village*. But his versatility was the most remarkable of his gifts, and each of his principal works has ministered to the fame of the others.

Appendixes

Appendix I

The History of Francis Wills and the Mystery of Goldsmith's Lost Novel[1]

I

Goldsmith is known to have written a novel at some date between early 1771 and late 1772. Neither Percy nor Johnson appears to have been aware of this, but Northcote speaks of it in his *Life of Reynolds* as follows: 'I have been informed by the lady who requested a lock of [Goldsmith's] hair before interment, that he once read to her several chapters of a novel in manuscript which he had in contemplation; but which he did not live to finish, now irrevocably lost'.[2] Prior received a different account of a novel from a Mr Harris who had succeeded to Francis Newbery's business:

'Being pressed by pecuniary difficulties in 1771–72, Goldsmith had ... obtained the advance of two or three hundred pounds from Newbery, under the engagement of writing a novel. ... Considerable delay took place in the execution of this undertaking, and when at length submitted to the perusal of the bookseller, it proved to be in great measure the plot of the "Good-Natured Man", turned into a tale. Objections being taken to this, the manuscript was returned. Goldsmith declared himself unable or unwilling to write another, but in liquidation of the debt ... said he should require time to look round for some means of raising the money, unless Mr Newbery

[1] See J. W. M. Gibbs, *The Works of Oliver Goldsmith*, 1885, vol I, pp 238–240; and A. Lytton Sells, ' "The History of Francis Wills": a Literary Mystery', in *Review of English Studies*, vol XI, No 41, January 1935.
[2] Vol I, p 327.

chose to take the chance of a play coming forward at Covent Garden . . . .'[1]

In short, he made over to Newbery the copyright of *She Stoops to Conquer*.

It will be noticed in the preceding records that Mrs Gwynne does not say *when* Goldsmith read to her 'several chapters of a novel', nor does she offer any opinion of its merits, or even mention its subject. She adds however that 'he did not live to finish it'. Harris, whose account is more circumstantial, makes it clear that the novel had been finished and submitted by, at latest, the autumn of 1772. It seems likely, however, that both Mrs Gwynne and Harris were referring to the same novel; and we now have to decide whether it has been lost or whether – as seems possible – it appeared anonymously as *The Triumph of Benevolence; or The History of Francis Wills*.

This novel, on which Browning poured so much scorn but which so few people have troubled to read, is now very rare. Of the first edition, published by Vernor and Chater, in two volumes, in 1772, no copy appears to have survived; but the *Critical Review* and the *Monthly Review* published indulgent notices of it, while the *London Magazine* was contemptuous.[2] Neglected in England, the novel won a certain esteem on the Continent. A version entitled *Histoire de François Wills, ou le triomphe de la bienfaisance. Par l'auteur du 'Ministre de Wakefield'. Traduction de l'Anglois*, was published at Amsterdam and Rotterdam in 1773. Another edition in French, with the same title – probably the same version – and also ascribed to the author of *The Vicar of Wakefield*, appeared at Neuchâtel in 1774. Later in 1786, there was published at Berlin what seems to have been a reprint of the first edition, in English; and finally, a last edition in English, with the original title, and not ascribed to Goldsmith, was published at Uppsala in 1799.[3] Thus the novel went through five separate editions, and, as we shall see, it was reviewed favourably and at some length by the *Année littéraire*.

---

[1] Prior, vol II, p 417.

[2] Our knowledge of the first edition and the reviews of it is due to an article by Edward Solly in *Notes and Queries*, 9 August 1884.

[3] For information about the Neuchâtel and Berlin editions I am indebted to the kindness of Professor Trench of Dublin and Professor Zachrisson of Uppsala.

No one in England appears to have associated the novel with Goldsmith until 1812 when Southey, in *Omniana*, wrote; 'A fraud has been practised in France upon Goldsmith's reputation. At the end of a volume which bears date 1774, is the following title in a list of new books: *Histoire de François Wills, ou le Triomphe de la Bienfaisance, par l'auteur du Ministre de Wakefield. Traduction de l'Anglois.*' But Southey gives no reason for supposing that it was a fraud. He says that the fraud was practised in France, whereas we know only of editions in French published in Holland and at Neuchâtel. Of greater weight with writers on Goldsmith has been the opinion of Robert Browning, which he communicated to John Forster: 'I read that *History of Francis Wills, or the Triumph of Benevolence*, some twenty years ago: a miserable, two volume, twaddling story of a sort of orphan, i.e. Wills – whom his maiden aunt – i.e. Benevolence Triumphant, – brings up against the opposition of her kindred; he proving a scapegrace, and she gracious to ... not the end; for at the decline of her life, Benevolence marries some stingy Scotch Captain Mac-something, and instantly turns as stingy as he ... till the very last of all ... when Benevolence does indeed triumph, in her return to the old way. So the poor author intended, whereas, you see ... Malevolence triumphed with a vengeance, in giving the paternity of the book to Goldsmith!'

One might be more impressed by all this, if Browning had not been writing from memory and if his account of the novel had been at all accurate. It is true that Francis's aunt Priscilla is benevolent and brings him up, but not against the wishes of her kinfolk. It is not true that Francis proves a scapegrace – on the contrary, he is a model of virtue; and it is not true that the aunt marries the Scottish Captain. The story of Francis Wills is romantic, idealistic and improbable; whether it can be described as twaddling is a matter of opinion.

II

The story opens one stormy evening at an inn on the Great North Road, where Francis Wills and his friends Lawson and Allen have been drying their clothes. While they are making a meal, Francis overhears an account of the troubles of a young labourer, whose

N

mother is threatened with eviction for non-paymnt of her rent. He gives him money – enough, presumably, to save the situation.

Our hero had been an orphan from childhood. His grandfather, a well-to-do man, had disinherited Francis's father and left his fortune to his sisters-in-law, the three Misses Kingley. Miss Priscilla Kingley had adopted Francis and engaged a Mr Brewer, an Oxford MA, as private tutor. Both she and the tutor encouraged him in benevolence; they had not objected when he once even gave his boots, in addition to money, to a poor boy who inspired his pity. At the age of nineteen he was taken by Brewer on a walking tour of the country, to inspect factories and farms and so fit himself to become an MP. This experience, Brewer thinks, would be 'of more service . . . than galloping through Europe under the tuition of a Swiss bear-leader'.

Soon after this, Brewer dies. Francis falls victim to the wiles of Charlotte Collins, a heartless coquette, who pretends to be attracted and then rejects him out of hand. He is strolling along a country road in an effort to soothe his feelings, when he comes on a solitary traveller who is being attacked by three highwaymen. Rushing to his assistance, he lays out two of the ruffians, while the third takes to his heels. It now transpires that the man he has saved is Captain MacGregor, a friend of Miss Kingley. The Captain is for having the miscreants arrested; but Frank demurs to this. 'Let them depart,' he urges, 'their own consciences . . . will be punishment' for them – 'Hoot awa' !' cries the other, 'they shall be hanged.' – 'Come, come, Captain, you,

> Taught by that pow'r that pities you
> Shou'd learn to pity them.'

Wills then delivers a sort of homily to the young men whom his blows have apparently disabled. He offers one of them a guinea, but the youth is so touched that he refuses the money and declares that he will forsake his evil ways. There follows between Wills and MacGregor a discussion of the penal laws, in which, as the reader will by now have foreseen, Frank uses arguments similar to those advanced by Dr Primrose in Chapter XXVII of the *Vicar of Wakefield*. He blames the law, 'for by the most equitable law, which is that of retaliation, *lex talionis*, an eye for any eye . . . is only required; but in cases of murder, I own there should be deprivation of life'. Where however there has only been robbery, the offender should be made to restore threefold, or to work to that end.

On his return to Chelsea where he has been living with his aunt Priscilla, Frank encounters a young girl who tells him that she and her father, imprisoned in the Marshalsea for debt, are going to die. He offers her two guineas, and accompanies her to the prison, the horrors of which are described. Resemblances between this story and the later chapters of *The Vicar* now become more numerous. The old man's name is Belton, his daughter's, Sophie. Frank's first care is to buy a new suit for Belton, and arrange for a good meal to be brought in for the sufferer, who now tells his story.

He had been steward to Lord Cotswold. The latter, being unhappy with his wife, had proposed a secret marriage with Sophie on the following terms: if he should predecease his wife, he would leave Sophie as much of his property as he could; but if he should be the survivor, he would declare Sophie his lawful wife. Belton rejected the proposal; but he had gone surety for a friend for £400 (a habit of young Honeywood's), and — needless to add — he now had to find the money. Cotswold advanced part of it, but Belton, being still £200 in debt, was thrown into prison with his wife and daughter; and his wife had died. Touched by this pitiful story, Frank raises £400 and has them released. But to find the money he has had to mortgage part of his capital. Captain MacGregor has heard of this. He informs Miss Kingley and she, now grown miserly (or perhaps more conscious of the need to make ends meet) is so displeased with Frank that she advises him to find lodgings elsewhere than under her roof. He takes rooms nearer the City and there meets Allen and Lawson, who are also short of cash and labouring under a cloud of disapproval. They decide to join forces, and the purpose of the journey north has been to enable Allen to effect a reconciliation with his father. It was at this point, when Frank and Lawson, having sped Allen on his way, were about to return to London, that we met them in the opening chapter.

They set off on foot. Owing to the previous day's storm the rivers are in flood, and at the first ford a fine carriage, with three ladies inside, has been halted in mid stream by the raging waters.

One of the horses has fallen. Our young men dash to the rescue, Frank seizing the youngest and most beautiful of the ladies and bringing her in a fainting condition to the bank. The sight of this fair creature inspires 'unknown and hitherto unexperienced transports in the breast of Wills'. He learns that she is Juliet Harcourt, and that the others are Mrs Kelsal, her aunt, and Miss Kelsal. Lawson, meanwhile, has obligingly rescued them, and the drivers have been able at last to bring the carriage to the bank.

Frank cannot refrain from declaring his passion. Miss Harcourt simply replies that her father lives near Nantwich and would be pleased to receive her rescuer. On his asking if her heart is engaged, she replies: 'It is not.'

    – 'May I be permitted to hope?'
    – 'I shall be glad to see you, Sir, at Nantwich.'

After renewing their wardrobe in London, Wills and Lawson again leave for the north. At a hostelry on the way, Frank is suspected of an intrigue with the host's wife, which gives rise to a grotesque episode imitated from the adventure of the Sieur de la Rappinière in *Le Roman comique*.[1] This is narrated with some verve. On reaching Nantwich, where they put up at the White Hart, they learn that Sir Lionel Harcourt lives at Pinehill, which is quite near. And the innkeeper's son – who turns out to be none other than the young highway robber whom Frank had spared – now gladly takes a message to Miss Harcourt. Thanks to this obliging intermediary, a secret meeting takes place at a room in the inn. Juliet is not now, she tells Frank, at liberty to hear his proposals, but confesses 'that I know no man with whom I would more willingly spend my life' – an avowal which appeared so unseemly to the Frenceh translator that he inserted the proviso: 'With my father's consent.' Juliet tells Frank that he may meet her at her married sister's, Lady Mannington, who also lives near by. He is taking tea here one day when Lord Cotswold unexpectedly calls. Since his harsh treatment of the Beltons he has lost his wife, and is now planning to marry Miss Harcourt; he has in fact come to escort her back to Pinehill.

On their way, Cotswold tells her that Wills had interceded with

---

[1] Book I, ch IV.

him on behalf of an old rascal who had swindled him, though he supposes that Wills's real motive was the old man's daughter. This to some extent damages Frank in Miss Harcourt's eyes; yet she remains perplexed, and when her father informs her that she is to marry Lord Cotswold, she passes a sleepless night. Frank, even more distressed by the turn of events, writes to her next day. In her reply she offers to meet him on the morrow after nightfall, inside the park-wall, which he can enter by a secret door. On reaching the rendezvous he swears that Cotswold had lied to her, but his sense of honour is such that he cannot divulge the story of the Beltons. Even so, she believes him. But at this moment a light is seen and Juliet urges him to escape. He runs inside the park-wall for some distance, then jumps over – into the arms of four gamekeepers who are on the lookout for deer-stealers.

Our hero is taken in custody to the White Hart, and next day both he and Lawson are put on trial before Mr Woodward, the local Justice. Obviously poor Frank cannot explain why he was in the park, and it looks as if Mr Woodward will be obliged to impose a sentence of imprisonment; but at this moment there is a stir in the anteroom and the Justice receives a message that two travellers desire urgently to communicate with him. Who, we ask, should they be but Mr Belton and Sophie, who are personal friends of Mr Woodward and who, since Frank had released them from the Marshalsea, have inherited a large fortune.

Events now move rapidly. Recognised by Mr Belton, Frank is released by the Justice as informally as George and Dr Primrose had been set at liberty by Sir William Thornhill. And at the touching moment when Frank rushes to support the fainting Juliet – who had secretly attended the trial – Sir Lionel and Lord Cotswold enter the room. Juliet decides to tell her father the whole story, while Wills confronts the infamous Cotswold with the much-wronged Belton. The latter now has no difficulty in clearing his benefactor of all suspicion, and throwing Cotswold into confusion. Thus has Benevolence come into her own. At the climax of this overpowering scene of revelations, recognitions and embracings, a courier bursts in, with a letter for Mr Wills, a letter from his aunt who is near her last hour and urges him to hasten to her side.

N*

It appears that the depraved MacGregor had been urging her to marry him, but that she had providentially continued to defer a decision. Then, quite by accident, she discovered that he was already married to a lady whom he had deprived of her money and deserted. In this situation her thoughts had returned to the nephew whom she had unkindly dismissed from her home; she had pictured him in poverty and affliction and these thoughts had so worked on her imagination that she fell grievously sick. It was only with difficulty that she discovered his whereabouts and sent for him. But he is now able to rejoin her, and they are reconciled before she dies.

In possession now of a handsome income, Frank returns to Pinehill. The haughty Sir Lionel, humiliated no doubt by his discovery that the man he had chosen as a son-in-law was a scoundrel, has become so 'generous and affable' as willingly to agree to Frank's marrying Juliet. Cotswold challenges him to a duel, but our hero merely disarms him, instead of killing him. He then marries Juliet; and, as the author concludes:

'The reward of guilt is misery; the tenaciousness of avarice brings its own punishment.... But peace and honour shall attend on him, whose honest and upright heart, . . . actuated by a principle of *universal benevolence*,[1] feels and relieves not only the distresses of virtue and merit, but even strives to assuage the anguish that is the eternal lot of the wicked: happiness shall stand at his right hand, and content shall crown his days.'

III

Two kinds of novel were gaining popularity in the later years of the century: the Gothic romance which developed into the 'roman noir' or tale of terror; and the sentimental novel of which Henry Mackenzie's *The Man of Feeling* (1771) is an example. *The History of Francis Wills* belongs of course to this class, and one is not surprised to hear Frank express his admiration for *The Man of Feeling*. Why the author should depict a Scotsman as a scoundrel is another matter. Francis Wills is the type of hero who filled the girlish imagination of Emma Rouhault and whom Flaubert un-

---

[1] My italics.

kindly describes as 'brave comme un lion, doux comme un agneau et vertueux comme on ne l'est pas'. And yet this type, less naïvely presented, figures in some of the best of Scott's and Dickens's novels and has pleased many thousands of intelligent readers. Small wonder then if the *Année littéraire* applauded it:

L'intrigue de ce Roman est assez compliquée, Monsieur; mais la façon dont elle se développe est ingénieuse. On peut lui reprocher aussi quelques longueurs, quelques détails d'un mauvais genre de plaisanterie, quelques épisodes inutiles. Il me paroît même assez peu décent que *Miss Harcourt* voie son amant dans le parc même du Château de son pére. Ce rendezvous eût été beaucoup moins repréhensible, si l'auteur l'eût placé chez la soeur de la jeune personne; ce qui, me semble, n'auroit pas été difficile . . . . Malgré ces défauts, l'ouvrage est très-estimable. . . . Le caractère du principal personnage est très-beau, très-bien tracé et se soutient jusqu'au dénoûment. Vous y trouverez de l'imagination dans le plan, du sentiment dans les situations, des scènes très-intéressantes. Cet ouvrage . . . respire sur-tout la bienfaisance; . . . cette vertu céleste qui feroit des hommes un peuple de frères et d'amis si tous étoient des Wills et s'il n'y avoit point de *Cotswolds* sur la terre.'

If this was the view of a leading French periodical, it must have been shared by a large part of the reading public whose attitude is not likely to have been more critical. It is to be judged then, less by the standards of the 1970s than of the 1770s. Goldsmith's most successful prose-works are full of improbabilities which would never pass muster today. As there appears no ground for supposing that any modern writer on Goldsmith has read *The History of Francis Wills*, none of their views regarding its authorship can be regarded as final. In the absence of further evidence one must therefore hesitate to take the responsibility of affirming that Goldsmith could not have written it.

The very title, and the concluding homily, read like signatures of Goldsmith. In *The Good-Natured Man*, Jarvis tells Sir William that young Honeywood calls his reckless open-handedness 'universal benevolence'. Francis Wills is another Honeywood and indeed might be Goldsmith himself. He gives his boots to a poor boy as Goldsmith had given his blankets to a poor woman. He goes surety for a man whom he scarcely knows with the lighthearted irresponsibility of a Honeywood or a Goldsmith. Many episodes are clearly imitated from *The Vicar of Wakefield*, and none is more striking than the adventure of the carriage in the flooded river, when Francis rescues Miss Harcourt just as 'Mr Burchell' rescues Sophie. The picture of the Marshalsea recalls the description of Dr Primrose's prison, and Dr Primrose's criticism of the penal laws is repeated more briefly by Francis Wills. Francis pardons the young highwayman, who later assists him in communicating with Miss Harcourt, just as the Vicar forgives Jenkinson, who later reveals the villainy of young Thornhill. Lord Cotswold is not an imitation of young Thornhill, but his attempt to seduce Sophie Belton, and to cast suspicion on Wills, shows that he would not have been averse from similar conduct. Other features of the novel recall Goldsmith's tastes or obsessions. In 1770 he had published a memoir of Parnell, and in the *History of Francis Wills* Parnell is quoted twice. The episode imitated from Scarron reminds us of Goldsmith's liking for the *Roman comique*, his later reference to Scarron in 'Retaliation', and his undertaking to translate the *Roman comique*. At the beginning of Chapter XX we read of 'the author of a certain voyage' who 'intends to give his readers a *minute* description of the *gigantic* people called Patagonians'. It may be recalled that Letter XXIV of *The Citizen of the World* had introduced 'the giant fair ones of Patagonia'; that in Act IV of *The Good-Natured Man*, where Olivia is anxious to start for Scotland even though Honeywood's bill has been protested, Jarvis damps her enthusiasm with the words 'Go to Scotland without money! ... We might as well set sail for Patagonia upon a cork-jacket'; and again that two or three pages of *Animated Nature* were to be devoted to the Patagonian giants. Finally the choice of a Scotsman as a minor villain is not out of keeping with the episode of the Scot and the Jew in 'The Haunch of Venison'.

It is true that the plot of *Francis Wills* is hardly, even 'in great measure the plot of "The Good-Natured Man"'; but Harris was recalling this impression after a period of sixty years, and even so there are striking resemblances. It is as though the author of *The*

Triumph of Benevolence had taken the character of young Honey-wood and, discarding all that is comical in his misadventures, had created from it, not merely Francis, but even Brewer and Belton. In this anonymous fiction Goldsmith's frailty of unintelligent kindness is raised to the level of a virtue and rewarded, as in the play, with the hand of a charming heiress.

Harassed for money as usual and faced with the necessity of fulfilling a contract, Goldsmith could perhaps have produced a novel as long as this by the autumn of 1772. He certainly produced a novel of some kind; and though he never exhibited any talent for the invention of plots, the plot of *The Triumph of Benevolence* seems more simple and less 'ingenious' than the *Année littéraire* considered it. Either, therefore, this was Goldsmith's 'lost novel', or it was deliberately imitated from his character and his earlier writings.

The objections to the theory of his authorship can be summarised as follows. The novel is altogether lacking in the whimsical humour of *The Vicar of Wakefield*; it lacks the irony, the ambiguity and the deliberate contradictions. But if this be the novel read to Mary Horneck, one would expect it to be so. He had lost, with success, the deeper causes of his resentment against society, and against women. The style, save in one passage in Chapter I where there is a reference to the 'Coterie',[1] would not discredit Goldsmith; for, except for its greater distinction, Goldsmith's style scarcely differs from that of a dozen of his contemporaries. It is not marked by any personal colour or mannerism. Among nineteenth-century prosateurs, one can distinguish without difficulty between the manners, respectively, of Carlyle, Ruskin, Arnold and Pater. In the eighteenth century, perhaps, only Gibbon and, in some measure, Johnson, had acquired a recognisable style of their own. Finally, if Goldsmith was not the author of *Francis Wills*, one is left with the equally puzzling problem of guessing who could possibly have thought of plagiarising him and who could have possessed the intimate knowledge to do so.

The summary of Chapter I points to Arthur Murphy, who was a friend of Goldsmith's and presumably familiar with his writings. This summary reads:

---

[1] i.e. 'the Ladies' Club' to which Marlow alludes in *She Stoops to Conquer*.

'In which the reader, according to Arthur Murphy Esquire's opinion, delivered in the first number of his Gray's Inn Journal,[1] will be much embarrassed, and suffer greatly from his natural diffidence, upon being introduced to some persons to whom he is, as yet, an entire stranger: but if he is well bred, and accustomed to see company, this remark will be deemed absurd.'

It would indeed, unless the whole passage were intended as a signature. Who, one may ask, would think of referring to a periodical which had appeared nearly twenty years before, if not Murphy himself? The author of the *Triumph of Benevolence* was obviously a well-read man, with at least some knowledge of French Literature (see chapter XXIV), a practised writer; a plagiarist; very much of a man about town; and quite possibly Irish, in view of the references to Parnell and the unpleasant attitude to the Scots. Now all this would fit Arthur Murphy.

Born in Dublin in 1727, he had been educated at the English College at Saint-Omer where he had spent six years before trying his luck as a journalist in London. In 1756 he had won a certain fame with his comedy *The Upholsterer*, and was on friendly terms with Foote, Garrick and Johnson; as also, as we have seen, with Goldsmith. 'Without enough originality to channel out his own way, he drifted easily with the tide, appropriating whatever came within easy reach' – so writes Professor Nettleton in Vol X of the *Cambridge History of English Literature*.[2] Thus the elder Crébillon, Voltaire, Metastasio were all put to contribution, while considerable portions of Molière and Destouches appeared at Drury Lane and Covent Garden in an English dress and under the name of Murphy. The description of Frank's emotions on revisiting the scene of his first meeting with *Juliet* are reminiscent of passages in the *Nouvelle Héloïse*, as for example Saint-Preux's winter visit to the rocks of Meillerie, when he recalls how he and *Julie* had rowed over there one summer day from Clarens.

The meals which Frank and his friends take at various hostelries, the cold mutton and porter, the copious draughts of hot punch, the

[1] In this number (21 October 1752) the sentiment is attributed, not to the reader but to the author.
[2] Edn 1921, vol X, pp 88–9.

even more copious libations of tea dispensed by Lady Mannington – these, and also the mention of Almack's, the Thatched House, Boodle's and 'the Coterie', – are details which we might expect from a friend of the Thrales and of Lord Loughborough, a man of whom it was said that he 'ate himself out of every tavern from the other side of Temple Bar to the West End'.[1]

As a vigorous and successful writer, skilled in effectively adapting other men's inventions, it seems that he could quite possibly have written the *Triumph of Benevolence*; the more so, as between the production of *Zenobia* (1768) and *The Grecian Daughter* (1772) he does not appear to have published anything. On the other hand one finds no record of his ever having written a novel, or of having been interested in any kind of writing but plays and translations from the Latin Classics. (Curiously, he is said to have translated Vida's *Scacchiae Ludus*; but whether this was the version which Gibbs ascribed to Goldsmith or another one, is uncertain.) If, notwithstanding, he had decided to attempt a novel, one asks why he should have so obviously imitated *The Vicar of Wakefield*, which had not hitherto been very popular, but which was the work of a personal friend. The plagiarism was certain to be noticed, Goldsmith and his friends would have heard about it, suspicion would have fallen on Murphy; he certainly would have been asked whether he was the author. The outcome could only have been unpleasant, and have received some publicity. Yet it appears that no questions were asked; indeed, no mention of *The Triumph of Benevolence* is to be found in records of Goldsmith's life. Again, if Murphy were the author, there were a dozen French plays, even novels, which he could have adapted to the English milieu; not perhaps *La fausse Agnès* (a general favourite and too well-known) or *L'Irrésolu*, both of which he had imitated on the stage, but *Le Glorieux*, which would have made a good didactic novel, or even *Le Philosophe marié*, or Gresset's *Le Méchant*. To plagiarise Goldsmith would not have been a friendly act, even under the veil of anonymity; and yet Murphy remained on good terms with Goldsmith, and wrote an epilogue for *She Stoops to Conquer*.

There are, in short, cogent objections to the theory that Murphy wrote this novel, or indeed that anyone else did, except Goldsmith

[1] J. Knight in *D.N.B.*, edn 1894, vol XXXIX, p 336.

himself. It seems unlikely that he would have thrown away a full-length novel just because Newbery had rejected it. He could have sold it for a moderate sum to Vernor and Chater, on the understanding that it should appear without the author's name. To the objection that it is ostensibly a serious sentimental novel, exempt from the deliberate inconsistencies and continual irony of *The Vicar of Wakefield*, one could reply that these features of *The Vicar* had not only not been appreciated but seem to have puzzled and even rather displeased certain readers, including Johnson. It would not therefore be unnatural to attempt a straightforward narrative, written still with his tongue in his cheek, but with the obvious intention of pleasing the average taste.

In the event, the *Triumph of Benevolence* made a stronger appeal to French, Dutch and Swiss readers than to English. This was due to its English provenance, for such fictions enjoyed greater prestige in France than French novels; and also partly because of their unabashed idealism. In the years approaching the Revolution a spirit of idealism as unpractical as that of Francis Wills, and far more dangerous, was permeating French opinion in all classes, including political opinion, and was so preparing the way for disillusion and violence.

All this is not to affirm that *The Triumph of Benevolence* is indeed Goldsmith's 'lost novel', but to suggest that, if no more likely author can be found for it, the probability of Goldsmith's having written it is a reasonable hypothesis.

Appendix II

A Note on Goldsmith's Influence on the French Stage¹

In tracing the literary fortune of a writer in a country other than his own, one observes that the number of translations of his work often bears no relation to his influence on writers. This was not true of Scott or Byron, who were not only translated by various hands (at least six or seven for Scott), but who inspired great numbers of poems and novels, and operas. But Goldsmith is an outstanding example to the contrary. *The Vicar of Wakefield* has remained in France his most popular work, it has been used as a textbook in French *lycées*, French critics rank it as his best; and yet it would be hard to find a trace of its influence. Henri Beyle – least Goldsmithian of writers – appears to allude to it on three occasions without mentioning it. When dedicating the *Chartreuse de Parme* 'To the Happy Few', he was almost certainly thinking of Dr Primrose on monogamy rather than of the passage in *Henry V*. The reason for this absence of influence is evident. The merit of the novel for most readers lay in Dr Primrose's humorous and quizzical comments and in such droll episodes as that of the gross of green spectacles; but the main interest is in character, and the Vicar's character has not lent itself to adaptation. A plot is easier to imitate than an attitude to life; but the plot of *The Vicar of Wakefield* is too slight, indeed too unimportant, to suggest a pastiche.

The plays are a different matter. A versatile writer could have

¹ From an article by the author, 'Oliver Goldsmith's Influence on the French Stage', *Durham University Journal*, 1941.

used *The Good-Natured Man* by developing young Honeywood's misfortunes; or by isolating Croaker and his family from Honeywood and writing the comedy of *L'Alarmiste*. This play never appealed much to the French. On the other hand *She Stoops to Conquer* was welcomed from the outset, and has been republished in the original, in France, or translated, many times since 1828, as well as being revived in 1927. Unlike *The Good-Natured Man* it has also inspired imitations. The first, as pointed out by Prior, was *La fausse Auberge*, a two-act comedy performed at the Théâtre Italien in Paris in 1789. Yet though it 'experienced tolerable success', according to Prior, this had no aftermath, since the years that followed drew men's eyes from the comic stage to a wider and more sensational theatre. If it was ever printed, the work is so rare that we know of it only through a summary in *Les Spectacles de Paris, ou Calendrier historique et chronologique des théâtres* for 1790. In a list of the new pieces performed at the Théâtre Italien in 1789 we read:

'La fausse Auberge.

comédie en 2 actes en prose, par M... le 16 juin.

'Deux valets, chassés pour friponnerie, imaginent, pour se venger, de faire manquer le mariage de la fille de leur maître. Ils attendent sur la route le prétendu, lui font accroire qu'il est éloigné du château, et l'engagent à loger dans une auberge voisine qui est le château. Le jeune homme traite lestement son [futur] beau–père qu'il prend pour un aubergiste. Le beau-père et le gendre se brouillent, ils se raccommodent bientôt; les jeunes gens sont unis, et l'on fait grâce aux valets.'[1]

Bare as is this notice, it shows that the play was closely imitated from Goldsmith, but that Tony Lumpkin, the most original character in *She Stoops to Conquer*, was replaced by two servants. Of the relations between 'le prétendu' and the girl whom he is to marry, one learns nothing. The play may have contained some study of character, some witty dialogue, but of this one cannot judge.

Tony's exploit in conducting his mother's carriage, in the hours of darkness, round and round the manor house and bringing it back almost to the starting point – an invention neglected in *La fausse*

[1] For the discovery of this notice and for the information immediately preceding, the writer has been indebted to the kindness of Mrs Francis Hood.

Auberge – inspired after the Restoration one of the most brilliant farces of the French Theatre. *Le Voyage à Dieppe* is a three act play by 'Wafflard et Fulgence', the nom de guerre of F.-J.-D. de Bury who, between 1820 and 1840, wrote some nineteen comedies or vaudevilles, including the libretto of an opera. The play in question was first performed in 1821.

Monsieur d'Herbelin, a retired business man who lives in the rue Buffon, near the Jardin des Plantes, is on the eve of starting for Dieppe with his wife and daughter, Isaure. To behold the sea has been his hope for the past thirty years, a hope always frustrated by the cares of his business; and there is indeed something poignant in the fact that this will be the fifth time that he has planned the journey. With him he will take *Les Voyages du Capitaine Cook* in two folio volumes. Now at a restaurant next door to his house young d'Hérigny, the son of a wealthy banker, is making merry with his friend Monbray. He confesses, however, that he cannot forget an attractive girl whom he had met the previous year at the Bal de Sceaux. As the young men are sitting at a table outside the restaurant, they overhear a conversation at d'Herbelin's door. It appears that a friend of d'Herbelin named Dumontel has called to explain that he cannot, as planned, accompany them in the diligence, but that his friend Monsieur de Saint-Valéry will put his private berline at their disposal.

This plan suggests to Monbray a practical joke which would have been heartless indeed, if in the event it had not brought good fortune to d'Hérigny. He at once arranges for d'Hérigny's carriage, driven by his coachman Dupré, to call for the d'Herbelin family, Monbray himself masquerading as Saint-Valéry. The ruse is successful. D'Herbelin and his family get into the carriage, and as night has now fallen, Dupré is able to drive them round Paris by way of Meudon, Sèvres, Neuilly, Saint-Denis and Vincennes, and at four in the early morning deposits them at d'Hérigny's house in the Marais. But young d'Hérigny has recognised in Isaure the unknown girl of the Bal de Sceaux, and Monbray insists that the d'Herbelins shall spend the rest of the night with him and his friend, a reasonable proposal from one who is supposed to be Saint-Valéry.

Everyone now retires to bed, but d'Herbelin is down betimes.

During the night he has heard 'l'ouragan qui agitait ses volets'; the sea will be rough and he is all agog to rush out and watch the breakers. And also he has a great appetite, due of course to the bracing sea-air. Isaure now for the first time recognises d'Hérigny, but keeps her own counsel. Dupré, however, has difficulty in restraining d'Herbelin's impatience, and succeeds in delaying his leaving the house only by informing him that a little later a frigate is to be launched. The appearance of Dumontel, who is supposed to have remained in Paris – as he has – dangerously complicates the situation. He happens to be a friend, or at least a client, of d'Hérigny's father, and has come to discuss business with him. Being unaware, like d'Herbelin, of the joke that has been perpetrated, he is equally mystified.

In the interval between Acts II and III the young people have come to an understanding. They now take Dumontel into their confidence. He agrees to try to help them and for a time contrives to keep their secret; but during the next few scenes, which are extremely funny, they are naturally on tenter-hooks. An element of pure farce, designed further to delay poor d'Herbelin, is furnished by the entry of a stockbroker named Lambert, dressed as a sea-captain and accompanied by his wife who is said to hail from the Caucasian Georgia. They engage d'Herbelin in conversation, although, after everyone has had lunch, he can hardly be restrained from rushing out to see the launch of the frigate: '36 canons, quel beau jour pour moi!' Lambert still detains him with an account of his first meeting with his wife in the Arabian deserts. She then describes the song she had sung for the Pacha Koulikad, the night before he was strangled. D'Herbelin innocently enquires if she had been one of the Pacha's favourites – a suggestion which provokes her husband's indignation and leads d'Hérigny to make peace between them.

Now, at long last, Monsieur d'Herbelin escapes from the house. The tension, which has been steadily increasing, may be imagined. He is soon back! Fortunately, however, the kind Dumontel has decided to face the music by pretending that the whole escapade has been of his invention: 'une revanche, un peu plus forte, j'en conviens, que tous les tours que tu m'as joués autrefois'. D'Herbelin's feelings can be well understood; but his wife pleads for indulgence, while Dumontel urges that if the joke had been practised by the young men, it would have transgressed all the proprieties, whereas, as it is, Isaure and d'Hérigny are in love, and it depends only on d'Herbelin to make them happy. Whereupon Monbray adds: 'Et nous partons pour Dieppe'.

The prospect, now certain, does something to placate d'Herbelin. This will be the sixth time that he will have set out for the seaport of his dreams: 'il en arrivera ce qu'il pourra'; but it will be only at Dieppe itself that he will listen to any talk of the marriage.

The play[1] has remained on the repertory of the Odéon, where it is still occasionally revived.

While *Le Voyage à Dieppe* cannot be described as an imitation, this word exactly fits Henry Crisafulli's *L'Hôtel Godelot*, a mediocre production which owed its performance, at the Théâtre du Gymnase on 13 May 1876, to the influence of Victorien Sardou.

Olivier and Paul, young men of fashion from Paris, descend one day on Monsieur Godelot, a man of property in Montélimar. Warned by a letter from Olivier's father, he is expecting them; although they, unaware of the arrangement, take his house for an hotel. Olivier falls in love with Miette, Godelot's daughter; while Paul tries to abduct his young cousin, Emma, from a neighbouring convent. In the opening scene Godelot is teaching his servants how to wait at table. The gardener is to stand behind his chair, 'et quand je lèverai l'index de la main droite, tu verseras du bordeaux; quand je lèverai celui de la gauche, tu verseras du bourgogne'. In another scene Godelot tells his wife, but not Miette, that his old friend Bertin, of Paris, has sent his 'mauvais sujet de fils' to travel in the south and has suggested that, if passing through Montélimar, he might put up at the 'Hôtel Godelot'. A mistake is rendered slightly plausible in this instance, since in France the word Hôtel designates a town-house as well as a hostelry. The arrangement between the parents is designed to induce Olivier to marry Miette. 'Et je compte, pour l'y décider, sur les charmes de ta fillette!', Bertin had explained; 'Mais nous sommes perdus s'il flaire le piège!' Olivier has a horror of marriage. Reserved and sheepish in presence of a lady,

---

[1] The text was first published by J. N. Barba in *Le Second Théâtre français*, 1821; it was reissued in the *Répertoire du Théâtre français*, 1824, and in apparently uniform reprints in later years.

he is bold enough with common women. He has been living, his father adds, 'dans un monde mêlé, très mêlé'; but at bottom he has 'un coeur d'or'.

The young men – to add to the invraisemblance – really take the house for an inn and behave even more rudely than Marlow and Hastings. Their servants get drunk. Olivier forces his way into the 'Chambre bleue', sacred to the memory of the Duc d'Angoulême who had slept there in 1815, and refuses to leave it. Later, however, he goes down to the salon to recover a cigar-case he had left there. He meets Miette and begins to pay court, while she accepts the misunderstanding and allows him to suppose her a servant. In Act II, scene XVII, he has almost decided to offer marriage.

But a fearful din is now heard outside, where a carriage has over-turned in the street; and Paul carries in a veiled woman, presumably the cousin, who has fainted. He and Olivier take her to Miette's room, but Godelot, outraged by these goings-on, arrives with an old sabre to attack and evict them. They reply by barricading the door, and they offer to leave only if a carriage is procured for them. Godelot pretends to agree, but retorts by locking them in. Miette, however, has slipped under the door a note for her father. Olivier now discovers that Miette is the daughter of Godelot, whom he still takes for an innkeeper; but he is so much in love that, when Godelot opens the door, he asks for Miette in marriage. Her father thinks him mad, but her mother persuades him to agree to this extra-ordinary match.

Meanwhile the veiled lady has turned out to be, not Paul's lovely young cousin Emma, but the elderly music mistress of the convent, who had happened to be emerging from the convent building at the moment when Emma was expected. She, however, has a letter for Paul which the young lady herself had asked her to post, and in which Emma announces that her family agree to the marriage.

It will be observed that the essentials of *She Stoops to Conquer* have been adapted, except for the only really original element in it; and that Marivaux's ingenious plot returns to the French stage, not improved in the interval. The play was dedicated to Sardou who, one suspects, had either put some touches to it or induced the Gymnase to stage it. 'Sans vous,' writes Crisafulli, 'Goldsmith et moi nous n'aurions peut-être pas fait si brillante figure . . . je vous suis vraiment reconnaissant du rude coup de main que vous m'avez donné.'

The play shows at least that Goldsmith's comedy was capable of kindling a certain enthusiasm in the dark years that followed 1870. It was studied in schools and universities, and a translation of it was produced in the Spring of 1927, with apparently great success, as reported by the *Figaro* of 2 April in an article by M. Charles Chassé:

'L'ombre aimable de Goldsmith aurait été satisfaite si elle avait pu assister à la série de représentations que la "Petite Scène" vient de donner avenue Hoche avec un brio extraordinairement élégant. M.X. de Courville . . . a présenté dans un texte français finement élaboré par M. de Heeckeren, *She stoops to conquer*. . .

'Félicitons-nous de ce que cet hommage posthume ait été rendu par un groupe de lettrés français à l'auteur du *Vicar of Wakefield*; nous avions en effet contracté à l'égard de Goldsmith, sans parler de notre reconnaissance de lecteurs émerveillés, une dette d'ordre diplomatique, car il a été outre–manche un des défenseurs les plus ardents de notre culture, un des partisans aussi les plus persuasifs d'une amitié durable entre les deux nations.'

No eighteenth-century writer could desire a warmer eulogy than is contained in these lines devoted to *Goldsmith en France*. They reveal, in artistic and literary circles, an interest which may be expected to revive from time to time.

One receives the impression that, prior to the time of Bernard Shaw, the French had no high opinion of the English comedies which have appeared since the time of Shakespeare. There was no reason why they should, since their own production was so much more abundant, and free also from the gross indecencies of Restoration comedy. Congreve might have been more acceptable, and of course Sheridan who renewed Congreve's manner. But Goldsmith's plays were marked by a French colouring and could also be read by children, without impropriety.

In 1822 Amédée Pichot, then the principal authority in France on Great Britain and things British, and also one of the best translators of the day, published *Les Méprises d'une nuit; ou, elle s'abaisse pour vaincre: comédie en cinq actes.* Editions of the English text were issued in 1828, 1837, 1873 (reprinted in 1899), 1878, 1891, 1892, and two in 1908, and a translation with notes in 1907. The 1873 edition was one of a series of English Classics edited by E. Sedley. The introduction contained an outline of Goldsmith's life, including the story of his visit to the Featherstones at Ardagh. *The Good-Natured Man* was not regarded as a masterpiece; its merit 'paraît résider tout entier dans le personnage vraiment ridicule de "Croaker, l'alarmiste," et dans une ou deux scènes de haute comédie'; but *She Stoops to Conquer* 'est une pièce qui durera'. Passing over the texts published in 1878 and 1891, it is worth pausing at Jules Guiraud's excellent edition of 1892, which was provided with an introduction and notes. This editor was the first critic to point to the analogy with *Le Jeu de l'Amour et du Hasard* – less perhaps an analogy than a case of imitation which some recent critics of Goldsmith seem unable to recognise. Equally good are the editions published by Professor A. Barbeau, of the University of Caen, in 1907 and 1908. The former is a very competent translation, with footnotes and a glossary of unusual words. The latter is an 'edition classique' on the lines of those already mentioned, but accompanied with a 'Vie de Goldsmith' and a detailed analysis of the play. After noting a few sources, including Marivaux, the editor concludes that these are insignificant borrowings and that Goldsmith transformed them to the point where we may regard both plot and character as his own. On the other hand, the character-drawing is rather superficial, there are weaknesses in the composition, an element of farce in the plot and a general lack of depth. The comedy is 'excellente dans son genre, mais dans un genre qui n'est pas le premier'. An appreciation which could hardly be more indulgent. The same year (1908) also saw an edition of the English text, with an outline of Goldsmith's life and works by Charles Petit, a professor at the Lycée d'Amiens. This edition has the merit of containing a study of the condition of English comedy towards 1773. Finally the appearance of three separate editions of this play in 1907 and 1908 may be explained, though only in part, by the political *rapprochement* between the two countries.

To conclude, in view of these facts and of the considerable number of editions of *The Vicar of Wakefield* in France, to say that

Goldsmith has remained almost as popular south of the Channel as in this country, would not be an exaggeration. Many recent editions of his works are designed mainly for the use of schools. Nor, amid the increasing number of 'classics' which many educated people read once in a lifetime – and often because it is the thing to read them – could Goldsmith easily maintain his hold beside such giants as Scott, Balzac, Dickens and the Russian novelists. But most of our own countrymen are likely, in the foreseeable future, to have some knowledge of *The Vicar of Wakefield*, *The Deserted Village* and at least one of the comedies. Whatever the defects of the latter, they are 'good theatre'; and their author, despite, or even because of his faults of character, will be remembered with indulgence as a good-natured man.

Appendix III

A Comparative Estimate of Money Values in Goldsmith's Time and in Ours

Some of Goldsmith's biographers have commiserated with him on the ground that he was badly, and even meanly, treated by the publishers. But a study of the relative value of money, in terms of purchasing power, between the decade 1761–70 and the year 1970 (since when there has of course been further inflation) reveals that, on the contrary, Goldsmith was extremely well paid for his work. Professor F. C. Spooner, of the Department of Economic History in the University of Durham, has kindly calculated for me the equivalents, in terms of purchasing power, between the value of the £ in the period 1761–70, and its value in 1970; while pointing out that, for various reasons, estimates can only be approximate. One should multiply the figure in Goldsmith's time by a little over ten. Thus £100 in the 1760s was worth about £1,042 in 1970 (and rather more today).

Nothing has been recorded of Goldsmith's income prior to 1759, when he received £20 for the *Memoir* on Voltaire. We do not know what Newbery paid him, in 1760 and 1761, for the 'Chinese Letters'; probably at least £100. On 5 March 1762, he received five guineas in final settlement. From 1762 onwards we have many exact figures of his income and some items of his expenditure, which almost always exceeded it.

In 1762:

for the *Life of Richard Nash* and some other work: £14 14s 0d

For the *Compendium of Biography*:[1]   £24 10s 0d
Between November 1762 and October 1763:   £63   0s 0d
(a figure which probably includes the above).
Towards the end of 1763 he received a further £30, making a total
of £93 which he acknowledged on 11 October.

In the meantime Newbery, who had taken Goldsmith's finances
in hand, had arranged for him to receive board and lodging with
Mrs Fleming at Canonbury House. She charged £50 per annum,
that is, about £521 in our currency, and for this provided his meals
and probably undertook his laundry. But he occasionally entertained and ordered additional luxuries, so that while Newbery had
credited his protégé with £63 for the period November 1762–
October 1763, he had paid out £111 1s 6d. Goldsmith owed him
£48 1s 6d, a debt reduced by £30 soon afterwards.

For *The Vicar of Wakefield*, for which Johnson obtained some
sort of contract in 1762 but which appeared only in 1766, Goldsmith received, probably at intervals, a total of sixty guineas, the
equivalent of £659 in the currency of 1970. That this was a handsome fee for a first novel, Goldsmith himself appears to have
recognised. He discovered, however, that popular compilations
were increasingly profitable. As he was paid £21 for *An History of
England in a series of Letters from a Nobleman* (1764), it became
clear that this was the easiest way of making money.

In 1764, Dodsley, another publisher, paid him forty guineas and
Newbery about twenty. It is not clear how much he made by the
collection of *Essays* published in 1765. In June 1766 he received
£127 for various pieces of work, including £21 for *The Traveller*
and £20 for a translation. The fee for the selection of *Poems for
Young Ladies* (early 1767) is not recorded; but for *The Beauties of
English Poesy* which he compiled soon afterwards, he is said to
have received, presumably from Griffin, £200, the equivalent of
£2,084 in the currency of our day.

It appears from the above figures that his income hitherto had
been very irregular, with good years and bad years, and substantial
debts. But from 1768 onwards he would have been really prosperous,
if he had not constantly overspent his earnings. In 1768 the author's

---

[1] An enterprise of Newbery's, to which Goldsmith contributed versions of some
of Plutarch's *Lives*.

benefit nights for *The Good-Natured Man* brought him about £400, and for the book, published by Griffin, about £50; that is, in all, the equivalent of £4,680 of present day money. This encouraged him to move to better chambers in Brick Court and to spend a good deal in furnishing them. He was now regarded by the reading public as a rising poet, and by the publishers as a furnisher of profitable compilations. Dodsley, Newbery, Griffin and Davies were all employing him. In 1768 he contracted with Davies to write a *History of Rome* for two hundred and fifty guineas (equivalent to £2,710). In February 1759 he embarked on a far more serious enterprise, that of composing for Griffin a Natural History in eight volumes, at one hundred guineas a volume. He was in fact paid £840 (the equivalent of £8,745 in the currency of 1970). This book took between four and five years of intermittent work, and was not finished until a few months before his death. Much easier to fulfil and comparatively more profitable was a contract with Davies, signed in June 1769, for a new *History of England* in four volumes, for £500 (£5,210).

It is not known what he received in 1770 for *The Deserted Village*, but it cannot have been less than £100. For an abridgment of the *History of England* he was paid £52 10s od.

In 1773 *She Stoops to Conquer* proved more successful than *The Good-Natured Man*, Goldsmith receiving just over £500 (£5,210). The printed version was extremely profitable, but Goldsmith ceded the profits to Francis Newbery, as he had no other means of repaying an advance which had been made to him in respect of a novel. It will be recalled that Newbery had rejected the manuscript of the novel. Finally, also in 1773, Goldsmith compiled a *Grecian History*, which was published in June 1774, after his death. But he had been paid £250 for it (£2,600).

While it is not easy to calculate Goldsmith's average minimum income per year between about January 1762 and the end of 1774, it can hardly have been less than about £330. After 1768 he was clearly making an average of £458 a year (£4,764 in terms of our money). As taxation was very low, service cheap, and coal for heating not expensive, this was a good income for a single man. Johnson lived comfortably on a pension of £300 a year, with a little extra money, and rather more after 1770.

Turning now to expenditure, the rent of his rooms in Brick Court

(1768–74) was probably not more than £60 a year, the cost of heating perhaps £15, and service £25. £100 p.a. would have easily covered these items. After 1768 he used to spend part of most summers in the farmer's house at Hyde, and paid probably an average of £20 or £25 p.a. for board and lodging. The furnishing of his rooms in Brick Court may well have cost £100 in 1768, but this was not a recurrent item. He may have spent £125 annually on food and drink. Apart from gambling, entertaining, and indiscriminate charity, the cost of clothes constituted a large item in his budget. Here are the figures that have been recorded from 1767 onwards:

1767	£52	5	2	
1768	£32	2	0	
1769	£33	13	5	
1770	£30	11	7	(and a coat in Paris)
1771	£42	4	2	
1772	£51	13	1	
1773	£80	0	10	
1774	£7	14	9	
	£330	5	0	

Thus, from 1767 to 1774 inclusive, he was spending an average of £41 5s 9d a year, equivalent to about £420 of our currency, while in 1773 his tailor's bill was equivalent to over £900.

One should recognise that in the eighteenth century a gentleman was obliged to spend relatively more on clothes than he is today, because the materials were finer and more costly, and because the dirt and pollution of London, and probably the wear and tear, rendered necessary a more frequent renewal of clothes. Even so, Goldsmith was notorious for his love of showy suits and breeches. He could have dressed decently, if not with distinction, on £20 a year.

The following table suggests what one may conjecture as the reasonable annual expenses of a man in Goldsmith's position, including, where possible, what he apparently had to pay during the period 1767–74.

o

Rent of Chambers	£60
Heating	£15
Service	£25
Board and lodging at Hyde	£25
Meals and wine	£125
Clothes	£20
Holidays	£60
Transport	£10
Charities	£10
Oddments	£5
	£355

The table below indicates in Column I Goldsmith's average annual income during these years; In Column II, an estimate of reasonable expenditure; in Column III, the apparent excess of expenditure over income; and in Column IV what appears to have been the real excess, in view of his leaving debts of at least £2,000 nett, that is, an average of £250 a year over a period of eight years. One may add £250 to £355 and deduct £458, to estimate the average excess of expenditure over income:

I Average annual income	II Estimate of necessary expenditure	III Apparent excess of expenditure over income	IV Real excess of expenditure over income
£458	£355	£103	£147 (£250 + 355 − 458)

Value in 1970

£4,764	£3,653	£1,052	(£1,553)

Thus, in the currency of 1770, Goldsmith was earning at least £458 a year. He could reasonably spend £355 a year, and save or invest £100. But in fact he was spending an average of £147 more than he earned. This circumstance probably explains the worry and anxiety which were a contributory cause of his death.

A Select Bibliography

Balderston, Katherine C. H., *The History and Sources of Percy's 'Memoir of Goldsmith'*, Cambridge University Press, 1926. *The Collected Letters of Oliver Goldsmith*, Cambridge University Press, 1928.

Black, William, *Goldsmith*, London, 1878.

Boswell, James, *The Life of Samuel Johnson*, ed G. B. Hill, revised by L. C. Powell, Oxford University Press, 1934–1950, 6 vols. *The Private Papers of James Boswell from Malahide Castle*, ed G. Scott and F. A. Pottle, Mount Vernon, 1928–34, 18 vols. *Boswell's London Journal*, ed F. A. Pottle, New York, 1950.

Boyle, the Reverend Patrick, *The Irish College in Paris from 1578 to 1901*, London, 1901.

Brooke, John, *King George III*, London, 1972.

Crane, Ronald S., *New Essays by O. G.*, Chicago, 1927.

Cumberland, Richard, *The West Indian*, London, 1771. *Memoirs*, London, 1806.

Dobson, Austin, *The Life of Oliver Goldsmith*, London, 1888. *The Complete Poetical Works of O. G.*, ed. with introduction and notes, London, 1907.

Forster John, *The Life and Adventures of O. G.*, London, 1848, 2nd edition, 1854, 2 vols.

Freeman, William, *Oliver Goldsmith*, London, 1951.

Freshfield, Douglas and Montagnier, H. F., *H.-B. de Saussure*, London, 1920.

Friedman, Arthur, ed. *The Complete Works of Oliver Goldsmith*, Oxford, 1966, 5 vols.

George, M. Dorothy, *London Life in the XVIIIth Century*, London, 1925.

Gibbon, Edward, *Memoirs of my Life and Writings*, ed G. B. Hill, London, 1900.

Gibbs, J. W. M., *The Works of Oliver Goldsmith*, London, 1884–86, 5 vols.

Hopkins, Robert, *The True Genius of Oliver Goldsmith*, Baltimore, 1969.

Irving, Washington, *Oliver Goldsmith: a Biography*, New York, 1844, 2 vols.

Kelly, Hugh, *False Delicacy*, London, 1768.

Ketton–Cremer, R. W., *Thomas Gray: a Biography*, Cambridge University Press, 1955.

Larroumet, G., *Marivaux: sa vie et ses oeuvres*, Paris, 1882.

Lecky, W. E. H., *A History of Ireland in the Eighteenth Century*, London, 1902, vol I.

Lynskey, Winifred, 'The Scientific Sources of Goldsmith's Animated Nature', in *Studies in Philology*, XI, (1943).

Lytton Sells, A., *Les Sources françaises de Goldsmith*, Paris, 1924.

Marivaux, Pierre Carlet de Chamblain de, *Le Legs*, Paris, 1736. *Le Jeu de l'Amour et du Hasard*, Paris, 1730.

Marshall, Dorothy, *English People in the XVIIIth Century*, London, 1956.

Martino, Pierre, *L'Orient dans la littérature française au XVII⁄e et au XVIII⁄e Siècle*, Paris, 1906.

Maxwell, Constantia, *A History of Trinity College, Dublin: 1571—1892*, Dublin, 1946.

Mornet, Daniel, *Le Romantisme en France au XVIII⁄e Siècle*, Paris, 1912.

Moore, F. Frankfort, *The Life of Oliver Goldsmith*, London, 1910.

Nicoll, J. R. Allardyce, *A History of late Eighteenth-Century Drama: 1750–1800*, Cambridge University Press, 1927.

Northcote, James, *The Life of Sir Joshua Reynolds*, London, 1818, 2 vols.

Pitman, J. H., *Goldsmith's 'Animated Nature'*, New Haven, 1924.

Plumb, J. H., *England in the Eighteenth Century*, London, 1950.

Prior, Sir James, *The Life of Oliver Goldsmith*, London, 1837, 2 vols.

Quintana, Ricardo, *Goldsmith: a Georgian Study*, London, 1967.

Reynolds, Sir Joshua, *Portraits by Sir Joshua Reynolds*, ed F. W. Hilles, New York, 1952.

Texte, Joseph, *Jean-Jacques Rousseau et les origines du cosmopolitisme littéraire*, Paris, 1895.

Traill, H. D., *Sterne*, London, 1888.

Walpole, Horace, *Correspondance*, ed W. S. Lewis and others, Oxford, 1955, 34 vols.

Wardle, Ralph M., *Oliver Goldsmith*, Lawrence (Kansas) and London, 1957.

Welsh, Charles, *A Bookseller of the Last Century*, (John Newbery), London, 1885.

Index